The Complete Book of
Bible Quotations from

THE NEW
TESTAMENT

Also edited by Mark L. Levine and Eugene Rachlis

The Complete Book of Bible Quotations
The Complete Book of Bible Quotations
from the Old Testament

Published by POCKET BOOKS

For orders other than by individual consumers, Pocket Books grants a discount on the purchase of **10 or more** copies of single titles for special markets or premium use. For further details, please write to the Vice-President of Special Markets, Pocket Books, 1633 Broadway, New York, NY 10019-6785 8th Floor.

For information on how individual consumers can place orders, please write to Mail Order Department, Simon & Schuster, Inc., 200 Old Tappan Road, Old Tappan, NJ 07675.

The Complete Book of Bible Quotations from

THE NEW TESTAMENT

Edited by MARK L. LEVINE
and EUGENE RACHLIS

POCKET BOOKS
New York   London   Toronto   Sydney   Tokyo   Singapore

This edition incorporates material from
The Complete Book of Bible Quotations.

An *Original* Publication of POCKET BOOKS

POCKET BOOKS, a division of Simon & Schuster Inc.
1230 Avenue of the Americas, New York, NY 10020

Copyright © 1986 by Mark L. Levine and Eugene Rachlis
Revised edition copyright © 1996 by Mark L. Levine
and the Estate of Eugene Rachlis

All rights reserved, including the right to reproduce
this book or portions thereof in any form whatsoever.
For information address Pocket Books, 1230 Avenue
of the Americas, New York, NY 10020

ISBN: 0-671-53797-0

First Pocket Books trade paperback printing April 1996

10 9 8 7 6 5 4 3 2 1

POCKET and colophon are registered trademarks of
Simon & Schuster Inc.

Cover design by Tom McKeveny

Printed in the U.S.A.

INTRODUCTION

Most books of quotations—Bartlett's and H.L. Mencken's come immediately to mind—contain only the most familiar quotations from the Bible, the popular phrases and verses that virtually everyone knows and is fond of. The Bible, however, contains thousands of additional phrases and verses that are just as beautiful and just as significant, yet are not as well known or used as often because they haven't been identified as "quotations."

The Old Testament and New Testament editions of *The Complete Book of Bible Quotations* contain not only the Bible's famous lines and phrases, but also those phrases that *should be* famous—by virtue of what is said or the way it is said. These editions are the definitive source books of quotations from the Bible, truly a "Bartlett's of the Bible."

"Quotability"—how the phrase sounds, in speech and on paper—was an essential element in every selection. We carefully reread the entire Bible and chose only those verses and phrases that we believed to be of such style, beauty and brevity that individuals would readily repeat them to make a point or illustrate an image in conversation, sermons, speeches and in writing.

In preparing the Old Testament and New Testament editions, we selected over 6,000 different quotations and classified them into more than 800 categories. There are quotations from every one of the Bible's books in these editions. Each quotation has been placed into an average of two categories (though some may only be in one, and a handful in as many as five). Cross-references to related categories with pertinent quotations are indicated where applicable.

Categorizing the quotations was difficult. We took particular care to make sure that each quotation was properly categorized and in context. We not only used our own judgment but consulted with clergy and Biblical scholars and availed ourselves of numerous translations and Biblical commentaries.

If not limited by space, we could have put each quotation into far more categories than we did. But of necessity, we made choices and selected only those that we considered most appropriate and most likely to be helpful to you; we also included in certain categories quotations about both the topic and its antonym. Please keep in mind that, because of the criteria used in selecting these quotations, the book is not intended to be a compilation of everything the Bible says on each subject.

We have given the chapter and verse citation for every quotation in the book and urge you to refer to the Bible for the full context in which each phrase appears. In the chapter and verse references, we have used *"e.g."* to indicate that the phrase appears several times in the Bible even though we have generally listed only one reference. We have used *"see also"* to indicate a verse similar but not identical to the one quoted where we thought you might want to consult that verse, too.

We also compiled an extensive Index which gives the key words in every quotation in the book, together with a few adjacent words to provide the context. This serves both as a supplement to the main categories in the book and to help readers find a quotation when they remember a word or two but not the entire quotation.

In addition, we have provided in an Appendix to this volume the full text of three lengthier passages from the New Testament that we consider particularly beautiful, meaningful and quotable in their entirety. Many more could, of course, have been included.

The translation used is the King James Version, universally renowned for its poetic and beautiful language. The only changes from the King James Version made in this New Testament edition were to capitalize second- and third-person pronouns which refer to Jesus, and first-, second- and third-person pronouns which refer to God.

Mark L. Levine
Eugene Rachlis

ACKNOWLEDGMENTS

No book of this size can be prepared without the assistance of a great many people.

In particular, we wish to thank Diana Bryant, Howard Cutler, Nick Egleson, Diana Finch, Sophie Greenblatt, Sheila Heyman, Sydny Miner, Katherine Romaine, Charles Salzberg, Jan Stone, Anna Van and Stephanie von Hirschberg.

We are also deeply indebted to Professor Douglas Stuart, chairman of the Biblical Studies Department and Professor of Old Testament at Gordon-Conwell Theological Seminary in South Hamilton, Massachusetts, and to Dr. Gregory K. Beale, Professor of New Testament at Gordon-Conwell, for reviewing the categorization of the quotations. Any errors in final placement, however, are not their fault but ours.

CONTENTS

Building
Burdens
Burial
Business

Calling—*See* Mission
Candor
Care—*See* Comfort, Devotion
Carnality
Caution—*See* Prudence, Vigilance,
   Warning
Celebration
Celibacy
Certainty
Challenges
Change
Chaos
Character
Charity
Chastisement
Cheating—*See* Honesty, Lies
Child-Rearing
Children
Choice
Christ—*See* Jesus, Messiah,
   Messianic Hopes and Prophecies
Christ Eternal
Christianity
Christians
Christmas
Church and State
Church Governance—*See* Clergy,
   Leadership
Churches
Circumcision
Clarity
Clergy
Comfort
Commandments
Commitment
Common Sense—*See* Wisdom
Communication
Communion
Companions
Compassion
Competition
Complacency
Complaints
Compromise
Conceit

Conduct—*See* Behavior
Conduct toward God—*See*
   Behavior, Fear of God, Love of
   God
Confession
Confidence
Conflict of Interest—*See* Allegiance,
   Loyalty
Conformity
Confusion
Conscience
Consecration
Consequences
Consistency
Conspiracy—*See* Betrayal
Contamination
Contemplation
Contempt
Contentment
Contrition
Controversy
Conversion
Cooperation
Corruption
Courage
Courtesy
Covenant
Cowardice—*See* Fear, Timidity
Creation
Creativity—*See* Achievement,
   Building
Credibility
Crime
Criticism
Crucifixion
Cruelty
Cultivation
Curses
Cynicism

Damnation
Dance
Danger
Darkness—*See* Enlightenment,
   Light and Darkness
Death
Decadence
Deception
Decisions
Deeds

Defeat

Defiance—*See* Audacity, Rebellion

Delay—*See* Patience,
  Procrastination

Deliverance

Denial

Dependence—*See* God's Protection,
  Reliance

Depravity

Deprivation

Desecration—*See* Sacrilege

Desire

Despair

Destruction

Determination

Devil—*See* Evil, Satan

Devotion

Diligence

Disappointment

Disbelief—*See* Doubt, Godlessness,
  Skepticism

Discernment

Disciples

Discipline

Discontent—*See* Contentment,
  Satisfaction

Dishonesty

Disobedience

Diversity

Divinity

Divorce

Doctrine

Doom—*See* Apocalypse,
  Destruction, Punishment, Terror

Doubt

Dreams

Drunkenness

Duty

Earth

Education

Effort

Ego—*See* Arrogance, Conceit,
  Humility

Eloquence

Embarrassment—*See* Shame

Emotions—*See* Fear, Happiness,
  Hatred, Love, Sorrow

Empathy

Employees

Encouragement

End Days

Endings

Endurance—*See* Diligence,
  Fortitude, Perseverance, Strength

Enemies

Enlightenment

Enthusiasm

Environment—*See* Nature

Envy

Ephemera—*See* Mortality,
  Permanence

Equality

Escape

Eternal Life

Eternity

Ethics—*See* Behavior, Honesty

Evangelism

Evidence—*See* Perjury, Proof

Evil

Exaltation

Exasperation

Excess

Excuses

Exercise—*See* Physical Fitness

Exile

Exorcism

Expectation

Experience

Exposure

Failure—*See* Success, Victory

Fairness

Faith

Faithfulness

Faithlessness—*See* Godlessness

False Gods—*See* Idolatry, Idols

False Prophets

Fame

Family

Famine—*See* Deprivation, Hunger

Farming—*See* Cultivation, Growth

Fashion—*See* Appearance, Change,
  Materialism

Fasting

Favoritism

Fear

Fear of God

Fellowship

Fidelity—*See* Commitment,
  Faithfulness, Loyalty

Firstborn

Flattery
Flavor
Folly
Food
Fools
Forgiveness
Fornication
Fortitude
Frailty
Freedom
Friendship
Frustration
Fulfillment
Futility
Future

Generosity
Gifts
Gloating—*See* Boasting, Conceit,
    Humility, Pride
Glory
Goals
God
God's Anger
God's Glory
God's Goodness—*See* Goodness
God's Greatness
God's Knowledge
God's Love
God's Mercy
God's People
God's Power
God's Presence
God's Protection
God's Support
God's Temple
God's Uniqueness
God's Will
God's Word
God, Traits of
Godlessness
Godliness
Good and Evil
Goodness
Gospel
Gossip—*See* Secrecy, Slander,
    Speech
Government
Grace
Gratitude
Greatness

Greed
Greetings—*See* Salutations
Grief
Growth
Grudges
Guidance
Guilt

Handicapped
Happiness
Hatred
Healing
Health—*See* Handicapped, Healing
Heaven
Heaven and Earth
Heedfulness
Height—*See* Size
Hell
Help—*See* Assistance, Deliverance
Heresy
Heritage
Heroism—*See* Courage, Leadership
Hierarchy—*See* Authority,
    Leadership
History
Holiness
Holy Spirit
Homage
Home
Homosexuality
Honesty
Honor—*See* Glory, Respect
Hope
Hospitality
Human Body—*See* Body, Physical
    Fitness
Human Nature
Humiliation
Humility
Hunger
Husband and Wife—*See* Marriage
Hypocrisy

Idolatry
Idols
Ignorance
Imagination—*See* Dreams, Future
Imminence
Immorality
Immortality—*See* Death, Eternal
    Life, Resurrection

Miracles
Misery—*See* Anguish
Misjudgment
Mission
Missionaries—*See* Evangelism
Mobs
Mockery
Models
Modesty
Monarchy
Money
Monotheism
Morality—*See* Decadence,
  Depravity, Immorality,
  Righteousness
Mortality
Motherhood—*See* Birth, Jesus
  (Birth of), Parents
Motivation
Mourning
Murder
Music—*See* Dance
Mystery
Myth

Naivete
Nature
Need
Neighbors
Neutrality
New Testament—*See* Covenant,
  Gospel, Scripture
News
Night

Oaths
Obedience
Obligation
Obstacles
Old Age—*See* Age
Old Testament—*See* Covenant,
  Scripture
Omens
Omnipotence—*See* God's Power
Omniscience—*See* God's
  Knowledge
Opportunism
Opportunity
Oppression
Optimism—*See* Hope
Oratory—*See* Preaching, Speech

Orphans—*See* Widows and
  Orphans
Ostentation
Outcast

Paganism—*See* Idolatry
Pain—*See* Anguish, Birth, Healing,
  Suffering
Paradise—*See* Heaven, Kingdom of
  God
Parents
Passion—*See* Carnality, Desire,
  Love, Lust
Patience
Peace
Pedantry
Perfection
Perjury
Permanence
Persecution
Perseverance
Perspective
Persuasion
Pessimism—*See* Despair, Hope
Philanthropy—*See* Charity,
  Generosity
Physical Fitness
Pity—*See* Compassion, Mercy
Plague
Planning
Pleas
Pleasure
Possibility
Posterity
Potential
Poverty
Power
Praise
Praise of God
Prayer
Preaching
Predictions—*See* Future, Prophecy
Prejudice—*See* Brotherhood,
  Equality
Preparedness—*See* Readiness,
  Second Coming, Vigilance
Pride
Principles—*See* Integrity
Priorities—*See* Goals, Values
Prison—*See* Imprisonment,
  Persecution

Procrastination
Profanity
Profit
Progress—*See* Success
Promises
Proof
Property—*See* Materialism, Wealth
Prophecy
Proselytization—*See* Evangelism
Prosperity—*See* Adversity, Reward,
 Success, Wealth
Prostitution—*See* Adultery,
 Carnality, Fornication,
 Immorality, Sin
Protection—*See* Deliverance, God's
 Protection, Safety, Vigilance
Provocation—*See* Instigation
Prudence
Public Opinion
Publicity
Punishment
Purity
Purpose

Quality
Quantity
Questioning—*See* Authority,
 Doctrine, Skepticism
Quotations

Rain
Rashness
Readiness
Rebellion
Rebirth—*See* Born Again, Jesus
 (Acceptance Of)
Reciprocity
Redemption
Refuge—*See* Safety
Regret
Rehabilitation
Rejection
Reliance
Remembrance
Renewal
Repentance
Representatives—*See* Spokesmen,
 Status
Reputation
Rescue—*See* Assistance, Danger,
 Deliverance

Respect
Responsibility
Restraint
Resurrection
Retribution
Revelation
Revenge
Reverence
Reversal
Revolution—*See* Rebellion, Strife
Reward
Righteousness
Risk
Rituals
Robbery
Romance—*See* Love

Sabbath
Sacrifice
Sacrifices
Sacrilege
Safety
Salutations
Salvation
Sarcasm—*See* Mockery
Satan
Satisfaction
Scorn
Scripture
Searching
Second Coming
Secrecy
Security
Seduction—*See* Temptation
Self-Awareness
Self-Confidence—*See* Confidence
Self-Control
Self-Deception
Self-Denial
Self-Hatred
Self-Incrimination
Self-Interest
Self-Righteousness
Selfishness
Selflessness
Separation
Serenity
Servants—*See* Employees, Freedom,
 Slavery, Work
Service—*See* Altruism, Charity,
 Ministry

Service to God
Severity
Sex—*See* Adultery, Carnality,
  Celibacy, Fornication,
  Homosexuality, Immorality, Lust
Shame
Sharing
Sharpness
Siblings
Sickness—*See* Healing, Miracles
Sight
Silence
Sin
Sincerity
Sinners
Size
Skepticism
Skill—*See* Ability
Slander
Slavery
Sleep
Sloth—*See* Laziness
Snakes
Snobbery—*See* Conceit
Sodomy—*See* Homosexuality
Soldiers—*See* Peace, War, Weapons
Sorrow
Soul
Sovereignty
Speech
Speed
Spies—*See* Betrayal
Spirit—*See* Holy Spirit, Inspiration
Spirituality
Spokesmen
Sportsmanship—*See* Competition
Stamina—*See* Fortitude
Status
Steadfastness
Stoicism—*See* Acceptance
Strangers—*See* Hospitality
Strategy
Strength
Strife
Stubbornness
Submission—*See* Acceptance,
  Authority, Marriage
Success
Suddenness
Suffering
Superstition

Support—*See* God's Support
Survival
Sustenance—*See* Bread of Life,
  Food
Swearing
Symbolism—*See* Omens
Sympathy

Talent—*See* Ability
Taste—*See* Flavor
Taxation
Teaching
Tears
Temper—*See* Anger, Patience,
  Restraint
Temperance—*See* Behavior, Excess
Temptation
Terror
Testimony
Testing—*See* Competition
Thanksgiving—*See* Gratitude
Thirst
Thoughts
Threat
Time
Timidity
Tolerance
Tongues
Torment
Tradition
Traitors—*See* Betrayal, Loyalty,
  Treachery
Traps—*See* Strategy
Treachery
Tribulation—*See* Suffering
Trinity
Trouble
Trust
Truth

Uncertainty—*See* Doubt
Underprivileged
Understanding
Unity
Universality
Universe—*See* Heaven and Earth,
  Nature
Urgency

Value
Values

THE BOOKS OF THE NEW TESTAMENT

Matthew
Mark
Luke
John
The Acts
Romans
I Corinthians
II Corinthians
Galatians
Ephesians
Philippians
Colossians
I Thessalonians
II Thessalonians

I Timothy
II Timothy
Titus
Philemon
Hebrews
James
I Peter
II Peter
I John
II John
III John
Jude
Revelation

ABBREVIATIONS

Acts	The Acts
Col.	Colossians
1 Cor.	I Corinthians
2 Cor.	II Corinthians
Eph.	Ephesians
Gal.	Galatians
Heb.	Hebrews
James	James
John	John
1 John	I John
2 John	II John
3 John	III John
Jude	Jude
Luke	Luke
Mark	Mark
Matt.	Matthew
1 Pet.	I Peter
2 Pet.	II Peter
Philem.	Philemon
Phil.	Philippians
Rev.	Revelation
Rom.	Romans
1 Thess.	I Thessalonians
2 Thess.	II Thessalonians
1 Tim.	I Timothy
2 Tim.	II Timothy
Titus	Titus

A

ABANDONMENT

My God, my God, why hast Thou forsaken me?
Jesus
Matt. 27:46, Mark 15:34
See also Ps. 22:1

I will not leave you comfortless: I will come to you.
Jesus
John 14:18

I will never leave thee, nor forsake thee.
(I: God)
Heb. 13:5
See also Deut. 31:6, Josh. 1:5

[*See also* Rejection]

ABILITY

Nothing shall be impossible unto you.
Jesus
Matt. 17:20

All things are possible to him that believeth.
Jesus
Mark 9:23

Every one that is perfect shall be as his master.
Jesus
Luke 6:40

The Son can do nothing of Himself, but what He seeth the Father do.
Jesus
John 5:19

I can of mine own self do nothing.
Jesus
John 5:30

There are diversities of gifts, but the same Spirit.
1 Cor. 12:4

Our sufficiency is of God.
2 Cor. 3:5

I can do all things through Christ which strengtheneth me.
Phil. 4:13

Neglect not the gift that is in thee.
1 Tim. 4:14

[*See also* Achievement, Character, Competition]

ABSENCE

Absent in body, but present in spirit.
1 Cor. 5:3

Though I be absent in the flesh, yet am I with you in the spirit.
Col. 2:5

ABUNDANCE

See Infinity, Quantity.

ACCEPTANCE

Not what I will, but what Thou wilt.
Jesus
Mark 14:36
See also Matt. 26:39, Luke 22:42

Father, into Thy hands I commend my spirit.
Jesus
Luke 23:46

The cup which my Father hath given me, shall I not drink it?
Jesus
John 18:11

He bearing His cross went forth.
(He: Jesus)
John 19:17

What was I, that I could withstand God?
Peter
Acts 11:17

The will of the Lord be done.
Acts 21:14

If a spirit or an angel hath spoken to him, let us not fight against God.
Pharisees, about Paul
Acts 23:9

Being reviled, we bless; being persecuted, we suffer it.
1 Cor. 4:12

Do all things without murmurings and disputings.
Phil. 2:14

Despise not thou the chastening of the Lord.
Heb. 12:5

Servants, be subject to your masters with all fear; not only to the good and gentle.
1 Pet. 2:18
See also Eph. 6:5

If, when ye do well, and suffer for it, ye take it patiently, this is acceptable with God.
1 Pet. 2:20

It is better, if the will of God be so, that ye suffer for well doing, than for evil doing.
1 Pet. 3:17

Here is the patience and the faith of the saints.
Rev. 13:10

[*See also* Contentment, Restraint]

ACCOUNTABILITY

See Obligation, Responsibility.

ACCUSATIONS

Doth our law judge any man, before it hear him, and know what he doeth?
Nicodemus
John 7:51

He that is without sin among you, let him first cast a stone.
Jesus
John 8:7

Woman, where are those thine accusers?
Jesus
John 8:10

If I have spoken evil, bear witness of the evil.
Jesus
John 18:23

If He were not a malefactor, we would not have delivered Him up unto thee.
John 18:30

Behold the man!
Pilate
John 19:5

[*See also* Criticism]

ACHIEVEMENT

By their fruits ye shall know them.
Jesus
Matt. 7:20
See also Matt. 7:16, Luke 6:44

All things are delivered to me of my Father.
Jesus
Luke 10:22
See also Matt. 11:27

Can a devil open the eyes of the blind?
John 10:21

The works that I do in my Father's name, they bear witness of me.
Jesus
John 10:25

For which of those works do ye stone me?
Jesus
John 10:32

Without me ye can do nothing.
Jesus
John 15:5

Do all to the glory of God.
1 Cor. 10:31

I have fought a good fight, I have finished my course, I have kept the faith.
2 Tim. 4:7

He who hath builded the house hath more honour than the house.
Heb. 3:3

Every house is builded by some man; but He that built all things is God.
Heb. 3:4

Look to yourselves, that we lose not those things which we have wrought.
2 John 8

It is done.
Rev. 16:17

[*See also* Deeds, Success, Victory]

ACKNOWLEDGMENT

Elias is come already, and they knew him not.
Jesus
Matt. 17:12

Truly this was the Son of God.
Matt. 27:54
See also Mark 15:39

Whosoever shall confess me before men, him shall the Son of man also confess before the angels of God.
Jesus
Luke 12:8
See also Matt. 10:32

Sir, I perceive that Thou art a prophet.
John 4:19

He that honoureth not the Son honoureth not the Father which hath sent Him.
Jesus
John 5:23

Every tongue should confess that Jesus Christ is Lord.
Phil. 2:11

All shall know Me, from the least to the greatest.
Heb. 8:11
See also Jer. 31:34

[*See also* Jesus (Acceptance of), Knowledge of God]

ACTION

See Deeds.

ADAPTABILITY

Unto the Jews I became as a Jew, that I might gain the Jews.
1 Cor. 9:20

To the weak became I as weak, that I might gain the weak.
1 Cor. 9:22

I am made all things to all men, that I might by all means save some.
1 Cor. 9:22

[*See also* Behavior, Conformity]

ADULTERY

Thou shalt not commit adultery.
Jesus
Matt. 5:27, 19:18
See also, e.g., Ex. 20:14, Mark 10:19, Luke 18:20

Whosoever looketh on a woman to lust after her hath committed adultery with her already in his heart.
Jesus
Matt. 5:28

Whosoever shall put away his wife, saving for the cause of fornication, causeth her to commit adultery.
Jesus
Matt. 5:32
See also Luke 16:18

Whosoever shall marry her that is divorced committeth adultery.
Jesus
Matt. 5:32
See also Matt. 19:9, Luke 16:18

It is not lawful for thee to have thy brother's wife.
John the Baptist to Herod
Mark 6:18

If a woman shall put away her husband, and be married to another, she committeth adultery.
Jesus
Mark 10:12

Thou that sayest a man should not commit adultery, dost thou commit adultery?
Rom. 2:22

Whoremongers and adulterers God will judge.
Heb. 13:4

He that said, Do not commit adultery, said also, Do not kill.
James 2:11

[*See also* Divorce]

ADVERSITY

We are perplexed, but not in despair; Persecuted, but not forsaken; cast down, but not destroyed.
2 Cor. 4:8–9

Behold, the devil shall cast some of you into prison, that ye may be tried.
Jesus
Rev. 2:10

ADVICE

He that heareth, and doeth not, is like a man that without a foundation built an house upon the earth.
Jesus
Luke 6:49
See also Matt. 7:26

These things I say, that ye might be saved.
Jesus
John 5:34

Thou therefore which teachest another, teachest thou not thyself?
Rom. 2:21

I have not written unto you because ye know not the truth, but because ye know it.
1 John 2:21

[*See also* Candor, Criticism, Guidance]

AGE

Rebuke not an elder, but intreat him as a father.
1 Tim. 5:1

Submit yourselves unto the elder.
1 Pet. 5:5

[*See also* Maturity, Mortality, Youth]

AGREEMENT

See Arguments.

ALCOHOL

See Drunkenness, Liquor.

ALLEGIANCE

He that taketh not his cross, and followeth after me, is not worthy of me.
Jesus
Matt. 10:38
See also Luke 14:27

This people honoureth me with their lips, but their heart is far from me.
Jesus
Mark 7:6
See also Matt. 15:8

Whosoever will come after me, let him deny himself, and take up his cross, and follow me.
Jesus
Mark 8:34
See also Matt. 16:24, Luke 9:23

Come, take up the cross, and follow me.
Jesus
Mark 10:21
See also Matt. 19:21, Luke 18:22

My sheep hear my voice, and I know them, and they follow me.
Jesus
John 10:27

Ye cannot drink the cup of the Lord, and the cup of devils.
1 Cor. 10:21

[*See also* Betrayal, Faithfulness, Loyalty]

ALLIES

He that is not against us is for us.
Jesus
Luke 9:50
See also Matt. 12:30, Mark 9:40

[*See also* Allegiance, Enemies, Loyalty]

ALTERNATIVES

See Choice, Compromise.

ALTRUISM

Whosoever will be great among you, let him be your minister.
Jesus
Matt. 20:26
See also Mark 10:43

The Son of man came not to be ministered unto, but to minister, and to give His life a ransom for many.
Jesus
Matt. 20:28, Mark 10:45

If ye lend to them of whom ye hope to receive, what thank have ye? for sinners also lend to sinners, to receive as much again.
Jesus
Luke 6:34

Give, and it shall be given unto you.
Jesus
Luke 6:38

Thou shalt be recompensed at the resurrection of the just.
Jesus
Luke 14:14

He that was healed wist not who it was.
John 5:13

It is more blessed to give than to receive.
Jesus
Acts 20:35

Even Christ pleased not Himself.
Rom. 15:3

Let no man seek his own, but every man another's wealth.
1 Cor. 10:24

By love serve one another.
Gal. 5:13

As we have therefore opportunity, let us do good unto all men.
Gal. 6:10

[*See also* Charity, Generosity, Selfishness]

AMBITION

He that seeketh findeth.
Jesus
Matt. 7:8, Luke 11:10

It is enough for the disciple that he be as his master, and the servant as his lord.
Jesus
Matt. 10:25

Whosoever will be great among you, let him be your minister.
Jesus
Matt. 20:26
See also Mark 10:43

If any man desire to be first, the same shall be last of all, and servant of all.
Jesus
Mark 9:35

Whosoever exalteth himself shall be abased; and he that humbleth himself shall be exalted.
Jesus
Luke 14:11
See also Matt. 23:12

Let us not be desirous of vain glory.
Gal. 5:26

Let nothing be done through strife or vainglory.
Phil. 2:3

I have learned, in whatsoever state I am, therewith to be content.
Phil. 4:11

Set your affection on things above, not on things on the earth.
Col. 3:2

If a man desire the office of a bishop, he desireth a good work.
1 Tim. 3:1

They that will be rich fall into temptation and a snare.
1 Tim. 6:9

The fruits that thy soul lusted after are departed from thee.
Rev. 18:14

[*See also* Goals, Leadership, Satisfaction]

ANCESTRY

See Heritage.

ANGELS

They are equal unto the angels; and are the children of God.
Jesus
Luke 20:36

A vision of angels, which said that He was alive.
Luke 24:23

Know ye not that we shall judge angels?
1 Cor. 6:3

Be not forgetful to entertain strangers: for thereby some have entertained angels unawares.
Heb. 13:2

God spared not the angels that sinned, but cast them down to hell.
2 Pet. 2:4

ANGER

Whosoever is angry with his brother without a cause shall be in danger of the judgment.
Jesus
Matt. 5:22

Let not the sun go down upon your wrath.
Eph. 4:26

Provoke not your children to wrath.
Eph. 6:4

Let every man be swift to hear, slow to speak, slow to wrath.
James 1:19

The wrath of man worketh not the righteousness of God.
James 1:20

[*See also* Arguments, Exasperation, God's Anger, Restraint]

ANGUISH

There shall be weeping and gnashing of teeth.
Jesus
E.g., Matt. 8:12

My soul is exceeding sorrowful, even unto death.
Jesus
Matt. 26:38
See also Mark 14:34

Eli, Eli, lama sabachthani?
Jesus
Matt. 27:46
See also Mark 15:34

My God, my God, why hast Thou forsaken me?
Jesus
Matt. 27:46, Mark 15:34
See also Ps. 22:1

O wretched man that I am! who shall deliver me from the body of this death?
Rom. 7:24

The merchants of the earth shall weep and mourn over her; for no man buyeth their merchandise any more.
(her: Babylon)
Rev. 18:11

[*See also* Despair, Grief, Mourning, Sorrow, Suffering, Torment]

ANNUNCIATION

See Jesus (Birth of).

ANTICHRIST

Antichrist shall come.
1 John 2:18

Even now are there many antichrists.
1 John 2:18

He is antichrist, that denieth the Father and the Son.
1 John 2:22

Even now already is it in the world.
1 John 4:3

ANXIETY

See Worry.

APOCALYPSE

Such things must needs be.
Jesus
Mark 13:7

When ye shall hear of wars and commotions, be not terrified: for these things must first come to pass.
Jesus
Luke 21:9
See also Matt. 24:6, Mark 13:7

Nation shall rise against nation, and kingdom against kingdom: And great earthquakes shall be in divers places, and famines, and pestilences; and fearful sights and great signs shall there be from heaven.
Jesus
Luke 21:10–11
See also Matt. 24:6, Mark 13:8

Watch ye therefore, and pray always, that ye may be accounted worthy to escape all these things.
Jesus
Luke 21:36

The end of all things is at hand: be ye therefore sober, and watch unto prayer.
1 Pet. 4:7

I looked, and behold a pale horse: and his name that sat on him was Death, and Hell followed with him.
Rev. 6:8

[*See also* End Days, Judgment Day, Second Coming]

APPEARANCE

Why take ye thought for raiment?
Jesus
Matt. 6:28

Consider the lilies of the field, how they grow; they toil not, neither do they spin: And yet I say unto you, That even Solomon in all his glory was not arrayed like one of these.
Jesus
Matt. 6:28–29
See also Luke 12:27

Ye are like unto whited sepulchres, which indeed appear beautiful outward.
Jesus
Matt. 23:27

Ye also outwardly appear righteous unto men, but within ye are full of hypocrisy and iniquity.
Jesus
Matt. 23:28

Judge not according to the appearance, but judge righteous judgment.
Jesus
John 7:24

Ye judge after the flesh; I judge no man.
Jesus
John 8:15

He is not a Jew, which is one outwardly.
Rom. 2:28

Neither is that circumcision, which is outward in the flesh.
Rom. 2:28

If a man have long hair, it is a shame unto him.
1 Cor. 11:14

If a woman have long hair, it is a glory to her.
1 Cor. 11:15

Let no man think me a fool; if otherwise, yet as a fool receive me.
2 Cor. 11:16

God accepteth no man's person.
Gal. 2:6

[*See also* Deception, Materialism, Ostentation, Status]

APPRECIATION

He was in the world, and the world was made by Him, and the world knew Him not.
> John 1:10

He came unto His own, and His own received Him not.
> John 1:11

[See also Contentment, Gratitude, Satisfaction]

APPROVAL

Well done, thou good and faithful servant. (parable of the talents)
> Matt. 25:21

I receive not honour from men.
> Jesus
> John 5:41

If I yet pleased men, I should not be the servant of Christ.
> Gal. 1:10

ARCHITECTURE

See Building.

ARGUMENTS

Agree with thine adversary quickly, whiles thou art in the way with him.
> Jesus
> Matt. 5:25

Sirs, ye are brethren; why do ye wrong one to another?
> Acts 7:26

Strive not about words to no profit.
> 2 Tim. 2:14

Follow peace with all men, and holiness, without which no man shall see the Lord.
> Heb. 12:14

[See also Anger, Controversy, Peace, Strife]

ARMIES

See Peace, War, War and Peace.

ARROGANCE

Why tempt ye me?
> Jesus
> Mark 12:15, Luke 20:23,
> Matt. 22:18

Dost thou teach us?
> John 9:34

Who art thou that judgest another man's servant?
> Rom. 14:4
> See also James 4:12

[See also Audacity, Boasting, Conceit, Humility, Pride]

ASCENSION

He was received up into heaven, and sat on the right hand of God.
> Mark 16:19

Whither I go, ye cannot come.
> Jesus
> John 8:21, John 13:33
> See also John 7:34

ASSISTANCE

They that be whole need not a physician, but they that are sick.
> Jesus
> Matt. 9:12
> See also Mark 2:17, Luke 5:31

He saved others; Himself He cannot save.
> Matt. 27:42, Mark 15:31
> See also Luke 23:35

Whosoever shall call on the name of the Lord shall be saved.
> E.g., Acts 2:21
> See also Joel 2:32

[See also Deliverance, God's Protection, Prayer, Safety]

ATHEISM

See Godlessness.

ATTITUDE

Thy heart is not right in the sight of God.
Acts 8:21

We should serve in newness of spirit, and not in the oldness of the letter.
Rom. 7:6

To be carnally minded is death; but to be spiritually minded is life and peace.
Rom. 8:6

There is nothing unclean of itself: but to him that esteemeth any thing to be unclean, to him it is unclean.
Rom. 14:14

God loveth a cheerful giver.
2 Cor. 9:7

Be renewed in the spirit of your mind.
Eph. 4:23

Unto the pure all things are pure.
Titus 1:15

Unto them that are defiled and unbelieving is nothing pure; but even their mind and conscience is defiled.
Titus 1:15

[*See also* Character, Motivation, Perspective]

AUDACITY

Be ye come out, as against a thief, with swords and staves?
Jesus
Luke 22:52

O man, who art thou that repliest against God?
Rom. 9:20

[*See also* Arrogance]

AUTHENTICITY

He whom God hath sent speaketh the words of God.
John 3:34

He that is of God heareth God's words.
Jesus
John 8:47

I am the true vine.
Jesus
John 15:1

The body is of Christ.
Col. 2:17

[*See also* Deception, False Prophets, Proof]

AUTHORITY

To sit on my right hand, and on my left, is not mine to give, but it shall be given to them for whom it is prepared of my Father.
Jesus
Matt. 20:23
See also Mark 10:40

He that cometh from above is above all.
John 3:31

The Father judgeth no man, but hath committed all judgment unto the Son.
Jesus
John 5:22

I am come in my Father's name, and ye receive me not.
Jesus
John 5:43

I have not spoken of myself; but the Father which sent me.
Jesus
John 12:49
See also John 14:10

My Father is greater than I.
Jesus
John 14:28

I am the vine, ye are the branches.
Jesus
John 15:5

My kingdom is not of this world.
Jesus
John 18:36

Thou couldest have no power at all against me, except it were given thee from above.
Jesus
John 19:11

If I will that he tarry till I come, what is that to thee?
Jesus to Peter, about John
John 21:22

Him shall ye hear in all things whatsoever He shall say unto you.
Acts 3:22
See also Deut. 18:15

By what power, or by what name, have ye done this?
(ye: Peter and John)
Acts 4:7

We ought to obey God rather than men.
Acts 5:29

Jesus I know, and Paul I know; but who are ye?
Acts 19:15

I appeal unto Caesar.
Acts 25:11

What things soever the law saith, it saith to them who are under the law.
Rom. 3:19

Let every soul be subject unto the higher powers.
Rom. 13:1

There is no power but of God.
Rom. 13:1

The powers that be are ordained of God.
Rom. 13:1

Pay ye tribute also: for they are God's ministers.
Rom. 13:6

He that judgeth me is the Lord.
1 Cor. 4:4

Shall I come unto you with a rod, or in love?
1 Cor. 4:21

The head of every man is Christ; and the head of the woman is the man; and the head of Christ is God.
1 Cor. 11:3

He is the head of the body, the church.
(He: Jesus)
Col. 1:18

Ye are complete in Him, which is the head of all principality and power.
(Him: Jesus)
Col. 2:10

I suffer not a woman to teach, nor to usurp authority over the man, but to be in silence.
1 Tim. 2:12

For Adam was first formed, then Eve.
1 Tim. 2:13

Without all contradiction the less is blessed of the better.
Heb. 7:7

[*See also* God's Power, Government, Leadership, Obedience]

AVARICE

See Greed.

AWE

What manner of man is this, that even the winds and the sea obey Him!
Matt. 8:27
See also Mark 4:41, Luke 8:25

A great prophet is risen up among us.
Luke 7:16

Sir, I perceive that Thou art a prophet.
John 4:19

Why marvel ye at this?
Acts 3:12

When He had opened the seventh seal, there was silence in heaven about the space of half an hour.
Rev. 8:1

[*See also* Reverence, Wonders]

B

Having begun in the Spirit, are ye now made perfect by the flesh?
> *Gal. 3:3*

Count him not as an enemy, but admonish him as a brother.
> *2 Thess. 3:15*

If any man draw back, My soul shall have no pleasure in him.
> *Heb. 10:38*

The dog is turned to his own vomit again.
> *2 Pet. 2:22*
> *See also Prov. 26:11*

Remember therefore from whence thou art fallen, and repent.
> *Jesus*
> *Rev. 2:5*

[*See also* Disobedience, Godlessness, Idolatry, Obedience]

BAPTISM

I indeed have baptized you with water: but He shall baptize you with the Holy Ghost.
> *John the Baptist*
> *Mark 1:8*
> *See also Matt. 3:11, Luke 3:16*

He that believeth and is baptized shall be saved; but he that believeth not shall be damned.
> *Jesus*
> *Mark 16:16*

Except a man be born of water and of the Spirit, he cannot enter into the kingdom of God.
> *Jesus*
> *John 3:5*

Repent, and be baptized every one of you in the name of Jesus Christ.
> *Acts 2:38*

Here is water; what doth hinder me to be baptized?
> *Acts 8:36*

Can any man forbid water?
> *Acts 10:47*

The baptism of repentance.
> *Acts 13:24*

Arise, and be baptized, and wash away thy sins.
> *Acts 22:16*

One Lord, one faith, one baptism.
> *Eph. 4:5*

Not by water only, but by water and blood.
> *1 John 5:6*

BATTLE CALLS

If the trumpet give an uncertain sound, who shall prepare himself to the battle?
> *1 Cor. 14:8*

BEATITUDES

See the Appendix at p. 200.

BEAUTY

Consider the lilies of the field, how they grow; they toil not, neither do they spin: And yet I say unto you, That even Solomon in all his glory was not arrayed like one of these.
> *Jesus*
> *Matt. 6:28–29*
> *See also Luke 12:27*

[*See also* Appearance]

BEGINNINGS

New wine must be put into new bottles.
> *Jesus*
> *Mark 2:22, Luke 5:38*
> *See also Matt. 9:17*

In the beginning was the Word, and the Word was with God, and the Word was God.
> *John 1:1*

He is before all things, and by Him all things consist.
(Him: Jesus)
Col. 1:17

Behold, how great a matter a little fire kindleth!
James 3:5

I am Alpha and Omega, the beginning and the end, the first and the last.
Jesus
Rev. 22:13
See also Rev. 1:8, 11, Rev. 21:6

[*See also* Creation]

BEHAVIOR

Bless them that curse you, do good to them that hate you.
Jesus
Matt. 5:44

All things whatsoever ye would that men should do to you, do ye even so to them.
Jesus
Matt. 7:12

Strait is the gate, and narrow is the way, which leadeth unto life, and few there be that find it.
Jesus
Matt. 7:14

As ye would that men should do to you, do ye also to them likewise.
Jesus
Luke 6:31

If ye do good to them which do good to you, what thank have ye? for sinners also do even the same.
Jesus
Luke 6:33
See also Matt. 5:46

Do as I have done to you.
Jesus
John 13:15

Love one another.
Jesus
E.g., John 13:34

Abhor that which is evil; cleave to that which is good.
Rom. 12:9

All things are lawful unto me, but all things are not expedient.
1 Cor. 6:12
See also 1 Cor. 10:23

They which preach the gospel should live of the gospel.
1 Cor. 9:14

Be ye followers of me, even as I also am of Christ.
1 Cor. 11:1

Let all things be done decently and in order.
1 Cor. 14:40

Awake to righteousness, and sin not.
1 Cor. 15:34

We walk by faith, not by sight.
2 Cor. 5:7

Walk in the Spirit, and ye shall not fulfil the lust of the flesh.
Gal. 5:16

If we live in the Spirit, let us also walk in the Spirit.
Gal. 5:25

Be ye kind one to another.
Eph. 4:32

Be ye therefore followers of God, as dear children.
Eph. 5:1

Walk in love, as Christ also hath loved us.
Eph. 5:2

Walk as children of light.
Eph. 5:8

Walk circumspectly, not as fools, but as wise.
Eph. 5:15

Walk worthy of the Lord.
Col. 1:10
See also 1 Thess. 2:12

As ye have therefore received Christ Jesus the Lord, so walk ye in Him.
Col. 2:6

Put off all these; anger, wrath, malice, blasphemy, filthy communication out of your mouth.
Col. 3:8

Study to be quiet, and to do your own business.
1 Thess. 4:11

Let us, who are of the day, be sober, putting on the breastplate of faith and love; and for an helmet, the hope of salvation.
1 Thess. 5:8

Abstain from all appearance of evil.
1 Thess. 5:22

Do good.
1 Tim. 6:18

Flee also youthful lusts: but follow righteousness, faith, charity, peace.
2 Tim. 2:22

Be sober, grave, temperate, sound in faith, in charity, in patience.
Titus 2:2

Be in behaviour as becometh holiness.
Titus 2:3

Make straight paths for your feet, lest that which is lame be turned out of the way.
Heb. 12:13

Love as brethren, be pitiful, be courteous.
1 Pet. 3:8

If we walk in the light, as He is in the light, we have fellowship one with another.
1 John 1:7

Keep yourselves in the love of God, looking for the mercy of our Lord Jesus Christ.
Jude 21

[*See also* Attitude, Conformity, Deeds, Good and Evil, Love, Sin]

BELIEF

Believe ye that I am able to do this?
Jesus
Matt. 9:28

Whosoever therefore shall confess me before men, him will I confess also before my Father which is in heaven. But whosoever shall deny me before men, him will I also deny before my Father which is in heaven.
Jesus
Matt. 10:32–33

Because they had no root, they withered away.
Jesus
Matt. 13:6
See also Mark 4:6

With God all things are possible.
Jesus
Matt. 19:26, Mark 10:27
See also Luke 18:27

Whatsoever ye shall ask in prayer, believing, ye shall receive.
Jesus
Matt. 21:22
See also Mark 11:24

He that believeth and is baptized shall be saved; but he that believeth not shall be damned.
Jesus
Mark 16:16

As many as received Him, to them gave He power to become the sons of God.
John 1:12

Ye receive not our witness.
Jesus
John 3:11

If I have told you earthly things, and ye believe not, how shall ye believe, if I tell you of heavenly things?
Jesus
John 3:12

He that believeth not is condemned already, because he hath not believed in the name of the only begotten Son of God.
Jesus
John 3:18

He that believeth not the Son shall not see life; but the wrath of God abideth on him.
John 3:36

Know that this is indeed the Christ, the Saviour of the world.
John 4:42

Except ye see signs and wonders, ye will not believe.
Jesus
John 4:48

He that heareth my word, and believeth on Him that sent me, hath everlasting life.
Jesus
John 5:24

Had ye believed Moses, ye would have believed me: for he wrote of me.
Jesus
John 5:46

No man can come to me, except the Father which hath sent me draw him.
Jesus
John 6:44
See also John 6:65

He that followeth me shall not walk in darkness.
Jesus
John 8:12

Lord, I believe.
John 9:38

Though ye believe not me, believe the works.
Jesus
John 10:38

He that believeth in me, though he were dead, yet shall he live.
Jesus
John 11:25

Whosoever liveth and believeth in me shall never die.
Jesus
John 11:26

He that believeth on me, believeth not on me, but on Him that sent me.
Jesus
John 12:44

Ye believe in God, believe also in me.
Jesus
John 14:1

Blessed are they that have not seen, and yet have believed.
Jesus
John 20:29

I believe that Jesus Christ is the Son of God.
Acts 8:37

By Him all that believe are justified.
Acts 13:39

Believe on the Lord Jesus Christ, and thou shalt be saved.
Acts 16:31

Whosoever believeth on Him shall not be ashamed.
Rom. 9:33, Rom. 10:11

With the heart man believeth unto righteousness.
Rom. 10:10

How shall they believe in Him of whom they have not heard?
Rom. 10:14

The woman which hath an husband that believeth not, and if he be pleased to dwell with her, let her not leave him.
1 Cor. 7:13

The unbelieving husband is sanctified by the wife, and the unbelieving wife is sanctified by the husband.
1 Cor. 7:14

If we believe not, yet He abideth faithful: He cannot deny Himself.
2 Tim. 2:13

If ye will hear His voice, harden not your hearts.
Heb. 3:15
See also, e.g., Ps. 95:7–8

He that cometh to God must believe that He is, and that He is a rewarder of them that diligently seek Him.
Heb. 11:6

Believe not every spirit.
1 John 4:1

He that believeth not God hath made Him a liar.
(Him: Jesus)
1 John 5:10

[*See also* Doubt, Faith, Jesus, Jesus (Acceptance of), Prayer, Sincerity, Skepticism]

BELIEVERS

Ye are the temple of God.
1 Cor. 3:16

The temple of God is holy, which temple ye are.
1 Cor. 3:17

Ye are Christ's; and Christ is God's.
1 Cor. 3:23

The saints shall judge the world.
1 Cor. 6:2

He that is called in the Lord, being a servant, is the Lord's freeman.
1 Cor. 7:22

Are not ye my work in the Lord?
1 Cor. 9:1

Ye are all one in Christ Jesus.
Gal. 3:28

We are the circumcision, which worship God in the spirit, and rejoice in Christ Jesus.
Phil. 3:3

Let us, who are of the day, be sober, putting on the breastplate of faith and love; and for an helmet, the hope of salvation.
1 Thess. 5:8

The Lord knoweth them that are His.
2 Tim. 2:19

[*See also* Christians, God's People]

BENEVOLENCE

See Altruism, Charity, Deeds.

BETRAYAL

Judas Iscariot.
E.g., Matt. 26:14

Thirty pieces of silver.
Matt. 26:15

Woe unto that man by whom the Son of man is betrayed! it had been good for that man if he had not been born.
Jesus
Matt. 26:24
See also Mark 14:21, Luke 22:22

Behold, the hour is at hand, and the Son of man is betrayed into the hands of sinners.
Jesus
Matt. 26:45
See also Mark 14:41

Whomsoever I shall kiss, that same is He: hold Him fast.
Matt. 26:48
See also Mark 14:44

One of you which eateth with me shall betray me.
Jesus
Mark 14:18
See also Matt. 26:21

He that betrayeth me is at hand.
Jesus
Mark 14:42
See also Matt. 26:46

The hand of him that betrayeth me is with me on the table.
Jesus
Luke 22:21
See also Matt. 26:21

Betrayest thou the Son of man with a kiss?
Jesus
Luke 22:48

Have not I chosen you twelve, and one of you is a devil?
Jesus
John 6:70

Ye are not all clean.
Jesus
John 13:11

He that eateth bread with me hath lifted up his heel against me.
Jesus
John 13:18

Verily, verily, I say unto you, that one of you shall betray me.
Jesus
John 13:21
See also Matt. 26:21

That thou doest, do quickly.
Jesus
John 13:27

Of your own selves shall men arise, speaking perverse things.
Acts 20:30

[*See also* Allegiance, Deception, Loyalty, Treachery]

BIRTH

That which is born of the flesh is flesh; and that which is born of the Spirit is spirit.
Jesus
John 3:6

As soon as she is delivered of the child, she remembereth no more the anguish.
Jesus
John 16:21

[*See also* Jesus (Birth of)]

BITTERNESS

It shall make thy belly bitter, but it shall be in thy mouth sweet as honey.
Rev. 10:9

[*See also* Anguish]

BLAME

If thy right hand offend thee, cut it off, and cast it from thee.
Jesus
Matt. 5:30
See also Matt. 18:8, Mark 9:43

Judge not, that ye be not judged.
Jesus
Matt. 7:1
See also Luke 6:37

Why beholdest thou the mote that is in thy brother's eye, but considerest not the beam that is in thine own eye?
Jesus
Matt. 7:3
See also Luke 6:41

Ye shall be hated of all men for my name's sake: but he that endureth to the end shall be saved.
Jesus
Matt. 10:22
See also Mark 13:13, Luke 21:17

If thine eye offend thee, pluck it out, and cast it from thee.
Jesus
Matt. 18:9
See also Matt. 5:29, Mark 9:47

I am innocent of the blood of this just person.
Pilate
Matt. 27:24

He that is without sin among you, let him first cast a stone.
Jesus
John 8:7

If I do that I would not, it is no more I that do it, but sin that dwelleth in me.
Rom. 7:20
See also Rom. 7:17

[*See also* Guilt, Responsibility]

BLASPHEMY

All manner of sin and blasphemy shall be forgiven unto men: but the blasphemy against the Holy Ghost shall not be forgiven unto men.
Jesus
Matt. 12:31
See also Matt. 12:32, Mark 3:29

Whosoever shall speak a word against the Son of man, it shall be forgiven him: but unto him that blasphemeth against the Holy Ghost it shall not be forgiven.
Jesus
Luke 12:10
See also Matt. 12:32

[*See also* Heresy, Profanity]

BLESSING

If the house be worthy, let your peace come upon it: but if it be not worthy, let your peace return to you.
Jesus
Matt. 10:13

He that is mighty hath done to me great things; and holy is His name.
Mary
Luke 1:49

To day shalt thou be with me in paradise.
Jesus to malefactor on cross
Luke 23:43

Receive ye the Holy Ghost.
Jesus
John 20:22

I will give you the sure mercies of David.
Acts 13:34
See also Isa. 55:3

I commend you to God, and to the word of His grace.
Paul
Acts 20:32

The gifts and calling of God are without repentance.
Rom. 11:29

The God of peace be with you all.
Rom. 15:33

Eye hath not seen, nor ear heard, neither have entered into the heart of man, the things which God hath prepared for them that love Him.
1 Cor. 2:9
See also Isa. 64:4

Grace be with all them that love our Lord Jesus Christ in sincerity.
Eph. 6:24

The grace of our Lord Jesus Christ be with you all.
Phil. 4:23

The Lord be with you all.
2 Thess. 3:16

Out of the same mouth proceedeth blessing and cursing.
James 3:10

Peace be with you all that are in Christ Jesus.
1 Pet. 5:14

Grace be with you, mercy, and peace.
2 John 3

Mercy unto you, and peace, and love.
Jude 2

[*See also* Curses, Reward, and the Appendix at p. 200]

BLINDNESS

If the blind lead the blind, both shall fall into the ditch.
Jesus
Matt. 15:14
See also Luke 6:39

[*See also* Enlightenment, Handicapped, Miracles, Sight, Stubbornness]

BLOOD

This is my blood of the new testament, which is shed for many for the remission of sins.
Jesus
Matt. 26:28
See also Mark 14:24, Luke 22:20

Without shedding of blood is no remission.
Heb. 9:22

The blood of Jesus Christ His Son cleanseth us from all sin.
1 John 1:7

[*See also* Guilt]

BOASTING

He that speaketh of himself seeketh his own glory.
Jesus
John 7:18

If I honour myself, my honour is nothing.
Jesus
John 8:54

If thou boast, thou bearest not the root, but the root thee.
Rom. 11:18

He that glorieth, let him glory in the Lord.
E.g., 1 Cor. 1:31
See also Jer. 9:24

Though I would desire to glory, I shall not be a fool; for I will say the truth.
2 Cor. 12:6

God forbid that I should glory, save in the cross of our Lord Jesus Christ.
Gal. 6:14

How much she hath glorified herself, and lived deliciously, so much torment and sorrow give her.
(she: Babylon)
Rev. 18:7

[*See also* Arrogance, Publicity]

The light of the body is the eye.
Jesus
Matt. 6:22, Luke 11:34

Fear not them which kill the body, but are not able to kill the soul.
Jesus
Matt. 10:28
See also Luke 12:4

The body is not for fornication, but for the Lord.
1 Cor. 6:13

Your bodies are the members of Christ.
1 Cor. 6:15

Your body is the temple of the Holy Ghost.
1 Cor. 6:19

Glorify God in your body, and in your spirit.
1 Cor. 6:20

It is sown in corruption; it is raised in incorruption.
1 Cor. 15:42

[*See also* Appearance, Carnality, Physical Fitness, Speech]

BOOKS

If they should be written every one, I suppose that even the world itself could not contain the books that should be written.
John 21:25

What thou seest, write in a book, and send it unto the seven churches.
Jesus
Rev. 1:11

[*See also* History]

BORN AGAIN

Except a man be born again, he cannot see the kingdom of God.
Jesus
John 3:3

Except a man be born of water and of the Spirit, he cannot enter into the kingdom of God.
Jesus
John 3:5

Ye must be born again.
Jesus
John 3:7

Though ye have ten thousand instructors in Christ, yet have ye not many fathers.
1 Cor. 4:15

If any man be in Christ, he is a new creature.
2 Cor. 5:17

Whosoever is born of God doth not commit sin.
1 John 3:9

[*See also* Jesus (Acceptance of)]

BORROWING

Give to him that asketh thee, and from him that would borrow of thee turn not thou away.
Jesus
Matt. 5:42
See also Luke 6:30

[*See also* Generosity]

BRAVERY

See Courage.

BREAD OF LIFE

Labour not for the meat which perisheth, but for that meat which endureth unto everlasting life.
Jesus
John 6:27

The bread of God is He which cometh down from heaven, and giveth life unto the world.
Jesus
John 6:33

I am the bread of life: he that cometh to me shall never hunger; and he that believeth on me shall never thirst.
Jesus
John 6:35

I am the living bread which came down from heaven: if any man eat of this bread, he shall live for ever.
Jesus
John 6:51
See also John 6:58

[*See also* Eternal Life, Food]

BRIBERY

See Corruption, Greed, Money.

BROTHERHOOD

Whosoever is angry with his brother without a cause shall be in danger of the judgment.
Jesus
Matt. 5:22

Thou shalt love thy neighbour as thyself.
Jesus
Matt. 19:19
See also, e.g., Lev. 19:18

On earth peace, good will toward men.
Luke 2:14

As ye would that men should do to you, do ye also to them likewise.
Jesus
Luke 6:31
See also Matt. 7:12

Love one another.
Jesus
E.g., John 13:34

Sirs, ye are brethren; why do ye wrong one to another?
Acts 7:26

Follow peace with all men, and holiness, without which no man shall see the Lord.
Heb. 12:14

Let brotherly love continue.
Heb. 13:1

He that saith he is in the light, and hateth his brother, is in darkness even until now.
1 John 2:9

He that loveth not his brother abideth in death.
1 John 3:14

He that loveth not his brother whom he hath seen, how can he love God whom he hath not seen?
1 John 4:20

He who loveth God love his brother also.
1 John 4:21

[*See also* Enemies, Equality, Fellowship, Friendship, Hatred, Love, Peace, Universality]

BROTHERS

See Siblings.

BUILDING

He who hath builded the house hath more honour than the house.
Heb. 3:3

Every house is builded by some man; but He that built all things is God.
Heb. 3:4

[*See also* Planning]

BURDENS

Come unto me, all ye that labour and are heavy laden, and I will give you rest.
Jesus
Matt. 11:28

Him they compelled to bear His cross.
(Him: Simon)
Matt. 27:32
See also John 19:17

Ye lade men with burdens grievous to be borne, and ye yourselves touch not the burdens with one of your fingers.
Jesus
Luke 11:46
See also Matt. 23:4

Bear ye one another's burdens.
Gal. 6:2

[*See also* Acceptance, Comfort, Responsibility, Worry]

BURIAL

The potter's field, to bury strangers in.
Matt. 27:7

[*See also* Death]

BUSINESS

The kingdom of heaven is like unto a merchant man, seeking goodly pearls.
Jesus
Matt. 13:45

The merchants of the earth shall weep and mourn over her; for no man buyeth their merchandise any more.
(her: Babylon)
Rev. 18:11

[*See also* Employees, Honesty, Leadership, Work]

CALLING

See Mission.

CANDOR

Though I would desire to glory, I shall not be a fool; for I will say the truth.
2 Cor. 12:6

If I yet pleased men, I should not be the servant of Christ.
Gal. 1:10

[*See also* Honesty, Truth]

CARE

See Comfort, Devotion.

CARNALITY

The law is spiritual: but I am carnal.
Rom. 7:14

In me (that is, in my flesh,) dwelleth no good thing.
Rom. 7:18

With the mind I myself serve the law of God; but with the flesh the law of sin.
Rom. 7:25

They that are after the flesh do mind the things of the flesh; but they that are after the Spirit the things of the Spirit.
Rom. 8:5

The carnal mind is enmity against God.
Rom. 8:7

They that are in the flesh cannot please God.
Rom. 8:8

If ye live after the flesh, ye shall die.
Rom. 8:13

[*See also* Fornication, Lust, Spirituality]

CAUTION

See Prudence, Vigilance, Warning.

CELEBRATION

When thou makest a feast, call the poor, the maimed, the lame, the blind: And thou shalt be blessed; for they cannot recompense thee.
Jesus
Luke 14:13–14

Bring hither the fatted calf.
Luke 15:23

Rejoice in the Lord alway.
E.g., Phil. 4:4

Rejoice evermore.
1 Thess. 5:16

[*See also* Happiness, Pleasure]

CELIBACY

He that is able to receive it, let him receive it.
Jesus
Matt. 19:12

It is good for a man not to touch a woman.
1 Cor. 7:1

It is better to marry than to burn.
1 Cor. 7:9

He that giveth her in marriage doeth well; but he that giveth her not in marriage doeth better.
1 Cor. 7:38

[*See also* Marriage]

CERTAINTY

Wheresoever the carcase is, there will the eagles be gathered together.
Jesus
Matt. 24:28
See also Luke 17:37

Though I should die with Thee, yet will I not deny Thee.
Peter to Jesus
Matt. 26:35
See also Mark 14:31

If the goodman of the house had known what hour the thief would come, he would have watched.
Jesus
Luke 12:39
See also Matt. 24:43

What I have written I have written.
Pilate
John 19:22

One man esteemeth one day above another: another esteemeth every day alike. Let every man be fully persuaded in his own mind.
Rom. 14:5

If the trumpet give an uncertain sound, who shall prepare himself to the battle?
1 Cor. 14:8

The word of God is quick, and powerful, and sharper than any twoedged sword.
Heb. 4:12

Ye ought to say, If the Lord will, we shall live, and do this, or that.
James 4:15

[*See also* Indecision]

If Thou be the Son of God, command that these stones be made bread.
Devil to Jesus
Matt. 4:3
See also Luke 4:3

Thou shalt not tempt the Lord thy God.
Jesus
Matt. 4:7, Luke 4:12
See also Deut. 6:16

Ye say that I am.
Jesus
Luke 22:70

Why tempt ye God?
Acts 15:10

[*See also* Competition]

CHANGE

New wine must be put into new bottles.
Jesus
Mark 2:22, Luke 5:38
See also Matt. 9:17

The fashion of this world passeth away.
1 Cor. 7:31

Old things are passed away; behold, all things are become new.
2 Cor. 5:17

He which persecuted us in times past now preacheth the faith which once he destroyed.
(He: Paul)
Gal. 1:23

Jesus Christ the same yesterday, and to day, and for ever.
Heb. 13:8

[*See also* Adaptability, Conversion]

CHAOS

God is not the author of confusion, but of peace.
1 Cor. 14:33

[*See also* Confusion]

CHARACTER

Ye are the salt of the earth.
Jesus
Matt. 5:13

If thine eye be evil, thy whole body shall be full of darkness.
Jesus
Matt. 6:23
See also Luke 11:34

Every good tree bringeth forth good fruit; but a corrupt tree bringeth forth evil fruit.
Jesus
Matt. 7:17
See also Luke 6:43

The tree is known by his fruit.
Jesus
Matt. 12:33
See also Luke 6:44

Out of the abundance of the heart the mouth speaketh.
Jesus
Matt. 12:34

A good man out of the good treasure of the heart bringeth forth good things: and an evil man out of the evil treasure bringeth forth evil things.
Jesus
Matt. 12:35

Because they had no root, they withered away.
Jesus
Matt. 13:6
See also Mark 4:6

Take heed therefore that the light which is in thee be not darkness.
Jesus
Luke 11:35

How can a man that is a sinner do such miracles?
Pharisees, about Jesus
John 9:16

They that are after the flesh do mind the things of the flesh; but they that are after the Spirit the things of the Spirit.
Rom. 8:5

We then that are strong ought to bear the infirmities of the weak.
Rom. 15:1

By the grace of God I am what I am: and His grace which was bestowed upon me was not in vain.
1 Cor. 15:10

Evil communications corrupt good manners.
1 Cor. 15:33

These are wells without water, clouds that are carried with a tempest.
2 Pet. 2:17

Clouds they are without water, carried about of winds; trees whose fruit withereth.
Jude 12

[*See also* Ability, Attitude, Behavior, Honesty, Integrity]

CHARITY

First be reconciled to thy brother, and then come and offer thy gift.
Jesus
Matt. 5:24

Do not your alms before men, to be seen of them: otherwise ye have no reward of your Father which is in heaven.
Jesus
Matt. 6:1

When thou doest thine alms, do not sound a trumpet before thee, as the hypocrites do.
Jesus
Matt. 6:2

When thou doest alms, let not thy left hand know what thy right hand doeth.
Jesus
Matt. 6:3

If thou wilt be perfect, go and sell that thou hast, and give to the poor, and thou shalt have treasure in heaven: and come and follow me.
Jesus
Matt. 19:21
See also Mark 10:21, Luke 18:22

Inasmuch as ye have done it unto one of the least of these my brethren, ye have done it unto me.
Jesus
Matt. 25:40
See also Matt. 25:45

Sell that ye have, and give alms.
Jesus
Luke 12:33

When thou makest a feast, call the poor, the maimed, the lame, the blind: And thou shalt be blessed; for they cannot recompense thee.
Jesus
Luke 14:13–14

Silver and gold have I none; but such as I have give I thee.
Acts 3:6

Thy money perish with thee, because thou hast thought that the gift of God may be purchased with money.
Acts 8:20

He that giveth, let him do it with simplicity.
Rom. 12:8

And though I bestow all my goods to feed the poor, and though I give my body to be burned, and have not charity, it profiteth me nothing.
(charity: love)
1 Cor. 13:3

Every man according as he purposeth in his heart, so let him give.
2 Cor. 9:7

God loveth a cheerful giver.
2 Cor. 9:7

Remember the poor.
Gal. 2:10

[*See also* Altruism, Generosity, Love, Poverty, Sharing, Underprivileged]

CHASTISEMENT

Neither do I condemn thee: go, and sin no more.
Jesus
John 8:11

Them that sin rebuke before all, that others also may fear.
(Them: church leaders)
1 Tim. 5:20

Despise not thou the chastening of the Lord.
Heb. 12:5

Whom the Lord loveth He chasteneth.
Heb. 12:6

[*See also* Discipline, Punishment]

CHEATING

See Honesty, Lies.

CHILD-REARING

Provoke not your children to wrath.
Eph. 6:4

Fathers, provoke not your children to anger, lest they be discouraged.
Col. 3:21

[*See also* Children, Parents]

CHILDREN

Whoso shall receive one such little child in my name receiveth me.
Jesus
Matt. 18:5
See also Mark 9:37, Luke 9:48

Out of the mouth of babes and sucklings Thou hast perfected praise.
Jesus
Matt. 21:16
See also Ps. 8:2

Whosoever shall offend one of these little ones that believe in me, it is better for him that a millstone were hanged about his neck, and he were cast into the sea.
Jesus
Mark 9:42
See also Matt. 18:6, Luke 17:2

Suffer the little children to come unto me, and forbid them not: for of such is the kingdom of God.
Jesus
Mark 10:14
See also Matt. 19:14, Luke 18:16

Whosoever shall not receive the kingdom

of God as a little child, he shall not enter therein.
Jesus
Mark 10:15
See also Luke 18:17

We are the children of God.
Rom. 8:16

When I was a child, I spake as a child, I understood as a child, I thought as a child: but when I became a man, I put away childish things.
1 Cor. 13:11

The desolate hath many more children than she which hath an husband.
Gal. 4:27
See also Isa. 54:1

Children, obey your parents in the Lord.
Eph. 6:1

What son is he whom the father chasteneth not?
Heb. 12:7

I have no greater joy than to hear that my children walk in truth.
3 John 4

[*See also* Birth, Child-Rearing, Firstborn, Maturity, Parents, Youth]

CHOICE

He shall separate them one from another, as a shepherd divideth his sheep from the goats.
Jesus
Matt. 25:32

Ye have not chosen me, but I have chosen you.
Jesus
John 15:16

Not this man, but Barabbas.
John 18:40
See also Luke 23:18

Seeing ye put it from you, and judge yourselves unworthy of everlasting life, lo, we turn to the Gentiles.
Paul to Jews
Acts 13:46

All things are lawful unto me, but all things are not expedient.
1 Cor. 6:12
See also 1 Cor. 10:23

Eschew evil, and do good.
1 Pet. 3:11

Follow not that which is evil, but that which is good.
3 John 11

[*See also* Good and Evil, Indecision, Loyalty]

CHRIST

See Jesus, Messiah, Messianic Hopes and Prophecies.

CHRIST ETERNAL

Heaven and earth shall pass away, but my words shall not pass away.
Jesus
Matt. 24:35, Mark 13:31,
Luke 21:33

Lo, I am with you alway, even unto the end of the world.
Jesus
Matt. 28:20

Of His kingdom there shall be no end.
(His: Jesus)
Luke 1:33

Before Abraham was, I am.
Jesus
John 8:58

Christ being raised from the dead dieth no more.
Rom. 6:9

Thy throne, O God, is for ever and ever.
Heb. 1:8

They shall perish; but Thou remainest.
Heb. 1:11

Jesus Christ the same yesterday, and to day, and for ever.
Heb. 13:8

I am alive for evermore.
Jesus
Rev. 1:18

I am Alpha and Omega, the beginning and the end, the first and the last.
Jesus
Rev. 22:13
See also Rev. 1:8, 11, Rev. 21:6

[See also Eternal Life, Eternity, Jesus, Resurrection]

CHRISTIANITY

Thou art Peter, and upon this rock I will build my church; and the gates of hell shall not prevail against it.
Jesus
Matt. 16:18

There shall be one fold, and one shepherd.
Jesus
John 10:16

CHRISTIANS

By this shall all men know that ye are my disciples, if ye have love one to another.
Jesus
John 13:35

The disciples were called Christians first in Antioch.
Acts 11:26

We are the children of God.
Rom. 8:16

Ye are the body of Christ.
1 Cor. 12:27

We are unto God a sweet savour of Christ.
2 Cor. 2:15

Thou art no more a servant, but a son.
Gal. 4:7

Ye who sometimes were far off are made nigh by the blood of Christ.
Eph. 2:13

Ye are no more strangers and foreigners, but fellowcitizens with the saints.
Eph. 2:19

Walk worthy of the vocation wherewith ye are called.
Eph. 4:1

Be ye therefore followers of God, as dear children.
Eph. 5:1

The dead in Christ shall rise first.
1 Thess. 4:16

Ye are all the children of light, and the children of the day.
1 Thess. 5:5

If any man suffer as a Christian, let him not be ashamed.
1 Pet. 4:16

The world knoweth us not, because it knew Him not.
1 John 3:1

[See also Believers, Christianity, God's People, Persecution]

CHRISTMAS

Unto you is born this day in the city of David a Saviour, which is Christ the Lord.
Luke 2:11

CHURCH AND STATE

Render therefore unto Caesar the things which are Caesar's; and unto God the things that are God's.
Jesus
Matt. 22:21
See also Mark 12:17, Luke 20:25

My kingdom is not of this world.
Jesus
John 18:36

Look ye to it; for I will be no judge of such matters.
Acts 18:15

I stand at Caesar's judgment seat, where I ought to be judged: to the Jews have I done no wrong.
Paul
Acts 25:10

[See also Government]

CHURCH GOVERNANCE

See Clergy, Leadership.

CHURCHES

Thou art Peter, and upon this rock I will build my church; and the gates of hell shall not prevail against it.
Jesus
Matt. 16:18

My house is the house of prayer: but ye have made it a den of thieves.
Jesus
Luke 19:46
See also Matt. 21:13, Mark 11:17

Heaven is My throne, and earth is My footstool: what house will ye build Me? saith the Lord.
Acts 7:49
See also Isa. 66:1

God that made the world and all things therein, seeing that He is Lord of heaven and earth, dwelleth not in temples made with hands.
Acts 17:24

We, being many, are one body in Christ, and every one members one of another.
Rom. 12:5

Let your women keep silence in the churches: for it is not permitted unto them to speak.
1 Cor. 14:34

It is a shame for women to speak in the church.
1 Cor. 14:35

He is the head of the body, the church.
(He: Jesus)
Col. 1:18

If a man know not how to rule his own house, how shall he take care of the church of God?
1 Tim. 3:5

[*See also* God's Presence, God's Temple, Prayer, Worship]

CIRCUMCISION

Neither is that circumcision, which is outward in the flesh.
Rom. 2:28

Circumcision is that of the heart, in the spirit, and not in the letter; whose praise is not of men, but of God.
Rom. 2:29

What advantage then hath the Jew? or what profit is there of circumcision?
Rom. 3:1

Circumcision is nothing, and uncircumcision is nothing, but the keeping of the commandments of God.
1 Cor. 7:19

In Jesus Christ neither circumcision availeth any thing, nor uncircumcision; but faith which worketh by love.
Gal. 5:6

We are the circumcision, which worship God in the spirit, and rejoice in Christ Jesus.
Phil. 3:3

[*See also* Rituals]

CLARITY

Now we see through a glass, darkly; but then face to face.
1 Cor. 13:12

[*See also* Communication, Eloquence, Speech]

CLERGY

They which preach the gospel should live of the gospel.
1 Cor. 9:14

Woe is unto me, if I preach not the gospel!
1 Cor. 9:16

Know them which labour among you, and are over you in the Lord.
1 Thess. 5:12

Esteem them very highly in love for their work's sake.
1 Thess. 5:13

Let the elders that rule well be counted worthy of double honour.
1 Tim. 5:17

[*See also* Ministry, Preaching]

COMFORT

Blessed are they that mourn: for they shall be comforted.
Jesus
Matt. 5:4

Come unto me, all ye that labour and are heavy laden, and I will give you rest.
Jesus
Matt. 11:28

I am meek and lowly in heart: and ye shall find rest unto your souls.
Jesus
Matt. 11:29

Be of good cheer; it is I; be not afraid.
Jesus
Matt. 14:27, Mark 6:50
See also John 6:20

Tarry ye here, and watch with me.
Jesus
Matt. 26:38
See also Mark 14:34

Whosoever shall give you a cup of water to drink in my name, because ye belong to Christ, verily I say unto you, he shall not lose his reward.
Jesus
Mark 9:41

In my Father's house are many mansions.
Jesus
John 14:2

He shall give you another Comforter, that He may abide with you for ever.
Jesus
John 14:16

I will not leave you comfortless: I will come to you.
Jesus
John 14:18

Peace I leave with you, my peace I give unto you.
Jesus
John 14:27

Let not your heart be troubled, neither let it be afraid.
Jesus
John 14:27
See also John 14:1

Be of good cheer; I have overcome the world.
Jesus
John 16:33

Woman, why weepest thou?
Jesus to Mary Magdalene
John 20:15

The Father of mercies, and the God of all comfort.
2 Cor. 1:3

[*See also* Anguish, Fear, Grief, Mourning]

COMMANDMENTS

Whosoever shall do and teach them, the same shall be called great in the kingdom of heaven.
Jesus
Matt. 5:19

All things whatsoever ye would that men should do to you, do ye even so to them.
Jesus
Matt. 7:12
See also Luke 6:31

If thou wilt enter into life, keep the commandments.
Jesus
Matt. 19:17

Thou shalt love the Lord thy God with all thy heart, and with all thy soul, and with all thy mind. This is the first and great commandment.
Jesus
Matt. 22:37–38
See also Mark 12:29–30, Luke 10:27

Thou knowest the commandments, Do not commit adultery, Do not kill, Do not steal, Do not bear false witness, Defraud not, Honour thy father and mother.
Jesus
Mark 10:19
See also Matt. 19:18–19, Luke 18:20

It is easier for heaven and earth to pass, than one tittle of the law to fail.
Jesus
Luke 16:17
See also Matt. 5:18

The law was given by Moses, but grace and truth came by Jesus Christ.
John 1:17

A new commandment I give unto you, That ye love one another.
Jesus
John 13:34

This is my commandment, That ye love one another, as I have loved you.
Jesus
John 15:12

As many as have sinned without law shall also perish without law.
Rom. 2:12

By the law is the knowledge of sin.
Rom. 3:20
See also Rom. 4:15

Do we then make void the law through faith? God forbid.
Rom. 3:31

I had not known sin, but by the law.
Rom. 7:7

When the commandment came, sin revived.
Rom. 7:9

The law is spiritual: but I am carnal.
Rom. 7:14

He that loveth another hath fulfilled the law.
Rom. 13:8
See also Rom. 13:10

The letter killeth, but the spirit giveth life.
2 Cor. 3:6

A man is not justified by the works of the law, but by the faith of Jesus Christ.
Gal. 2:16

By the works of the law shall no flesh be justified.
Gal. 2:16

I through the law am dead to the law, that I might live unto God.
Gal. 2:19

If righteousness come by the law, then Christ is dead in vain.
Gal. 2:21

No man is justified by the law in the sight of God.
Gal. 3:11

Christ hath redeemed us from the curse of the law.
Gal. 3:13

It was ordained by angels in the hand of a mediator.
Gal. 3:19

Before faith came, we were kept under the law.
Gal. 3:23

The law was our schoolmaster to bring us unto Christ, that we might be justified by faith.
Gal. 3:24

All the law is fulfilled in one word, even in this; Thou shalt love thy neighbour as thyself.
Gal. 5:14

I will put My laws into their hearts, and in their minds will I write them.
Heb. 10:16
See also Jer. 31:33

He that said, Do not commit adultery, said also, Do not kill.
James 2:11

I write no new commandment unto you.
1 John 2:7

This is His commandment, That we should believe on the name of His Son Jesus Christ, and love one another.
1 John 3:23

[*See also* God's Word, Gospel, Law, Obedience, Sin]

COMMITMENT

Because they had no root, they withered away.
Jesus
Matt. 13:6
See also Mark 4:6

I seek not your's, but you.
2 Cor. 12:14

Let us run with patience the race that is set before us.
Heb. 12:1

Because thou art lukewarm, and neither cold nor hot, I will spue thee out of my mouth.
Jesus
Rev. 3:16
See also Rev. 3:15

[*See also* Devotion, Neutrality, Perseverance, Sincerity]

COMMON SENSE

See Wisdom.

COMMUNICATION

He that speaketh in an unknown tongue speaketh not unto men, but unto God: for no man understandeth him.
1 Cor. 14:2

He that speaketh in an unknown tongue edifieth himself; but he that prophesieth edifieth the church.
1 Cor. 14:4

Greater is he that prophesieth than he that speaketh with tongues.
1 Cor. 14:5

Except ye utter by the tongue words easy to be understood, how shall it be known what is spoken? for ye shall speak into the air.
1 Cor. 14:9

If I know not the meaning of the voice, I shall be unto him that speaketh a barbarian, and he that speaketh shall be a barbarian unto me.
1 Cor. 14:11

[*See also* Eloquence, News, Speech]

COMMUNION

Take, eat; this is my body.
Jesus
Matt. 26:26, Mark 14:22

This is my blood of the new testament,

which is shed for many for the remission of sins.
Jesus
Matt. 26:28
See also Mark 14:24, Luke 22:20

Except ye eat the flesh of the Son of man, and drink His blood, ye have no life in you.
Jesus
John 6:53
See also John 6:54

He that eateth me, even he shall live by me.
Jesus
John 6:57

This is my body, which is broken for you: this do in remembrance of me.
Jesus
1 Cor. 11:24
See also Luke 22:19

This cup is the new testament in my blood: this do ye, as oft as ye drink it, in remembrance of me.
Jesus
1 Cor. 11:25
See also Luke 22:20

[*See also* Bread of Life]

COMPANIONS

Depart from me, all ye workers of iniquity.
Jesus
Luke 13:27
See also Matt. 7:23

Evil communications corrupt good manners.
1 Cor. 15:33

Withdraw yourselves from every brother that walketh disorderly.
2 Thess. 3:6

[*See also* Fellowship, Friendship]

COMPASSION

Pray for them which despitefully use you, and persecute you.
Jesus
Matt. 5:44
See also Luke 6:28

For I was an hungred, and ye gave me meat: I was thirsty, and ye gave me drink: I was a stranger, and ye took me in: Naked, and ye clothed me: I was sick, and ye visited me: I was in prison, and ye came unto me.
Jesus
Matt. 25:35–36

Inasmuch as ye have done it unto one of the least of these my brethren, ye have done it unto me.
Jesus
Matt. 25:40
See also Matt. 25:45

He hath filled the hungry with good things; and the rich He hath sent empty away.
Luke 1:53

The law was given by Moses, but grace and truth came by Jesus Christ.
John 1:17

Neither do I condemn thee: go, and sin no more.
Jesus
John 8:11

Comfort the feebleminded, support the weak, be patient toward all men.
1 Thess. 5:14

Remember them that are in bonds, as bound with them; and them which suffer adversity, as being yourselves also in the body.
Heb. 13:3

Love as brethren, be pitiful, be courteous.
1 Pet. 3:8

[*See also* Charity, Comfort, Empathy, God's Mercy, Kindness, Mercy, Suffering, Sympathy]

COMPETITION

They which run in a race run all, but one receiveth the prize.
1 Cor. 9:24

Run, that ye may obtain.
1 Cor. 9:24

They do it to obtain a corruptible crown; but we an incorruptible.
1 Cor. 9:25

I press toward the mark for the prize of the high calling of God in Christ Jesus.
Phil. 3:14

I have fought a good fight, I have finished my course, I have kept the faith.
2 Tim. 4:7

Let us run with patience the race that is set before us.
Heb. 12:1

[*See also* Loss]

COMPLACENCY

Because thou art lukewarm, and neither cold nor hot, I will spue thee out of my mouth.
Jesus
Rev. 3:16
See also Rev. 3:15

COMPLAINTS

Neither murmur ye.
1 Cor. 10:10

Do all things without murmurings and disputings.
Phil. 2:14

Murmurers, complainers, walking after their own lusts.
Jude 16

[*See also* Acceptance, Contentment]

COMPROMISE

Ye cannot serve God and mammon.
Jesus
Matt. 6:24, Luke 16:13

Ye cannot drink the cup of the Lord, and the cup of devils.
1 Cor. 10:21

[*See also* Arguments, Grudges, Mediation]

CONCEIT

Every one that exalteth himself shall be abased; and he that humbleth himself shall be exalted.
Jesus
Luke 18:14
See also Luke 14:11

They loved the praise of men more than the praise of God.
John 12:43

Jesus I know, and Paul I know; but who are ye?
Acts 19:15

Professing themselves to be wise, they became fools.
Rom. 1:22

Be not wise in your own conceits.
Rom. 12:16

I will destroy the wisdom of the wise, and will bring to nothing the understanding of the prudent.
1 Cor. 1:19
See also Isa. 29:14

Let no man deceive himself.
1 Cor. 3:18

Knowledge puffeth up, but charity edifieth.
(charity: love)
1 Cor. 8:1

Let us not be desirous of vain glory.
Gal. 5:26

If a man think himself to be something, when he is nothing, he deceiveth himself.
Gal. 6:3

Let nothing be done through strife or vainglory.
Phil. 2:3

[*See also* Arrogance, Boasting, Humility, Pride, Self-Awareness, Self-Righteousness]

CONDUCT

See Behavior.

CONDUCT TOWARD GOD

See Behavior, Fear of God, Love of God.

CONFESSION

Depart from me; for I am a sinful man, O Lord.
Luke 5:8

Father, I have sinned against heaven, and before thee.
Luke 15:18
See also Luke 15:21

Confess your faults one to another.
James 5:16

If we confess our sins, He is faithful and just to forgive us our sins.
1 John 1:9

[*See also* Acknowledgment, Forgiveness, Repentance]

CONFIDENCE

With God all things are possible.
Jesus
Matt. 19:26, Mark 10:27
See also Luke 18:27

All things are possible to him that believeth.
Jesus
Mark 9:23

If God be for us, who can be against us?
Rom. 8:31

Let him that thinketh he standeth take heed lest he fall.
1 Cor. 10:12

I can do all things through Christ which strengtheneth me.
Phil. 4:13

Fathers, provoke not your children to anger, lest they be discouraged.
Col. 3:21

Be not soon shaken in mind.
2 Thess. 2:2

God hath not given us the spirit of fear; but of power, and of love, and of a sound mind.
2 Tim. 1:7

I am not ashamed: for I know whom I have believed.
2 Tim. 1:12

Cast not away therefore your confidence, which hath great recompence of reward.
Heb. 10:35

Lift up the hands which hang down, and the feeble knees.
Heb. 12:12

The Lord is my helper, and I will not fear what man shall do unto me.
Heb. 13:6
See also Ps. 118:6

[*See also* Courage, Faith, Pride, Timidity]

CONFLICT OF INTEREST

See Allegiance, Loyalty.

CONFORMITY

Be not conformed to this world.
Rom. 12:2

For though we walk in the flesh, we do not war after the flesh.
2 Cor. 10:3

Know ye not that the friendship of the world is enmity with God?
James 4:4

They think it strange that ye run not with them to the same excess of riot.
1 Pet. 4:4

Love not the world, neither the things that are in the world.
1 John 2:15

[*See also* Behavior, Worldliness]

CONFUSION

Where envying and strife is, there is confusion and every evil work.
James 3:16

[*See also* Chaos]

CONSCIENCE

Whether it be right in the sight of God to hearken unto you more than unto God, judge ye.
Acts 4:19

I have lived in all good conscience before God until this day.
Acts 23:1

Herein do I exercise myself, to have always a conscience void of offence toward God, and toward men.
Acts 24:16

We trust we have a good conscience, in all things willing to live honestly.
Heb. 13:18

[*See also* Guilt, Honesty, Integrity, Soul]

CONSECRATION

Every male that openeth the womb shall be called holy to the Lord.
Luke 2:23
See also Ex. 13:2, 12

[*See also* Holiness]

CONSEQUENCES

With what measure ye mete, it shall be measured to you.
Jesus
Mark 4:24
See also Luke 6:38

Give, and it shall be given unto you.
Jesus
Luke 6:38

By one man's disobedience many were made sinners.
Rom. 5:19

He that soweth to his flesh shall of the

flesh reap corruption; but he that soweth to the Spirit shall of the Spirit reap life everlasting.
Gal. 6:8

If we deny Him, He also will deny us.
2 Tim. 2:12

[*See also* Punishment, Reciprocity, Retribution, Revenge, Reward]

CONSISTENCY

Of thorns men do not gather figs, nor of a bramble bush gather they grapes.
Jesus
Luke 6:44

He that is faithful in that which is least is faithful also in much.
Jesus
Luke 16:10

He that is unjust in the least is unjust also in much.
Jesus
Luke 16:10

Doth a fountain send forth at the same place sweet water and bitter?
James 3:11

Can the fig tree, my brethren, bear olive berries?
James 3:12

[*See also* Adaptability, Character]

CONSPIRACY

See Betrayal.

CONTAMINATION

A little leaven leaveneth the whole lump.
1 Cor. 5:6, Gal. 5:9

Be not partakers of her sins.
(her: Babylon)
Rev. 18:4

[*See also* Corruption, Purity]

CONTEMPLATION

Whatsoever things are true, whatsoever things are honest, whatsoever things are just, whatsoever things are pure, whatsoever things are lovely, whatsoever things are of good report; if there be any virtue, and if there be any praise, think on these things.
Phil. 4:8

[*See also* Thoughts]

CONTEMPT

Blessed are ye, when men shall revile you, and persecute you, and shall say all manner of evil against you falsely, for my sake.
Jesus
Matt. 5:11

[*See also* Hatred, Scorn]

CONTENTMENT

Mine eyes have seen Thy salvation, Which Thou hast prepared before the face of all people.
Simeon
Luke 2:30–31

We have peace with God through our Lord Jesus Christ.
Rom. 5:1

As the Lord hath called every one, so let him walk.
1 Cor. 7:17

Let every man abide in the same calling wherein he was called.
1 Cor. 7:20

The peace of God, which passeth all understanding.
Phil. 4:7

I have learned, in whatsoever state I am, therewith to be content.
Phil. 4:11

Godliness with contentment is great gain.
1 Tim. 6:6

Be content with such things as ye have.
Heb. 13:5

They shall hunger no more, neither thirst

any more; neither shall the sun light on them, nor any heat.
   Rev. 7:16

[*See also* Greed, Happiness, Satisfaction, Serenity]

CONTRITION

God be merciful to me a sinner.
   Luke 18:13

Lord, remember me when Thou comest into Thy kingdom.
   Malefactor, on cross, to Jesus
   Luke 23:42

Many of the saints did I shut up in prison.
   Paul
   Acts 26:10

[*See also* Confession, Humility, Regret]

CONTROVERSY

Him that is weak in the faith receive ye, but not to doubtful disputations.
   Rom. 14:1

Foolish and unlearned questions avoid, knowing that they do gender strifes.
   2 Tim. 2:23

The servant of the Lord must not strive.
   2 Tim. 2:24

Avoid foolish questions.
   Titus 3:9

A man that is an heretick after the first and second admonition reject.
   Titus 3:10

[*See also* Anger, Arguments, Strife]

CONVERSION

Except ye be converted, and become as little children, ye shall not enter into the kingdom of heaven.
   Jesus
   Matt. 18:3

Repent ye therefore, and be converted, that your sins may be blotted out.
   Acts 3:19

Lord, what wilt Thou have me to do?
   Saul to Jesus
   Acts 9:6

There fell from his eyes as it had been scales: and he received sight forthwith, and arose, and was baptized.
   (he: Saul)
   Acts 9:18

The hand of the Lord was with them: and a great number believed.
   Acts 11:21

Seeing ye put it from you, and judge yourselves unworthy of everlasting life, lo, we turn to the Gentiles.
   Paul to Jews
   Acts 13:46

I have set thee to be a light of the Gentiles, that thou shouldest be for salvation unto the ends of the earth.
   Acts 13:47
   See also Isa. 49:6

God, which knoweth the hearts, bare them witness, giving them the Holy Ghost.
   Acts 15:8

I was found of them that sought me not.
   Rom. 10:20
   See also Isa. 65:1

He which persecuted us in times past now preacheth the faith which once he destroyed.
   (He: Paul)
   Gal. 1:23

[*See also* Born Again, Evangelism, Jesus (Acceptance of)]

COOPERATION

Whosoever shall compel thee to go a mile, go with him twain.
   Jesus
   Matt. 5:41

One soweth, and another reapeth.
   Jesus
   John 4:37

He that planteth and he that watereth are one.
1 Cor. 3:8

Let us walk by the same rule, let us mind the same thing.
Phil. 3:16

He that biddeth him God speed is partaker of his evil deeds.
2 John 11

[*See also* Brotherhood, Unity, Work]

CORRUPTION

Do violence to no man, neither accuse any falsely.
Luke 3:14

Save yourselves from this untoward generation.
Acts 2:40

There is none that doeth good, no, not one.
Rom. 3:12, Ps. 14:3, Ps. 53:3
See also Rom. 3:10

Keep thyself pure.
1 Tim. 5:22

Unto them that are defiled and unbelieving is nothing pure; but even their mind and conscience is defiled.
Titus 1:15

The law maketh men high priests which have infirmity.
Heb. 7:28

If ye have respect to persons, ye commit sin.
James 2:9

All nations have drunk of the wine of the wrath of her fornication.
(her: Babylon)
Rev. 18:3

The merchants of the earth are waxed rich through the abundance of her delicacies.
(her: Babylon)
Rev. 18:3

[*See also* Decadence, Good and Evil, Honesty, Injustice, Purity, Wickedness]

COURAGE

The voice of one crying in the wilderness.
Matt. 3:3, Mark 1:3, Luke 3:4,
John 1:23
See also Isa. 40:3

Let them come themselves and fetch us out.
Acts 16:37

As thou hast testified of me in Jerusalem, so must thou bear witness also at Rome.
Jesus
Acts 23:11

Be strong in the Lord, and in the power of His might.
Eph. 6:10

Fear none of those things which thou shalt suffer.
Jesus
Rev. 2:10

[*See also* Confidence, Encouragement, Fear]

COURTESY

Give none offence.
1 Cor. 10:32

Let your speech be alway with grace, seasoned with salt, that ye may know how ye ought to answer every man.
Col. 4:6

Love as brethren, be pitiful, be courteous.
1 Pet. 3:8

[*See also* Behavior, Hospitality]

COVENANT

This is my blood of the new testament, which is shed for many for the remission of sins.
Jesus
Matt. 26:28
See also Mark 14:24, Luke 22:20

This cup is the new testament in my blood: this do ye, as oft as ye drink it, in remembrance of me.
Jesus
1 Cor. 11:25
See also Luke 22:20

If that first covenant had been faultless, then should no place have been sought for the second.
> *Heb. 8:7*

In that He saith, A new covenant, He hath made the first old.
> *Heb. 8:13*

COWARDICE

See Fear, Timidity.

CREATION

Without Him was not any thing made.
> *John 1:3*

Lord, Thou art God, which hast made heaven, and earth, and the sea.
> *Acts 4:24*

Hath not My hand made all these things?
> *Acts 7:50*
> *See also Isa. 66:2*

The man is not of the woman; but the woman of the man.
> *1 Cor. 11:8*

By Him were all things created, that are in heaven, and that are in earth.
> *(Him: Jesus)*
> *Col. 1:16*

Every house is builded by some man; but He that built all things is God.
> *Heb. 3:4*

[*See also* Beginnings]

CREATIVITY

See Achievement, Building.

CREDIBILITY

How can ye, being evil, speak good things?
> *Jesus*
> *Matt. 12:34*

If I bear witness of myself, my witness is not true.
> *Jesus*
> *John 5:31*

If we receive the witness of men, the witness of God is greater.
> *1 John 5:9*

[*See also* Belief, Doubt, Skepticism]

CRIME

Thou shalt not steal.
> *Jesus*
> *Matt. 19:18*
> *See also, e.g., Ex. 20:15, Mark 10:19, Luke 18:20*

The thief cometh not, but for to steal, and to kill, and to destroy.
> *Jesus*
> *John 10:10*

Let him that stole steal no more: but rather let him labour, working with his hands.
> *Eph. 4:28*

[*See also* Evil]

CRITICISM

Judge not, that ye be not judged.
> *Jesus*
> *Matt. 7:1*

With what judgment ye judge, ye shall be judged.
> *Jesus*
> *Matt. 7:2*

First cast out the beam out of thine own eye; and then shalt thou see clearly to cast out the mote out of thy brother's eye.
> *Jesus*
> *Matt. 7:5*
> *See also Luke 6:42*

Physician, heal thyself.
> *Luke 4:23*

Judge not, and ye shall not be judged: condemn not, and ye shall not be condemned.
> *Jesus*
> *Luke 6:37*

If thy brother trespass against thee, rebuke him; and if he repent, forgive him.
> *Jesus*
> *Luke 17:3*

Ye judge after the flesh; I judge no man.
Jesus
John 8:15

Wherein thou judgest another, thou condemnest thyself.
Rom. 2:1

Who art thou that judgest another man's servant?
Rom. 14:4

No chastening for the present seemeth to be joyous.
Heb. 12:11

Who art thou that judgest another?
James 4:12

What glory is it, if, when ye be buffeted for your faults, ye shall take it patiently?
1 Pet. 2:20

If, when ye do well, and suffer for it, ye take it patiently, this is acceptable with God.
1 Pet. 2:20

[*See also* Accusations, Chastisement, Discipline, Public Opinion, Scorn, Slander]

CRUCIFIXION

They shall mock Him, and shall scourge Him, and shall spit upon Him, and shall kill Him: and the third day He shall rise again.
Jesus
Mark 10:34
See also Luke 18:33

Father, into Thy hands I commend my spirit.
Jesus
Luke 23:46

Ye shall weep and lament, but the world shall rejoice.
Jesus
John 16:20

They cried out, saying, Crucify Him, crucify Him.
John 19:6, Luke 23:21
See also, e.g., Matt. 27:23,
Mark 15:13

He bowed His head, and gave up the ghost.
John 19:30

Through ignorance ye did it.
Acts 3:17

Christ died for the ungodly.
Rom. 5:6

Christ died for us.
Rom. 5:8

In that He died, He died unto sin once: but in that He liveth, He liveth unto God.
Rom. 6:10

We preach Christ crucified, unto the Jews a stumblingblock, and unto the Greeks foolishness.
1 Cor. 1:23

Had they known it, they would not have crucified the Lord.
1 Cor. 2:8

Christ died for our sins.
1 Cor. 15:3

He died for all.
2 Cor. 5:15

I am crucified with Christ: nevertheless I live.
Gal. 2:20

Ye who sometimes were far off are made nigh by the blood of Christ.
Eph. 2:13

If God so loved us, we ought also to love one another.
1 John 4:11

Worthy is the Lamb that was slain.
Rev. 5:12

[*See also* Jesus (Last Words on the Cross), Martyrdom, Sacrifice]

CRUELTY

I was an hungred, and ye gave me no meat: I was thirsty, and ye gave me no drink.
Jesus
Matt. 25:42

He shall have judgment without mercy,
that hath showed no mercy.
James 2:13

[*See also* Persecution]

CULTIVATION

I have planted, Apollos watered; but God
gave the increase.
1 Cor. 3:6

He that planteth and he that watereth are
one.
1 Cor. 3:8

[*See also* Growth, Nature]

CURSES

Bless them that curse you.
Jesus
Matt. 5:44, Luke 6:28

Bless them which persecute you: bless,
and curse not.
Rom. 12:14

If any man love not the Lord Jesus Christ,
let him be Anathema.
1 Cor. 16:22

[*See also* Blasphemy, Blessing, Profanity,
Speech]

CYNICISM

Can there any good thing come out of
Nazareth?
John 1:46

If ye believe not his writings, how shall ye
believe my words?
Jesus, about Moses
John 5:47

[*See also* Doubt, Skepticism]

DAMNATION

If thy right eye offend thee, pluck it out,
and cast it from thee: for it is profitable
for thee that one of thy members should
perish, and not that thy whole body
should be cast into hell.
Jesus
Matt. 5:29
See also Matt. 18:9

Wide is the gate, and broad is the way,
that leadeth to destruction.
Jesus
Matt. 7:13

Ye serpents, ye generation of vipers, how
can ye escape the damnation of hell?
Jesus
Matt. 23:33

If thy foot offend thee, cut it off: it is better
for thee to enter halt into life, than having
two feet to be cast into hell.
Jesus
Mark 9:45
See also Matt. 18:8

He that believeth not shall be damned.
Jesus
Mark 16:16

Fear Him, which after He hath killed hath
power to cast into hell; yea, I say unto you,
Fear Him.
Jesus
Luke 12:5
See also Matt. 10:28

He that believeth not is condemned already, because he hath not believed in the
name of the only begotten Son of God.
Jesus
John 3:18

They that have done good, unto the resurrection of life; and they that have done
evil, unto the resurrection of damnation.
Jesus
John 5:29

We are not of them who draw back unto

perdition; but of them that believe to the saving of the soul.
Heb. 10:39

God spared not the angels that sinned, but cast them down to hell.
2 Pet. 2:4

Whosoever was not found written in the book of life was cast into the lake of fire.
Rev. 20:15

[*See also* Death, Hell, Salvation, Wickedness]

DANCE

We have piped unto you, and ye have not danced; we have mourned unto you, and ye have not lamented.
Jesus
Matt. 11:17
See also Luke 7:32

DANGER

I send you forth as sheep in the midst of wolves: be ye therefore wise as serpents, and harmless as doves.
Jesus
Matt. 10:16

Behold, I send you forth as lambs among wolves.
Jesus
Luke 10:3

In perils in the city, in perils in the wilderness, in perils in the sea, in perils among false brethren.
2 Cor. 11:26

Behold, how great a matter a little fire kindleth!
James 3:5

The second woe is past; and, behold, the third woe cometh quickly.
Rev. 11:14

[*See also* Safety, Trouble]

DARKNESS

See Enlightenment, Light and Darkness.

DEATH

There be some standing here, which shall not taste of death, till they see the Son of man coming in His kingdom.
Jesus
Matt. 16:28
See also Mark 9:1, Luke 9:27

Wheresoever the carcase is, there will the eagles be gathered together.
Jesus
Matt. 24:28
See also Luke 17:37

Except ye repent, ye shall all likewise perish.
Jesus
Luke 13:3

Whosoever believeth in Him should not perish, but have eternal life.
Jesus
John 3:15
See also John 3:16

If a man keep my saying, he shall never see death.
Jesus
John 8:51

Yet a little while, and the world seeth me no more.
Jesus
John 14:19

I come to Thee.
Jesus
John 17:11

It is finished.
Jesus
John 19:30

As a sheep to the slaughter.
Acts 8:32
See also Isa. 53:7, Jer. 11:19

Scarcely for a righteous man will one die:

yet peradventure for a good man some would even dare to die.
Rom. 5:7

He that is dead is freed from sin.
Rom. 6:7

If ye live after the flesh, ye shall die.
Rom. 8:13

No man dieth to himself.
Rom. 14:7

The last enemy that shall be destroyed is death.
1 Cor. 15:26

Death is swallowed up in victory.
1 Cor. 15:54

O death, where is thy sting? O grave, where is thy victory?
1 Cor. 15:55
See also Hos. 13:14

The sting of death is sin; and the strength of sin is the law.
1 Cor. 15:56

We brought nothing into this world, and it is certain we can carry nothing out.
1 Tim. 6:7

Where a testament is, there must also of necessity be the death of the testator.
Heb. 9:16

Sin, when it is finished, bringeth forth death.
James 1:15

As the body without the spirit is dead, so faith without works is dead also.
James 2:26
See also James 2:24

Shortly I must put off this my tabernacle.
2 Pet. 1:14

I looked, and behold a pale horse: and his name that sat on him was Death, and Hell followed with him.
Rev. 6:8

In those days shall men seek death, and shall not find it; and shall desire to die, and death shall flee from them.
Rev. 9:6

Blessed are the dead which die in the Lord from henceforth.
Rev. 14:13

Blessed and holy is he that hath part in the first resurrection: on such the second death hath no power.
Rev. 20:6

Death and hell were cast into the lake of fire. This is the second death.
Rev. 20:14

There shall be no more death, neither sorrow, nor crying, neither shall there be any more pain: for the former things are passed away.
Rev. 21:4

[*See also* Burial, Crucifixion, Damnation, Destruction, Eternal Life, Life, Life and Death, Martyrdom, Mortality, Mourning, Punishment, Resurrection]

DECADENCE

Ye are like unto whited sepulchres, which indeed appear beautiful outward.
Jesus
Matt. 23:27

Wasted his substance with riotous living.
(his: the prodigal son)
Luke 15:13

Clouds they are without water, carried about of winds; trees whose fruit withereth.
Jude 12

Babylon the great is fallen, is fallen, and is become the habitation of devils.
Rev. 18:2

All nations have drunk of the wine of the wrath of her fornication.
(her: Babylon)
Rev. 18:3

Be not partakers of her sins.
(her: Babylon)
Rev. 18:4

How much she hath glorified herself, and lived deliciously, so much torment and sorrow give her.
(she: Babylon)
Rev. 18:7

Alas, alas that great city Babylon, that mighty city! for in one hour is thy judgment come.
Rev. 18:10

The fruits that thy soul lusted after are departed from thee.
Rev. 18:14

Without are dogs, and sorcerers, and whoremongers, and murderers, and idolaters, and whosoever loveth and maketh a lie.
Rev. 22:15

[*See also* Corruption, Depravity, Evil, Immorality, Wickedness]

DECEPTION

Beware of false prophets, which come to you in sheep's clothing, but inwardly they are ravening wolves.
Jesus
Matt. 7:15

Take heed that ye be not deceived.
Jesus
Luke 21:8
See also Matt. 24:4, Mark 13:5

Let no man deceive himself.
1 Cor. 3:18

Who hath bewitched you, that ye should not obey the truth?
Gal. 3:1

Let no man deceive you with vain words.
Eph. 5:6

Beware lest any man spoil you through philosophy and vain deceit.
Col. 2:8

By thy sorceries were all nations deceived.
Rev. 18:23

[*See also* Appearance, Dishonesty, Hypocrisy, Lies, Self-Deception, Truth]

DECISIONS

Not as I will, but as Thou wilt.
Jesus
Matt. 26:39
See also Mark 14:36, Luke 22:42

[*See also* Certainty, Choice, Compromise, Indecision, Time]

DEEDS

Let your light so shine before men, that they may see your good works.
Jesus
Matt. 5:16

By their fruits ye shall know them.
Jesus
Matt. 7:20
See also Matt. 7:16

Whosoever heareth these sayings of mine, and doeth them, I will liken him unto a wise man, which built his house upon a rock.
Jesus
Matt. 7:24

He shall reward every man according to his works.
Jesus
Matt. 16:27
See also Ps. 62:12

Bring forth therefore fruits worthy of repentance.
Luke 3:8

Every tree is known by his own fruit.
Jesus
Luke 6:44
See also Matt. 7:17, Matt. 12:33

Why call ye me, Lord, Lord, and do not the things which I say?
Jesus
Luke 6:46

He that doeth truth cometh to the light, that his deeds may be made manifest.
Jesus
John 3:21

If this counsel or this work be of men, it will come to nought: But if it be of God, ye cannot overthrow it.
Acts 5:38–39

Glory, honour, and peace, to every man that worketh good.
Rom. 2:10

Not the hearers of the law are just before God, but the doers of the law shall be justified.
Rom. 2:13

A man is justified by faith without the deeds of the law.
    Rom. 3:28

By the works of the law shall no flesh be justified.
    Gal. 2:16

Whatsoever ye do in word or deed, do all in the name of the Lord Jesus.
    Col. 3:17

Be rich in good works.
    1 Tim. 6:18

They profess that they know God; but in works they deny Him.
    Titus 1:16

Not by works of righteousness which we have done, but according to His mercy He saved us.
    Titus 3:5

With such sacrifices God is well pleased.
    Heb. 13:16

Be ye doers of the word, and not hearers only.
    James 1:22

Faith without works is dead.
    James 2:20
    See also James 2:17

By works was faith made perfect.
    James 2:22

By works a man is justified, and not by faith only.
    James 2:24
    See also James 2:26

So is the will of God, that with well doing ye may put to silence the ignorance of foolish men.
    1 Pet. 2:15

It is better, if the will of God be so, that ye suffer for well doing, than for evil doing.
    1 Pet. 3:17

Let us not love in word, neither in tongue; but in deed and in truth.
    1 John 3:18

I have not found thy works perfect before God.
    Jesus
    Rev. 3:2

[*See also* Achievement, Ministry]

DEFEAT

The light of a candle shall shine no more at all in thee.
    Rev. 18:23

The voice of the bridegroom and of the bride shall be heard no more at all in thee.
    Rev. 18:23

[*See also* Success, Victory]

DEFIANCE

See Audacity, Rebellion.

DELAY

See Patience, Procrastination.

DELIVERANCE

He hath sent me to heal the broken-hearted, to preach deliverance to the captives.
    Jesus
    Luke 4:18
    See also Isa. 61:1

O wretched man that I am! who shall deliver me from the body of this death?
    Rom. 7:24

I was delivered out of the mouth of the lion.
    2 Tim. 4:17

The Lord knoweth how to deliver the godly out of temptations.
    2 Pet. 2:9

[*See also* Escape, Exile, Freedom, Safety, Salvation]

DENIAL

Whosoever shall deny me before men, him will I also deny before my Father which is in heaven.
    Jesus
    Matt. 10:33
    See also Luke 12:9

Before the cock crow, thou shalt deny me thrice.
Jesus
Matt. 26:34, 75
See also Mark 14:30, John 13:38,
    Luke 22:34

Though I should die with Thee, yet will I not deny Thee.
Peter to Jesus
Matt. 26:35
See also Mark 14:31

And immediately the cock crew.
Matt. 26:74, John 18:27
See also Luke 22:60

I know not this man of whom ye speak.
Peter of Jesus
Mark 14:71
See also, e.g., Matt. 26:74

If I should say, I know Him not, I shall be a liar like unto you: but I know Him, and keep His saying.
Jesus
John 8:55

If we deny Him, He also will deny us.
2 Tim. 2:12

If we believe not, yet He abideth faithful: He cannot deny Himself.
2 Tim. 2:13

Whosoever denieth the Son, the same hath not the Father.
1 John 2:23

[*See also* Godlessness, Self-Denial]

DEPENDENCE

See God's Protection, Reliance.

DEPRAVITY

The great whore that sitteth upon many waters.
(Babylon)
Rev. 17:1

Babylon the Great, the Mother of Harlots and Abominations of the Earth.
Rev. 17:5

[*See also* Decadence, Evil, Immorality, Sin, Wickedness]

DEPRIVATION

If any man thirst, let him come unto me, and drink.
Jesus
John 7:37

They shall hunger no more, neither thirst any more; neither shall the sun light on them, nor any heat.
Rev. 7:16

I will give unto him that is athirst of the fountain of the water of life freely.
Jesus
Rev. 21:6

[*See also* Bread of Life, Hunger, Thirst]

DESECRATION

See Sacrilege.

DESIRE

We should not lust after evil things.
1 Cor. 10:6

When lust hath conceived, it bringeth forth sin.
James 1:15

Ye lust, and have not.
James 4:2

The world passeth away, and the lust thereof: but he that doeth the will of God abideth for ever.
1 John 2:17

[*See also* Carnality, Greed, Lust]

DESPAIR

Eli, Eli, lama sabachthani?
Jesus
Matt. 27:46
See also Mark 15:34

He that cometh to me shall never hunger; and he that believeth on me shall never thirst.
Jesus
John 6:35

There is none that doeth good, no, not one.
> Rom. 3:12, Ps. 14:3, Ps. 53:3
> See also Rom. 3:10

Strangers from the covenants of promise, having no hope, and without God in the world.
> Eph. 2:12

Alas, alas that great city Babylon, that mighty city! for in one hour is thy judgment come.
> Rev. 18:10

[See also Anguish, Faith, Hope]

DESTRUCTION

The abomination of desolation.
> Jesus
> Matt. 24:15, Mark 13:14

Destroy this temple, and in three days I will raise it up.
> Jesus
> John 2:19

The second woe is past; and, behold, the third woe cometh quickly.
> Rev. 11:14

Armageddon.
> Rev. 16:16

It is done.
> Rev. 16:17

Every island fled away, and the mountains were not found.
> Rev. 16:20

Alas, alas that great city Babylon, that mighty city! for in one hour is thy judgment come.
> Rev. 18:10

The merchants of the earth shall weep and mourn over her; for no man buyeth their merchandise any more.
> (her: Babylon)
> Rev. 18:11

[See also Defeat, Terror, Violence]

DETERMINATION

Stand fast in the faith.
> 1 Cor. 16:13

Lift up the hands which hang down, and the feeble knees.
> Heb. 12:12

[See also Diligence, Effort, Fortitude, Perseverance, Work]

DEVIL

See Evil, Satan.

DEVOTION

With all thy heart, and with all thy soul, and with all thy mind.
> Jesus
> Matt. 22:37, Mark 12:29
> See also, e.g., Deut. 10:12

Whosoever he be of you that forsaketh not all that he hath, he cannot be my disciple.
> Jesus
> Luke 14:33

The good shepherd giveth his life for the sheep.
> Jesus
> John 10:11

The hireling fleeth, because he is an hireling, and careth not for the sheep.
> Jesus
> John 10:13

I am ready not to be bound only, but also to die at Jerusalem for the name of the Lord Jesus.
> Acts 21:13

Neither is that circumcision, which is outward in the flesh.
> Rom. 2:28

Who shall separate us from the love of Christ? shall tribulation, or distress, or persecution, or famine, or nakedness, or peril, or sword?
> Rom. 8:35

He that is unmarried careth for the things that belong to the Lord, how he may please the Lord: But he that is married

careth for the things that are of the world, how he may please his wife.
1 Cor. 7:32–33

She that is married careth for the things of the world, how she may please her husband.
1 Cor. 7:34

Ye would have plucked out your own eyes, and have given them to me.
Gal. 4:15

Sanctify the Lord God in your hearts.
1 Pet. 3:15

[*See also* Allegiance, Commitment, Faithfulness, Love, Love of God, Loyalty, Service to God, Sincerity, Worship]

DILIGENCE

Seek, and ye shall find.
Jesus
Matt. 7:7, Luke 11:9

No man, having put his hand to the plough, and looking back, is fit for the kingdom of God.
Jesus
Luke 9:62

Be ye stedfast, unmoveable, always abounding in the work of the Lord.
1 Cor. 15:58

He which soweth bountifully shall reap also bountifully.
2 Cor. 9:6

Stand fast in the Lord, my dearly beloved.
Phil. 4:1

Study to be quiet, and to do your own business.
1 Thess. 4:11

Study to show thyself approved unto God, a workman that needeth not to be ashamed.
2 Tim. 2:15

[*See also* Effort, Laziness, Perseverance, Steadfastness]

DISAPPOINTMENT

What, could ye not watch with me one hour?
Jesus
Matt. 26:40
See also Mark 14:37

[*See also* Effort, Frustration, Futility, Hope]

DISBELIEF

See Doubt, Godlessness, Skepticism.

DISCERNMENT

O ye hypocrites, ye can discern the face of the sky; but can ye not discern the signs of the times?
Jesus
Matt. 16:3
See also Luke 12:56

[*See also* Folly, Understanding]

DISCIPLES

Follow me, and I will make you fishers of men.
Jesus
Matt. 4:19
See also Mark 1:17

I send you forth as sheep in the midst of wolves: be ye therefore wise as serpents, and harmless as doves.
Jesus
Matt. 10:16

The disciple is not above his master, nor the servant above his lord.
Jesus
Matt. 10:24
See also Luke 6:40, John 13:16

He that taketh not his cross, and followeth after me, is not worthy of me.
Jesus
Matt. 10:38
See also Luke 14:27

Whosoever will come after me, let him

deny himself, and take up his cross, and follow me.
> *Jesus*
> *Mark 8:34*
> *See also Matt. 16:24, Luke 9:23*

Go ye into all the world, and preach the gospel to every creature.
> *Jesus*
> *Mark 16:15*

He that despiseth you despiseth me; and he that despiseth me despiseth Him that sent me.
> *Jesus*
> *Luke 10:16*

Whosoever he be of you that forsaketh not all that he hath, he cannot be my disciple.
> *Jesus*
> *Luke 14:33*

Have not I chosen you twelve, and one of you is a devil?
> *Jesus*
> *John 6:70*

If ye continue in my word, then are ye my disciples indeed.
> *Jesus*
> *John 8:31*

If any man serve me, him will my Father honour.
> *Jesus*
> *John 12:26*

By this shall all men know that ye are my disciples, if ye have love one to another.
> *Jesus*
> *John 13:35*

I am the vine, ye are the branches.
> *Jesus*
> *John 15:5*

Ye have not chosen me, but I have chosen you.
> *Jesus*
> *John 15:16*

Follow me.
> *Jesus*
> *John 21:19*

[*See also* Evangelism, Leadership]

DISCIPLINE

Shall I come unto you with a rod, or in love?
> *1 Cor. 4:21*

What son is he whom the father chasteneth not?
> *Heb. 12:7*

No chastening for the present seemeth to be joyous.
> *Heb. 12:11*

It yieldeth the peaceable fruit of righteousness unto them which are exercised thereby.
> *Heb. 12:11*

As many as I love, I rebuke and chasten.
> *Jesus*
> *Rev. 3:19*

[*See also* Chastisement, Criticism, Punishment, Self-Control]

DISCONTENT

See Contentment, Satisfaction.

DISHONESTY

He that is unjust in the least is unjust also in much.
> *Jesus*
> *Luke 16:10*

Thou hast not lied unto men, but unto God.
> *Acts 5:4*

[*See also* Candor, Honesty, Lies, Truth]

DISOBEDIENCE

Every one that heareth these sayings of mine, and doeth them not, shall be likened unto a foolish man, which built his house upon the sand.
> *Jesus*
> *Matt. 7:26*
> *See also Luke 6:49*

Laying aside the commandment of God, ye hold the tradition of men.
> *Jesus*
> *Mark 7:8*

Remember Lot's wife.
Jesus
Luke 17:32

He that loveth me not keepeth not my sayings.
Jesus
John 14:24

By one man's disobedience many were made sinners.
Rom. 5:19

If I do that I would not, it is no more I that do it, but sin that dwelleth in me.
Rom. 7:20
See also Rom. 7:17

Who hath bewitched you, that ye should not obey the truth?
Gal. 3:1

The wrath of God cometh on the children of disobedience.
Col. 3:6

He therefore that despiseth, despiseth not man, but God.
1 Thess. 4:8

Whosoever shall keep the whole law, and yet offend in one point, he is guilty of all.
James 2:10

He that saith, I know Him, and keepeth not His commandments, is a liar.
(Him: Jesus)
1 John 2:4

[*See also* Backsliding, Blame, Curses, Obedience, Punishment, Rebellion, Sin]

DIVERSITY

There are diversities of gifts, but the same Spirit.
1 Cor. 12:4

There are differences of administrations, but the same Lord.
1 Cor. 12:5

In a great house there are not only vessels of gold and of silver, but also of wood and of earth.
2 Tim. 2:20

DIVINITY

Of a truth Thou art the Son of God.
Matt. 14:33

Truly this was the Son of God.
Matt. 27:54
See also Mark 15:39

Ye say that I am.
Jesus
Luke 22:70

I saw, and bare record that this is the Son of God.
John 1:34

He that cometh from above is above all.
John 3:31

I and my Father are one.
Jesus
John 10:30

He was come from God, and went to God.
(He: Jesus)
John 13:3

He that hath seen me hath seen the Father.
Jesus
John 14:9

I am in the Father, and the Father in me.
Jesus
John 14:11

I believe that Jesus Christ is the Son of God.
Acts 8:37

One Lord, one faith, one baptism.
Eph. 4:5

In Him dwelleth all the fulness of the Godhead bodily.
(Him: Jesus)
Col. 2:9

[*See also* Acknowledgment, God, Jesus]

Whosoever shall put away his wife, saving for the cause of fornication, causeth her to commit adultery.
Jesus
Matt. 5:32

Whosoever shall marry her that is divorced committeth adultery.
Jesus
Matt. 5:32
See also Matt. 19:9, Luke 16:18

What therefore God hath joined together, let not man put asunder.
Jesus
Matt. 19:6, Mark 10:9

Whosoever shall put away his wife, except it be for fornication, and shall marry another, committeth adultery.
Jesus
Matt. 19:9
See also Mark 10:11

If a woman shall put away her husband, and be married to another, she committeth adultery.
Jesus
Mark 10:12

Whosoever putteth away his wife, and marrieth another, committeth adultery.
Jesus
Luke 16:18

Let not the husband put away his wife.
1 Cor. 7:11

Art thou bound unto a wife? seek not to be loosed.
1 Cor. 7:27

[*See also* Marriage]

DOCTRINE

My doctrine is not mine, but His that sent me.
Jesus
John 7:16

We henceforth be no more children, tossed to and fro, and carried about with every wind of doctrine, by the sleight of men, and cunning craftiness, whereby they lie in wait to deceive.
Eph. 4:14

Give attendance to reading, to exhortation, to doctrine.
1 Tim. 4:13

Speak thou the things which become sound doctrine.
Titus 2:1

Avoid foolish questions.
Titus 3:9

[*See also* Controversy]

DOOM

See Apocalypse, Destruction, Punishment, Terror.

DOUBT

Art thou He that should come, or do we look for another?
Matt. 11:3
See also Luke 7:19

We have here but five loaves, and two fishes.
His disciples to Jesus
Matt. 14:17
See also Luke 9:13

O thou of little faith, wherefore didst thou doubt?
Jesus
Matt. 14:31

O ye of little faith.
Jesus
E.g., Matt. 16:8

O faithless and perverse generation, how long shall I be with you? how long shall I suffer you?
Jesus
Matt. 17:17
See also Mark 9:19, Luke 9:41

Help Thou mine unbelief.
Mark 9:24

How shall this be, seeing I know not a man?
Luke 1:34

Except I shall see in His hands the print of the nails, and put my finger into the print

of the nails, and thrust my hand into His side, I will not believe.
Thomas
John 20:25

Reach hither thy hand, and thrust it into my side: and be not faithless, but believing.
Jesus
John 20:27

Him that is weak in the faith receive ye, but not to doubtful disputations.
Rom. 14:1

Stand fast, and hold the traditions which ye have been taught.
2 Thess. 2:15

He that wavereth is like a wave of the sea driven with the wind.
James 1:6

[*See also* Belief, Faith, Hope, Skepticism]

DREAMS

Your young men shall see visions, and your old men shall dream dreams.
Acts 2:17
See also Joel 2:28

DRUNKENNESS

Be not drunk with wine, wherein is excess; but be filled with the Spirit.
Eph. 5:18

[*See also* Liquor]

DUTY

It becometh us to fulfil all righteousness.
Jesus
Matt. 3:15

Wist ye not that I must be about my Father's business?
Jesus
Luke 2:49

Go thou and preach the kingdom of God.
Jesus
Luke 9:60

This is the work of God, that ye believe on Him whom He hath sent.
Jesus
John 6:29

I must work the works of Him that sent me, while it is day.
Jesus
John 9:4

The cup which my Father hath given me, shall I not drink it?
Jesus
John 18:11

It shall be told thee what thou must do.
Jesus to Saul
Acts 9:6

I go bound in the spirit unto Jerusalem, not knowing the things that shall befall me there.
Acts 20:22

Feed the church of God, which He hath purchased with His own blood.
Paul
Acts 20:28

As the Lord hath called every one, so let him walk.
1 Cor. 7:17

Woe is unto me, if I preach not the gospel!
1 Cor. 9:16

If I yet pleased men, I should not be the servant of Christ.
Gal. 1:10

Walk worthy of the vocation wherewith ye are called.
Eph. 4:1

[*See also* Goals, Mission, Responsibility]

EARTH

The earth is the Lord's, and the fulness thereof.
1 Cor. 10:26, 28
See also Ps. 24:1

[*See also* Creation, God's Presence, Heaven and Earth, Nature]

EDUCATION

Understandest thou what thou readest?
Acts 8:30

How can I, except some man should guide me?
Acts 8:31

Paul, thou art beside thyself; much learning doth make thee mad.
Festus
Acts 26:24

How shall they hear without a preacher?
Rom. 10:14

I have fed you with milk, and not with meat.
1 Cor. 3:2

Beware lest any man spoil you through philosophy and vain deceit.
Col. 2:8

Let the woman learn in silence with all subjection.
1 Tim. 2:11

I suffer not a woman to teach, nor to usurp authority over the man, but to be in silence.
1 Tim. 2:12

[*See also* Enlightenment, Instruction, Knowledge, Teaching, Wisdom]

EFFORT

Whosoever shall compel thee to go a mile, go with him twain.
Jesus
Matt. 5:41

He that seeketh findeth.
Jesus
Matt. 7:8, Luke 11:10

To him that knocketh it shall be opened.
Jesus
Matt. 7:8, Luke 11:10

With what measure ye mete, it shall be measured to you.
Jesus
Mark 4:24
See also Luke 6:38

He which soweth sparingly shall reap also sparingly.
2 Cor. 9:6

Whatsoever a man soweth, that shall he also reap.
Gal. 6:7

Whatsoever ye do, do it heartily, as to the Lord, and not unto men.
Col. 3:23

I have fought a good fight, I have finished my course, I have kept the faith.
2 Tim. 4:7

[*See also* Diligence, Patience, Work]

EGO

See Arrogance, Conceit, Humility.

ELOQUENCE

Paul, Almost thou persuadest me to be a Christian.
Agrippa
Acts 26:28

Though I speak with the tongues of men and of angels, and have not charity, I am become as sounding brass, or a tinkling cymbal.
(charity: love)
1 Cor. 13:1

Though I be rude in speech, yet not in knowledge.
2 Cor. 11:6

[*See also* Speech, Verbosity]

EMBARRASSMENT

See Shame.

EMOTIONS

See Fear, Happiness, Hatred, Love, Sorrow.

EMPATHY

Rejoice with them that do rejoice, and weep with them that weep.
Rom. 12:15

Absent in body, but present in spirit.
1 Cor. 5:3

Who is weak, and I am not weak? who is offended, and I burn not?
2 Cor. 11:29

Though I be absent in the flesh, yet am I with you in the spirit.
Col. 2:5

[*See also* Compassion, Sympathy]

EMPLOYEES

The workman is worthy of his meat.
Jesus
Matt. 10:10
See also Luke 10:7, 1 Tim. 5:18

Every man shall receive his own reward according to his own labour.
1 Cor. 3:8

Give unto your servants that which is just and equal; knowing that ye also have a Master in heaven.
Col. 4:1

[*See also* Reward, Wages, Work]

ENCOURAGEMENT

Be of good cheer; thy sins be forgiven thee.
Jesus
Matt. 9:2
See also Mark 2:5

When thou art converted, strengthen thy brethren.
Jesus
Luke 22:32

Be not afraid, but speak, and hold not thy peace: For I am with thee.
Jesus to Paul
Acts 18:9–10

Exhort one another daily, while it is called To day.
Heb. 3:13

Lift up the hands which hang down, and the feeble knees.
Heb. 12:12

[*See also* Courage, Fear, God's Protection, Hope]

END DAYS

Watch ye therefore: for ye know not when the master of the house cometh.
Jesus
Mark 13:35

When ye shall see Jerusalem compassed with armies, then know that the desolation thereof is nigh.
Jesus
Luke 21:20

The sun shall be turned into darkness, and the moon into blood, before that great and notable day of the Lord come.
Acts 2:20

[*See also* Apocalypse, Judgment Day, Second Coming]

ENDINGS

Of His kingdom there shall be no end.
(His: Jesus)
Luke 1:33

The night cometh, when no man can work.
Jesus
John 9:4

I have fought a good fight, I have finished my course, I have kept the faith.
2 Tim. 4:7

[*See also* Apocalypse, Beginnings, Death, Permanence]

ENDURANCE

See Diligence, Fortitude, Perseverance, Strength.

ENEMIES

Love your enemies.
Jesus
Matt. 5:44, Luke 6:27
See also Luke 6:35

Bless them that curse you, do good to them that hate you.
Jesus
Matt. 5:44

If ye love them which love you, what reward have ye? do not even the publicans the same?
Jesus
Matt. 5:46
See also Luke 6:32

If ye do good to them which do good to you, what thank have ye? for sinners also do even the same.
Jesus
Luke 6:33

He that hateth me hateth my Father also.
Jesus
John 15:23

If God be for us, who can be against us?
Rom. 8:31

If thine enemy hunger, feed him; if he thirst, give him drink.
Rom. 12:20
See also Prov. 25:21

We wrestle not against flesh and blood, but against principalities, against powers, against the rulers of the darkness.
Eph. 6:12

[*See also* Allies, Brotherhood, God's Protection, Hatred, Persecution, Revenge]

ENLIGHTENMENT

To give light to them that sit in darkness.
Luke 1:79

He hath anointed me to preach the gospel to the poor.
Jesus
Luke 4:18
See also Isa. 61:1

The light shineth in darkness; and the darkness comprehended it not.
John 1:5

I am come a light into the world, that whosoever believeth on me should not abide in darkness.
Jesus
John 12:46

Open their eyes.
Jesus to Paul
Acts 26:18

Ye are all the children of light, and the children of the day.
1 Thess. 5:5

The darkness is past, and the true light now shineth.
1 John 2:8

[*See also* Education, Knowledge, Light and Darkness]

ENTHUSIASM

Whatsoever ye do, do it heartily, as to the Lord, and not unto men.
Col. 3:23

I know thy works, that thou art neither cold nor hot: I would thou wert cold or hot.
Jesus
Rev. 3:15
See also Rev. 3:16

I heard as it were the voice of a great multitude, and as the voice of many waters, and as the voice of mighty thunderings.
Rev. 19:6

[*See also* Contentment, Zeal]

ENVIRONMENT

See Nature.

ENVY

Is thine eye evil, because I am good?
Jesus
Matt. 20:15

For envy they had delivered Him.
Pilate
Matt. 27:18

Thou art in the gall of bitterness, and in the bond of iniquity.
Acts 8:23

I had not known lust, except the law had said, Thou shalt not covet.
Rom. 7:7

Thou shalt not covet.
E.g., Rom. 13:9, Ex. 20:17

Where envying and strife is, there is confusion and every evil work.
James 3:16

[*See also* Contentment, Greed, Jealousy]

EPHEMERA

See Mortality, Permanence.

EQUALITY

The last shall be first, and the first last.
Jesus
Matt. 20:16
See also Matt. 19:30, Mark 10:31

The servant is not greater than his lord; neither he that is sent greater than he that sent him.
Jesus
John 13:16
See also John 15:20, Matt. 10:24

There is no difference between the Jew and the Greek: for the same Lord over all is rich unto all that call upon Him.
Rom. 10:12

We shall all stand before the judgment seat of Christ.
Rom. 14:10
See also 2 Cor. 5:10

Ye are all the children of God by faith in Christ Jesus.
Gal. 3:26

There is neither Jew nor Greek, there is neither bond nor free, there is neither

male nor female: for ye are all one in Christ Jesus.
Gal. 3:28

Be as I am; for I am as ye are.
Gal. 4:12

There is neither Greek nor Jew, circumcision nor uncircumcision, Barbarian, Scythian, bond nor free: but Christ is all, and in all.
Col. 3:11

[*See also* Brotherhood, Humility, Impartiality]

ESCAPE

O generation of vipers, who hath warned you to flee from the wrath to come?
Matt. 3:7, Luke 3:7

Whosoever shall seek to save his life shall lose it; and whosoever shall lose his life shall preserve it.
Jesus
Luke 17:33
See also Matt. 16:25, Mark 8:35

Save yourselves from this untoward generation.
Acts 2:40

Behold, the men whom ye put in prison are standing in the temple.
Acts 5:25

[*See also* Deliverance, Safety]

ETERNAL LIFE

He that loseth his life for my sake shall find it.
Jesus
Matt. 10:39

There be some standing here, which shall not taste of death, till they see the Son of man coming in His kingdom.
Jesus
Matt. 16:28
See also Mark 9:1, Luke 9:27

If thou wilt enter into life, keep the commandments.
Jesus
Matt. 19:17

Go and sell that thou hast, and give to the

poor, and thou shalt have treasure in heaven.
Jesus
Matt. 19:21
See also Mark 10:21, Luke 18:22

Thou knowest the commandments, Do not commit adultery, Do not kill, Do not steal, Do not bear false witness, Defraud not, Honour thy father and mother.
Jesus
Mark 10:19
See also Matt. 19:18–19, Luke 18:20

Come, take up the cross, and follow me.
Jesus
Mark 10:21
See also Matt. 19:21, Luke 18:22

How hard is it for them that trust in riches to enter into the kingdom of God!
Jesus
Mark 10:24
See also Matt. 19:23, Luke 18:24

Many that are first shall be last; and the last first.
Jesus
Mark 10:31
See also Matt. 19:30, Matt. 20:16

Whosoever believeth in Him should not perish, but have eternal life.
Jesus
John 3:15

For God so loved the world, that He gave His only begotten Son, that whosoever believeth in Him should not perish, but have everlasting life.
Jesus
John 3:16
See also John 3:36, John 6:47

Living water.
John 4:11

Whosoever drinketh of this water shall thirst again: But whosoever drinketh of the water that I shall give him shall never thirst.
Jesus
John 4:13–14

He that reapeth receiveth wages, and gathereth fruit unto life eternal.
Jesus
John 4:36

He that heareth my word, and believeth on Him that sent me, hath everlasting life.
Jesus
John 5:24

I am the living bread which came down from heaven: if any man eat of this bread, he shall live for ever.
Jesus
John 6:51
See also John 6:58

Whoso eateth my flesh, and drinketh my blood, hath eternal life; and I will raise him up at the last day.
Jesus
John 6:54

If a man keep my saying, he shall never see death.
Jesus
John 8:51

I am the resurrection, and the life.
Jesus
John 11:25

Whosoever liveth and believeth in me shall never die.
Jesus
John 11:26

I go to prepare a place for you.
Jesus
John 14:2

The wages of sin is death; but the gift of God is eternal life through Jesus Christ our Lord.
Rom. 6:23

Thanks be to God, which giveth us the victory through our Lord Jesus Christ.
1 Cor. 15:57

He that soweth to the Spirit shall of the Spirit reap life everlasting.
Gal. 6:8

Lay hold on eternal life, whereunto thou art also called.
1 Tim. 6:12

The world passeth away, and the lust thereof: but he that doeth the will of God abideth for ever.
1 John 2:17

God hath given to us eternal life, and this life is in His Son.
1 John 5:11

Be thou faithful unto death, and I will give thee a crown of life.
Jesus
Rev. 2:10

I will give unto him that is athirst of the fountain of the water of life freely.
Jesus
Rev. 21:6

Let him that is athirst come. And whosoever will, let him take the water of life freely.
Rev. 22:17

[*See also* Bread of Life, Christ Eternal, Life, Resurrection, Reward, Salvation]

ETERNITY

For Thine is the kingdom, and the power, and the glory, for ever.
Jesus
Matt. 6:13

Holy, holy, holy, Lord God Almighty, which was, and is, and is to come.
Rev. 4:8

[*See also* Christ Eternal, Eternal Life, Permanence]

ETHICS

See Behavior, Honesty.

EVANGELISM

The voice of one crying in the wilderness.
Matt. 3:3, Mark 1:3, Luke 3:4,
John 1:23
See also Isa. 40:3

Follow me, and I will make you fishers of men.
Jesus
Matt. 4:19
See also Mark 1:17

Why eateth your Master with publicans and sinners?
Matt. 9:11
See also Luke 5:30

The harvest truly is plenteous, but the labourers are few.
Jesus
Matt. 9:37
See also Luke 10:2

I send you forth as sheep in the midst of wolves: be ye therefore wise as serpents, and harmless as doves.
Jesus
Matt. 10:16

I am not sent but unto the lost sheep of the house of Israel.
Jesus
Matt. 15:24

Go ye therefore, and teach all nations, baptizing them in the name of the Father, and of the Son, and of the Holy Ghost.
Jesus
Matt. 28:19

The sower soweth the word.
Jesus
Mark 4:14

The gospel must first be published among all nations.
Jesus
Mark 13:10

Go ye into all the world, and preach the gospel to every creature.
Jesus
Mark 16:15

Go thou and preach the kingdom of God.
Jesus
Luke 9:60

Repentance and remission of sins should be preached in His name among all nations.
Jesus
Luke 24:47

He that reapeth receiveth wages, and gathereth fruit unto life eternal.
Jesus
John 4:36

Other sheep I have, which are not of this fold.
Jesus
John 10:16

He that receiveth whomsoever I send receiveth me.
Jesus
John 13:20

Go and bring forth fruit.
Jesus
John 15:16

Ye also shall bear witness, because ye have been with me from the beginning.
Jesus
John 15:27

He is a chosen vessel unto me, to bear my name.
Jesus, about Saul
Acts 9:15

The hand of the Lord was with them: and a great number believed.
Acts 11:21

The word of God grew and multiplied.
Acts 12:24

Open their eyes.
Jesus to Paul
Acts 26:18

Turn them from darkness to light, and from the power of Satan unto God.
Jesus to Paul
Acts 26:18

The salvation of God is sent unto the Gentiles.
Acts 28:28

How shall they believe in Him of whom they have not heard?
Rom. 10:14

To whom He was not spoken of, they shall see: and they that have not heard shall understand.
Rom. 15:21
See also Isa. 52:15

Christ sent me not to baptize, but to preach the gospel.
1 Cor. 1:17

I seek not your's, but you.
2 Cor. 12:14

[*See also* Gospel, Ministry, Mission, Praise of God, Preaching, Testimony]

EVIDENCE

See Perjury, Proof.

EVIL

O generation of vipers.
E.g., Matt. 3:7, Luke 3:7

Lead us not into temptation, but deliver us from evil.
Jesus
Matt. 6:13, Luke 11:4

If thine eye be evil, thy whole body shall be full of darkness.
Jesus
Matt. 6:23
See also Luke 11:34

Wherefore think ye evil in your hearts?
Jesus
Matt. 9:4
See also Luke 6:22

When the unclean spirit is gone out of a man, he walketh through dry places, seeking rest, and findeth none.
Jesus
Matt. 12:43
See also Luke 11:24

My name is Legion: for we are many.
Mark 5:9

This is an evil generation: they seek a sign.
Jesus
Luke 11:29
See also Matt. 12:39, Matt. 16:4

Depart from me, all ye workers of iniquity.
Jesus
Luke 13:27
See also Matt. 7:23

Men loved darkness rather than light, because their deeds were evil.
Jesus
John 3:19

Every one that doeth evil hateth the light.
Jesus
John 3:20

Ye are of your father the devil, and the lusts of your father ye will do.
Jesus
John 8:44

If I have spoken evil, bear witness of the evil.
Jesus
John 18:23

Thou child of the devil, thou enemy of all righteousness.
Acts 13:10

Their feet are swift to shed blood.
Rom. 3:15

A little leaven leaveneth the whole lump.
1 Cor. 5:6, Gal. 5:9

In malice be ye children, but in understanding be men.
1 Cor. 14:20

Evil communications corrupt good manners.
1 Cor. 15:33

Abstain from all appearance of evil.
1 Thess. 5:22

The love of money is the root of all evil.
1 Tim. 6:10

The tongue is a fire, a world of iniquity.
James 3:6

He that will love life, and see good days, let him refrain his tongue from evil.
1 Pet. 3:10
See also Ps. 34:13

The face of the Lord is against them that do evil.
1 Pet. 3:12

He that biddeth him God speed is partaker of his evil deeds.
2 John 11

Let him that hath understanding count the number of the beast.
Rev. 13:18

His number is Six hundred threescore and six.
Rev. 13:18

The Lamb shall overcome them: for He is Lord of lords, and King of kings.
Rev. 17:14

Receive not of her plagues.
(her: Babylon)
Rev. 18:4

Reward her even as she rewarded you,

and double unto her double according to her works.
(her: Babylon)
Rev. 18:6

By thy sorceries were all nations deceived.
Rev. 18:23

[*See also* Behavior, Depravity, Godlessness, Good and Evil, Immorality, Purity, Righteousness, Satan, Sin, Wickedness]

EXALTATION

Hereafter shall the Son of man sit on the right hand of the power of God.
Jesus
Luke 22:69
See also Matt. 26:64, Mark 14:62

Sit Thou on my right hand, Until I make Thy foes Thy footstool.
Acts 2:34–35
See also Ps. 110:1, Matt. 22:44

EXASPERATION

O faithless and perverse generation, how long shall I be with you? how long shall I suffer you?
Jesus
Matt. 17:17
See also Mark 9:19, Luke 9:41

From henceforth I will go unto the Gentiles.
Acts 18:6

[*See also* Anger, God's Anger, Patience]

EXCESS

Be not drunk with wine, wherein is excess; but be filled with the Spirit.
Eph. 5:18

EXCUSES

Now they have no cloak for their sin.
Jesus
John 15:22

EXERCISE

See Physical Fitness.

EXILE

I will carry you away beyond Babylon.
Acts 7:43

[*See also* Freedom, Outcast]

EXORCISM

How can Satan cast out Satan?
Jesus
Mark 3:23

Come out of the man, thou unclean spirit.
Jesus
Mark 5:8

In my name shall they cast out devils.
Jesus
Mark 16:17

I command thee in the name of Jesus Christ to come out of her.
Acts 16:18

EXPECTATION

To whom men have committed much, of him they will ask the more.
Jesus
Luke 12:48

[*See also* Disappointment, Hope]

EXPERIENCE

Whether He be a sinner or no, I know not: one thing I know, that, whereas I was blind, now I see.
John 9:25

[*See also* Age, Maturity, Wisdom, Youth]

EXPOSURE

That which ye have spoken in the ear in closets shall be proclaimed upon the housetops.
Jesus
Luke 12:3
See also Matt. 10:27

All things that are reproved are made manifest by the light.
Eph. 5:13

[*See also* Light and Darkness, Secrecy]

FAILURE

See Success, Victory.

FAIRNESS

With what judgment ye judge, ye shall be judged.
Jesus
Matt. 7:2

All things whatsoever ye would that men should do to you, do ye even so to them.
Jesus
Matt. 7:12
See also Luke 6:31

Whatsoever is right, that shall ye receive.
Jesus
Matt. 20:7

With what measure ye mete, it shall be measured to you.
Jesus
Mark 4:24
See also Luke 6:38

Sittest thou to judge me after the law, and commandest me to be smitten contrary to the law?
Paul to Ananias
Acts 23:3

Give unto your servants that which is just

and equal; knowing that ye also have a Master in heaven.
Col. 4:1

The labourer is worthy of his reward.
1 Tim. 5:18
See also Luke 10:7

[*See also* Impartiality, Justice]

FAITH

If Thou wilt, Thou canst make me clean.
Leper to Jesus
Matt. 8:2, Mark 1:40, Luke 5:12

Speak the word only, and my servant shall be healed.
Centurion to Jesus
Matt. 8:8

Verily I say unto you, I have not found so great faith, no, not in Israel.
Jesus, about the centurion
Matt. 8:10
See also Luke 7:9

As thou hast believed, so be it done unto thee.
Jesus
Matt. 8:13

Why are ye fearful, O ye of little faith?
Jesus
Matt. 8:26
See also Mark 4:40

If I may but touch His garment, I shall be whole.
Matt. 9:21
See also Mark 5:28

Thy faith hath made thee whole.
Jesus
Matt. 9:22, Mark 5:34, Mark 10:52,
Luke 8:48
See also Luke 17:19

According to your faith be it unto you.
Jesus
Matt. 9:29

As many as touched were made perfectly whole.
Matt. 14:36
See also Mark 6:56

Great is thy faith: be it unto thee even as thou wilt.
Jesus
Matt. 15:28

O ye of little faith.
Jesus
E.g., Matt. 16:8

If ye have faith as a grain of mustard seed, ye shall say unto this mountain, Remove hence to yonder place; and it shall remove.
Jesus
Matt. 17:20

Nothing shall be impossible unto you.
Jesus
Matt. 17:20

If ye shall say unto this mountain, Be thou removed, and be thou cast into the sea; it shall be done.
Jesus
Matt. 21:21
See also Mark 11:23

Be not afraid, only believe.
Jesus
Mark 5:36

All things are possible to him that believeth.
Jesus
Mark 9:23

Whosoever shall offend one of these little ones that believe in me, it is better for him that a millstone were hanged about his neck, and he were cast into the sea.
Jesus
Mark 9:42
See also Matt. 18:6, Luke 17:2

Have faith in God.
Jesus
Mark 11:22

What things soever ye desire, when ye pray, believe that ye receive them, and ye shall have them.
Jesus
Mark 11:24
See also Matt. 21:22

Thy faith hath saved thee.
Jesus
E.g., Luke 7:50

Increase our faith.
Apostles to Jesus
Luke 17:5

Father, into Thy hands I commend my spirit.
Jesus
Luke 23:46

For God so loved the world, that He gave His only begotten Son, that whosoever believeth in Him should not perish, but have everlasting life.
Jesus
John 3:16
See also John 3:36, John 6:47

Blessed are they that have not seen, and yet have believed.
Jesus
John 20:29

The just shall live by faith.
E.g., Rom. 1:17

A man is justified by faith without the deeds of the law.
Rom. 3:28

Do we then make void the law through faith? God forbid.
Rom. 3:31

The righteousness of faith.
Rom. 4:13

Ye are not in the flesh, but in the Spirit.
Rom. 8:9

All things work together for good to them that love God.
Rom. 8:28

Faith cometh by hearing, and hearing by the word of God.
Rom. 10:17

Him that is weak in the faith receive ye, but not to doubtful disputations.
Rom. 14:1

Hast thou faith? have it to thyself before God.
Rom. 14:22

Whatsoever is not of faith is sin.
Rom. 14:23

Faith should not stand in the wisdom of men, but in the power of God.
1 Cor. 2:5

Be not deceived.
E.g., 1 Cor. 6:9

Though I have all faith, so that I could remove mountains, and have not charity, I am nothing.
(charity: love)
1 Cor. 13:2

And now abideth faith, hope, charity, these three; but the greatest of these is charity.
(charity: love)
1 Cor. 13:13

If Christ be not raised, your faith is vain; ye are yet in your sins.
1 Cor. 15:17

Stand fast in the faith.
1 Cor. 16:13

By faith ye stand.
2 Cor. 1:24

We walk by faith, not by sight.
2 Cor. 5:7

Having nothing, and yet possessing all things.
2 Cor. 6:10

A man is not justified by the works of the law, but by the faith of Jesus Christ.
Gal. 2:16

I am crucified with Christ: nevertheless I live.
Gal. 2:20

Before faith came, we were kept under the law.
Gal. 3:23

The law was our schoolmaster to bring us unto Christ, that we might be justified by faith.
Gal. 3:24

By grace are ye saved through faith.
Eph. 2:8

The shield of faith, wherewith ye shall be able to quench all the fiery darts of the wicked.
Eph. 6:16

Stand fast in the Lord, my dearly beloved.
Phil. 4:1

Now we live, if ye stand fast in the Lord.
1 Thess. 3:8

Quench not the Spirit.
1 Thess. 5:19

Be not soon shaken in mind.
2 Thess. 2:2

Stand fast, and hold the traditions which ye have been taught.
2 Thess. 2:15

All men have not faith.
2 Thess. 3:2

Fight the good fight of faith.
1 Tim. 6:12

I am not ashamed: for I know whom I have believed.
2 Tim. 1:12

I have fought a good fight, I have finished my course, I have kept the faith.
2 Tim. 4:7

Let us hold fast the profession of our faith without wavering.
Heb. 10:23

We are not of them who draw back unto perdition; but of them that believe to the saving of the soul.
Heb. 10:39

Faith is the substance of things hoped for, the evidence of things not seen.
Heb. 11:1

Without faith it is impossible to please Him.
Heb. 11:6

Ask in faith, nothing wavering.
James 1:6

Faith without works is dead.
James 2:20
See also James 2:17, James 2:26

By works was faith made perfect.
James 2:22

Draw nigh to God, and He will draw nigh to you.
James 4:8

Add to your faith virtue; and to virtue knowledge.
2 Pet. 1:5

Earnestly contend for the faith which was once delivered unto the saints.
Jude 3

Buy of me gold tried in the fire, that thou mayest be rich; and white raiment, that thou mayest be clothed.
Jesus
Rev. 3:18

Here is the patience and the faith of the saints.
Rev. 13:10

He that overcometh shall inherit all things.
Rev. 21:7

[*See also* Belief, Doubt, Fear of God, Healing, Jesus (Acceptance of), Monotheism, Sin, Trust]

FAITHFULNESS

Examine yourselves, whether ye be in the faith.
2 Cor. 13:5

As ye have therefore received Christ Jesus the Lord, so walk ye in Him.
Col. 2:6

The Lord is faithful, who shall stablish you, and keep you from evil.
2 Thess. 3:3

Be thou faithful unto death, and I will give thee a crown of life.
Jesus
Rev. 2:10

They that are with Him are called, and chosen, and faithful.
Rev. 17:14

Behold a white horse; and he that sat upon him was called Faithful and True.
Rev. 19:11

[*See also* Allegiance, Devotion, Faith, Loyalty]

FAITHLESSNESS

See Godlessness.

FALSE GODS

See Idolatry, Idols.

FALSE PROPHETS

Beware of false prophets, which come to you in sheep's clothing, but inwardly they are ravening wolves.
Jesus
Matt. 7:15

Take heed that no man deceive you. For many shall come in my name, saying, I am Christ.
Jesus
Matt. 24:4–5
See also Mark 13:6, Luke 21:8

Thou child of the devil, thou enemy of all righteousness.
Acts 13:10

Wilt thou not cease to pervert the right ways of the Lord?
Acts 13:10

Many shall follow their pernicious ways.
2 Pet. 2:2

These are wells without water, clouds that are carried with a tempest.
2 Pet. 2:17

They are of the world: therefore speak they of the world.
1 John 4:5

[*See also* Heresy, Prophecy]

FAME

A city that is set on an hill cannot be hid.
Jesus
Matt. 5:14

[*See also* Boasting, Deeds, Glory, God's Glory, Modesty, Reputation, Respect]

FAMILY

He that loveth father or mother more than me is not worthy of me: and he that loveth son or daughter more than me is not worthy of me.
Jesus to disciples
Matt. 10:37

Whosoever shall do the will of my Father which is in heaven, the same is my brother, and sister, and mother.
Jesus
Matt. 12:50
See also Mark 3:35

My mother and my brethren are these which hear the word of God, and do it.
Jesus
Luke 8:21

The father shall be divided against the son, and the son against the father; the mother against the daughter, and the daughter against the mother.
Jesus
Luke 12:53
See also Matt. 10:35

[*See also* Children, Parents, Strife]

FAMINE

See Deprivation, Hunger.

FARMING

See Cultivation, Growth.

FASHION

See Appearance, Change, Materialism.

FASTING

When thou fastest, anoint thine head, and wash thy face.
Jesus
Matt. 6:17

Appear not unto men to fast, but unto thy Father.
Jesus
Matt. 6:18

There is no respect of persons with God.
> *Rom. 2:11*
> *See also Acts 10:34*

[*See also* Equality, Impartiality]

FEAR

Why are ye fearful, O ye of little faith?
> *Jesus*
> *Matt. 8:26*
> *See also Mark 4:40*

Fear not them which kill the body, but are not able to kill the soul.
> *Jesus*
> *Matt. 10:28*
> *See also Luke 12:4*

Be of good cheer; it is I; be not afraid.
> *Jesus*
> *Matt. 14:27, Mark 6:50*
> *See also John 6:20*

Be not afraid, only believe.
> *Jesus*
> *Mark 5:36*

Fear Him, which after He hath killed hath power to cast into hell; yea, I say unto you, Fear Him.
> *Jesus*
> *Luke 12:5*
> *See also Matt. 10:28*

Let not your heart be troubled, neither let it be afraid.
> *Jesus*
> *John 14:27*
> *See also John 14:1*

If thou do that which is evil, be afraid; for he beareth not the sword in vain.
> *(he: civil authorities)*
> *Rom. 13:4*

Tribute to whom tribute is due; custom to whom custom; fear to whom fear; honour to whom honour.
> *Rom. 13:7*

The Lord is my helper, and I will not fear what man shall do unto me.
> *Heb. 13:6*
> *See also Ps. 118:6*

Perfect love casteth out fear.
> *1 John 4:18*

[*See also* Courage, Encouragement, God's Protection, Terror, Timidity]

FEAR OF GOD

His mercy is on them that fear Him from generation to generation.
> *Mary, mother of Jesus*
> *Luke 1:50*

Whosoever among you feareth God, to you is the word of this salvation sent.
> *Acts 13:26*

The devils also believe, and tremble.
> *James 2:19*

[*See also* Reverence]

FELLOWSHIP

Whosoever shall do the will of my Father which is in heaven, the same is my brother, and sister, and mother.
> *Jesus*
> *Matt. 12:50*
> *See also Mark 3:35*

Where two or three are gathered together in my name, there am I in the midst of them.
> *Jesus*
> *Matt. 18:20*

Have salt in yourselves, and have peace one with another.
> *Jesus*
> *Mark 9:50*

He that loveth me shall be loved of my Father.
> *Jesus*
> *John 14:21*

I am the vine, ye are the branches.
> *Jesus*
> *John 15:5*

Woman, behold thy son!
> *Jesus (son: John)*
> *John 19:26*

We, being many, are one body in Christ, and every one members one of another.
Rom. 12:5

Him that is weak in the faith receive ye, but not to doubtful disputations.
Rom. 14:1

Receive ye one another, as Christ also received us to the glory of God.
Rom. 15:7

We being many are one bread, and one body: for we are all partakers of that one bread.
1 Cor. 10:17

Ye are no more strangers and foreigners, but fellowcitizens with the saints.
Eph. 2:19

Speak every man truth with his neighbour: for we are members one of another.
Eph. 4:25

Though I be absent in the flesh, yet am I with you in the spirit.
Col. 2:5
See also 1 Cor. 5:3

Not now as a servant, but above a servant, a brother beloved.
Philem. 16

Greet ye one another with a kiss of charity.
1 Pet. 5:14

Our fellowship is with the Father, and with His Son Jesus Christ.
1 John 1:3

If we walk in the light, as He is in the light, we have fellowship one with another.
1 John 1:7

[*See also* Brotherhood, Companions, Friendship]

FIDELITY

See Commitment, Faithfulness, Loyalty.

FIRSTBORN

Every male that openeth the womb shall be called holy to the Lord.
Luke 2:23
See also Ex. 13:2, 12

The elder shall serve the younger.
Rom. 9:12, Gen. 25:23

FLATTERY

Get thee behind me, Satan: thou art an offence unto me.
Jesus
Matt. 16:23
See also Matt. 4:10, Mark 8:33,
Luke 4:8

Woe unto you, when all men shall speak well of you!
Jesus
Luke 6:26

FLAVOR

If the salt have lost his savour, wherewith shall it be salted? it is thenceforth good for nothing.
Jesus
Matt. 5:13
See also Mark 9:50, Luke 14:34

It shall make thy belly bitter, but it shall be in thy mouth sweet as honey.
Rev. 10:9

FOLLY

Every one that heareth these sayings of mine, and doeth them not, shall be likened unto a foolish man, which built his house upon the sand.
Jesus
Matt. 7:26
See also Luke 6:49

God hath chosen the foolish things of the world to confound the wise.
1 Cor. 1:27

Walk circumspectly, not as fools, but as wise.
Eph. 5:15

Shun profane and vain babblings: for they will increase unto more ungodliness.
2 Tim. 2:16

Avoid foolish questions.
Titus 3:9

[*See also* Fools, Wisdom]

Give us this day our daily bread.
Jesus
Matt. 6:11
See also Luke 11:3

Not that which goeth into the mouth defileth a man; but that which cometh out of the mouth, this defileth a man.
Jesus
Matt. 15:11
See also Mark 7:15

Take no thought for your life, what ye shall eat; neither for the body, what ye shall put on.
Jesus
Luke 12:22
See also Matt. 6:25

Labour not for the meat which perisheth, but for that meat which endureth unto everlasting life.
Jesus
John 6:27

Rise, Peter; kill, and eat.
Acts 10:13

Every creature of God is good, and nothing to be refused, if it be received with thanksgiving.
1 Tim. 4:4

[*See also* Bread of Life, Celebration, Deprivation, Flavor, Hunger, Materialism, Pleasure, Thirst]

FOOLS

For ye suffer fools gladly, seeing ye yourselves are wise.
2 Cor. 11:19

[*See also* Folly]

FORGIVENESS

Whosoever shall smite thee on thy right cheek, turn to him the other also.
Jesus
Matt. 5:39

Pray for them which despitefully use you, and persecute you.
Jesus
Matt. 5:44
See also Luke 6:28

Forgive us our debts, as we forgive our debtors.
Jesus
Matt. 6:12
See also Luke 11:4

If ye forgive men their trespasses, your heavenly Father will also forgive you.
Jesus
Matt. 6:14

Be of good cheer; thy sins be forgiven thee.
Jesus
Matt. 9:2
See also Mark 2:5

The Son of man hath power on earth to forgive sins.
Jesus
Matt. 9:6, Mark 2:10
See also Luke 5:24

All manner of sin and blasphemy shall be forgiven unto men: but the blasphemy against the Holy Ghost shall not be forgiven unto men.
Jesus
Matt. 12:31
See also Matt. 12:32, Mark 3:29,
Luke 12:10

Until seventy times seven.
Jesus
Matt. 18:22

Unto him that smiteth thee on the one cheek offer also the other.
Jesus
Luke 6:29
See also Matt. 5:39

Forgive, and ye shall be forgiven.
Jesus
Luke 6:37

To whom little is forgiven, the same loveth little.
Jesus
Luke 7:47

Forgive us our sins.
Jesus
Luke 11:4

If thy brother trespass against thee, rebuke him; and if he repent, forgive him.
Jesus
Luke 17:3

If he trespass against thee seven times in a day, and seven times in a day turn again to thee, saying, I repent; thou shalt forgive him.
Jesus
Luke 17:4

Father, forgive them; for they know not what they do.
Jesus
Luke 23:34

To day shalt thou be with me in paradise.
Jesus to malefactor on cross
Luke 23:43

Him that cometh to me I will in no wise cast out.
Jesus
John 6:37

Lord, lay not this sin to their charge.
Stephen, dying
Acts 7:60

Whosoever believeth in Him shall receive remission of sins.
Acts 10:43

Through this man is preached unto you the forgiveness of sins.
Paul, about Jesus
Acts 13:38

Blessed are they whose iniquities are forgiven, and whose sins are covered.
Rom. 4:7

Blessed is the man to whom the Lord will not impute sin.
Rom. 4:8

As by one man's disobedience many were made sinners, so by the obedience of one shall many be made righteous.
Rom. 5:19

Where sin abounded, grace did much more abound.
Rom. 5:20

Bless them which persecute you: bless, and curse not.
Rom. 12:14

If thine enemy hunger, feed him; if he thirst, give him drink.
Rom. 12:20
See also Prov. 25:21

Let not the sun go down upon your wrath.
Eph. 4:26

God for Christ's sake hath forgiven you.
Eph. 4:32

We have redemption through His blood, even the forgiveness of sins.
Col. 1:14

Even as Christ forgave you, so also do ye.
Col. 3:13

Without shedding of blood is no remission.
Heb. 9:22

It is not possible that the blood of bulls and of goats should take away sins.
Heb. 10:4

Your sins are forgiven you for His name's sake.
1 John 2:12

[*See also* Anger, Confession, Grudges, Intercession, Repentance, Retribution, Revenge, Sin]

FORNICATION

The body is not for fornication, but for the Lord.
1 Cor. 6:13

Flee fornication.
1 Cor. 6:18

He that committeth fornication sinneth against his own body.
1 Cor. 6:18

To avoid fornication, let every man have his own wife, and let every woman have her own husband.
1 Cor. 7:2

[*See also* Adultery, Carnality, Immorality, Lust]

The spirit indeed is willing, but the flesh is weak.

> Jesus
> Matt. 26:41
> See also Mark 14:38

Being reviled, we bless; being persecuted, we suffer it.

> 1 Cor. 4:12

Though our outward man perish, yet the inward man is renewed day by day.

> 2 Cor. 4:16

Be strong in the Lord, and in the power of His might.

> Eph. 6:10

Fight the good fight of faith.

> 1 Tim. 6:12

Be strong in the grace that is in Christ Jesus.

> 2 Tim. 2:1

Lift up the hands which hang down, and the feeble knees.

> Heb. 12:12

Hold fast till I come.

> Jesus
> Rev. 2:25

[See also Diligence, Patience, Perseverance, Strength, Temptation]

The law maketh men high priests which have infirmity.

> Heb. 7:28

[See also Fortitude, Mortality, Strength]

Ye shall know the truth, and the truth shall make you free.

> Jesus
> John 8:32

If the Son therefore shall make you free, ye shall be free indeed.

> John 8:36

But I was free born.

> Paul
> Acts 22:28

He that is called in the Lord, being a servant, is the Lord's freeman.

> 1 Cor. 7:22

He that is called, being free, is Christ's servant.

> 1 Cor. 7:22

Ye are bought with a price; be not ye the servants of men.

> 1 Cor. 7:23

Where the Spirit of the Lord is, there is liberty.

> 2 Cor. 3:17

Christ hath made us free.

> Gal. 5:1

Use not liberty for an occasion to the flesh.

> Gal. 5:13

Of whom a man is overcome, of the same is he brought in bondage.

> 2 Pet. 2:19

[See also Deliverance, Exile, Imprisonment, Slavery]

Greater love hath no man than this, that a man lay down his life for his friends.

> Jesus
> John 15:13

I have called you friends; for all things that I have heard of my Father I have made known unto you.

> Jesus
> John 15:15

Salute one another with an holy kiss.

> Rom. 16:16

If thou count me therefore a partner, receive him as myself.

> Philem. 17

[See also Brotherhood, Companions, Fellowship]

FRUSTRATION

In those days shall men seek death, and shall not find it; and shall desire to die, and death shall flee from them.
Rev. 9:6

[*See also* Disappointment, Futility]

FULFILLMENT

I am not come to destroy, but to fulfil.
Jesus
Matt. 5:17

Ye are complete in Him, which is the head of all principality and power.
(Him: Jesus)
Col. 2:10

[*See also* Contentment, Reward, Satisfaction]

FUTILITY

The Lord knoweth the thoughts of the wise, that they are vain.
1 Cor. 3:20

[*See also* Frustration]

FUTURE

Take therefore no thought for the morrow: for the morrow shall take thought for the things of itself.
Jesus
Matt. 6:34

Sufficient unto the day is the evil thereof.
Jesus
Matt. 6:34

It is not for you to know the times or the seasons.
Jesus
Acts 1:7

Known unto God are all His works from the beginning of the world.
Acts 15:18

Ye know not what shall be on the morrow.
James 4:14

Ye ought to say, If the Lord will, we shall live, and do this, or that.
James 4:15

[*See also* Ambition, Dreams, Posterity, Visions, Worry]

G

GENEROSITY

If any man will sue thee at the law, and take away thy coat, let him have thy cloak also.
Jesus
Matt. 5:40

Whosoever shall compel thee to go a mile, go with him twain.
Jesus
Matt. 5:41

Give to him that asketh thee, and from him that would borrow of thee turn not thou away.
Jesus
Matt. 5:42
See also Luke 6:30

If ye then, being evil, know how to give good gifts unto your children, how much more shall your Father which is in heaven give good things to them that ask Him?
Jesus
Matt. 7:11
See also Luke 11:13

Freely ye have received, freely give.
Jesus
Matt. 10:8

If ye lend to them of whom ye hope to receive, what thank have ye? for sinners also lend to sinners, to receive as much again.
Jesus
Luke 6:34

Of a truth I say unto you, that this poor widow hath cast in more than they all.
Jesus
Luke 21:3
See also Mark 12:43

Silver and gold have I none; but such as I have give I thee.
Acts 3:6

It is more blessed to give than to receive.
Jesus
Acts 20:35

He which soweth sparingly shall reap also sparingly.
2 Cor. 9:6

[*See also* Altruism, Charity, Greed, Selfishness, Selflessness, Sharing]

GIFTS

They presented unto Him gifts; gold, and frankincense, and myrrh.
Matt. 2:11

[*See also* Altruism, Generosity]

GLOATING

See Boasting, Conceit, Humility, Pride.

GLORY

Ye are our glory and joy.
1 Thess. 2:20

All flesh is as grass, and all the glory of man as the flower of grass.
1 Pet. 1:24
See also Isa. 40:6

[*See also* Fame, God's Glory, Respect]

GOALS

Seek ye first the kingdom of God, and His righteousness.
Jesus
Matt. 6:33
See also Luke 12:31

Great is thy faith: be it unto thee even as thou wilt.
Jesus
Matt. 15:28

Not as I will, but as Thou wilt.
Jesus
Matt. 26:39
See also Mark 14:36, Luke 22:42

What things soever ye desire, when ye pray, believe that ye receive them, and ye shall have them.
Jesus
Mark 11:24
See also Matt. 21:22

A man can receive nothing, except it be given him from heaven.
John 3:27

I seek not mine own will, but the will of the Father.
Jesus
John 5:30

He that planteth and he that watereth are one.
1 Cor. 3:8

Run, that ye may obtain.
1 Cor. 9:24

We should not lust after evil things.
1 Cor. 10:6

Be ye stedfast, unmoveable, always abounding in the work of the Lord.
1 Cor. 15:58

Whether in pretence, or in truth, Christ is preached; and I therein do rejoice.
Phil. 1:18

I press toward the mark for the prize of the high calling of God in Christ Jesus.
Phil. 3:14

Seek those things which are above, where Christ sitteth on the right hand of God.
Col. 3:1

Walk worthy of God, who hath called you unto His kingdom and glory.
1 Thess. 2:12

Follow after righteousness, godliness, faith, love, patience, meekness.
1 Tim. 6:11

[*See also* Ambition, Duty, Mission, Values]

GOD

Our Father which art in heaven, Hallowed be Thy name. Thy kingdom come. Thy will be done in earth, as it is in heaven.
Jesus
Matt. 6:9–10
See also Luke 11:2

God is not the God of the dead, but of the living.
Jesus
Matt. 22:32
See also Mark 12:27, Luke 20:38

Call no man your father upon the earth: for one is your Father, which is in heaven.
Jesus
Matt. 23:9

God is true.
John 3:33

He that sent me is true, whom ye know not.
Jesus
John 7:28

He giveth to all life, and breath, and all things.
Acts 17:25

Is He the God of the Jews only? is He not also of the Gentiles?
Rom. 3:29

The same Lord over all is rich unto all that call upon Him.
Rom. 10:12

There is no power but of God.
Rom. 13:1

The things of God knoweth no man.
1 Cor. 2:11

Faithful is He that calleth you.
1 Thess. 5:24

The foundation of God standeth sure.
2 Tim. 2:19

He that cometh to God must believe that He is, and that He is a rewarder of them that diligently seek Him.
Heb. 11:6

There is one lawgiver, who is able to save and to destroy: who art thou that judgest another?
James 4:12

God is light, and in Him is no darkness at all.
1 John 1:5

God is love.
1 John 4:8, 16

We love Him, because He first loved us.
1 John 4:19

Holy, holy, holy, Lord God Almighty, which was, and is, and is to come.
Rev. 4:8

[*See also* Fear of God, Goodness, Holiness, Jesus, Knowledge of God, Love of God, Praise of God, Reverence, Service to God, Sovereignty, Trust, and the categories which follow]

GOD'S ANGER

O generation of vipers, who hath warned you to flee from the wrath to come?
Matt. 3:7, Luke 3:7

The wrath of God cometh on the children of disobedience.
Col. 3:6

It is a fearful thing to fall into the hands of the living God.
Heb. 10:31

Our God is a consuming fire.
Heb. 12:29
See also Deut. 4:24

The great day of His wrath is come; and who shall be able to stand?
Rev. 6:17

The great winepress of the wrath of God.
Rev. 14:19

Pour out the vials of the wrath of God upon the earth.
Rev. 16:1

[*See also* Exasperation, Forgiveness, Judgment]

GOD'S GLORY

Peace in heaven, and glory in the highest.
Luke 19:38

Ye shall see heaven open, and the angels of

God ascending and descending upon the Son of man.
Jesus
John 1:51

This sickness is not unto death, but for the glory of God.
Jesus
John 11:4

The hour is come, that the Son of man should be glorified.
Jesus
John 12:23

Father, glorify Thy name.
Jesus
John 12:28

Now is the Son of man glorified, and God is glorified in Him.
Jesus
John 13:31

Whatsoever ye shall ask in my name, that will I do, that the Father may be glorified in the Son.
Jesus
John 14:13
See also John 14:14

Glorify Thy Son, that Thy Son also may glorify Thee.
Jesus
John 17:1

The city had no need of the sun, neither of the moon, to shine in it: for the glory of God did lighten it, and the Lamb is the light thereof.
Rev. 21:23

GOD'S GOODNESS

See Goodness.

GOD'S GREATNESS

For Thine is the kingdom, and the power, and the glory, for ever.
Jesus
Matt. 6:13

My Father is greater than I.
Jesus
John 14:28

Every house is builded by some man; but He that built all things is God.
Heb. 3:4

Great and marvellous are Thy works, Lord God Almighty.
Rev. 15:3

GOD'S KNOWLEDGE

Your Father knoweth what things ye have need of, before ye ask Him.
Jesus
Matt. 6:8

Are not five sparrows sold for two farthings, and not one of them is forgotten before God?
Jesus
Luke 12:6
See also Matt. 10:29

Even the very hairs of your head are all numbered.
Jesus
Luke 12:7
See also Matt. 10:30

God knoweth your hearts.
Jesus
Luke 16:15

Known unto God are all His works from the beginning of the world.
Acts 15:18

He that searcheth the hearts knoweth what is the mind of the Spirit.
Rom. 8:27

How unsearchable are His judgments, and His ways past finding out!
Rom. 11:33

Who hath known the mind of the Lord, that he may instruct Him?
1 Cor. 2:16

The Lord knoweth the thoughts of the wise, that they are vain.
1 Cor. 3:20

God is greater than our heart, and knoweth all things.
1 John 3:20

[*See also* God's Presence, Secrecy]

GOD'S LOVE

For God so loved the world, that He gave His only begotten Son, that whosoever believeth in Him should not perish, but have everlasting life.
> *Jesus*
> *John 3:16*
> *See also John 3:36, John 6:47*

Whom the Lord loveth He chasteneth.
> *Heb. 12:6*

Draw nigh to God, and He will draw nigh to you.
> *James 4:8*

[*See also* God's Mercy, Love]

GOD'S MERCY

His mercy is on them that fear Him from generation to generation.
> *Mary, mother of Jesus*
> *Luke 1:50*

I will have mercy on whom I will have mercy, and I will have compassion on whom I will have compassion.
> *Rom. 9:15*
> *See also Ex. 33:19*

[*See also* Compassion, God's Love, Mercy]

GOD'S PEOPLE

God is able of these stones to raise up children unto Abraham.
> *Matt. 3:9, Luke 3:8*

As many as received Him, to them gave He power to become the sons of God.
> *John 1:12*

He that is of God heareth God's words.
> *Jesus*
> *John 8:47*

Other sheep I have, which are not of this fold.
> *Jesus*
> *John 10:16*

I will call them My people, which were not My people; and her beloved, which was not beloved.
> *Rom. 9:25*
> *See also Hos. 2:23*

I will be their God, and they shall be My people.
> *2 Cor. 6:16*
> *See also Lev. 26:12*

Ye are all the children of God by faith in Christ Jesus.
> *Gal. 3:26*

Ye who sometimes were far off are made nigh by the blood of Christ.
> *Eph. 2:13*

Unto us was the gospel preached, as well as unto them.
> *Heb. 4:2*

I will be to them a God, and they shall be to Me a people.
> *Heb. 8:10*
> *See also Jer. 31:33*

[*See also* Believers, Christians]

GOD'S POWER

God is able of these stones to raise up children unto Abraham.
> *Matt. 3:9, Luke 3:8*

For Thine is the kingdom, and the power, and the glory, for ever.
> *Jesus*
> *Matt. 6:13*

Father, all things are possible unto Thee.
> *Jesus*
> *Mark 14:36*

With God nothing shall be impossible.
> *Luke 1:37*

All things are delivered to me of my Father.
> *Jesus*
> *Luke 10:22*
> *See also Matt. 11:27*

Without Him was not any thing made.
> *John 1:3*

The Son can do nothing of Himself, but what He seeth the Father do.
> *Jesus*
> *John 5:19*

If it be of God, ye cannot overthrow it.
Acts 5:39

What was I, that I could withstand God?
Peter
Acts 11:17

All things are of God.
2 Cor. 5:18

To Him be glory and dominion for ever
and ever.
1 Pet. 5:11

The Lamb shall overcome them: for He is
Lord of lords, and King of kings.
Rev. 17:14

Alleluia: for the Lord God omnipotent
reigneth.
Rev. 19:6

[*See also* God's Knowledge]

GOD'S PRESENCE

Thy Father which seeth in secret shall
reward thee openly.
Jesus
Matt. 6:6, Matt. 6:18

Where two or three are gathered together
in my name, there am I in the midst of
them.
Jesus
Matt. 18:20

God that made the world and all things
therein, seeing that He is Lord of heaven
and earth, dwelleth not in temples made
with hands.
Acts 17:24

He be not far from every one of us.
Acts 17:27

Ye are the temple of the living God.
2 Cor. 6:16

The Lord is at hand.
Phil 4:5

[*See also* Churches, God's Temple]

GOD'S PROTECTION

I commend you to God, and to the word
of His grace.
Paul
Acts 20:32

Shall their unbelief make the faith of God
without effect?
Rom. 3:3

If God be for us, who can be against us?
Rom. 8:31

Take unto you the whole armour of God,
that ye may be able to withstand in the
evil day.
Eph. 6:13

The shield of faith, wherewith ye shall be
able to quench all the fiery darts of the
wicked.
Eph. 6:16

The Lord is faithful, who shall stablish
you, and keep you from evil.
2 Thess. 3:3

The eyes of the Lord are over the righteous, and His ears are open unto their
prayers.
1 Pet. 3:12

The face of the Lord is against them that
do evil.
1 Pet. 3:12

They shall hunger no more, neither thirst
any more; neither shall the sun light on
them, nor any heat.
Rev. 7:16

[*See also* Assistance, Enemies, Fear,
God's Presence, God's Support, Reliance,
Trust]

GOD'S SUPPORT

Consider the lilies of the field, how they
grow; they toil not, neither do they spin:
And yet I say unto you, That even Solo-
mon in all his glory was not arrayed like
one of these.
Jesus
Matt. 6:28–29
See also Luke 12:27

No man can do these miracles that Thou doest, except God be with him.
John 3:2

I will never leave thee, nor forsake thee.
Heb. 13:5
See also Deut. 31:6, Josh. 1:5

The Lamb which is in the midst of the throne shall feed them, and shall lead them unto living fountains of waters.
Rev. 7:17

[*See also* Abandonment, Encouragement, Faith, God's Protection]

GOD'S TEMPLE

The temple of God is holy, which temple ye are.
1 Cor. 3:17

Behold, the tabernacle of God is with men, and He will dwell with them.
Rev. 21:3

I saw no temple therein: for the Lord God Almighty and the Lamb are the temple of it.
Rev. 21:22

[*See also* Churches]

GOD'S UNIQUENESS

To us there is but one God, the Father, of whom are all things, and we in Him.
1 Cor. 8:6

God is one.
Gal. 3:20

There is one God, and one mediator between God and men, the man Christ Jesus.
1 Tim. 2:5

[*See also* Monotheism]

GOD'S WILL

Our Father which art in heaven, Hallowed be Thy name. Thy kingdom come. Thy will be done in earth, as it is in heaven.
Jesus
Matt. 6:9–10
See also Luke 11:2

Not my will, but Thine, be done.
Jesus
Luke 22:42
See also Mark 14:36

The will of the Lord be done.
Acts 21:14

Ye ought to say, If the Lord will, we shall live, and do this, or that.
James 4:15

The world passeth away, and the lust thereof: but he that doeth the will of God abideth for ever.
1 John 2:17

[*See also* Certainty]

GOD'S WORD

My doctrine is not mine, but His that sent me.
Jesus
John 7:16

Thy word is truth.
Jesus to God
John 17:17

Let the word of Christ dwell in you.
Col. 3:16

The word of God is quick, and powerful, and sharper than any twoedged sword.
Heb. 4:12

The grass withereth, and the flower thereof falleth away: But the word of the Lord endureth forever.
1 Pet. 1:24–25
See also Isa. 40:8

As newborn babes, desire the sincere milk of the word, that ye may grow thereby.
1 Pet. 2:2

[*See also* Commandments, Gospel, Scripture]

GOD, TRAITS OF

We ought not to think that the Godhead is like unto gold, or silver, or stone, graven by art and man's device.
Acts 17:29

God is faithful.
E.g., 1 Cor. 1:9

The Father of mercies, and the God of all comfort.
2 Cor. 1:3

GODLESSNESS

O faithless and perverse generation.
Jesus
Matt. 17:17

It shall be more tolerable for Sodom and Gomorrha in the day of judgment than for that city.
Jesus
Mark 6:11
See also Matt. 10:15

He that denieth me before men shall be denied before the angels of God.
Jesus
Luke 12:9
See also Matt. 10:33

Ye are of your father the devil, and the lusts of your father ye will do.
Jesus
John 8:44

Ye stiffnecked and uncircumcised in heart and ears, ye do always resist the Holy Ghost.
Acts 7:51

Wilt thou not cease to pervert the right ways of the Lord?
Acts 13:10

Turn them from darkness to light, and from the power of Satan unto God.
Jesus to Paul
Acts 26:18

When they knew God, they glorified Him not as God.
Rom 1:21

Shall their unbelief make the faith of God without effect?
Rom. 3:3

If the unbelieving depart, let him depart.
1 Cor. 7:15

The things which the Gentiles sacrifice, they sacrifice to devils, and not to God.
1 Cor. 10:20

If any man love not the Lord Jesus Christ, let him be Anathema.
1 Cor. 16:22

If our gospel be hid, it is hid to them that are lost.
2 Cor. 4:3

Strangers from the covenants of promise, having no hope, and without God in the world.
Eph. 2:12

The enemies of the cross of Christ: Whose end is destruction, whose god is their belly, and whose glory is in their shame.
Phil. 3:18–19

They that sleep sleep in the night; and they that be drunken are drunken in the night.
1 Thess. 5:7

The Lord Jesus shall be revealed from heaven with His mighty angels, In flaming fire taking vengeance on them that know not God, and that obey not the gospel.
2 Thess. 1:7–8

All men have not faith.
2 Thess. 3:2

Shun profane and vain babblings: for they will increase unto more ungodliness.
2 Tim. 2:16

Unto them that are defiled and unbelieving is nothing pure; but even their mind and conscience is defiled.
Titus 1:15

Ye were as sheep going astray; but are now returned unto the Shepherd.
1 Pet. 2:25

If the righteous scarcely be saved, where shall the ungodly and the sinner appear?
1 Pet. 4:18

Whosoever denieth the Son, the same hath not the Father.
1 John 2:23

The world knoweth us not, because it knew Him not.
1 John 3:1

He that believeth not God hath made Him a liar.
(Him: Jesus)
1 John 5:10

Woe unto them! for they have gone in the way of Cain.
Jude 11

Clouds they are without water, carried about of winds; trees whose fruit withereth.
Jude 12

Murmurers, complainers, walking after their own lusts.
Jude 16

Babylon the Great, the Mother of Harlots and Abominations of the Earth.
Rev. 17:5

Babylon the great is fallen, is fallen, and is become the habitation of devils.
Rev. 18:2

Her sins have reached unto heaven, and God hath remembered her iniquities.
(her: Babylon)
Rev. 18:5

With violence shall that great city Babylon be thrown down.
Rev. 18:21

[See also Backsliding, Faith, Godliness, Idolatry, Rebellion, Sin]

GODLINESS

Ye cannot serve God and mammon.
Jesus
Matt. 6:24, Luke 16:13

None of us liveth to himself.
Rom. 14:7

The unbelieving husband is sanctified by the wife, and the unbelieving wife is sanctified by the husband.
1 Cor. 7:14

He that soweth to the Spirit shall of the Spirit reap life everlasting.
Gal. 6:8

Great is the mystery of godliness.
1 Tim. 3:16

Bodily exercise profiteth little: but godliness is profitable unto all things.
1 Tim. 4:8

Godliness with contentment is great gain.
1 Tim. 6:6

All that will live godly in Christ Jesus shall suffer persecution.
2 Tim. 3:12

Whosoever is born of God doth not commit sin.
1 John 3:9

Whosoever shall confess that Jesus is the Son of God, God dwelleth in him, and he in God.
1 John 4:15

If a man say, I love God, and hateth his brother, he is a liar.
1 John 4:20

Whatsoever is born of God overcometh the world.
1 John 5:4

I have no greater joy than to hear that my children walk in truth.
3 John 4

He that doeth good is of God: but he that doeth evil hath not seen God.
3 John 11

Keep yourselves in the love of God, looking for the mercy of our Lord Jesus Christ.
Jude 21

[See also Righteousness]

GOOD AND EVIL

He maketh His sun to rise on the evil and on the good, and sendeth rain on the just and on the unjust.
Jesus
Matt. 5:45

Every good tree bringeth forth good fruit; but a corrupt tree bringeth forth evil fruit.
Jesus
Matt. 7:17
See also Luke 6:43

How can ye, being evil, speak good things?
Jesus
Matt. 12:34

A good man out of the good treasure of the heart bringeth forth good things: and an evil man out of the evil treasure bringeth forth evil things.
Jesus
Matt. 12:35

They that have done good, unto the resurrection of life; and they that have done evil, unto the resurrection of damnation.
Jesus
John 5:29

Ye are from beneath; I am from above: ye are of this world; I am not of this world.
Jesus
John 8:23

Abhor that which is evil; cleave to that which is good.
Rom. 12:9

Be not overcome of evil, but overcome evil with good.
Rom. 12:21

Let us therefore cast off the works of darkness, and let us put on the armour of light.
Rom. 13:12

I would have you wise unto that which is good, and simple concerning evil.
Rom. 16:19

To him that knoweth to do good, and doeth it not, to him it is sin.
James 4:17

Eschew evil, and do good.
1 Pet. 3:11

We know that we are of God, and the whole world lieth in wickedness.
1 John 5:19

Follow not that which is evil, but that which is good.
3 John 11

He that doeth good is of God: but he that doeth evil hath not seen God.
3 John 11

[*See also* Corruption, Evil, Wickedness]

He maketh His sun to rise on the evil and on the good, and sendeth rain on the just and on the unjust.
Jesus
Matt. 5:45

Why callest thou me good? there is none good but one, that is, God.
Jesus
Matt. 19:17, Mark 10:18
See also Luke 18:19

Is thine eye evil, because I am good?
Jesus
Matt. 20:15

If ye do good to them which do good to you, what thank have ye? for sinners also do even the same.
Jesus
Luke 6:33
See also Matt. 5:46

Take care of him; and whatsoever thou spendest more, when I come again, I will repay thee.
(I: The Good Samaritan)
Luke 10:35

Go, and do thou likewise.
Jesus
Luke 10:37

The goodness of God leadeth thee to repentance.
Rom. 2:4

Whatsoever good thing any man doeth, the same shall he receive of the Lord.
Eph. 6:8

Hold fast to that which is good.
1 Thess. 5:21

Do good.
1 Tim. 6:18

Every good gift and every perfect gift is from above.
James 1:17

[*See also* Altruism, Good and Evil, Kindness, Righteousness, Virtue]

GOSPEL

The care of this world, and the deceitfulness of riches, choke the word.
Jesus
Matt. 13:22
See also Mark 4:19

Repent ye, and believe the gospel.
Jesus
Mark 1:15

Whosoever shall lose his life for my sake and the gospel's, the same shall save it.
Jesus
Mark 8:35
See also Matt. 16:25, Luke 9:24

The gospel must first be published among all nations.
Jesus
Mark 13:10

Go ye into all the world, and preach the gospel to every creature.
Jesus
Mark 16:15

Man shall not live by bread alone, but by every word of God.
Jesus
Luke 4:4
See also Deut. 8:3, Matt. 4:4

He hath anointed me to preach the gospel to the poor.
Jesus
Luke 4:18
See also Isa. 61:1

Whosoever shall be ashamed of me and of my words, of him shall the Son of man be ashamed.
Jesus
Luke 9:26

Blessed are they that hear the word of God, and keep it.
Jesus
Luke 11:28

He that heareth my word, and believeth on Him that sent me, hath everlasting life.
Jesus
John 5:24

The promise which was made unto the fathers, God hath fulfilled the same unto us their children.
Acts 13:32–33

Seeing ye put it from you, and judge yourselves unworthy of everlasting life, lo, we turn to the Gentiles.
Paul to Jews
Acts 13:46

Remember the words of the Lord Jesus.
Acts 20:35

I am not ashamed of the gospel of Christ.
Rom. 1:16

It is the power of God unto salvation to every one that believeth.
Rom. 1:16

The word is nigh thee.
Rom. 10:8

How shall they hear without a preacher?
Rom. 10:14

How beautiful are the feet of them that preach the gospel of peace.
Rom. 10:15

In Christ Jesus I have begotten you through the gospel.
1 Cor. 4:15

If our gospel be hid, it is hid to them that are lost.
2 Cor. 4:3

The gospel which was preached of me is not after man.
Gal. 1:11

I neither received it of man, neither was I taught it, but by the revelation of Jesus Christ.
Gal. 1:12

I am set for the defence of the gospel.
Phil. 1:17

Whether in pretence, or in truth, Christ is preached; and I therein do rejoice.
Phil. 1:18

Be not moved away from the hope of the gospel.
Col. 1:23

The word of God is not bound.
2 Tim. 2:9

Preach the word.
2 Tim. 4:2

Unto us was the gospel preached, as well as unto them.
Heb. 4:2

[See also Evangelism, God's Word, Preaching, Scripture]

GOSSIP

See Secrecy, Slander, Speech.

GOVERNMENT

If a kingdom be divided against itself, that kingdom cannot stand.
Jesus
Mark 3:24
See also Matt. 12:25, Luke 11:17

Whether it be right in the sight of God to hearken unto you more than unto God, judge ye.
Acts 4:19

Thou shalt not speak evil of the ruler of thy people.
Acts 23:5
See also Ex. 22:28

Let every soul be subject unto the higher powers.
Rom. 13:1

The powers that be are ordained of God.
Rom. 13:1

Rulers are not a terror to good works, but to the evil.
Rom. 13:3

He is the minister of God, a revenger to execute wrath upon him that doeth evil.
Rom. 13:4

Fear God. Honour the king.
1 Pet. 2:17

[See also Church and State, Leadership, Monarchy, Obedience, Rebellion, Taxation]

GRACE

The law was given by Moses, but grace and truth came by Jesus Christ.
John 1:17

No man can come unto me, except it were given unto him of my Father.
Jesus
John 6:65

Where sin abounded, grace did much more abound.
Rom. 5:20

Sin shall not have dominion over you: for ye are not under the law, but under grace.
Rom. 6:14

The gift of God is eternal life through Jesus Christ our Lord.
Rom. 6:23

If by grace, then is it no more of works: otherwise grace is no more grace.
Rom. 11:6

By grace are ye saved through faith.
Eph. 2:8

It is the gift of God.
Eph. 2:8

Grace be with all them that love our Lord Jesus Christ in sincerity.
Eph. 6:24

GRATITUDE

He that is mighty hath done to me great things; and holy is His name.
Mary
Luke 1:49

To whom little is forgiven, the same loveth little.
Jesus
Luke 7:47

All things are delivered to me of my Father.
Jesus
Luke 10:22
See also Matt. 11:27

Thanks be to God, which giveth us the victory through our Lord Jesus Christ.
1 Cor. 15:57

Thanks be unto God for His unspeakable gift.
2 Cor. 9:15

In every thing give thanks: for this is the will of God in Christ Jesus.
1 Thess. 5:18

Every creature of God is good, and noth-

ing to be refused, if it be received with thanksgiving.
1 Tim. 4:4

[*See also* Appreciation, Ingratitude, Praise of God]

GREATNESS

He that cometh after me is mightier than I, whose shoes I am not worthy to bear.
John the Baptist
Matt. 3:11
See also Mark 1:7, Luke 3:16

Whosoever shall do and teach them, the same shall be called great in the kingdom of heaven.
Jesus (them: commandments)
Matt. 5:19

He that is least among you all, the same shall be great.
Jesus
Luke 9:48

The servant is not greater than his lord; neither he that is sent greater than he that sent him.
Jesus
John 13:16
See also John 15:20, Matt. 10:24

[*See also* God's Greatness, Size, Status]

GREED

Exact no more than that which is appointed you.
Luke 3:13

Beware of covetousness.
Jesus
Luke 12:15

Having food and raiment let us be therewith content.
1 Tim. 6:8

The love of money is the root of all evil.
1 Tim. 6:10

Be content with such things as ye have.
Heb. 13:5

[*See also* Ambition, Contentment, Envy, Satisfaction]

GREETINGS
See Salutations.

GRIEF

Weep not for me, but weep for yourselves, and for your children.
Jesus
Luke 23:28

Ye shall weep and lament, but the world shall rejoice.
Jesus
John 16:20

[*See also* Anguish, Mourning, Sorrow, Tears]

GROWTH

First the blade, then the ear, after that the full corn in the ear.
Jesus
Mark 4:28

It is like a grain of mustard seed, which a man took, and cast into his garden; and it grew, and waxed a great tree.
Jesus
Luke 13:19
See also Matt. 13:31, Mark 4:31

I have fed you with milk, and not with meat.
1 Cor. 3:2

[*See also* Cultivation, Maturity]

GRUDGES

Agree with thine adversary quickly, whiles thou art in the way with him.
Jesus
Matt. 5:25

When ye stand praying, forgive, if ye have ought against any: that your Father also which is in heaven may forgive you your trespasses.
Jesus
Mark 11:25

If ye do not forgive, neither will your

Father which is in heaven forgive your trespasses.
Jesus
Mark 11:26

Let not the sun go down upon your wrath.
Eph. 4:26

[*See also* Anger, Arguments, Forgiveness]

GUIDANCE

I am the light of the world.
Jesus
John 8:12

I am the way, the truth, and the life: no man cometh unto the Father, but by me.
Jesus
John 14:6

Lord, what wilt Thou have me to do?
Saul to Jesus
Acts 9:6

It shall be told thee what thou must do.
Jesus to Saul
Acts 9:6

Remember the words of the Lord Jesus.
Acts 20:35

Let the word of Christ dwell in you.
Col. 3:16

Make straight paths for your feet, lest that which is lame be turned out of the way.
Heb. 12:13

[*See also* Advice, Behavior, Instruction]

GUILT

He that is without sin among you, let him first cast a stone.
Jesus
John 8:7

Woman, where are those thine accusers?
Jesus
John 8:10

Ye are not all clean.
Jesus
John 13:11

He that delivered me unto thee hath the greater sin.
Jesus
John 19:11

Your blood be upon your own heads; I am clean.
Acts 18:6

If I build again the things which I destroyed, I make myself a transgressor.
Gal. 2:18

Whosoever shall keep the whole law, and yet offend in one point, he is guilty of all.
James 2:10

[*See also* Blame, Innocence, Justice, Responsibility, Self-Incrimination]

HANDICAPPED

He maketh both the deaf to hear, and the dumb to speak.
(He: Jesus)
Mark 7:37

The blind see, the lame walk, the lepers are cleansed, the deaf hear, the dead are raised, to the poor the gospel is preached.
Jesus
Luke 7:22
See also Matt. 11:5

When thou makest a feast, call the poor, the maimed, the lame, the blind: And thou shalt be blessed; for they cannot recompense thee.
Jesus
Luke 14:13–14

[*See also* Blindness, Healing, Obstacles, Sight]

HAPPINESS

I bring you good tidings of great joy.
Luke 2:10

Rejoice not, that the spirits are subject unto you; but rather rejoice, because your names are written in heaven.
Jesus
Luke 10:20

Rejoice with me; for I have found my sheep which was lost.
Jesus
Luke 15:6

If ye know these things, happy are ye if ye do them.
Jesus
John 13:17

Ask, and ye shall receive, that your joy may be full.
Jesus
John 16:24

Rejoice with them that do rejoice, and weep with them that weep.
Rom. 12:15

Rejoice in the Lord.
E.g., Phil. 3:1

We count them happy which endure.
James 5:11

He that will love life, and see good days, let him refrain his tongue from evil.
1 Pet. 3:10
See also Ps. 34:13

Let us be glad and rejoice, and give honour to Him.
Rev. 19:7

Blessed are they which are called unto the marriage supper of the Lamb.
Rev. 19:9

[*See also* Celebration, Contentment, Laughter, Pleasure, Satisfaction]

HATRED

Do good to them that hate you.
Jesus
Matt. 5:44
See also Luke 6:27

If the world hate you, ye know that it hated me before it hated you.
Jesus
John 15:18

The poison of asps is under their lips.
Rom. 3:13
See also Ps. 140:3

He that saith he is in the light, and hateth his brother, is in darkness even until now.
1 John 2:9

Whosoever hateth his brother is a murderer.
1 John 3:15

He that loveth not knoweth not God; for God is love.
1 John 4:8

If a man say, I love God, and hateth his brother, he is a liar.
1 John 4:20

[*See also* Brotherhood, Contempt, Enemies, Love, Persecution, Self-Hatred]

HEALING

If Thou wilt, Thou canst make me clean.
Leper to Jesus
Matt. 8:2, Mark 1:40, Luke 5:12

They that be whole need not a physician, but they that are sick.
Jesus
Matt. 9:12
See also Mark 2:17, Luke 5:31

If I may but touch His garment, I shall be whole.
Matt. 9:21
See also Mark 5:28

Thy faith hath made thee whole.
Jesus
Matt. 9:22, Mark 5:34, Mark 10:52, Luke 8:48
See also Luke 17:19

Heal the sick, cleanse the lepers, raise the dead, cast out devils.
Jesus
Matt. 10:8

As many as touched were made perfectly whole.
Matt. 14:36
See also Mark 6:56

Ephphatha, that is, Be opened.
Jesus
Mark 7:34

He maketh both the deaf to hear, and the dumb to speak.
(He: Jesus)
Mark 7:37

They shall lay hands on the sick, and they shall recover.
Jesus
Mark 16:18

He hath sent me to heal the broken-hearted, to preach deliverance to the captives.
Jesus
Luke 4:18
See also Isa. 61:1

Physician, heal thyself.
Luke 4:23

He laid His hands on every one of them, and healed them.
Luke 4:40

Go thy way; thy son liveth.
Jesus
John 4:50

Rise, take up thy bed, and walk.
Jesus
John 5:8
See also Matt. 9:6, Mark 2:9,
   Luke 5:24

Go, wash in the pool of Siloam.
Jesus
John 9:7

In the name of Jesus Christ of Nazareth rise up and walk.
Acts 3:6

By Him doth this man stand here before you whole.
Acts 4:10

And they were healed every one.
Acts 5:16

Jesus Christ maketh thee whole: arise, and make thy bed.
Acts 9:34

He had faith to be healed.
Acts 14:9

And he leaped and walked.
Acts 14:10

The prayer of faith shall save the sick.
James 5:15

[*See also* Faith, Miracles]

HEALTH

See Handicapped, Healing.

HEAVEN

It is better for thee to enter into the kingdom of God with one eye, than having two eyes to be cast into hell fire.
Jesus
Mark 9:47
See also Matt. 18:9

In my Father's house are many mansions.
Jesus
John 14:2

I go to prepare a place for you.
Jesus
John 14:2

Whither I go ye know, and the way ye know.
Jesus
John 14:4

Heaven is My throne, and earth is My footstool: what house will ye build Me? saith the Lord.
Acts 7:49
See also Isa. 66:1, Matt. 5:34–35

The gates of it shall not be shut at all by day: for there shall be no night there.
Rev. 21:25

[*See also* Creation, Damnation, Eternal Life, God's Presence, Kingdom of God, Kingdom of Heaven]

HEAVEN AND EARTH

One star differeth from another star in glory.
1 Cor. 15:41

They shall perish; but Thou remainest.
Heb. 1:11

I saw a new heaven and a new earth: for the first heaven and the first earth were passed away.
Rev. 21:1

[*See also* Creation, Earth]

HEEDFULNESS

We have piped unto you, and ye have not danced; we have mourned unto you, and ye have not lamented.
Jesus
Matt. 11:17
See also Luke 7:32

Who hath ears to hear, let him hear.
Jesus
Matt. 13:9, Matt. 13:43
See also, e.g., Matt. 11:15, Mark 4:9,
*   Rev. 13:9*

Hear, and understand.
Jesus
Matt. 15:10

Ye that fear God, give audience.
Acts 13:16

Let every man be swift to hear, slow to speak, slow to wrath.
James 1:19

He that hath an ear, let him hear what the Spirit saith unto the churches.
Jesus
E.g., Rev. 2:7

[*See also* Obedience, Pleas, Prayer, Preaching, Warning]

HEIGHT

See Size.

HELL

The fire that never shall be quenched.
Jesus
Mark 9:43, 45

Where their worm dieth not, and the fire is not quenched.
Jesus
Mark 9:44, 46, 48

I am tormented in this flame.
Luke 16:24

Between us and you there is a great gulf fixed: so that they which would pass from hence to you cannot.
Luke 16:26

I looked, and behold a pale horse: and his name that sat on him was Death, and Hell followed with him.
Rev. 6:8

The bottomless pit.
Rev. 9:1

Death and hell were cast into the lake of fire. This is the second death.
Rev. 20:14

[*See also* Damnation, Death, Torment]

HELP

See Assistance, Deliverance.

HERESY

In vain they do worship me, teaching for doctrines the commandments of men.
Jesus
Matt. 15:9, Mark 7:7
See also Isa. 29:13

False Christs and false prophets shall rise, and shall show signs and wonders, to seduce, if it were possible, even the elect.
Jesus
Mark 13:22
See also Matt. 24:24

After the way which they call heresy, so worship I the God of my fathers.
Paul
Acts 24:14

If any man preach any other gospel unto you than that ye have received, let him be accursed.
Gal. 1:9

Beware lest any man spoil you through philosophy and vain deceit.
Col. 2:8

A man that is an heretick after the first and second admonition reject.
Titus 3:10

There shall be false teachers among you.
2 Pet. 2:1

He that biddeth him God speed is partaker of his evil deeds.
2 John 11

Woe unto them! for they have gone in the way of Cain.
Jude 11

[*See also* Blasphemy, False Prophets]

HERITAGE

The God of Abraham, and the God of Isaac, and the God of Jacob.
Mark 12:26
See also, e.g., Ex. 3:6

Who shall declare His generation? for His life is taken from the earth.
Acts 8:33
See also Isa. 53:8

I am a Pharisee, the son of a Pharisee.
Paul
Acts 23:6

I am debtor both to the Greeks, and to the Barbarians; both to the wise, and to the unwise.
Rom. 1:14

If the root be holy, so are the branches.
Rom. 11:16

We are not children of the bondwoman, but of the free.
Gal. 4:31

[*See also* Character, Tradition]

HEROISM

See Courage, Leadership.

HIERARCHY

See Authority, Leadership.

HISTORY

He that saw it bare record, and his record is true.
John 19:35

If they should be written every one, I suppose that even the world itself could not contain the books that should be written.
John 21:25

That which we have seen and heard declare we unto you.
1 John 1:3

[*See also* Testimony]

HOLINESS

Now ye are clean through the word which I have spoken unto you.
Jesus
John 15:3

Sanctify them through Thy truth.
Jesus
John 17:17

If the root be holy, so are the branches.
Rom. 11:16

The temple of God is holy, which temple ye are.
1 Cor. 3:17

God hath not called us unto uncleanness, but unto holiness.
1 Thess. 4:7

Both He that sanctifieth and they who are sanctified are all of one.
Heb. 2:11

As He which hath called you is holy, so be ye holy.
1 Pet. 1:15
See also, e.g., Lev. 19:2, 1 Pet. 1:16

Holy, holy, holy, Lord God Almighty, which was, and is, and is to come.
Rev. 4:8
See also Isa. 6:3

Thou only art holy.
Rev. 15:4

[*See also* Consecration]

HOLY SPIRIT

The Spirit of God descending like a dove.
Matt. 3:16
See also Mark 1:10

Whosoever speaketh against the Holy Ghost, it shall not be forgiven him, neither in this world, neither in the world to come.
Jesus
Matt. 12:32
See also Mark 3:29, Luke 12:10

I indeed have baptized you with water: but He shall baptize you with the Holy Ghost.
John the Baptist
Mark 1:8
See also Matt. 3:11, Luke 3:16

I saw the Spirit descending from heaven like a dove, and it abode upon Him.
John 1:32

Except a man be born of water and of the Spirit, he cannot enter into the kingdom of God.
Jesus
John 3:5

It is the Spirit that quickeneth; the flesh profiteth nothing.
Jesus
John 6:63

He shall give you another Comforter, that He may abide with you for ever.
Jesus
John 14:16

The Comforter, which is the Holy Ghost.
Jesus
John 14:26

If I go not away, the Comforter will not come unto you.
Jesus
John 16:7

Receive ye the Holy Ghost.
Jesus
John 20:22

Wait for the promise of the Father.
Jesus
Acts 1:4

The promise is unto you, and to your children, and to all that are afar off.
Acts 2:39

They that are after the flesh do mind the things of the flesh; but they that are after the Spirit the things of the Spirit.
Rom. 8:5

Ye are not in the flesh, but in the Spirit.
Rom. 8:9

As many as are led by the Spirit of God, they are the sons of God.
Rom. 8:14

The kingdom of God is not meat and drink; but righteousness, and peace, and joy in the Holy Ghost.
Rom. 14:17

The Spirit searcheth all things.
1 Cor. 2:10

The Spirit of God dwelleth in you.
1 Cor. 3:16

There are diversities of gifts, but the same Spirit.
1 Cor. 12:4

Walk in the Spirit, and ye shall not fulfil the lust of the flesh.
Gal. 5:16

The fruit of the Spirit is love, joy, peace, longsuffering, gentleness, goodness, faith, meekness, temperance.
Gal. 5:22–23

If we live in the Spirit, let us also walk in the Spirit.
Gal. 5:25

Be not drunk with wine, wherein is excess; but be filled with the Spirit.
Eph. 5:18

Quench not the Spirit.
1 Thess. 5:19

It is the Spirit that beareth witness, because the Spirit is truth.
1 John 5:6

Out of His mouth goeth a sharp sword, that with it He should smite the nations.
Rev. 19:15

HOMAGE

We have seen His star in the east, and are come to worship Him.
Matt. 2:2

Whosoever shall receive me, receiveth not me, but Him that sent me.
Jesus
Mark 9:37
See also Luke 9:48

He that honoureth not the Son honoureth not the Father which hath sent Him.
Jesus
John 5:23

I receive not honour from men.
Jesus
John 5:41

He that receiveth whomsoever I send receiveth me.
Jesus
John 13:20

He that regardeth the day, regardeth it unto the Lord.
Rom. 14:6

He that eateth, eateth to the Lord, for he giveth God thanks.
Rom. 14:6

At the name of Jesus every knee should bow.
Phil. 2:10

[*See also* Respect]

HOME

Foxes have holes, and birds of the air have nests; but the Son of man hath not where to lay His head.
Jesus
Luke 9:58
See also Matt. 8:20

[*See also* Building, Family, Marriage]

HOMOSEXUALITY

Their women did change the natural use into that which is against nature.
Rom. 1:26

Men, leaving the natural use of the woman, burned in their lust one toward another.
Rom. 1:27

Men with men working that which is unseemly.
Rom. 1:27

HONESTY

Exact no more than that which is appointed you.
Luke 3:13

He that is faithful in that which is least is faithful also in much.
Jesus
Luke 16:10

God is my witness.
Rom. 1:9

Speak every man truth with his neighbour: for we are members one of another.
Eph. 4:25

Lie not one to another.
Col. 3:9

He that will love life, and see good days, let him refrain his tongue from evil.
1 Pet. 3:10
See also Ps. 34:13

Ye know that our record is true.
3 John 12

[*See also* Candor, Corruption, Dishonesty, Integrity, Lies, Perjury, Truth]

HONOR

See Glory, Respect.

HOPE

The last shall be first.
Jesus
Matt. 19:30
See also, e.g., Mark 10:31

Ye shall be sorrowful, but your sorrow shall be turned into joy.
Jesus
John 16:20

Tribulation worketh patience; And patience, experience; and experience, hope.
Rom. 5:3–4

Hope maketh not ashamed.
Rom. 5:5

We are saved by hope.
Rom. 8:24

Hope that is seen is not hope.
Rom. 8:24

And now abideth faith, hope, charity, these three; but the greatest of these is charity.
(charity: love)
1 Cor. 13:13

We are perplexed, but not in despair;

Persecuted, but not forsaken; cast down, but not destroyed.
2 Cor. 4:8–9

Be not moved away from the hope of the gospel.
Col. 1:23

Faith is the substance of things hoped for, the evidence of things not seen.
Heb. 11:1

I will give unto him that is athirst of the fountain of the water of life freely.
Jesus
Rev. 21:6

[*See also* Despair, Encouragement, Expectation, Prayer]

HOSPITALITY

If the house be worthy, let your peace come upon it: but if it be not worthy, let your peace return to you.
Jesus
Matt. 10:13

He that receiveth a prophet in the name of a prophet shall receive a prophet's reward.
Jesus
Matt. 10:41

He that receiveth a righteous man in the name of a righteous man shall receive a righteous man's reward.
Jesus
Matt. 10:41

For I was an hungred, and ye gave me meat: I was thirsty, and ye gave me drink: I was a stranger, and ye took me in: Naked, and ye clothed me: I was sick, and ye visited me: I was in prison, and ye came unto me.
Jesus
Matt. 25:35–36

Inasmuch as ye have done it unto one of the least of these my brethren, ye have done it unto me.
Jesus
Matt. 25:40
See also Matt. 25:45

Whosoever shall give you a cup of water to drink in my name, because ye belong to Christ, verily I say unto you, he shall not lose his reward.
Jesus
Mark 9:41

Every man at the beginning doth set forth good wine.
John 2:10

He that receiveth whomsoever I send receiveth me.
Jesus
John 13:20

Be not forgetful to entertain strangers: for thereby some have entertained angels unawares.
Heb. 13:2

Use hospitality one to another without grudging.
1 Pet. 4:9

[*See also* Brotherhood, Kindness]

HUMAN BODY

See Body, Physical Fitness.

HUMAN NATURE

Destruction and misery are in their ways: And the way of peace have they not known.
Rom. 3:16–17
See also Isa. 59:7–8

The law is spiritual: but I am carnal.
Rom. 7:14

In me (that is, in my flesh,) dwelleth no good thing.
Rom. 7:18

The flesh lusteth against the Spirit, and the Spirit against the flesh.
Gal. 5:17

[*See also* Behavior, Carnality, Mankind, Sin]

HUMILIATION

God hath chosen the foolish things of the world to confound the wise.
  1 Cor. 1:27

[*See also* Contempt, Defeat, Outcast, Shame]

HUMILITY

He that cometh after me is mightier than I, whose shoes I am not worthy to bear.
  John the Baptist
  Matt. 3:11
  See also Mark 1:7, Luke 3:16

Blessed are the poor in spirit: for their's is the kingdom of heaven.
  Jesus
  Matt. 5:3
  See also Luke 6:20

Blessed are the meek: for they shall inherit the earth.
  Jesus
  Matt. 5:5
  See also Ps. 37:11

I am meek and lowly in heart: and ye shall find rest unto your souls.
  Jesus
  Matt. 11:29

Except ye be converted, and become as little children, ye shall not enter into the kingdom of heaven.
  Jesus
  Matt. 18:3

Whosoever will be great among you, let him be your minister.
  Jesus
  Matt. 20:26
  See also Mark 10:43

Whosoever will be chief among you, let him be your servant.
  Jesus
  Matt. 20:27
  See also Matt. 23:11, Mark 10:44

Whosoever shall exalt himself shall be abased; and he that shall humble himself shall be exalted.
  Jesus
  Matt. 23:12
  See also Luke 14:11

If any man desire to be first, the same shall be last of all, and servant of all.
  Jesus
  Mark 9:35

He that is least among you all, the same shall be great.
  Jesus
  Luke 9:48

I am among you as He that serveth.
  Jesus
  Luke 22:27

I can of mine own self do nothing.
  Jesus
  John 5:30

The servant is not greater than his lord; neither he that is sent greater than he that sent him.
  Jesus
  John 13:16
  See also John 15:20, Matt. 10:24

Stand up; I myself also am a man.
  Acts 10:26

What was I, that I could withstand God?
  Peter
  Acts 11:17

Serving the Lord with all humility of mind, and with many tears.
  Acts 20:19

In me (that is, in my flesh,) dwelleth no good thing.
  Rom. 7:18

Think soberly.
  Rom. 12:3

I have planted, Apollos watered; but God gave the increase.
  1 Cor. 3:6

Let him become a fool, that he may be wise.
  1 Cor. 3:18

I know nothing by myself.
  1 Cor. 4:4

By the grace of God I am what I am: and

His grace which was bestowed upon me was not in vain.
1 Cor. 15:10

Our sufficiency is of God.
2 Cor. 3:5

My strength is made perfect in weakness.
Jesus
2 Cor. 12:9

God resisteth the proud, but giveth grace unto the humble.
James 4:6

Humble yourselves in the sight of the Lord, and He shall lift you up.
James 4:10

Confess your faults one to another.
James 5:16

Be clothed with humility.
1 Pet. 5:5

God resisteth the proud, and giveth grace to the humble.
1 Pet. 5:5

Remember therefore from whence thou art fallen, and repent.
Jesus
Rev. 2:5

[*See also* Arrogance, Audacity, Conceit, Equality, Meekness, Modesty, Pride]

HUNGER

He that cometh to me shall never hunger; and he that believeth on me shall never thirst.
Jesus
John 6:35

If thine enemy hunger, feed him; if he thirst, give him drink.
Rom. 12:20
See also Prov. 25:21

If any would not work, neither should he eat.
2 Thess. 3:10

[*See also* Bread of Life, Deprivation, Food, Thirst]

HUSBAND AND WIFE

See Marriage.

HYPOCRISY

They love to pray standing in the synagogues and in the corners of the streets, that they may be seen of men.
Jesus
Matt. 6:5

They have their reward.
Jesus
Matt. 6:5

They disfigure their faces, that they may appear unto men to fast.
Jesus
Matt. 6:16

Why beholdest thou the mote that is in thy brother's eye, but considerest not the beam that is in thine own eye?
Jesus
Matt. 7:3
See also Luke 6:41

In vain they do worship me, teaching for doctrines the commandments of men.
Jesus
Matt. 15:9, Mark 7:7
See also Isa. 29:13

O ye hypocrites, ye can discern the face of the sky; but can ye not discern the signs of the times?
Jesus
Matt. 16:3
See also Luke 12:56

Do not ye after their works: for they say, and do not.
Jesus
Matt. 23:3

They bind heavy burdens and grievous to be borne, and lay them on men's shoulders; but they themselves will not move them with one of their fingers.
Jesus
Matt. 23:4
See also Luke 11:46

All their works they do for to be seen of men.
Jesus
Matt. 23:5

Woe unto you, scribes and Pharisees, hypocrites!
>Jesus
>E.g., Matt. 23:14

Ye blind guides, which strain at a gnat, and swallow a camel.
>Jesus
>Matt. 23:24

Ye also outwardly appear righteous unto men, but within ye are full of hypocrisy and iniquity.
>Jesus
>Matt. 23:28

This people honoureth me with their lips, but their heart is far from me.
>Jesus
>Mark 7:6
>See also Matt. 15:8

Ye reject the commandment of God, that ye may keep your own tradition.
>Jesus
>Mark 7:9
>See also Matt. 15:3

Beware of the scribes, which love to go in long clothing, and love salutations in the marketplaces, And the chief seats in the synagogues, and the uppermost rooms at feasts.
>Jesus
>Mark 12:38–40
>See also Matt. 23:5–6,
>Luke 20:46–47

Woe unto you also, ye lawyers!
>Jesus
>Luke 11:46

Beware ye of the leaven of the Pharisees, which is hypocrisy.
>Jesus
>Luke 12:1
>See also Matt. 16:6, Mark 8:15

He that is without sin among you, let him first cast a stone.
>Jesus
>John 8:7

If ye were Abraham's children, ye would do the works of Abraham.
>Jesus
>John 8:39

Thou that sayest a man should not commit adultery, dost thou commit adultery?
>Rom. 2:22

The name of God is blasphemed among the Gentiles through you.
>(you: hypocrites)
>Rom. 2:24

They profess that they know God; but in works they deny Him.
>Titus 1:16

Out of the same mouth proceedeth blessing and cursing.
>James 3:10

Doth a fountain send forth at the same place sweet water and bitter?
>James 3:11

If we say that we have not sinned, we make Him a liar.
>1 John 1:10

He that saith, I know Him, and keepeth not His commandments, is a liar.
>(Him: Jesus)
>1 John 2:4

He that saith he is in the light, and hateth his brother, is in darkness even until now.
>1 John 2:9

If a man say, I love God, and hateth his brother, he is a liar.
>1 John 4:20

[See also Deception, Lies, Rituals, Sincerity]

I

IDOLATRY

We ought not to think that the Godhead is like unto gold, or silver, or stone, graven by art and man's device.
>Acts 17:29

Served the creature more than the Creator.
>Rom. 1:25

Flee from idolatry.
>1 Cor. 10:14

Little children, keep yourselves from idols.
1 John 5:21

They have no rest day nor night, who worship the beast and his image.
Rev. 14:11

[See also Backsliding, Godlessness, Worship]

IDOLS

Turn from these vanities unto the living God.
Acts 14:15

They be no gods, which are made with hands.
Acts 19:26

[See also Godlessness, Idolatry, Worship]

IGNORANCE

They seeing see not; and hearing they hear not, neither do they understand.
Jesus
Matt. 13:13
See also Isa. 6:9, Isa. 42:20,
Acts 28:26

If the blind lead the blind, both shall fall into the ditch.
Jesus
Matt. 15:14
See also Luke 6:39

O ye hypocrites, ye can discern the face of the sky; but can ye not discern the signs of the times?
Jesus
Matt. 16:3
See also Luke 12:56

Father, forgive them; for they know not what they do.
Jesus
Luke 23:34

He was in the world, and the world was made by Him, and the world knew Him not.
John 1:10

Art thou a master of Israel, and knoweth not these things?
Jesus
John 3:10

Ye worship ye know not what.
Jesus
John 4:22

He that followeth me shall not walk in darkness.
Jesus
John 8:12

He that walketh in darkness knoweth not whither he goeth.
Jesus
John 12:35

Who art Thou, Lord?
Saul to Jesus
Acts 9:5

Whom therefore ye ignorantly worship, Him declare I unto you.
Acts 17:23

The heart of this people is waxed gross, and their ears are dull of hearing, and their eyes have they closed.
Acts 28:27

I had not known sin, but by the law.
Rom. 7:7
See also Rom. 3:20, Rom. 4:15

They have a zeal of God, but not according to knowledge.
Rom. 10:2

How shall they believe in Him of whom they have not heard?
Rom. 10:14

Had they known it, they would not have crucified the Lord.
1 Cor. 2:8

We know in part, and we prophesy in part.
1 Cor. 13:9

Foolish and unlearned questions avoid, knowing that they do gender strifes.
2 Tim. 2:23

Every one that useth milk is unskilful in the word of righteousness: for he is a babe.
Heb. 5:13

[See also Knowledge, Naivete, Understanding, Wisdom]

IMAGINATION

See Dreams, Future.

IMMINENCE

My time is at hand.
> Jesus
> Matt. 26:18

Behold, the hour is at hand, and the Son of man is betrayed into the hands of sinners.
> Jesus
> Matt. 26:45
> See also Mark 14:41

The hour is coming, in the which all that are in the graves shall hear His voice.
> Jesus
> John 5:28

The hour is come, that the Son of man should be glorified.
> Jesus
> John 12:23

Yet a little while, and the world seeth me no more.
> Jesus
> John 14:19

Behold, the hour cometh.
> Jesus
> John 16:32

The Lord is at hand.
> Phil 4:5

The coming of the Lord draweth nigh.
> James 5:8

Behold, the judge standeth before the door.
> James 5:9

The end of all things is at hand: be ye therefore sober, and watch unto prayer.
> 1 Pet. 4:7

The time is at hand.
> E.g., Rev. 1:3

[See also Second Coming, Time]

IMMORALITY

Flee fornication.
> 1 Cor. 6:18

She that liveth in pleasure is dead while she liveth.
> 1 Tim. 5:6

Whoremongers and adulterers God will judge.
> Heb. 13:4

Woe unto them! for they have gone in the way of Cain.
> Jude 11

[See also Carnality, Decadence, Depravity, Fornication, Lust, Sin]

IMMORTALITY

See Death, Eternal Life, Resurrection.

IMPARTIALITY

He maketh His sun to rise on the evil and on the good, and sendeth rain on the just and on the unjust.
> Jesus
> Matt. 5:45

God is no respecter of persons.
> Acts 10:34
> See also Rom. 2:11

God accepteth no man's person.
> Gal. 2:6

If ye have respect to persons, ye commit sin.
> James 2:9

[See also Equality, Fairness, Justice, Neutrality]

IMPENITENCE

It shall be more tolerable for the land of Sodom in the day of judgment, than for thee.
> Jesus
> Matt. 11:24
> See also Luke 10:14

Harden not your hearts.
E.g., Heb. 3:8

[*See also* Repentance, Stubbornness]

IMPOSSIBILITY

See God's Power, Possibility.

IMPRISONMENT

For the hope of Israel I am bound with this chain.
Acts 28:20

I am an ambassador in bonds.
Eph. 6:20

Remember my bonds.
Col. 4:18

Remember them that are in bonds, as bound with them; and them which suffer adversity, as being yourselves also in the body.
Heb. 13:3

[*See also* Freedom, Persecution]

INDECISION

No man, having put his hand to the plough, and looking back, is fit for the kingdom of God.
Jesus
Luke 9:62

We henceforth be no more children, tossed to and fro, and carried about with every wind of doctrine, by the sleight of men, and cunning craftiness, whereby they lie in wait to deceive.
Eph. 4:14

He that wavereth is like a wave of the sea driven with the wind.
James 1:6

A double minded man is unstable in all his ways.
James 1:8

[*See also* Certainty, Neutrality]

INDEPENDENCE

See Freedom.

INDIVIDUAL, IMPORTANCE OF

Ye are of more value than many sparrows.
Jesus
Matt. 10:31, Luke 12:7

Are not five sparrows sold for two farthings, and not one of them is forgotten before God?
Jesus
Luke 12:6
See also Matt. 10:29

Rejoice with me; for I have found my sheep which was lost.
Jesus
Luke 15:6

Joy shall be in heaven over one sinner that repenteth, more than over ninety and nine just persons, which need no repentance.
Jesus
Luke 15:7

There is joy in the presence of the angels of God over one sinner that repenteth.
Jesus
Luke 15:10

By one man sin entered into the world.
Rom. 5:12

As by one man's disobedience many were made sinners, so by the obedience of one shall many be made righteous.
Rom. 5:19

Every man hath his proper gift of God.
1 Cor. 7:7

One star differeth from another star in glory.
1 Cor. 15:41

I seek not your's, but you.
2 Cor. 12:14

What is man, that Thou art mindful of him? or the son of man, that Thou visitest him?
Heb. 2:6
See also Ps. 8:4

[*See also* Mankind]

INEVITABILITY

See Certainty, Death, Mortality.

INFINITY

Even the very hairs of your head are all numbered.
Jesus
Luke 12:7
See also Matt. 10:30

INGRATITUDE

Give not that which is holy unto the dogs, neither cast ye your pearls before swine, lest they trample them under their feet, and turn again and rend you.
Jesus
Matt. 7:6

When they knew God, they glorified Him not as God.
Rom 1:21

[*See also* Gratitude]

INHERITANCE

See Heritage, Reward.

INJUSTICE

Sittest thou to judge me after the law, and commandest me to be smitten contrary to the law?
Paul to Ananias
Acts 23:3

Remember my bonds.
Col. 4:18

If, when ye do well, and suffer for it, ye take it patiently, this is acceptable with God.
1 Pet. 2:20

[*See also* Corruption, Judgment, Justice]

INNOCENCE

If ye were blind, ye should have no sin.
Jesus
John 9:41

Whom seek ye?
Jesus to His captors
John 18:4, 7

As a sheep to the slaughter.
Acts 8:32
See also Isa. 53:7, Jer. 11:19

Neither against the law of the Jews, neither against the temple, nor yet against Caesar, have I offended any thing at all.
Acts 25:8

I stand at Caesar's judgment seat, where I ought to be judged: to the Jews have I done no wrong.
Paul
Acts 25:10

If I be an offender, or have committed any thing worthy of death, I refuse not to die.
Acts 25:11

Unto the pure all things are pure.
Titus 1:15

If we say that we have no sin, we deceive ourselves.
1 John 1:8

If we say that we have not sinned, we make Him a liar.
1 John 1:10

In their mouth was found no guile: for they are without fault before the throne of God.
Rev. 14:5

[*See also* Guilt, Naivete]

INNOVATION

No man also having drunk old wine straightway desireth new.
Jesus
Luke 5:39

See Madness.

See Hypocrisy, Sincerity.

It is not ye that speak, but the Spirit of your Father which speaketh in you.
> Jesus
> Matt. 10:20

A man can receive nothing, except it be given him from heaven.
> John 3:27

He was a burning and a shining light: and ye were willing for a season to rejoice in his light.
> Jesus (He: John the Baptist)
> John 5:35

Your young men shall see visions, and your old men shall dream dreams.
> Acts 2:17
> See also Joel 2:28

Write the things which thou hast seen, and the things which are, and the things which shall be hereafter.
> Jesus
> Rev. 1:19

See Indecision.

Woe to that man by whom the offence cometh!
> Jesus
> Matt. 18:7

He that hath ears to hear, let him hear.
> Jesus
> Luke 14:35
> See also, e.g., Matt. 13:9

Though ye have ten thousand instructors in Christ, yet have ye not many fathers.
> 1 Cor. 4:15

[See also Criticism, Education, Guidance, Heedfulness, Knowledge]

What shall a man give in exchange for his soul?
> Jesus
> Matt. 16:26, Mark 8:37

What shall it profit a man, if he shall gain the whole world, and lose his own soul?
> Jesus
> Mark 8:36
> See also Matt. 16:26, Luke 9:25

I have coveted no man's silver, or gold, or apparel.
> Acts 20:33

I have lived in all good conscience before God until this day.
> Acts 23:1

Walk as children of light.
> Eph. 5:8

Unto the pure all things are pure.
> Titus 1:15

Swear not, neither by heaven, neither by the earth, neither by any other oath: but let your yea be yea; and your nay, nay.
> James 5:12

[See also Character, Conscience, Corruption, Honesty, Righteousness]

See Education, Ignorance, Knowledge, Understanding.

Whosoever looketh on a woman to lust after her hath committed adultery with her already in his heart.
> Jesus
> Matt. 5:28

Wherefore think ye evil in your hearts?
Jesus
Matt. 9:4
See also Luke 6:22

The good that I would I do not: but the evil which I would not, that I do.
Rom. 7:19

[*See also* Motivation, Purpose]

INTERCESSION

All things are delivered unto me of my Father.
Jesus
Matt. 11:27
See also Luke 10:22

No man cometh unto the Father, but by me.
Jesus
John 14:6

There is one God, and one mediator between God and men, the man Christ Jesus.
1 Tim. 2:5

If any man sin, we have an advocate with the Father.
1 John 2:1

INTOXICATION

See Drunkenness.

J

JEALOUSY

Charity envieth not.
(charity: love)
1 Cor. 13:4

[*See also* Envy, Greed]

JERUSALEM

The city of the great King.
Jesus
Matt. 5:35, Ps. 48:2

O Jerusalem, Jerusalem, thou that killest the prophets, and stonest them which are sent unto thee.
Jesus
Matt. 23:37
See also Luke 13:34

JESUS

He shall save His people from their sins.
Matt. 1:21

We have seen His star in the east, and are come to worship Him.
Matt. 2:2

He that cometh after me is mightier than I, whose shoes I am not worthy to bear.
John the Baptist
Matt. 3:11
See also Mark 1:7, Luke 3:16

This is My beloved Son, in whom I am well pleased.
Matt. 3:17
See also Mark 1:11, Luke 3:22

What manner of man is this, that even the winds and the sea obey Him!
Matt. 8:27
See also Mark 4:41, Luke 8:25

The Son of man hath power on earth to forgive sins.
Jesus
Matt. 9:6, Mark 2:10
See also Luke 5:24

Whosoever therefore shall confess me before men, him will I confess also before my Father which is in heaven. But whosoever shall deny me before men, him will I also deny before my Father which is in heaven.
Jesus
Matt. 10:32–33

He that taketh not his cross, and followeth after me, is not worthy of me.
Jesus
Matt. 10:38
See also Luke 14:27

In His name shall the Gentiles trust.
Matt. 12:21

He that is not with me is against me.
Jesus
Matt. 12:30, Luke 11:23

Behold, a greater than Solomon is here.
Jesus
Matt. 12:42, Luke 11:31

Is not this the carpenter's son?
Matt. 13:55
See also Mark 6:3, John 6:42

The Son of man is come to save that which was lost.
Jesus
Matt. 18:11

Art Thou the King of the Jews?
Pilate to Jesus
Matt. 27:11, Mark 15:2, Luke 23:3, John 18:33

Come, take up the cross, and follow me.
Jesus
Mark 10:21
See also Matt. 19:21, Luke 18:22

In my name shall they cast out devils.
Jesus
Mark 16:17

A great prophet is risen up among us.
Luke 7:16

The Son of man is come to seek and to save that which was lost.
Jesus
Luke 19:10

In the beginning was the Word, and the Word was with God, and the Word was God.
John 1:1

Without Him was not any thing made.
John 1:3

In Him was life; and the life was the light of men.
John 1:4

He was in the world, and the world was made by Him, and the world knew Him not.
John 1:10

The Word was made flesh, and dwelt among us.
John 1:14

Behold the Lamb of God, which taketh away the sin of the world.
John the Baptist
John 1:29

Whosoever believeth in Him should not perish, but have eternal life.
Jesus
John 3:15

For God so loved the world, that He gave His only begotten Son, that whosoever believeth in Him should not perish, but have everlasting life.
Jesus
John 3:16
See also John 3:36, John 6:47

God sent not His Son into the world to condemn the world; but that the world through Him might be saved.
Jesus
John 3:17

He that believeth not the Son shall not see life; but the wrath of God abideth on him.
John 3:36

He told me all that ever I did.
Woman of Samaria
John 4:39

Know that this is indeed the Christ, the Saviour of the world.
John 4:42

He that was healed wist not who it was.
John 5:13

He that honoureth not the Son honoureth not the Father which hath sent Him.
Jesus
John 5:23

He that heareth my word, and believeth on Him that sent me, hath everlasting life.
Jesus
John 5:24

I came down from heaven, not to do mine own will, but the will of Him that sent me.
Jesus
John 6:38

He that eateth my flesh, and drinketh my blood, dwelleth in me, and I in him.
Jesus
John 6:56

If any man thirst, let him come unto me, and drink.
Jesus
John 7:37

If ye had known me, ye should have known my Father also.
Jesus
John 8:19

If God were your Father, ye would love me: for I proceeded forth and came from God.

Jesus
John 8:42

As long as I am in the world, I am the light of the world.

Jesus
John 9:5

I am the door: by me if any man enter in, he shall be saved.

Jesus
John 10:9

I am the resurrection, and the life.

Jesus
John 11:25

He that believeth in me, though he were dead, yet shall he live.

Jesus
John 11:25

I am come a light into the world, that whosoever believeth on me should not abide in darkness.

Jesus
John 12:46

I am the way, the truth, and the life.

Jesus
John 14:6

If ye shall ask any thing in my name, I will do it.

Jesus
John 14:14

If ye love me, keep my commandments.

Jesus
John 14:15
See also John 14:23

Whatsoever ye shall ask the Father in my name, He will give it you.

Jesus
John 16:23

I am He.

Jesus
John 18:5

Follow me.

Jesus
John 21:19

Him hath God exalted with His right hand to be a Prince and a Saviour.

Acts 5:31

Who shall declare His generation? for His life is taken from the earth.

Acts 8:33
See also Isa. 53:8

Whosoever believeth in Him shall receive remission of sins.

Acts 10:43

Through this man is preached unto you the forgiveness of sins.

Paul, about Jesus
Acts 13:38

I have set thee to be a light of the Gentiles, that thou shouldest be for salvation unto the ends of the earth.

Acts 13:47
See also Isa. 49:6

We have peace with God through our Lord Jesus Christ.

Rom. 5:1

In that He died, He died unto sin once: but in that He liveth, He liveth unto God.

Rom. 6:10

The wages of sin is death; but the gift of God is eternal life through Jesus Christ our Lord.

Rom. 6:23

Whosoever believeth on Him shall not be ashamed.

Rom. 9:33, Rom. 10:11

Ye are Christ's; and Christ is God's.

1 Cor. 3:23

In Christ Jesus I have begotten you through the gospel.

1 Cor. 4:15

We being many are one bread, and one body: for we are all partakers of that one bread.

1 Cor. 10:17

Maranatha.

1 Cor. 16:22

Though He was rich, yet for your sakes He became poor, that ye through His poverty might be rich.

2 Cor. 8:9

Thanks be unto God for His unspeakable gift.
2 Cor. 9:15

Christ liveth in me.
Gal. 2:20

The Son of God, who loved me, and gave Himself for me.
Gal. 2:20

Ye are all one in Christ Jesus.
Gal. 3:28

Christ hath made us free.
Gal. 5:1

He is our peace.
Eph. 2:14

God for Christ's sake hath forgiven you.
Eph. 4:32

We are members of His body, of His flesh, and of His bones.
Eph. 5:30

At the name of Jesus every knee should bow.
Phil. 2:10

He is before all things, and by Him all things consist.
Col. 1:17

He is the head of the body, the church.
Col. 1:18

Ye are complete in Him, which is the head of all principality and power.
Col. 2:10

Christ is all, and in all.
Col. 3:11

Let the word of Christ dwell in you.
Col. 3:16

Christ Jesus came into the world to save sinners.
1 Tim. 1:15

God was manifest in the flesh, justified in the Spirit, seen of angels, preached unto the Gentiles, believed on in the world, received up into glory.
1 Tim. 3:16

Be not thou therefore ashamed of the testimony of our Lord.
2 Tim. 1:8

Be strong in the grace that is in Christ Jesus.
2 Tim. 2:1

If we be dead with Him, we shall also live with Him.
2 Tim. 2:11

If we deny Him, He also will deny us.
2 Tim. 2:12

If we believe not, yet He abideth faithful: He cannot deny Himself.
2 Tim. 2:13

Though He were a Son, yet learned He obedience by the things which He suffered.
Heb. 5:8

Jesus the author and finisher of our faith.
Heb. 12:2

Ye should follow His steps: Who did no sin.
1 Pet. 2:21–22

To Him be glory both now and for ever.
2 Pet. 3:18

Whosoever denieth the Son, the same hath not the Father.
1 John 2:23

In Him is no sin.
1 John 3:5

Whosoever sinneth hath not seen Him, neither known Him.
1 John 3:6

Greater is He that is in you, than he that is in the world.
1 John 4:4

God sent His only begotten Son into the world, that we might live through Him.
1 John 4:9

The Father sent the Son to be the Saviour of the world.
1 John 4:14

To Him be glory and dominion for ever and ever.
Rev. 1:6

I am He which searcheth the reins and hearts.
Jesus
Rev. 2:23

The marriage of the Lamb is come, and His wife hath made herself ready.
Rev. 19:7

I will give unto him that is athirst of the fountain of the water of life freely.
Jesus
Rev. 21:6

I am the root and the offspring of David, and the bright and morning star.
Jesus
Rev. 22:16

[*See also* Authority, Bread of Life, Christ Eternal, Crucifixion, Intercession, Messiah, Messianic Hopes and Prophecies, Redemption, Resurrection, Revelation, Sacrifice, Second Coming, and the categories which follow]

JESUS, ACCEPTANCE OF

Take my yoke upon you, and learn of me; for I am meek and lowly in heart: and ye shall find rest unto your souls.
Jesus
Matt. 11:29

Flesh and blood hath not revealed it unto thee, but my Father which is in heaven.
Jesus
Matt. 16:17

Whosoever will come after me, let him deny himself, and take up his cross, and follow me.
Jesus
Mark 8:34
See also Matt. 16:24, Luke 9:23

Whosoever shall confess me before men, him shall the Son of man also confess before the angels of God.
Jesus
Luke 12:8
See also Matt. 10:32

Whosoever he be of you that forsaketh not all that he hath, he cannot be my disciple.
Jesus
Luke 14:33

As many as received Him, to them gave He power to become the sons of God.
John 1:12

Ye must be born again.
Jesus
John 3:7

This is the work of God, that ye believe on Him whom He hath sent.
Jesus
John 6:29

He that cometh to me shall never hunger; and he that believeth on me shall never thirst.
Jesus
John 6:35

No man can come to me, except the Father which hath sent me draw him.
Jesus
John 6:44
See also John 6:65

Lord, I believe.
John 9:38

I believe that Thou art the Christ, the Son of God.
John 11:27

He that believeth on me, believeth not on me, but on Him that sent me.
Jesus
John 12:44

He that receiveth me receiveth Him that sent me.
Jesus
John 13:20

Ye believe in God, believe also in me.
Jesus
John 14:1

He that loveth me shall be loved of my Father.
Jesus
John 14:21

If a man love me, he will keep my words.
Jesus
John 14:23

If thou shalt confess with thy mouth the Lord Jesus, and shalt believe in thine heart that God hath raised Him from the dead, thou shalt be saved.
Rom. 10:9

To whom He was not spoken of, they shall see: and they that have not heard shall understand.
Rom. 15:21
See also Isa. 52:15

Ye were sometimes darkness, but now are ye light in the Lord.
Eph. 5:8

Every tongue should confess that Jesus Christ is Lord.
Phil. 2:11

What things were gain to me, those I counted loss for Christ.
Phil. 3:7

Ye are dead, and your life is hid with Christ in God.
Col. 3:3

He that acknowledgeth the Son hath the Father also.
1 John 2:23

Whosoever shall confess that Jesus is the Son of God, God dwelleth in him, and he in God.
1 John 4:15

He that hath the Son hath life.
1 John 5:12

If any man hear my voice, and open the door, I will come in to him.
Jesus
Rev. 3:20

[*See also* Born Again, Conversion, Faith, Redemption]

JESUS, BIRTH OF

She shall bring forth a son, and thou shalt call His name JESUS.
Matt. 1:21

Behold, a virgin shall be with child, and shall bring forth a son.
Matt. 1:23
See also Isa. 7:14

They presented unto Him gifts; gold, and frankincense, and myrrh.
Matt. 2:11

The Lord is with thee: blessed art thou among women.
Angel to Mary
Luke 1:28

Behold, thou shalt conceive in thy womb,

and bring forth a son, and shalt call His name JESUS.
Luke 1:31

How shall this be, seeing I know not a man?
Luke 1:34

With God nothing shall be impossible.
Luke 1:37

He that is mighty hath done to me great things; and holy is His name.
Mary
Luke 1:49

There was no room for them in the inn.
Luke 2:7

Unto you is born this day in the city of David a Saviour, which is Christ the Lord.
Luke 2:11

His name was called JESUS.
Luke 2:21

To this end was I born, and for this cause came I into the world, that I should bear witness unto the truth.
Jesus
John 18:37

JESUS, LAST WORDS ON THE CROSS

Eli, Eli, lama sabachthani?
Matt. 27:46
See also Mark 15:34

My God, my God, why hast Thou forsaken me?
Matt. 27:46, Mark 15:34
See also Ps. 22:1

Father, forgive them; for they know not what they do.
Luke 23:34

Verily I say unto thee, To day shalt thou be with me in paradise.
Luke 23:43

Father, into Thy hands I commend my spirit.
Luke 23:46

Woman, behold thy son!
(son: John)
John 19:26

Behold thy mother!
John 19:27

I thirst.
John 19:28

It is finished.
John 19:30

JESUS, TITLES OF

They shall call His name Emmanuel.
Matt. 1:23

Thou art the Christ, the Son of the living God.
Simon Peter
Matt. 16:16
See also Mark 8:29, Luke 9:20,
* John 6:69*

A Saviour, which is Christ the Lord.
Luke 2:11

His name was called JESUS.
Luke 2:21

The Lamb of God.
E.g., John 1:29

The Son of God.
E.g., John 1:34

The Messiah.
John 1:41

The Son of man.
E.g., John 1:51

The bread of life.
Jesus
E.g., John 6:35

I am the light of the world.
Jesus
John 8:12

I am the door.
E.g., John 10:9

The good shepherd.
Jesus
John 10:11

I am the way, the truth, and the life.
Jesus
John 14:6

I am the true vine.
Jesus
John 15:1

Jesus of Nazareth the King of the Jews.
John 19:19
See also Matt. 27:37, Mark 15:26,
* Luke 23:38*

The Holy One and the Just.
Acts 3:14

The Deliverer.
Rom. 11:26

That great shepherd of the sheep.
Heb. 13:20

The judge.
James 5:9

The chief Shepherd.
1 Pet. 5:4

The true light.
1 John 2:8

The faithful witness.
Rev. 1:5

The prince of the kings of the earth.
Rev. 1:5

The morning star.
Rev. 2:28

The Word of God.
Rev. 19:13

KING OF KINGS, AND LORD OF LORDS.
Rev. 19:16

I am Alpha and Omega, the beginning and the end, the first and the last.
Jesus
Rev. 22:13
See also Rev. 1:8, 11, Rev. 21:6

JEWS

The lost sheep of the house of Israel.
Jesus
Matt. 15:24

He came unto His own, and His own received Him not.
John 1:11

Forty years suffered He their manners in the wilderness.
Acts 13:18

I am a Pharisee, the son of a Pharisee.
Paul
Acts 23:6

He is not a Jew, which is one outwardly.
Rom. 2:28

What advantage then hath the Jew? or what profit is there of circumcision?
Rom. 3:1

Unto them were committed the oracles of God.
Rom. 3:2

They have a zeal of God, but not according to knowledge.
Rom. 10:2

Hath God cast away His people? God forbid.
Rom. 11:1

I also am an Israelite, of the seed of Abraham.
Paul
Rom. 11:1

Through their fall salvation is come unto the Gentiles.
Rom. 11:11

Unto the Jews I became as a Jew, that I might gain the Jews.
1 Cor. 9:20

Are they Hebrews? so am I. Are they Israelites? so am I. Are they the seed of Abraham? so am I.
Paul
2 Cor. 11:22

JOHN THE BAPTIST

Elias is come already, and they knew him not.
Jesus
Matt. 17:12

One mightier than I cometh, the latchet of whose shoes I am not worthy to unloose.
Luke 3:16
See also Matt. 3:11, Mark 1:7,
John 1:27

He was not that Light, but was sent to bear witness of that Light.
John 1:8

I am the voice of one crying in the wilderness, Make straight the way of the Lord.
John the Baptist
John 1:23
See also Matt. 3:3, Mark 1:3,
Luke 3:4

He was a burning and a shining light: and ye were willing for a season to rejoice in his light.
Jesus
John 5:35

JOY

See Happiness, Laughter, Tears.

JUDAS

None of them is lost, but the son of perdition.
Jesus
John 17:12

[*See also* Betrayal]

JUDGING

See Fairness, Justice.

JUDGMENT

By thy words thou shalt be justified, and by thy words thou shalt be condemned.
Jesus
Matt. 12:37

He shall reward every man according to his works.
Jesus
Matt. 16:27
See also Ps. 62:12

It shall be more tolerable for Sodom and Gomorrha in the day of judgment than for that city.
Jesus
Mark 6:11
See also Matt. 10:15

The Father judgeth no man, but hath committed all judgment unto the Son.
Jesus
John 5:22

As I hear, I judge: and my judgment is just.
Jesus
John 5:30

If I judge, my judgment is true: for I am not alone.
Jesus
John 8:16

Now is the judgment of this world: now shall the prince of this world be cast out.
Jesus
John 12:31

I came not to judge the world, but to save the world.
Jesus
John 12:47

He will judge the world in righteousness.
Acts 17:31

As many as have sinned in the law shall be judged by the law.
Rom. 2:12

We shall all stand before the judgment seat of Christ.
Rom. 14:10
See also 2 Cor. 5:10

He that judgeth me is the Lord.
1 Cor. 4:4

The saints shall judge the world.
1 Cor. 6:2

God hath not appointed us to wrath, but to obtain salvation.
1 Thess. 5:9

Whoremongers and adulterers God will judge.
Heb. 13:4

There is one lawgiver, who is able to save and to destroy: who art thou that judgest another?
James 4:12

Behold, the judge standeth before the door.
James 5:9

Judgment must begin at the house of God.
1 Pet. 4:17

If the righteous scarcely be saved, where shall the ungodly and the sinner appear?
1 Pet. 4:18

Thrust in Thy sickle, and reap.
Rev. 14:15

Gather the clusters of the vine of the earth; for her grapes are fully ripe.
Rev. 14:18

Pour out the vials of the wrath of God upon the earth.
Rev. 16:1

With violence shall that great city Babylon be thrown down.
Rev. 18:21

True and righteous are His judgments.
Rev. 19:2
See also Rev. 16:7

In righteousness He doth judge and make war.
Rev. 19:11

[*See also* Criticism, Judgment Day, Punishment, Responsibility, Retribution]

JUDGMENT DAY

He shall separate them one from another, as a shepherd divideth his sheep from the goats.
Jesus
Matt. 25:32

These be the days of vengeance, that all things which are written may be fulfilled.
Luke 21:22

He hath appointed a day, in the which He will judge the world in righteousness.
Acts 17:31

We must all appear before the judgment seat of Christ.
2 Cor. 5:10

The great day of His wrath is come; and who shall be able to stand?
Rev. 6:17

Fear God, and give glory to Him; for the hour of His judgment is come.
Rev. 14:7

I saw the dead, small and great, stand before God.
Rev. 20:12

Death and hell delivered up the dead which were in them: and they were judged every man according to their works.
Rev. 20:13

Whosoever was not found written in the book of life was cast into the lake of fire.
Rev. 20:15

[*See also* Apocalypse, End Days, Second Coming]

JUSTICE

He hath filled the hungry with good things; and the rich He hath sent empty away.
Luke 1:53

Judge not according to the appearance, but judge righteous judgment.
Jesus
John 7:24

Doth our law judge any man, before it hear him, and know what he doeth?
Nicodemus
John 7:51

Men, brethren, and fathers, hear ye my defence.
Paul
Acts 22:1

Is it lawful for you to scourge a man that is a Roman, and uncondemned?
Acts 22:25

Take heed what thou doest: for this man is a Roman.
Acts 22:26

I appeal unto Caesar.
Acts 25:11

He shall have judgment without mercy, that hath showed no mercy.
James 2:13

He that leadeth into captivity shall go into captivity.
Rev. 13:10

[*See also* Fairness, Guilt, Impartiality, Injustice, Innocence, Judgment, Law, Wickedness]

JUSTIFICATION

By Him all that believe are justified.
Acts 13:39

A man is justified by faith without the deeds of the law.
Rom. 3:28

It is God that justifieth.
Rom. 8:33

Ye are justified in the name of the Lord Jesus, and by the Spirit of our God.
1 Cor. 6:11

No man is justified by the law in the sight of God.
Gal. 3:11

KINDNESS

What man is there of you, whom if his son ask bread, will he give him a stone?
Jesus
Matt. 7:9
See also Luke 11:11

If thine enemy hunger, feed him; if he thirst, give him drink.
Rom. 12:20
See also Prov. 25:21

Be ye kind one to another.
Eph. 4:32

Be gentle unto all men, apt to teach, patient.
2 Tim. 2:24

[*See also* Altruism, Compassion, Cruelty, Generosity, Hospitality, Humility]

KINGDOM OF GOD

It is easier for a camel to go through the eye of a needle, than for a rich man to enter into the kingdom of God.
Jesus
Matt. 19:24, Mark 10:25
See also Luke 18:25

Whosoever shall not receive the kingdom of God as a little child, he shall not enter therein.
Jesus
Mark 10:15
See also Luke 18:17

No man, having put his hand to the plough, and looking back, is fit for the kingdom of God.
Jesus
Luke 9:62

The kingdom of God is come nigh unto you.
Jesus
Luke 10:9

Seek ye the kingdom of God; and all these things shall be added unto you.
Jesus
Luke 12:31
See also Matt. 6:33

Fear not, little flock; for it is your Father's good pleasure to give you the kingdom.
Jesus
Luke 12:32

It is like a grain of mustard seed, which a man took, and cast into his garden; and it grew, and waxed a great tree.
Jesus
Luke 13:19
See also Matt. 13:31, Mark 4:31

The law and the prophets were until John: since that time the kingdom of God is preached.
Jesus
Luke 16:16

The kingdom of God cometh not with observation.
Jesus
Luke 17:20

The kingdom of God is within you.
Jesus
Luke 17:21

Except a man be born again, he cannot see the kingdom of God.
Jesus
John 3:3

Except a man be born of water and of the Spirit, he cannot enter into the kingdom of God.
Jesus
John 3:5

We must through much tribulation enter into the kingdom of God.
Acts 14:22

The kingdom of God is not meat and drink; but righteousness, and peace, and joy in the Holy Ghost.
Rom. 14:17

The kingdom of God is not in word, but in power.
1 Cor. 4:20

The unrighteous shall not inherit the kingdom of God.
1 Cor. 6:9

Flesh and blood cannot inherit the kingdom of God.
1 Cor. 15:50

[*See also* Heaven, Kingdom of Heaven, Salvation]

KINGDOM OF HEAVEN

Repent, for the kingdom of heaven is at hand.
Jesus
Matt. 4:17
See also Matt. 3:2, Matt. 10:7,
Mark 1:15

Blessed are the poor in spirit: for their's is the kingdom of heaven.
Jesus
Matt. 5:3
See also Luke 6:20

Blessed are they which are persecuted for righteousness' sake: for their's is the kingdom of heaven.
Jesus
Matt. 5:10

Not every one that saith unto me, Lord, Lord, shall enter into the kingdom of heaven.
Jesus
Matt. 7:21

The kingdom of heaven is like unto treasure hid in a field.
Jesus
Matt. 13:44

I will give unto thee the keys of the kingdom of heaven.
Jesus to Peter
Matt. 16:19

Except ye be converted, and become as little children, ye shall not enter into the kingdom of heaven.
Jesus
Matt. 18:3

A rich man shall hardly enter into the kingdom of heaven.
Jesus
Matt. 19:23
See also Mark 10:24

[See also Heaven, Kingdom of God, Salvation]

KINGS

See Monarchy.

KNOWLEDGE

Hear, and understand.
Jesus
Matt. 15:10

Flesh and blood hath not revealed it unto thee, but my Father which is in heaven.
Jesus
Matt. 16:17

If ye were blind, ye should have no sin.
Jesus
John 9:41

Walk while ye have the light, lest darkness come upon you.
Jesus
John 12:35

It is not for you to know the times or the seasons.
Jesus
Acts 1:7

I had not known lust, except the law had said, Thou shalt not covet.
Rom. 7:7

I would have you wise unto that which is good, and simple concerning evil.
Rom. 16:19

I know nothing by myself.
1 Cor. 4:4

If any man think that he knoweth any thing, he knoweth nothing yet as he ought to know.
1 Cor. 8:2

Though I be rude in speech, yet not in knowledge.
2 Cor. 11:6

Ye know not what shall be on the morrow.
James 4:14

To him that knoweth to do good, and doeth it not, to him it is sin.
James 4:17

As newborn babes, desire the sincere milk of the word, that ye may grow thereby.
1 Pet. 2:2

Add to your faith virtue; and to virtue knowledge.
2 Pet. 1:5

[See also Education, Experience, God's Knowledge, Ignorance, Understanding, Wisdom]

KNOWLEDGE OF GOD

No man knoweth the Son, but the Father; neither knoweth any man the Father, save the Son, and he to whomsoever the Son will reveal Him.
Jesus
Matt. 11:27
See also Luke 10:22

I know Him: for I am from Him, and He hath sent me.
Jesus
John 7:29

If ye had known me, ye should have known my Father also.
Jesus
John 8:19

If I should say, I know Him not, I shall be a liar like unto you: but I know Him, and keep His saying.
Jesus
John 8:55

As the Father knoweth me, even so know I the Father.
Jesus
John 10:15

They know not Him that sent me.
Jesus
John 15:21

Who hath known the mind of the Lord? or who hath been His counsellor?
Rom. 11:34

They profess that they know God; but in works they deny Him.
Titus 1:16

Grace and peace be multiplied unto you through the knowledge of God, and of Jesus our Lord.
2 Pet. 1:2

Grow in grace, and in the knowledge of our Lord.
2 Pet. 3:18

[*See also* Acknowledgment, Disobedience, Salvation, Testimony]

L

LABOR

See Work.

LAMENT

O faithless and perverse generation.
Jesus
Matt. 17:17

[*See also* Anguish, Grief, Jerusalem, Mourning]

LANGUAGE

See Communication, Eloquence, Speech.

LAST JUDGMENT

See Apocalypse, Judgment Day.

LAUGHTER

Blessed are ye that weep now: for ye shall laugh.
Jesus
Luke 6:21

Woe unto you that laugh now! for ye shall mourn and weep.
Jesus
Luke 6:25

Let your laughter be turned to mourning, and your joy to heaviness.
James 4:9

LAW

If any man will sue thee at the law, and take away thy coat, let him have thy cloak also.
Jesus
Matt. 5:40

Woe unto you also, ye lawyers!
Jesus
Luke 11:46

What things soever the law saith, it saith to them who are under the law.
Rom. 3:19

Where no law is, there is no transgression.
Rom. 4:15
See also Rom. 3:20

Sin is not imputed when there is no law.
Rom. 5:13

Brother goeth to law with brother, and that before the unbelievers.
1 Cor. 6:6

There is utterly a fault among you, because ye go to law one with another.
1 Cor. 6:7

It was added because of transgressions.
Gal. 3:19

The law is good, if a man use it lawfully.
1 Tim. 1:8

The law is not made for a righteous man, but for the lawless and disobedient, for the ungodly and for sinners.
1 Tim. 1:9

Submit yourselves to every ordinance of man for the Lord's sake.
1 Pet. 2:13

[*See also* Commandments, Justice, Scripture]

LAWLESSNESS

See Corruption, Crime, Injustice, Wickedness.

LAZINESS

If any would not work, neither should he eat.
>*2 Thess. 3:10*

[*See also* Diligence, Work]

LEADERSHIP

Ye are the light of the world. A city that is set on an hill cannot be hid.
>*Jesus*
>*Matt. 5:14*

Let your light so shine before men, that they may see your good works.
>*Jesus*
>*Matt. 5:16*

Follow me.
>*Jesus*
>*Matt. 9:9, Luke 5:27*
>*See also Matt. 4:19, Mark 1:17*

If the blind lead the blind, both shall fall into the ditch.
>*Jesus*
>*Matt. 15:14*
>*See also Luke 6:39*

Whosoever will be chief among you, let him be your servant.
>*Jesus*
>*Matt. 20:27*
>*See also Mark 10:44*

He that is greatest among you shall be your servant.
>*Jesus*
>*Matt. 23:11*

As a hen gathereth her chickens under her wings.
>*Jesus*
>*Matt. 23:37*

As sheep not having a shepherd.
>*Mark 6:34*

Smite the shepherd, and the sheep shall be scattered.
>*Mark 14:27, Zech. 13:7*
>*See also Matt. 26:31*

He that entereth in by the door is the shepherd of the sheep.
>*Jesus*
>*John 10:2*

The good shepherd giveth his life for the sheep.
>*Jesus*
>*John 10:11*

My sheep hear my voice, and I know them, and they follow me.
>*Jesus*
>*John 10:27*

Ye have not chosen me, but I have chosen you.
>*Jesus*
>*John 15:16*

He is the minister of God, a revenger to execute wrath upon him that doeth evil.
>*Rom. 13:4*

Who then is Paul, and who is Apollos, but ministers by whom ye believed?
>*1 Cor. 3:5*

If a man desire the office of a bishop, he desireth a good work.
>*1 Tim. 3:1*

If a man know not how to rule his own house, how shall he take care of the church of God?
>*1 Tim. 3:5*

Let the elders that rule well be counted worthy of double honour.
>*1 Tim. 5:17*

Them that sin rebuke before all, that others also may fear.
>*(Them: church leaders)*
>*1 Tim. 5:20*

A bishop must be blameless, as the steward of God.
>*Titus 1:7*

For love's sake I rather beseech thee.
>*Philem. 9*

Feed the flock of God which is among you.
>*1 Pet. 5:2*

There shall be false teachers among you.
>*2 Pet. 2:1*

[*See also* Ambition, Authority, Corruption, Disciples, Government, Models, Monarchy]

See Compassion, Forgiveness, Punishment.

LIES

He is a liar, and the father of it.
Jesus (He: Satan)
John 8:44

Thou hast not lied unto men, but unto God.
Acts 5:4

The poison of asps is under their lips.
Rom. 3:13
See also Ps. 140:3

No lie is of the truth.
1 John 2:21

Who is a liar but he that denieth that Jesus is the Christ?
1 John 2:22

[*See also* Deception, Dishonesty, Honesty, Hypocrisy, Perjury, Truth]

LIFE

In Him was life; and the life was the light of men.
John 1:4

Except ye eat the flesh of the Son of man, and drink His blood, ye have no life in you.
Jesus
John 6:53
See also John 6:54

It is the Spirit that quickeneth; the flesh profiteth nothing.
Jesus
John 6:63

As long as I am in the world, I am the light of the world.
Jesus
John 9:5

He that loveth his life shall lose it; and he that hateth his life in this world shall keep it unto life eternal.
Jesus
John 12:25

I am the way, the truth, and the life: no man cometh unto the Father, but by me.
Jesus
John 14:6

Because I live, ye shall live also.
Jesus
John 14:19

In Him we live, and move, and have our being.
Acts 17:28

None of us liveth to himself.
Rom. 14:7

Now we live, if ye stand fast in the Lord.
1 Thess. 3:8

God sent His only begotten Son into the world, that we might live through Him.
1 John 4:9

He that hath the Son hath life.
1 John 5:12

Blessed are they that do His commandments, that they may have right to the tree of life.
Rev. 22:14

[*See also* Death, Eternal Life, Mortality]

LIFE AND DEATH

Whosoever will save his life shall lose it: and whosoever will lose his life for my sake shall find it.
Jesus
Matt. 16:25
See also Mark 8:35, Luke 9:24

God is not the God of the dead, but of the living.
Jesus
Matt. 22:32
See also Mark 12:27, Luke 20:38

The damsel is not dead, but sleepeth.
Jesus
Mark 5:39
See also Matt. 9:24

He that believeth in me, though he were dead, yet shall he live.
Jesus
John 11:25

If I will that he tarry till I come, what is that to thee?
Jesus to Peter, about John
John 21:22

In that He died, He died unto sin once: but in that He liveth, He liveth unto God.
Rom. 6:10

The wages of sin is death; but the gift of God is eternal life through Jesus Christ our Lord.
Rom. 6:23

Whether we live therefore, or die, we are the Lord's.
Rom. 14:8

As in Adam all die, even so in Christ shall all be made alive.
1 Cor. 15:22

Whilst we are at home in the body, we are absent from the Lord.
2 Cor. 5:6

I through the law am dead to the law, that I might live unto God.
Gal. 2:19

To live is Christ, and to die is gain.
Phil. 1:21

Ye are dead, and your life is hid with Christ in God.
Col. 3:3

If we be dead with Him, we shall also live with Him.
2 Tim. 2:11

[*See also* Christ Eternal, Death, Eternal Life, Life, Mortality]

LIGHT AND DARKNESS

Ye are the light of the world. A city that is set on an hill cannot be hid.
Jesus
Matt. 5:14

Take heed therefore that the light which is in thee be not darkness.
Jesus
Luke 11:35

The light shineth in darkness; and the darkness comprehended it not.
John 1:5

Men loved darkness rather than light, because their deeds were evil.
Jesus
John 3:19

Every one that doeth evil hateth the light.
Jesus
John 3:20

As long as I am in the world, I am the light of the world.
Jesus
John 9:5

Turn them from darkness to light, and from the power of Satan unto God.
Jesus to Paul
Acts 26:18

All things that are reproved are made manifest by the light.
Eph. 5:13

God is light, and in Him is no darkness at all.
1 John 1:5

The city had no need of the sun, neither of the moon, to shine in it: for the glory of God did lighten it, and the Lamb is the light thereof.
Rev. 21:23

[*See also* Enlightenment, Night, Spirituality]

LIQUOR

No man also having drunk old wine straightway desireth new.
Jesus
Luke 5:39

Use a little wine for thy stomach's sake.
1 Tim. 5:23

[*See also* Drunkenness]

LISTENING

See Heedfulness.

LONELINESS

I am not alone, because the Father is with me.
Jesus
John 16:32

None of us liveth to himself.
Rom. 14:7

[*See also* Abandonment, Fellowship]

LONGEVITY

See Age, Mortality.

LOSS

If the salt have lost his savour, wherewith shall it be salted? it is thenceforth good for nothing.
Jesus
Matt. 5:13
See also Mark 9:50, Luke 14:34

The last shall be first.
Jesus
Matt. 19:30
See also, e.g., Mark 10:31

Many are called, but few are chosen.
Jesus
Matt. 22:14
See also Matt. 20:16

From him that hath not shall be taken away even that which he hath.
Jesus
Matt. 25:29

He that hath, to him shall be given: and he that hath not, from him shall be taken even that which he hath.
Jesus
Mark 4:25
See also Matt. 13:12, Luke 8:18,
Luke 19:26

What shall it profit a man, if he shall gain the whole world, and lose his own soul?
Jesus
Mark 8:36
See also Matt. 16:26, Luke 9:25

The fruits that thy soul lusted after are departed from thee.
Rev. 18:14

[*See also* Acceptance, Profit, Reward]

LOVE

Love your enemies.
Jesus
Matt. 5:44, Luke 6:27
See also Luke 6:35

Bless them that curse you, do good to them that hate you.
Jesus
Matt. 5:44

If ye love them which love you, what reward have ye? do not even the publicans the same?
Jesus
Matt. 5:46
See also Luke 6:32

He that loveth father or mother more than me is not worthy of me: and he that loveth son or daughter more than me is not worthy of me.
Jesus to disciples
Matt. 10:37

Thou shalt love thy neighbour as thyself.
Jesus
Matt. 19:19
See also, e.g., Lev. 19:18

This do, and thou shalt live.
Jesus
Luke 10:28

A new commandment I give unto you, That ye love one another.
Jesus
John 13:34

By this shall all men know that ye are my disciples, if ye have love one to another.
Jesus
John 13:35

He that loveth me shall be loved of my Father.
Jesus
John 14:21

This is my commandment, That ye love one another, as I have loved you.
Jesus
John 15:12

Greater love hath no man than this, that a man lay down his life for his friends.
Jesus
John 15:13

Let love be without dissimulation.
Rom. 12:9

Owe no man any thing, but to love one another.
Rom. 13:8

He that loveth another hath fulfilled the law.
Rom. 13:8
See also Rom. 13:10

Love worketh no ill to his neighbour.
Rom. 13:10

Shall I come unto you with a rod, or in love?
1 Cor. 4:21

[Note: The following quotations from 1 Corinthians contain the word "charity." This is an Elizabethan translation from the Latin "caritas" and the Greek "agape." Recent versions of the Bible translate the word more accurately, as "love." See Appendix, p. 202]

Knowledge puffeth up, but charity edifieth.
1 Cor. 8:1

Though I speak with the tongues of men and of angels, and have not charity, I am become as sounding brass, or a tinkling cymbal.
1 Cor. 13:1

Though I have all faith, so that I could remove mountains, and have not charity, I am nothing.
1 Cor. 13:2

And though I bestow all my goods to feed the poor, and though I give my body to be burned, and have not charity, it profiteth me nothing.
1 Cor. 13:3

Charity suffereth long, and is kind; charity envieth not; charity vaunteth not itself, is not puffed up.
1 Cor. 13:4

Charity envieth not.
1 Cor. 13:4

Beareth all things, believeth all things, hopeth all things, endureth all things.
1 Cor. 13:7

Charity never faileth.
1 Cor. 13:8

And now abideth faith, hope, charity, these three; but the greatest of these is charity.
1 Cor. 13:13

Let all your things be done with charity.
1 Cor. 16:14

By love serve one another.
Gal. 5:13

All the law is fulfilled in one word, even in this; Thou shalt love thy neighbour as thyself.
Gal. 5:14

Walk in love, as Christ also hath loved us.
Eph. 5:2

Husbands, love your wives, even as Christ also loved the church.
Eph. 5:25

He that loveth his wife loveth himself.
Eph. 5:28

Above all these things put on charity, which is the bond of perfectness.
(charity: love)
Col. 3:14

The end of the commandment is charity out of a pure heart, and of a good conscience, and of faith unfeigned.
1 Tim. 1:5

Above all things have fervent charity among yourselves.
1 Pet. 4:8

Charity shall cover the multitude of sins.
(charity: love)
1 Pet. 4:8

He that loveth his brother abideth in the light.
1 John 2:10

This is the message that ye heard from the beginning, that we should love one another.
1 John 3:11

Let us not love in word, neither in tongue; but in deed and in truth.
1 John 3:18

Let us love one another: for love is of God.
1 John 4:7

Every one that loveth is born of God, and knoweth God.
1 John 4:7

He that loveth not knoweth not God.
1 John 4:8

God is love.
1 John 4:8, 16

If God so loved us, we ought also to love one another.
1 John 4:11

If we love one another, God dwelleth in us.
1 John 4:12

He that dwelleth in love dwelleth in God, and God in him.
1 John 4:16

Perfect love casteth out fear.
1 John 4:18

We love Him, because He first loved us.
1 John 4:19

As many as I love, I rebuke and chasten.
Jesus
Rev. 3:19

[*See also* Brotherhood, Friendship, God's Love, God's Mercy, Hatred, and the Appendix at p. 202]

LOVE OF GOD

Thou shalt love the Lord thy God with all thy heart, and with all thy soul, and with all thy mind. This is the first and great commandment.
Jesus
Matt. 22:37–38
See also Deut. 6:5, Mark 12:29–30, Luke 10:27

All things work together for good to them that love God.
Rom. 8:28

Who shall separate us from the love of Christ? shall tribulation, or distress, or persecution, or famine, or nakedness, or peril, or sword?
Rom. 8:35

Eye hath not seen, nor ear heard, neither have entered into the heart of man, the things which God hath prepared for them that love Him.
1 Cor. 2:9
See also Isa. 64:4

Whosoever therefore will be a friend of the world is the enemy of God.
James 4:4

If any man love the world, the love of the Father is not in him.
1 John 2:15

He that loveth not his brother whom he hath seen, how can he love God whom he hath not seen?
1 John 4:20

He who loveth God love his brother also.
1 John 4:21

We love the children of God, when we love God, and keep His commandments.
1 John 5:2

Keep yourselves in the love of God, looking for the mercy of our Lord Jesus Christ.
Jude 21

[*See also* Reverence]

LOYALTY

Where your treasure is, there will your heart be also.
Jesus
Matt. 6:21, Luke 12:34

Ye cannot serve God and mammon.
Jesus
Matt. 6:24, Luke 16:13

No man can serve two masters: for either he will hate the one, and love the other; or else he will hold to the one, and despise the other.
Jesus
Matt. 6:24, Luke 16:13

He that is not with me is against me.
Jesus
Matt. 12:30, Luke 11:23

Render therefore unto Caesar the things which are Caesar's; and unto God the things that are God's.
Jesus
Matt. 22:21
See also Mark 12:17, Luke 20:25

Though I should die with Thee, yet will I not deny Thee.
Peter to Jesus
Matt. 26:35
See also Mark 14:31

We have no king but Caesar.
John 19:15

God is faithful.
E.g., 1 Cor. 1:9

Faithful is He that calleth you.
1 Thess. 5:24

All men have not faith. But the Lord is faithful.
2 Thess. 3:2–3

The Lord knoweth them that are His.
2 Tim. 2:19

I will never leave thee, nor forsake thee.
(I: God)
Heb. 13:5
See also Deut. 31:6, Josh. 1:5

They went out from us, but they were not of us.
1 John 2:19

[*See also* Allegiance, Allies, Betrayal, Faithfulness]

LUST

Whosoever looketh on a woman to lust after her hath committed adultery with her already in his heart.
Jesus
Matt. 5:28

I had not known lust, except the law had said, Thou shalt not covet.
Rom. 7:7

To be carnally minded is death; but to be spiritually minded is life and peace.
Rom. 8:6

Use not liberty for an occasion to the flesh.
Gal. 5:13

Walk in the Spirit, and ye shall not fulfil the lust of the flesh.
Gal. 5:16

The flesh lusteth against the Spirit, and the Spirit against the flesh.
Gal. 5:17

He that soweth to his flesh shall of the flesh reap corruption.
Gal. 6:8

Abstain from fleshly lusts, which war against the soul.
1 Pet. 2:11

[*See also* Adultery, Carnality, Desire, Fornication, Immorality]

MADNESS

They say, He hath a devil.
Jesus (He: John the Baptist)
Matt. 11:18
See also Luke 7:33

These are not the words of him that hath a devil.
John 10:21

Paul, thou art beside thyself; much learning doth make thee mad.
Festus
Acts 26:24

I am not mad, most noble Festus; but speak forth the words of truth and soberness.
Paul
Acts 26:25

[*See also* Exorcism]

MAN AND WOMAN

He is the image and glory of God: but the woman is the glory of the man.
1 Cor. 11:7

The man is not of the woman; but the woman of the man.
1 Cor. 11:8

Neither was the man created for the woman; but the woman for the man.
1 Cor. 11:9

I suffer not a woman to teach, nor to usurp authority over the man, but to be in silence.
1 Tim. 2:12

For Adam was first formed, then Eve.
1 Tim. 2:13

[*See also* Mankind, Marriage, Women]

MANAGEMENT

See Leadership.

MANKIND

With men it is impossible, but not with God.
Jesus
Mark 10:27
See also Matt. 19:26, Luke 18:27

That which is born of the flesh is flesh; and that which is born of the Spirit is spirit.
Jesus
John 3:6

They are all under sin.
Rom. 3:9

There is none righteous, no, not one.
Rom. 3:10
See also Ps. 14:3, Ps. 53:3

All have sinned, and come short of the glory of God.
Rom. 3:23

Ye are the temple of God.
1 Cor. 3:16

The Spirit of God dwelleth in you.
1 Cor. 3:16

There is neither Jew nor Greek, there is neither bond nor free, there is neither male nor female: for ye are all one in Christ Jesus.
Gal. 3:28

There is neither Greek nor Jew, circumcision nor uncircumcision, Barbarian, Scythian, bond nor free: but Christ is all, and in all.
Col. 3:11

What is man, that Thou art mindful of

him? or the son of man, that Thou visitest him?
Heb. 2:6
See also Ps. 8:4

A little lower than the angels.
Heb. 2:7, Ps. 8:5

Thou crownedst him with glory and honour, and didst set him over the works of Thy hands.
Heb. 2:7

All flesh is as grass, and all the glory of man as the flower of grass.
1 Pet. 1:24
See also Isa. 40:6

[*See also* Human Nature, Individual (Importance of), Man and Woman, Mortality]

MANNERS

See Courtesy.

MARRIAGE

What therefore God hath joined together, let not man put asunder.
Jesus
Matt. 19:6, Mark 10:9

They twain shall be one flesh.
Jesus
Mark 10:8
See also Matt. 19:6, Eph. 5:31

To avoid fornication, let every man have his own wife, and let every woman have her own husband.
1 Cor. 7:2

Let the husband render unto the wife due benevolence: and likewise also the wife unto the husband.
1 Cor. 7:3

It is better to marry than to burn.
1 Cor. 7:9

The woman which hath an husband that believeth not, and if he be pleased to dwell with her, let her not leave him.
1 Cor. 7:13

The unbelieving husband is sanctified by

the wife, and the unbelieving wife is sanctified by the husband.
1 Cor. 7:14

If the unbelieving depart, let him depart.
1 Cor. 7:15

Such shall have trouble in the flesh.
1 Cor. 7:28

He that is unmarried careth for the things that belong to the Lord, how he may please the Lord: But he that is married careth for the things that are of the world, how he may please his wife.
1 Cor. 7:32–33

She that is married careth for the things of the world, how she may please her husband.
1 Cor. 7:34

He that giveth her in marriage doeth well; but he that giveth her not in marriage doeth better.
1 Cor. 7:38

Wives, submit yourselves unto your own husbands, as unto the Lord.
Eph. 5:22
See also Col. 3:18

The husband is the head of the wife, even as Christ is the head of the church.
Eph. 5:23

As the church is subject unto Christ, so let the wives be to their own husbands in every thing.
Eph. 5:24

Husbands, love your wives, even as Christ also loved the church.
Eph. 5:25

He that loveth his wife loveth himself.
Eph. 5:28

Husbands, love your wives, and be not bitter against them.
Col. 3:19

Teach the young women to be sober, to love their husbands, to love their children.
Titus 2:4

Wives, be in subjection to your own husbands.
1 Pet. 3:1

Giving honour unto the wife, as unto the weaker vessel.
1 Pet. 3:7

[*See also* Adultery, Divorce, Strife, Women]

MARTYRDOM

Blessed are they which are persecuted for righteousness' sake: for their's is the kingdom of heaven.
Jesus
Matt. 5:10

Great is your reward in heaven.
Jesus
Matt. 5:12

Whosoever shall lose his life for my sake and the gospel's, the same shall save it.
Jesus
Mark 8:35
See also Matt. 16:25, Luke 9:24

If we let Him thus alone, all men will believe on Him.
John 11:48

Behold, I see the heavens opened, and the Son of man standing on the right hand of God.
Stephen
Acts 7:56

Lord Jesus, receive my spirit.
Stephen
Acts 7:59

I am ready not to be bound only, but also to die at Jerusalem for the name of the Lord Jesus.
Acts 21:13

And though I bestow all my goods to feed the poor, and though I give my body to be burned, and have not charity, it profiteth me nothing.
(charity: love)
1 Cor. 13:3

I am set for the defence of the gospel.
Phil. 1:17

All that will live godly in Christ Jesus shall suffer persecution.
2 Tim. 3:12

They shall hunger no more, neither thirst

any more; neither shall the sun light on them, nor any heat.
Rev. 7:16

The Lamb which is in the midst of the throne shall feed them, and shall lead them unto living fountains of waters.
Rev. 7:17

Blessed are the dead which die in the Lord from henceforth.
Rev. 14:13

They have shed the blood of saints and prophets, and Thou hast given them blood to drink.
Rev. 16:6

I saw the souls of them that were beheaded for the witness of Jesus, and for the word of God.
Rev. 20:4

[*See also* Persecution, Sacrifice]

MATERIALISM

Lay not up for yourselves treasures upon earth, where moth and rust doth corrupt, and where thieves break through and steal.
Jesus
Matt. 6:19

Ye cannot serve God and mammon.
Jesus
Matt. 6:24, Luke 16:13

Take no thought for your life, what ye shall eat, or what ye shall drink; nor yet for your body, what ye shall put on.
Jesus
Matt. 6:25
See also Luke 12:22

Is not the life more than meat, and the body than raiment?
Jesus
Matt. 6:25
See also Luke 12:23

Why take ye thought for raiment?
Jesus
Matt. 6:28

What shall it profit a man, if he shall gain the whole world, and lose his own soul?
Jesus
Mark 8:36
See also Matt. 16:26, Luke 9:25

Man shall not live by bread alone, but by every word of God.
Jesus
Luke 4:4
See also Deut. 8:3, Matt. 4:4

A man's life consisteth not in the abundance of the things which he possesseth.
Jesus
Luke 12:15

That which is highly esteemed among men is abomination in the sight of God.
Jesus
Luke 16:15

Labour not for the meat which perisheth, but for that meat which endureth unto everlasting life.
Jesus
John 6:27

The kingdom of God is not meat and drink; but righteousness, and peace, and joy in the Holy Ghost.
Rom. 14:17

He that is unmarried careth for the things that belong to the Lord, how he may please the Lord: But he that is married careth for the things that are of the world, how he may please his wife.
1 Cor. 7:32–33

She that is married careth for the things of the world, how she may please her husband.
1 Cor. 7:34

The things which are seen are temporal; but the things which are not seen are eternal.
2 Cor. 4:18

Set your affection on things above, not on things on the earth.
Col. 3:2

Having food and raiment let us be therewith content.
1 Tim. 6:8

Love not the world, neither the things that are in the world.
1 John 2:15

Thou sayest, I am rich, and increased with goods, and have need of nothing; and knowest not that thou art wretched, and miserable, and poor, and blind, and naked.

Jesus
Rev. 3:17

[*See also* Greed, Spirituality, Wealth, Worldliness]

MATURITY

He is of age; ask him.
John 9:21, 23

When I was a child, I spake as a child, I understood as a child, I thought as a child: but when I became a man, I put away childish things.
1 Cor. 13:11

Be not children in understanding.
1 Cor. 14:20

In malice be ye children, but in understanding be men.
1 Cor. 14:20

We henceforth be no more children, tossed to and fro, and carried about with every wind of doctrine, by the sleight of men, and cunning craftiness, whereby they lie in wait to deceive.
Eph. 4:14

Flee also youthful lusts: but follow righteousness, faith, charity, peace.
2 Tim. 2:22

Strong meat belongeth to them that are of full age.
Heb. 5:14

Grow in grace, and in the knowledge of our Lord.
2 Pet. 3:18

The time is come for Thee to reap; for the harvest of the earth is ripe.
Rev. 14:15

Gather the clusters of the vine of the earth; for her grapes are fully ripe.
Rev. 14:18

[*See also* Children, Growth]

MEDIATION

A mediator is not a mediator of one.
Gal. 3:20

Jesus the mediator of the new covenant.
Heb. 12:24

[*See also* Compromise, Intercession]

MEDICINE

See Healing.

MEEKNESS

Blessed are the meek: for they shall inherit the earth.
Jesus
Matt. 5:5
See also Ps. 37:11

Behold, I send you forth as lambs among wolves.
Jesus
Luke 10:3
See also Matt. 10:16

As a sheep to the slaughter.
Acts 8:32
See also Isa. 53:7, Jer. 11:19

Like a lamb dumb before His shearer, so opened He not His mouth.
Acts 8:32
See also Isa. 53:7

[*See also* Humility]

MERCY

Blessed are the merciful: for they shall obtain mercy.
Jesus
Matt. 5:7

Be ye therefore merciful, as your Father also is merciful.
Jesus
Luke 6:36

It is not of him that willeth, nor of him

that runneth, but of God that showeth mercy.
Rom. 9:16

[*See also* Compassion, Forgiveness, God's Mercy, Kindness, Suffering]

MERIT

See Justice, Reward, Success, Worthiness.

MESSIAH

Art thou He that should come, or do we look for another?
Matt. 11:3
See also Luke 7:19

But whom say ye that I am?
Jesus
Matt. 16:15, Mark 8:29, Luke 9:20

This is My beloved Son, in whom I am well pleased; hear ye Him.
Matt. 17:5
See also Mark 9:7, Luke 9:35

Blessed is He that cometh in the name of the Lord.
Matt. 21:9, Matt. 23:39
See also Mark 11:9, John 12:13,
Ps. 118:26

Take heed that no man deceive you. For many shall come in my name, saying, I am Christ.
Jesus
Matt. 24:4–5
See also Mark 13:6, Luke 21:8

If Thou be the Son of God, come down from the cross.
Passers-by to Jesus
Matt. 27:40
See also Mark 15:30

Truly this was the Son of God.
Matt. 27:54
See also Mark 15:39

False Christs and false prophets shall rise, and shall show signs and wonders, to seduce, if it were possible, even the elect.
Jesus
Mark 13:22
See also Matt. 24:24

Mine eyes have seen Thy salvation,

Which Thou hast prepared before the face of all people.
Simeon
Luke 2:30–31

The Son of man is not come to destroy men's lives, but to save them.
Jesus
Luke 9:56

He was not that Light, but was sent to bear witness of that Light.
(He: John the Baptist)
John 1:8

I am the voice of one crying in the wilderness, Make straight the way of the Lord.
John the Baptist
John 1:23
See also Matt. 3:3, Mark 1:3,
Luke 3:4

He whom God hath sent speaketh the words of God.
John 3:34

I that speak unto thee am He.
Jesus
John 4:26

Whom He hath sent, Him ye believe not.
Jesus
John 5:38

The bread of God is He which cometh down from heaven, and giveth life unto the world.
Jesus
John 6:33

If ye believe not that I am He, ye shall die in your sins.
Jesus
John 8:24

It is He that talketh with thee.
Jesus
John 9:37

This Jesus, whom I preach unto you, is Christ.
Acts 17:3

Who is a liar but he that denieth that Jesus is the Christ?
1 John 2:22

Whosoever believeth that Jesus is the Christ is born of God.
1 John 5:1

[See also False Prophets, Jesus, Second Coming]

MESSIANIC HOPES AND PROPHECIES

I am not come to destroy, but to fulfil.
Jesus
Matt. 5:17

This is he, of whom it is written, Behold, I send my messenger before Thy face, which shall prepare Thy way before Thee.
Jesus (he: John the Baptist)
Matt. 11:10, Luke 7:27
See also Mal. 3:1

All this was done, that the scriptures of the prophets might be fulfilled.
Jesus
Matt. 26:56

Every valley shall be filled, and every mountain and hill shall be brought low.
Luke 3:5
See also Isa. 40:4

This day is this scripture fulfilled in your ears.
Jesus
Luke 4:21

We have found Him, of whom Moses in the law, and the prophets, did write.
John 1:45

Search the scriptures.
Jesus
John 5:39

Had ye believed Moses, ye would have believed me: for he wrote of me.
Jesus
John 5:46

Of a truth this is the Prophet.
John 7:40

These things were done, that the scripture should be fulfilled.
John 19:36

Of whom speaketh the prophet this? of himself, or of some other man?
Acts 8:34

They have fulfilled them in condemning Him.
(them: Scripture)
Acts 13:27

The promise which was made unto the fathers, God hath fulfilled the same unto us their children.
Acts 13:32–33

[See also Jesus, Messiah]

MINISTRY

The harvest truly is plenteous, but the labourers are few.
Jesus
Matt. 9:37
See also Luke 10:2

Freely ye have received, freely give.
Jesus
Matt. 10:8

Feed my lambs.
Jesus
John 21:15

Feed my sheep.
Jesus
John 21:16, 17

It is not reason that we should leave the word of God, and serve tables.
Acts 6:2

Serving the Lord with all humility of mind, and with many tears.
Acts 20:19

Feed the church of God, which He hath purchased with His own blood.
Paul
Acts 20:28

We are labourers together with God.
1 Cor. 3:9

We are fools for Christ's sake.
1 Cor. 4:10

Being reviled, we bless; being persecuted, we suffer it.
1 Cor. 4:12

Are not ye my work in the Lord?
1 Cor. 9:1

Though I be free from all men, yet have I made myself servant unto all.
1 Cor. 9:19

I am made all things to all men, that I might by all means save some.
1 Cor. 9:22

Let all things be done decently and in order.
1 Cor. 14:40

Be ye stedfast, unmoveable, always abounding in the work of the Lord.
1 Cor. 15:58

We are ambassadors for Christ.
2 Cor. 5:20

As we have therefore opportunity, let us do good unto all men.
Gal. 6:10

If any man minister, let him do it as of the ability which God giveth.
1 Pet. 4:11

Feed the flock of God which is among you.
1 Pet. 5:2

[*See also* Clergy, Disciples, Evangelism, Preaching, Service to God, Underprivileged]

MIRACLES

An evil and adulterous generation seeketh after a sign; and there shall no sign be given to it, but the sign of the prophet Jonas.
Jesus
Matt. 12:39
See also Matt. 16:4, Mark 8:12,
Luke 11:29

We have here but five loaves, and two fishes.
His disciples to Jesus
Matt. 14:17
See also Luke 9:13

Jesus went unto them, walking on the sea.
Matt. 14:25
See also Mark 6:48

In my name shall they cast out devils.
Jesus
Mark 16:17

He laid His hands on every one of them, and healed them.
Luke 4:40

We have seen strange things to day.
Luke 5:26

The blind see, the lame walk, the lepers are cleansed, the deaf hear, the dead are raised, to the poor the gospel is preached
Jesus
Luke 7:22
See also Matt. 11:5

No man can do these miracles that Thou doest, except God be with him.
John 3:2

Go thy way; thy son liveth.
Jesus
John 4:50

How can a man that is a sinner do such miracles?
Pharisees, about Jesus
John 9:16

Whether He be a sinner or no, I know not: one thing I know, that, whereas I was blind, now I see.
John 9:25

Can a devil open the eyes of the blind?
John 10:21

If they should be written every one, I suppose that even the world itself could not contain the books that should be written.
John 21:25

Why marvel ye at this?
Acts 3:12

And he leaped and walked.
Acts 14:10

The gods are come down to us in the likeness of men.
Acts 14:11

[*See also* God's Power, Healing, Wonders]

MISERY

See Anguish.

MISJUDGMENT

How can a man that is a sinner do such miracles?
Pharisees, about Jesus
John 9:16

[*See also* Rashness]

Heal the sick, cleanse the lepers, raise the dead, cast out devils.
Jesus
Matt. 10:8

He hath sent me to heal the broken-hearted, to preach deliverance to the captives.
Jesus
Luke 4:18
See also Isa. 61:1

Behold, I send you forth as lambs among wolves.
Jesus
Luke 10:3
See also Matt. 10:16

My meat is to do the will of Him that sent me, and to finish His work.
Jesus
John 4:34

I came down from heaven, not to do mine own will, but the will of Him that sent me.
Jesus
John 6:38

I know Him: for I am from Him, and He hath sent me.
Jesus
John 7:29

But for this cause came I unto this hour.
Jesus
John 12:27

To this end was I born, and for this cause came I into the world, that I should bear witness unto the truth.
Jesus
John 18:37

As my Father hath sent me, even so send I you.
Jesus
John 20:21

Arise, and go into Damascus.
Jesus to Saul
Acts 22:10
See also Acts 9:6

I have appeared unto thee for this purpose, to make thee a minister and a witness.
Jesus to Saul
Acts 26:16

Let us run with patience the race that is set before us.
Heb. 12:1

[*See also* Duty, Goals, Purpose]

MISSIONARIES

See Evangelism.

MOBS

Not this man, but Barabbas.
John 18:40
See also Luke 23:18

They cried out, saying, Crucify Him, crucify Him.
John 19:6, Luke 23:21
See also, e.g., Matt. 27:23,
Mark 15:13

Take ye Him, and crucify Him: for I find no fault in Him.
Pilate
John 19:6
See also Luke 23:4

They stoned Stephen.
Acts 7:59

[*See also* Public Opinion]

MOCKERY

If Thou be the Son of God, come down from the cross.
Passers-by to Jesus
Matt. 27:40
See also Mark 15:30

He saved others; Himself He cannot save.
Matt. 27:42, Mark 15:31
See also Luke 23:35

Can there any good thing come out of Nazareth?
John 1:46

Art thou also of Galilee?
John 7:52

God is not mocked.
Gal. 6:7

[*See also* Contempt, Scorn]

Ye are the light of the world. A city that is set on an hill cannot be hid.
Jesus
Matt. 5:14

Let your light so shine before men, that they may see your good works.
Jesus
Matt. 5:16

It is enough for the disciple that he be as his master, and the servant as his lord.
Jesus
Matt. 10:25

Do not ye after their works: for they say, and do not.
Jesus
Matt. 23:3

Go, and do thou likewise.
Jesus
Luke 10:37

He was a burning and a shining light: and ye were willing for a season to rejoice in his light.
Jesus (He: John the Baptist)
John 5:35

Do as I have done to you.
Jesus
John 13:15

Be ye followers of me, even as I also am of Christ.
1 Cor. 11:1

Be as I am; for I am as ye are.
Gal. 4:12

Be ye therefore followers of God, as dear children.
Eph. 5:1

Mark them which walk so as ye have us for an ensample.
Phil. 3:17

Ye should follow His steps: Who did no sin.
1 Pet. 2:21-22

[*See also* Leadership]

When thou doest thine alms, do not sound a trumpet before thee, as the hypocrites do.
Jesus
Matt. 6:2

Appear not unto men to fast, but unto thy Father.
Jesus
Matt. 6:18

See that no man know it.
Jesus to blind men He healed
Matt. 9:30

Thou sayest it.
Jesus to Pilate
Mark 15:2, Luke 23:3
See also Matt. 27:11

He must increase, but I must decrease.
John the Baptist
John 3:30

[*See also* Conceit, Humility, Ostentation, Pride, Publicity]

We have no king but Caesar.
John 19:15

Fear God. Honour the king.
1 Pet. 2:17

[*See also* Government, Leadership, Sovereignty]

Ye cannot serve God and mammon.
Jesus
Matt. 6:24, Luke 16:13

Thy money perish with thee, because thou hast thought that the gift of God may be purchased with money.
Acts 8:20

Filthy lucre.
E.g., 1 Tim. 3:3

The love of money is the root of all evil.
1 Tim. 6:10

[*See also* Borrowing, Materialism, Wealth]

MONOTHEISM

Thou shalt worship the Lord thy God, and Him only shalt thou serve.
> *Jesus*
> *Matt. 4:10*
> *See also Deut. 6:13*

Hear, O Israel; The Lord our God is one Lord.
> *Jesus*
> *Mark 12:29*
> *See also, e.g., Deut. 6:4*

The devils also believe, and tremble.
> *James 2:19*

[*See also* God's Uniqueness, Idolatry]

MORALITY

See Decadence, Depravity, Immorality, Righteousness.

MORTALITY

Which of you by taking thought can add one cubit unto his stature?
> *Jesus*
> *Matt. 6:27*
> *See also Luke 12:25*

Be not afraid of them that kill the body, and after that have no more that they can do.
> *Jesus*
> *Luke 12:4*
> *See also Matt. 10:28*

What is man, that Thou art mindful of him? or the son of man, that Thou visitest him?
> *Heb. 2:6*
> *See also Ps. 8:4*

For what is your life? It is even a vapour, that appeareth for a little time, and then vanisheth away.
> *James 4:14*

All flesh is as grass, and all the glory of man as the flower of grass.
> *1 Pet. 1:24*
> *See also Isa. 40:6*

The grass withereth, and the flower there-of falleth away: But the word of the Lord endureth forever.
> *1 Pet. 1:24–25*
> *See also Isa. 40:8*

[*See also* Death, Eternal Life, Life, Life and Death, Mankind]

MOTHERHOOD

See Birth, Jesus (Birth of), Parents.

MOTIVATION

Out of the heart proceed evil thoughts, murders, adulteries, fornications, thefts, false witness, blasphemies.
> *Jesus*
> *Matt. 15:19*
> *See also Mark 7:21*

Ye ask, and receive not, because ye ask amiss.
> *James 4:3*

Not for filthy lucre.
> *1 Pet. 5:2*

[*See also* Attitude, Behavior, Intentions, Self-Interest]

MOURNING

Blessed are they that mourn: for they shall be comforted.
> *Jesus*
> *Matt. 5:4*

We have piped unto you, and ye have not danced; we have mourned unto you, and ye have not lamented.
> *Jesus*
> *Matt. 11:17*
> *See also Luke 7:32*

[*See also* Anguish, Death, Grief, Sorrow]

MURDER

Thou shalt do no murder.
> *Jesus*
> *Matt. 19:18*
> *See also, e.g., Ex. 20:13, Mark 10:19, Luke 18:20*

No murderer hath eternal life abiding in him.
1 John 3:15

[*See also* Death, Violence]

MUSIC

See Dance.

MYSTERY

The wind bloweth where it listeth, and thou hearest the sound thereof, but canst not tell whence it cometh, and whither it goeth.
Jesus
John 3:8

He that was healed wist not who it was.
John 5:13

Who is worthy to open the book, and to loose the seals thereof?
Rev. 5:2

When He had opened the seventh seal, there was silence in heaven about the space of half an hour.
Rev. 8:1

[*See also* Secrecy, Wonders]

MYTH

Refuse profane and old wives' fables.
1 Tim. 4:7

NAIVETE

Ye know not what ye ask.
Jesus
Matt. 20:22, Mark 10:38

Sir, Thou hast nothing to draw with, and the well is deep.
John 4:11

Whither will He go, that we shall not find Him?
Pharisees about Jesus
John 7:35

Who art Thou, Lord?
Saul to Jesus
Acts 9:5

We henceforth be no more children, tossed to and fro, and carried about with every wind of doctrine, by the sleight of men, and cunning craftiness, whereby they lie in wait to deceive.
Eph. 4:14

[*See also* Innocence]

NATURE

Consider the lilies of the field, how they grow; they toil not, neither do they spin: And yet I say unto you, That even Solomon in all his glory was not arrayed like one of these.
Jesus
Matt. 6:28–29
See also Luke 12:27

The wind bloweth where it listeth, and thou hearest the sound thereof, but canst not tell whence it cometh, and whither it goeth.
Jesus
John 3:8

Hath not My hand made all these things?
Acts 7:50
See also Isa. 66:2

The earth is the Lord's, and the fulness thereof.
1 Cor. 10:26, 28
See also Ps. 24:1

Can the fig tree, my brethren, bear olive berries?
James 3:12

The grass withereth, and the flower thereof falleth away: But the word of the Lord endureth forever.
1 Pet. 1:24–25
See also Isa. 40:8

[*See also* Creation, Cultivation, Heaven and Earth, Night, Rain]

NEED

Your Father knoweth what things ye have need of, before ye ask Him.
Jesus
Matt. 6:8

They that be whole need not a physician, but they that are sick.
Jesus
Matt. 9:12
See also Mark 2:17, Luke 5:31

Let him that is athirst come. And whosoever will, let him take the water of life freely.
Rev. 22:17

[*See also* Charity, Poverty, Underprivileged]

NEIGHBORS

Thou shalt love thy neighbour as thyself.
Jesus
Matt. 19:19
See also, e.g., Lev. 19:18

Love worketh no ill to his neighbour.
Rom. 13:10

[*See also* Brotherhood, Fellowship]

NEUTRALITY

He that is not with me is against me.
Jesus
Matt. 12:30, Luke 11:23

He that is not against us is for us.
Jesus
Luke 9:50
See also Mark 9:40

I know thy works, that thou art neither cold nor hot: I would thou wert cold or hot.
Jesus
Rev. 3:15

Because thou art lukewarm, and neither cold nor hot, I will spue thee out of my mouth.
Jesus
Rev. 3:16

[*See also* Choice, Impartiality]

NEW TESTAMENT

See Covenant, Gospel, Scripture.

NEWS

I bring you good tidings of great joy.
Luke 2:10

[*See also* Gospel]

NIGHT

They that sleep sleep in the night; and they that be drunken are drunken in the night.
1 Thess. 5:7

[*See also* Light and Darkness]

OATHS

Swear not at all; neither by heaven; for it is God's throne: Nor by the earth; for it is His footstool: neither by Jerusalem; for it is the city of the great King.
Jesus
Matt. 5:34–35

Neither shalt thou swear by thy head, because thou canst not make one hair white or black.
Jesus
Matt. 5:36

He that shall swear by heaven, sweareth by the throne of God, and by Him that sitteth thereon.
Jesus
Matt. 23:22

Swear not, neither by heaven, neither by the earth, neither by any other oath: but let your yea be yea; and your nay, nay.
James 5:12

[*See also* Profanity, Promises]

OBEDIENCE

Whosoever heareth these sayings of mine, and doeth them, I will liken him unto a wise man, which built his house upon a rock.
Jesus
Matt. 7:24

Whosoever shall do the will of my Father which is in heaven, the same is my brother, and sister, and mother.
Jesus
Matt. 12:50
See also Mark 3:35

Blessed are they that hear the word of God, and keep it.
Jesus
Luke 11:28

Not my will, but Thine, be done.
Jesus
Luke 22:42
See also Mark 14:36

My meat is to do the will of Him that sent me, and to finish His work.
Jesus
John 4:34

If ye continue in my word, then are ye my disciples indeed.
Jesus
John 8:31

He that is of God heareth God's words.
Jesus
John 8:47

If a man keep my saying, he shall never see death.
Jesus
John 8:51

If ye know these things, happy are ye if ye do them.
Jesus
John 13:17

If ye love me, keep my commandments.
Jesus
John 14:15
See also John 14:23

If ye keep my commandments, ye shall abide in my love.
Jesus
John 15:10

Follow me.
Jesus
John 21:19

Whether it be right in the sight of God to hearken unto you more than unto God, judge ye.
Acts 4:19

We ought to obey God rather than men.
Acts 5:29

Not the hearers of the law are just before God, but the doers of the law shall be justified.
Rom. 2:13

As by one man's disobedience many were made sinners, so by the obedience of one shall many be made righteous.
Rom. 5:19

With the mind I myself serve the law of God; but with the flesh the law of sin.
Rom. 7:25

Let every soul be subject unto the higher powers.
Rom. 13:1

Circumcision is nothing, and uncircumcision is nothing, but the keeping of the commandments of God.
1 Cor. 7:19

Children, obey your parents in the Lord.
Eph. 6:1

Let us walk by the same rule, let us mind the same thing.
Phil. 3:16

Children, obey your parents in all things: for this is well pleasing unto the Lord.
Col. 3:20

Though He were a Son, yet learned He obedience by the things which He suffered.
Heb. 5:8

We put bits in the horses' mouths, that they may obey us.
James 3:3

Submit yourselves to every ordinance of man for the Lord's sake.
1 Pet. 2:13

Servants, be subject to your masters with all fear; not only to the good and gentle.
1 Pet. 2:18
See also Eph. 6:5

Whoso keepeth His word, in him verily is the love of God perfected.
(His: Jesus)
1 John 2:5

Whosoever abideth in Him sinneth not.
1 John 3:6

He that keepeth His commandments dwelleth in Him.
1 John 3:24

We love the children of God, when we love God, and keep His commandments.
1 John 5:2

He that hath an ear, let him hear what the Spirit saith unto the churches.
Jesus
E.g., Rev. 2:7

Blessed is he that keepeth the sayings of the prophecy of this book.
Rev. 22:7

Blessed are they that do His commandments, that they may have right to the tree of life.
Rev. 22:14

[*See also* Acceptance, Authority, Backsliding, Commandments, Disobedience, Law, Rebellion, Reward, Sin]

OBLIGATION

Unto whomsoever much is given, of him shall be much required.
Jesus
Luke 12:48

To whom men have committed much, of him they will ask the more.
Jesus
Luke 12:48

Owe no man any thing, but to love one another.
Rom. 13:8

Though I be free from all men, yet have I made myself servant unto all.
1 Cor. 9:19

[*See also* Borrowing, Duty]

OBSTACLES

Every valley shall be filled, and every mountain and hill shall be brought low.
Luke 3:5
See also Isa. 40:4

The crooked shall be made straight, and the rough ways shall be made smooth.
Luke 3:5
See also Isa. 40:4

Make straight paths for your feet, lest that which is lame be turned out of the way.
Heb. 12:13

OLD AGE

See Age.

OLD TESTAMENT

See Covenant, Scripture.

OMENS

An evil and adulterous generation seeketh after a sign; and there shall no sign be given to it, but the sign of the prophet Jonas.
Jesus
Matt. 12:39
See also Matt. 16:4, Mark 8:12,
Luke 11:29

O ye hypocrites, ye can discern the face of the sky; but can ye not discern the signs of the times?
Jesus
Matt. 16:3
See also Luke 12:56

OMNIPOTENCE

See God's Power.

OMNISCIENCE

See God's Knowledge.

OPPORTUNISM

O generation of vipers, who hath warned you to flee from the wrath to come?
Matt. 3:7, Luke 3:7

Wheresoever the carcase is, there will the eagles be gathered together.
Jesus
Matt. 24:28
See also Luke 17:37

OPPORTUNITY

Seek, and ye shall find.
Jesus
Matt. 7:7, Luke 11:9

Knock, and it shall be opened unto you.
Jesus
Matt. 7:7, Luke 11:9

Many are called, but few are chosen.
Jesus
Matt. 22:14
See also Matt. 20:16

Lift up your eyes, and look on the fields; for they are white already to harvest.
Jesus
John 4:35

I must work the works of Him that sent me, while it is day.
Jesus
John 9:4

The night cometh, when no man can work.
Jesus
John 9:4

I am the door: by me if any man enter in, he shall be saved.
Jesus
John 10:9

This sickness is not unto death, but for the glory of God.
Jesus
John 11:4

Walk while ye have the light, lest darkness come upon you.
Jesus
John 12:35

The time is short.
1 Cor. 7:29

Behold, I have set before thee an open door, and no man can shut it.
Jesus
Rev. 3:8

If any man hear my voice, and open the door, I will come in to him.
Jesus
Rev. 3:20

Thrust in Thy sickle, and reap.
Rev. 14:15

The time is come for Thee to reap; for the harvest of the earth is ripe.
Rev. 14:15

Let him that is athirst come. And whosoever will, let him take the water of life freely.
Rev. 22:17

OPPRESSION

The word of God is not bound.
2 Tim. 2:9

[*See also* Burdens, Cruelty, Persecution]

OPTIMISM

See Hope.

ORATORY

See Preaching, Speech.

ORPHANS

See Widows and Orphans.

OSTENTATION

Do not your alms before men, to be seen of them: otherwise ye have no reward of your Father which is in heaven.
Jesus
Matt. 6:1

They love to pray standing in the synagogues and in the corners of the streets, that they may be seen of men.
Jesus (they: hypocrites)
Matt. 6:5

All their works they do for to be seen of men.
Jesus
Matt. 23:5

Beware of the scribes, which love to go in long clothing, and love salutations in the marketplaces, And the chief seats in the synagogues, and the uppermost rooms at feasts.
Jesus
Mark 12:38–40
See also Matt. 23:5–6,
Luke 20:46–47

[*See also* Boasting, Humility, Modesty]

OUTCAST

The stone which the builders rejected is become the head of the corner.
Jesus
Mark 12:10
See also Ps. 118:22, Matt. 21:42,
Luke 20:17

If any man love not the Lord Jesus Christ, let him be Anathema.
1 Cor. 16:22

He was cast out into the earth, and his angels were cast out with him.
Rev. 12:9

[*See also* Exile, Rejection]

PAGANISM

See Idolatry.

PAIN

See Anguish, Birth, Healing, Suffering.

PARADISE

See Heaven, Kingdom of God.

PARENTS

What man is there of you, whom if his son ask bread, will he give him a stone?
Jesus
Matt. 7:9
See also Luke 11:11

He that curseth father or mother, let him die the death.
Jesus
Matt. 15:4
See also, e.g., Ex. 20:12

Honour thy father and thy mother.
Jesus
Matt. 19:19, Luke 18:20, Ex. 20:14
See also, e.g., Mark 10:19

Call no man your father upon the earth: for one is your Father, which is in heaven.
Jesus
Matt. 23:9

The children ought not to lay up for the parents, but the parents for the children.
2 Cor. 12:14

Children, obey your parents in all things: for this is well pleasing unto the Lord.
Col. 3:20

[*See also* Age, Children, Family, Marriage]

PASSION

See Carnality, Desire, Love, Lust.

PATIENCE

The end is not yet.
> Jesus
> Matt. 24:6
> See also Mark 13:7

If he trespass against thee seven times in a day, and seven times in a day turn again to thee, saying, I repent; thou shalt forgive him.
> Jesus
> Luke 17:4

Wait for the promise of the Father.
> Jesus
> Acts 1:4

Forty years suffered He their manners in the wilderness.
> Acts 13:18

Tribulation worketh patience; And patience, experience; and experience, hope.
> Rom. 5:3–4

Let us not be weary in well doing: for in due season we shall reap.
> Gal. 6:9
> See also 2 Thess. 3:13

Be patient toward all men.
> 1 Thess. 5:14

The servant of the Lord must not strive.
> 2 Tim. 2:24

Be gentle unto all men, apt to teach, patient.
> 2 Tim. 2:24

Reprove, rebuke, exhort with all longsuffering and doctrine.
> 2 Tim. 4:2

Ye have need of patience, that, after ye have done the will of God, ye might receive the promise.
> Heb. 10:36

He that shall come will come, and will not tarry.
> Heb. 10:37
> See also Hab. 2:3

Let every man be swift to hear, slow to speak, slow to wrath.
> James 1:19

The coming of the Lord draweth nigh.
> James 5:8

The patience of Job.
> James 5:11

What glory is it, if, when ye be buffeted for your faults, ye shall take it patiently?
> 1 Pet. 2:20

If, when ye do well, and suffer for it, ye take it patiently, this is acceptable with God.
> 1 Pet. 2:20

One day is with the Lord as a thousand years, and a thousand years as one day.
> 2 Pet. 3:8

The longsuffering of our Lord is salvation.
> 2 Pet. 3:15

Rest yet for a little season.
> Rev. 6:11

The patience of the saints.
> Rev. 14:12
> See also Rev. 13:10

[See also Anger, Exasperation, Fortitude, Restraint]

PEACE

Blessed are the peacemakers: for they shall be called the children of God.
> Jesus
> Matt. 5:9

Agree with thine adversary quickly, whiles thou art in the way with him.
> Jesus
> Matt. 5:25

Have salt in yourselves, and have peace one with another.
> Jesus
> Mark 9:50

On earth peace, good will toward men.
> Luke 2:14

Suppose ye that I am come to give peace on earth? I tell you, Nay; but rather division.
> Jesus
> Luke 12:51
> See also Matt. 10:34

Peace in heaven, and glory in the highest.
Luke 19:38

Peace I leave with you, my peace I give unto you.
Jesus
John 14:27

We have peace with God through our Lord Jesus Christ.
Rom. 5:1

How beautiful are the feet of them that preach the gospel of peace.
Rom. 10:15
See also Isa. 52:7, Nah. 1:15

God is not the author of confusion, but of peace.
1 Cor. 14:33

He is our peace.
(He: Jesus)
Eph. 2:14

Let the peace of God rule in your hearts.
Col. 3:15

Be at peace among yourselves.
1 Thess. 5:13

The fruit of righteousness is sown in peace of them that make peace.
James 3:18

[*See also* Brotherhood, Serenity, War, War and Peace]

PEDANTRY

Ye blind guides, which strain at a gnat, and swallow a camel.
Jesus
Matt. 23:24

The letter killeth, but the spirit giveth life.
2 Cor. 3:6

If righteousness come by the law, then

Christ is dead in vain.
Gal. 2:21

Strive not about words to no profit.
2 Tim. 2:14

PERFECTION

Be ye therefore perfect, even as your Father which is in heaven is perfect.
Jesus
Matt. 5:48

If thou wilt be perfect, go and sell that thou hast, and give to the poor, and thou shalt have treasure in heaven: and come and follow me.
Jesus
Matt. 19:21
See also Mark 10:21, Luke 18:22

The crooked shall be made straight, and the rough ways shall be made smooth.
Luke 3:5
See also Isa. 40:4

Every good gift and every perfect gift is from above.
James 1:17

Whosoever shall keep the whole law, and yet offend in one point, he is guilty of all.
James 2:10

I have not found thy works perfect before God.
Jesus
Rev. 3:2

[*See also* Models]

PERJURY

Thou shalt not bear false witness.
Jesus
Matt. 19:18
See also, e.g., Ex. 20:16, Mark 10:19, Luke 18:20

[*See also* Dishonesty, Honesty, Lies]

PERMANENCE

If this counsel or this work be of men, it will come to nought: But if it be of God, ye cannot overthrow it.
Acts 5:38-39

If it be of God, ye cannot overthrow it.
Acts 5:39

Not in tables of stone, but in fleshy tables of the heart.
2 Cor. 3:3

The foundation of God standeth sure.
2 Tim. 2:19

Jesus Christ the same yesterday, and to day, and for ever.
Heb. 13:8

The grass withereth, and the flower thereof falleth away: But the word of the Lord endureth forever.
1 Pet. 1:24-25
See also Isa. 40:8

The world passeth away, and the lust thereof: but he that doeth the will of God abideth for ever.
1 John 2:17

[*See also* Christ Eternal, Eternal Life, Eternity, Mortality]

PERSECUTION

Blessed are they which are persecuted for righteousness' sake: for their's is the kingdom of heaven.
Jesus
Matt. 5:10

Blessed are ye, when men shall revile you, and persecute you, and shall say all manner of evil against you falsely, for my sake.
Jesus
Matt. 5:11

Pray for them which despitefully use you, and persecute you.
Jesus
Matt. 5:44
See also Luke 6:28

Ye shall be hated of all men for my name's

sake: but he that endureth to the end shall be saved.
Jesus
Matt. 10:22
See also Mark 13:13, Luke 21:17

Fear not them which kill the body, but are not able to kill the soul.
Jesus
Matt. 10:28
See also Luke 12:4

O Jerusalem, Jerusalem, thou that killest the prophets, and stonest them which are sent unto thee.
Jesus
Matt. 23:37
See also Luke 13:34

They shall mock Him, and shall scourge Him, and shall spit upon Him, and shall kill Him: and the third day He shall rise again.
Jesus
Mark 10:34
See also Luke 18:33

In the synagogues ye shall be beaten: and ye shall be brought before rulers and kings for my sake.
Jesus
Mark 13:9

He that despiseth you despiseth me; and he that despiseth me despiseth Him that sent me.
Jesus
Luke 10:16

For which of those works do ye stone me?
Jesus
John 10:32

If we let Him thus alone, all men will believe on Him.
John 11:48

If the world hate you, ye know that it hated me before it hated you.
Jesus
John 15:18

If they have persecuted me, they will also persecute you.
Jesus
John 15:20

They know not Him that sent me.
Jesus
John 15:21

He that hateth me hateth my Father also.
Jesus
John 15:23

The time cometh, that whosoever killeth you will think that he doeth God service.
Jesus
John 16:2

He that delivered me unto thee hath the greater sin.
Jesus
John 19:11

He bearing His cross went forth.
(He: Jesus)
John 19:17

As your fathers did, so do ye.
Acts 7:51

Which of the prophets have not your fathers persecuted?
Acts 7:52

Saul, Saul, why persecutest thou me?
Jesus
E.g., Acts 9:4

I am Jesus whom thou persecutest.
Jesus to Saul
Acts 9:5, Acts 26:15

If a spirit or an angel hath spoken to him, let us not fight against God.
Pharisees, about Paul
Acts 23:9

I stand at Caesar's judgment seat, where I ought to be judged: to the Jews have I done no wrong.
Paul
Acts 25:10

I stand and am judged for the hope of the promise made of God unto our fathers.
Paul
Acts 26:6

Many of the saints did I shut up in prison.
Paul
Acts 26:10

I persecuted them even unto strange cities.
Paul
Acts 26:11

Bless them which persecute you: bless, and curse not.
Rom. 12:14

Being reviled, we bless; being persecuted, we suffer it.
1 Cor. 4:12

Why stand we in jeopardy every hour?
1 Cor. 15:30

In labours more abundant, in stripes above measure, in prisons more frequent, in deaths oft.
2 Cor. 11:23

Let no man trouble me: for I bear in my body the marks of the Lord Jesus.
Gal. 6:17

I am an ambassador in bonds.
Eph. 6:20

Endure hardness, as a good soldier of Jesus Christ.
2 Tim. 2:3

All that will live godly in Christ Jesus shall suffer persecution.
2 Tim. 3:12

If ye be reproached for the name of Christ, happy are ye.
1 Pet. 4:14

If any man suffer as a Christian, let him not be ashamed.
1 Pet. 4:16

Marvel not, my brethren, if the world hate you.
1 John 3:13

Fear none of those things which thou shalt suffer.
Jesus
Rev. 2:10

Behold, the devil shall cast some of you into prison, that ye may be tried.
Jesus
Rev. 2:10

[*See also* Martyrdom, Suffering]

PERSEVERANCE

Ye shall be hated of all men for my name's sake: but he that endureth to the end shall be saved.
Jesus
Matt. 10:22
See also Mark 13:13, Luke 21:17

Tribulation worketh patience; And patience, experience; and experience, hope.
Rom. 5:3–4

Who shall separate us from the love of Christ? shall tribulation, or distress, or persecution, or famine, or nakedness, or peril, or sword?
Rom. 8:35

Let us not be weary in well doing: for in due season we shall reap.
Gal. 6:9
See also 2 Thess. 3:13

Endure hardness, as a good soldier of Jesus Christ.
2 Tim. 2:3

Let us hold fast the profession of our faith without wavering.
Heb. 10:23

Let us run with patience the race that is set before us.
Heb. 12:1

We count them happy which endure.
James 5:11

The patience of Job.
James 5:11

Hope to the end.
1 Pet. 1:13

He that overcometh shall inherit all things.
Rev. 21:7

[*See also* Determination, Diligence, Effort, Fortitude]

PERSPECTIVE

If thy right eye offend thee, pluck it out, and cast it from thee: for it is profitable for thee that one of thy members should perish, and not that thy whole body should be cast into hell.
Jesus
Matt. 5:29
See also Matt. 18:9

If a man have an hundred sheep, and one of them be gone astray, doth he not leave the ninety and nine, and goeth into the mountains, and seeketh that which is gone astray?
Jesus
Matt. 18:12
See also Luke 15:4

The last shall be first, and the first last.
Jesus
Matt. 20:16
See also Matt. 19:30, Mark 10:31

If thy foot offend thee, cut it off: it is better for thee to enter halt into life, than having two feet to be cast into hell.
Jesus
Mark 9:45
See also Matt. 18:8

Woe unto you that laugh now! for ye shall mourn and weep.
Jesus
Luke 6:25

Ye shall be sorrowful, but your sorrow shall be turned into joy.
Jesus
John 16:20

Be of good cheer; I have overcome the world.
Jesus
John 16:33

[*See also* Attitude]

PERSUASION

If they hear not Moses and the prophets, neither will they be persuaded, though one rose from the dead.
Jesus
Luke 16:31

Paul, Almost thou persuadest me to be a Christian.
Agrippa
Acts 26:28

Some believed the things which were spoken, and some believed not.
Acts 28:24

Let no man deceive you with vain words.
Eph. 5:6

For love's sake I rather beseech thee.
Philem. 9

[*See also* Eloquence, Proof]

PESSIMISM

See Despair, Hope.

PHILANTHROPY

See Charity, Generosity.

PHYSICAL FITNESS

Bodily exercise profiteth little: but godliness is profitable unto all things.
1 Tim. 4:8

[*See also* Body]

PITY

See Compassion, Mercy.

PLAGUE

Heal the sick, cleanse the lepers.
Jesus
Matt. 10:8

Pour out the vials of the wrath of God upon the earth.
Rev. 16:1

Receive not of her plagues.
(her: Babylon)
Rev. 18:4

Therefore shall her plagues come in one day, death, and mourning, and famine.
(her: Babylon)
Rev. 18:8

If any man shall add unto these things, God shall add unto him the plagues that are written in this book.
Rev. 22:18

[*See also* Healing]

PLANNING

A wise man, which built his house upon a rock.
Jesus
Matt. 7:24

A foolish man, which built his house upon the sand.
Jesus
Matt. 7:26

Which of you, intending to build a tower, sitteth not down first, and counteth the cost, whether he have sufficient to finish it?
Jesus
Luke 14:28

Let all things be done decently and in order.
1 Cor. 14:40

[*See also* Cooperation, Readiness]

PLEAS

Men, brethren, and fathers, hear ye my defence.
Paul
Acts 22:1

Maranatha.
1 Cor. 16:22

[*See also* Prayer]

PLEASURE

Let us eat and drink; for to morrow we shall die.
1 Cor. 15:32, Isa. 22:13

She that liveth in pleasure is dead while she liveth.
1 Tim. 5:6

Lovers of pleasures more than lovers of God.
2 Tim. 3:4

[*See also* Happiness, Laughter]

POSSIBILITY

If ye have faith as a grain of mustard seed, ye shall say unto this mountain, Remove hence to yonder place; and it shall remove.
Jesus
Matt. 17:20

It is easier for a camel to go through the

eye of a needle, than for a rich man to enter into the kingdom of God.
Jesus
Matt. 19:24, Mark 10:25
See also Luke 18:25

With God all things are possible.
Jesus
Matt. 19:26, Mark 10:27
See also Luke 18:27

Ye know not what ye ask.
Jesus
Matt. 20:22, Mark 10:38

If ye shall say unto this mountain, Be thou removed, and be thou cast into the sea; it shall be done.
Jesus
Matt. 21:21
See also Mark 11:23

All things are possible to him that believeth.
Jesus
Mark 9:23

With men it is impossible, but not with God.
Jesus
Mark 10:27
See also Matt. 19:26, Luke 18:27

With God nothing shall be impossible.
Luke 1:37

[*See also* Ability, God's Power, Skepticism]

POSTERITY

The promise is unto you, and to your children, and to all that are afar off.
Acts 2:39

[*See also* Heritage]

POTENTIAL

Other sheep I have, which are not of this fold.
Jesus
John 10:16

A little leaven leaveneth the whole lump.
1 Cor. 5:6, Gal. 5:9

Behold, how great a matter a little fire kindleth!
James 3:5

POVERTY

Ye have the poor always with you; but me ye have not always.
Jesus
Matt. 26:11
See also Mark 14:7, John 12:8

Having nothing, and yet possessing all things.
2 Cor. 6:10

Remember the poor.
Gal. 2:10

[*See also* Charity, Underprivileged, Wealth]

POWER

What manner of man is this, that even the winds and the sea obey Him!
Matt. 8:27
See also Mark 4:41, Luke 8:25

Whatsoever thou shalt bind on earth shall be bound in heaven.
Jesus to Peter
Matt. 16:19
See also Matt. 18:18

If ye have faith as a grain of mustard seed, ye shall say unto this mountain, Remove hence to yonder place; and it shall remove.
Jesus
Matt. 17:20

If Thou be the Son of God, come down from the cross.
Passers-by to Jesus
Matt. 27:40
See also Mark 15:30

Rejoice not, that the spirits are subject unto you; but rather rejoice, because your names are written in heaven.
Jesus
Luke 10:20

Thou couldest have no power at all against me, except it were given thee from above.
Jesus
John 19:11

Hath not the potter power over the clay?
Rom. 9:21

The kingdom of God is not in word, but in power.
1 Cor. 4:20

Of whom a man is overcome, of the same is he brought in bondage.
2 Pet. 2:19

[*See also* Authority, God's Power, Strength]

PRAISE

Out of the mouth of babes and sucklings Thou hast perfected praise.
Jesus
Matt. 21:16
See also Ps. 8:2

If I honour myself, my honour is nothing: it is my Father that honoureth me.
Jesus
John 8:54

Hosanna.
John 12:13

They loved the praise of men more than the praise of God.
John 12:43

Nor of men sought we glory, neither of you, nor yet of others.
1 Thess. 2:6

I heard as it were the voice of a great multitude, and as the voice of many waters, and as the voice of mighty thunderings.
Rev. 19:6

[*See also* Flattery]

PRAISE OF GOD

Glory to God in the highest, and on earth peace, good will toward men.
Luke 2:14

Praise the Lord.
E.g., Rom. 15:11

Unto God and our Father be glory for ever.
Phil. 4:20

Who shall not fear Thee, O Lord, and glorify Thy name?
Rev. 15:4

Alleluia: for the Lord God omnipotent reigneth.
Rev. 19:6

Let us be glad and rejoice, and give honour to Him.
Rev. 19:7

[*See also* Gratitude, Testimony]

PRAYER

They love to pray standing in the synagogues and in the corners of the streets, that they may be seen of men.
Jesus (They: hypocrites)
Matt. 6:5

When thou prayest, enter into thy closet.
Jesus
Matt. 6:6

Use not vain repetitions, as the heathen do.
Jesus
Matt. 6:7

They think that they shall be heard for their much speaking.
Jesus (They: heathens praying)
Matt. 6:7

Your Father knoweth what things ye have need of, before ye ask Him.
Jesus
Matt. 6:8

Our Father which art in heaven, Hallowed be Thy name. Thy kingdom come. Thy will be done in earth, as it is in heaven.
Jesus
Matt. 6:9–10
See also Luke 11:2

Ask, and it shall be given you; seek, and ye shall find; knock, and it shall be opened unto you.
Jesus
Matt. 7:7, Luke 11:9

Every one that asketh receiveth.
Jesus
Matt. 7:8, Luke 11:10

If ye then, being evil, know how to give good gifts unto your children, how much more shall your Father which is in heaven give good things to them that ask Him?
Jesus
Matt. 7:11
See also Luke 11:13

Where two or three are gathered together in my name, there am I in the midst of them.
Jesus
Matt. 18:20

Whatsoever ye shall ask in prayer, believing, ye shall receive.
Jesus
Matt. 21:22
See also Mark 11:24

When ye stand praying, forgive, if ye have ought against any: that your Father also which is in heaven may forgive you your trespasses.
Jesus
Mark 11:25

Take ye heed, watch and pray: for ye know not when the time is.
Jesus
Mark 13:33
See also Matt. 13:23

Not what I will, but what Thou wilt.
Jesus
Mark 14:36
See also Matt. 26:39, Luke 22:42

Men ought always to pray.
Luke 18:1

Watch ye therefore, and pray always.
Jesus
Luke 21:36

Whatsoever ye shall ask in my name, that will I do, that the Father may be glorified in the Son.
Jesus
John 14:13
See also John 14:14

Whatsoever ye shall ask the Father in my name, He will give it you.
Jesus
John 16:23

Ask, and ye shall receive, that your joy may be full.
Jesus
John 16:24

Whosoever shall call on the name of the Lord shall be saved.
E.g., Acts 2:21
See also Joel 2:32

Lord Jesus, receive my spirit.
Stephen
Acts 7:59

The same Lord over all is rich unto all that call upon Him.
Rom. 10:12

If I pray in an unknown tongue, my spirit prayeth, but my understanding is unfruitful.
1 Cor. 14:14

By prayer and supplication with thanksgiving let your requests be made known unto God.
Phil. 4:6

Pray without ceasing.
1 Thess. 5:17

Pray every where, lifting up holy hands, without wrath and doubting.
1 Tim. 2:8

Ask in faith, nothing wavering.
James 1:6

Ye fight and war, yet ye have not, because ye ask not.
James 4:2

Ye ask, and receive not, because ye ask amiss.
James 4:3

The prayer of faith shall save the sick.
James 5:15

Pray one for another, that ye may be healed.
James 5:16

The effectual fervent prayer of a righteous man availeth much.
James 5:16

The eyes of the Lord are over the righteous, and His ears are open unto their prayers.
1 Pet. 3:12

Whatsoever we ask, we receive of Him, because we keep His commandments.
1 John 3:22

[*See also* Worship and the Appendix at p. 201]

PREACHING

I am not come to call the righteous, but sinners to repentance.
> *Jesus*
> *Matt. 9:13*
> *See also Mark 2:17, Luke 5:32*

Preach ye upon the housetops.
> *Jesus*
> *Matt. 10:27*
> *See also Luke 12:3*

Who hath ears to hear, let him hear.
> *Jesus*
> *Matt. 13:9, Matt. 13:43*
> *See also, e.g., Matt. 11:15, Mark 4:9, Rev. 13:9*

Hear, O Israel; The Lord our God is one Lord.
> *Jesus*
> *Mark 12:29*
> *See also, e.g., Deut. 6:4*

He hath anointed me to preach the gospel to the poor.
> *Jesus*
> *Luke 4:18*
> *See also Isa. 61:1*

He whom God hath sent speaketh the words of God.
> *John 3:34*

Ye that fear God, give audience.
> *Acts 13:16*

From henceforth I will go unto the Gentiles.
> *Acts 18:6*

Be not afraid, but speak, and hold not thy peace: For I am with thee.
> *Jesus to Paul*
> *Acts 18:9–10*

How shall they hear without a preacher?
> *Rom. 10:14*

How beautiful are the feet of them that preach the gospel of peace.
> *Rom. 10:15*

Faith cometh by hearing, and hearing by the word of God.
> *Rom. 10:17*

We preach Christ crucified.
> *1 Cor. 1:23*

Woe is unto me, if I preach not the gospel!
> *1 Cor. 9:16*

We preach not ourselves, but Christ Jesus the Lord.
> *2 Cor. 4:5*

We are ambassadors for Christ.
> *2 Cor. 5:20*

If any man preach any other gospel unto you than that ye have received, let him be accursed.
> *Gal. 1:9*

Give attendance to reading, to exhortation, to doctrine.
> *1 Tim. 4:13*

Fight the good fight of faith.
> *1 Tim. 6:12*

Preach the word.
> *2 Tim. 4:2*

If any man speak, let him speak as the oracles of God.
> *1 Pet. 4:11*

He that hath an ear, let him hear what the Spirit saith unto the churches.
> *Jesus*
> *E.g., Rev. 2:7*

[*See also* Communication, Evangelism, God's Word, Ministry, Speech, Testimony]

PREDICTIONS

See Future, Prophecy.

PREJUDICE

See Brotherhood, Equality.

PREPAREDNESS

See Readiness, Second Coming, Vigilance.

PRIDE

Whosoever shall exalt himself shall be abased; and he that shall humble himself shall be exalted.
Jesus
Matt. 23:12
See also Luke 14:11

If I honour myself, my honour is nothing.
Jesus
John 8:54

God resisteth the proud, and giveth grace to the humble.
1 Pet. 5:5

[*See also* Arrogance, Boasting, Conceit, Confidence, Humility]

PRINCIPLES

See Integrity.

PRIORITIES

See Goals, Values.

PRISON

See Imprisonment, Persecution.

PROCRASTINATION

Exhort one another daily, while it is called To day.
Heb. 3:13

PROFANITY

Put off all these; anger, wrath, malice, blasphemy, filthy communication out of your mouth.
Col. 3:8

[*See also* Blasphemy]

PROFIT

Godliness is profitable unto all things.
1 Tim. 4:8

[*See also* Loss, Reward, Values, Wealth]

PROGRESS

See Success.

PROMISES

Whatsoever thou shalt ask of me, I will give it thee, unto the half of my kingdom.
Herod to his daughter
Mark 6:23

If ye shall ask any thing in my name, I will do it.
Jesus
John 14:14

The Lord is not slack concerning His promise.
2 Pet. 3:9

[*See also* Covenant, Oaths]

PROOF

An evil and adulterous generation seeketh after a sign; and there shall no sign be given to it, but the sign of the prophet Jonas.
Jesus
Matt. 12:39
See also Matt. 16:4, Mark 8:12,
Luke 11:29

Why doth this generation seek after a sign?
Jesus about Pharisees
Mark 8:12

Physician, heal thyself.
Luke 4:23

If they hear not Moses and the prophets, neither will they be persuaded, though one rose from the dead.
Jesus
Luke 16:31

Search the scriptures.
Jesus
John 5:39

Whether He be a sinner or no, I know not: one thing I know, that, whereas I was blind, now I see.
John 9:25

Though ye believe not me, believe the works.
Jesus
John 10:38

Reach hither thy hand, and thrust it into my side: and be not faithless, but believing.
Jesus
John 20:27

Him God raised up the third day, and showed Him openly; Not to all the people, but unto witnesses chosen before of God.
Acts 10:40–41

God is my witness.
Rom. 1:9

The Jews require a sign, and the Greeks seek after wisdom.
1 Cor. 1:22

Prove all things; hold fast that which is good.
1 Thess. 5:21

Where a testament is, there must also of necessity be the death of the testator.
Heb. 9:16

[*See also* Doubt, Testimony]

PROPERTY

See Materialism, Wealth.

PROPHECY

The voice of one crying in the wilderness.
Matt. 3:3, Mark 1:3, Luke 3:4,
John 1:23
See also Isa. 40:3

A prophet is not without honour, save in his own country, and in his own house.
Jesus
Matt. 13:57
See also Mark 6:4, Luke 4:24,
John 4:44

Behold, I have foretold you all things.
Jesus
Mark 13:23

O fools, and slow of heart to believe all that the prophets have spoken.
Jesus
Luke 24:25

Well spake the Holy Ghost by Esaias the prophet unto our fathers.
Acts 28:25

Greater is he that prophesieth than he that speaketh with tongues.
1 Cor. 14:5

Prophesying serveth not for them that believe not, but for them which believe.
1 Cor. 14:22

Despise not prophesyings.
1 Thess. 5:20

No prophecy of the Scripture is of any private interpretation.
2 Pet. 1:20

Blessed is he that readeth, and they that hear the words of this prophecy.
Rev. 1:3

What thou seest, write in a book, and send it unto the seven churches.
Jesus
Rev. 1:11

Write the things which thou hast seen, and the things which are, and the things which shall be hereafter.
Jesus
Rev. 1:19

If any man have an ear, let him hear.
E.g., Rev. 13:9

The testimony of Jesus is the spirit of prophecy.
Rev. 19:10

Blessed is he that keepeth the sayings of the prophecy of this book.
Rev. 22:7

If any man shall add unto these things, God shall add unto him the plagues that are written in this book.
Rev. 22:18

If any man shall take away from the words of the book of this prophecy, God shall take away his part out of the book of life.
Rev. 22:19

[*See also* False Prophets, Future, Messiah, Messianic Hopes and Prophecies, Scripture]

PROSELYTIZATION

See Evangelism.

PROSPERITY

See Adversity, Reward, Success, Wealth.

PROSTITUTION

See Adultery, Carnality, Fornication, Immorality, Sin.

PROTECTION

See Deliverance, God's Protection, Safety, Vigilance.

PROVOCATION

See Instigation.

PRUDENCE

Let him that thinketh he standeth take heed lest he fall.
1 Cor. 10:12

[*See also* Rashness, Warning]

PUBLIC OPINION

They feared the people, lest they should have been stoned.
(They: apostles)
Acts 5:26

[*See also* Mobs]

PUBLICITY

A city that is set on an hill cannot be hid.
Jesus
Matt. 5:14

Neither do men light a candle, and put it under a bushel, but on a candlestick.
Jesus
Matt. 5:15
See also Mark 4:21, Luke 11:33

Let your light so shine before men, that they may see your good works.
Jesus
Matt. 5:16

He that doeth truth cometh to the light, that his deeds may be made manifest.
Jesus
John 3:21

PUNISHMENT

It shall be more tolerable for the land of Sodom in the day of judgment, than for thee.
Jesus
Matt. 11:24
See also Luke 10:14

Let him die the death.
Jesus
Matt. 15:4
See also, e.g., Ex. 20:12

God sent not His Son into the world to condemn the world; but that the world through Him might be saved.
Jesus
John 3:17

As many as have sinned without law shall also perish without law.
Rom. 2:12

If thou do that which is evil, be afraid; for he beareth not the sword in vain.
(he: civil authorities)
Rom. 13:4

The Lord reward him according to his works.
2 Tim. 4:14

It is a fearful thing to fall into the hands of the living God.
Heb. 10:31

God spared not the angels that sinned, but cast them down to hell.
2 Pet. 2:4

Behold, the Lord cometh with ten thousands of His saints, To execute judgment upon all.
Jude 14–15

The time is come for Thee to reap; for the harvest of the earth is ripe.
Rev. 14:15

True and righteous are Thy judgments.
Rev. 16:7
See also Rev. 19:2

Great Babylon came in remembrance before God.
Rev. 16:19

How much she hath glorified herself, and lived deliciously, so much torment and sorrow give her.
(she: Babylon)
Rev. 18:7

Strong is the Lord God who judgeth her.
(her: Babylon)
Rev. 18:8

The lake of fire and brimstone.
Rev. 20:10

If any man shall add unto these things, God shall add unto him the plagues that are written in this book.
Rev. 22:18

If any man shall take away from the words of the book of this prophecy, God shall take away his part out of the book of life.
Rev. 22:19

[See also Discipline, Forgiveness, God's Anger, Judgment, Plague, Retribution, Revenge, Reward, Sin]

PURITY

Blessed are the pure in heart: for they shall see God.
Jesus
Matt. 5:8

Not that which goeth into the mouth defileth a man; but that which cometh out of the mouth, this defileth a man.
Jesus
Matt. 15:11
See also Mark 7:15

To eat with unwashen hands defileth not a man.
Jesus
Matt. 15:20

If thy foot offend thee, cut it off: it is better for thee to enter halt into life, than having two feet to be cast into hell.
Jesus
Mark 9:45
See also Matt. 18:8

Now ye are clean through the word which I have spoken unto you.
Jesus
John 15:3

What God hath cleansed, that call not thou common.
Acts 10:15, Acts 11:9

There is nothing unclean of itself: but to him that esteemeth any thing to be unclean, to him it is unclean.
Rom. 14:14

The temple of God is holy, which temple ye are.
1 Cor. 3:17

Glorify God in your body, and in your spirit.
1 Cor. 6:20

God hath not called us unto uncleanness, but unto holiness.
1 Thess. 4:7

Keep thyself pure.
1 Tim. 5:22

Cleanse your hands, ye sinners; and purify your hearts, ye double minded.
James 4:8

They shall walk with me in white: for they are worthy.
Jesus
Rev. 3:4

[See also Contamination, Corruption, Evil]

PURPOSE

The thief cometh not, but for to steal, and to kill, and to destroy.
Jesus
John 10:10

Do all to the glory of God.
1 Cor. 10:31

What advantageth it me, if the dead rise not?

1 Cor. 15:32

[*See also* Duty, Goals, Intentions, Mission]

QUALITY

Every good tree bringeth forth good fruit; but a corrupt tree bringeth forth evil fruit.

Jesus
Matt. 7:17
See also Luke 6:43

No man also having drunk old wine straightway desireth new.

Jesus
Luke 5:39

Of thorns men do not gather figs, nor of a bramble bush gather they grapes.

Jesus
Luke 6:44

[*See also* Perfection, Purity, Value]

QUANTITY

My name is Legion: for we are many.

Mark 5:9

Behold, how great a matter a little fire kindleth!

James 3:5

[*See also* Infinity, Size]

QUESTIONING

See Authority, Doctrine, Skepticism.

QUOTATIONS

This is a faithful saying and worthy of all acceptation.

1 Tim. 4:9

[*See also* Speech]

RAIN

He maketh His sun to rise on the evil and on the good, and sendeth rain on the just and on the unjust.

Jesus
Matt. 5:45

He left not Himself without witness, in that He did good, and gave us rain from heaven.

Acts 14:17

RASHNESS

Whatsoever thou shalt ask of me, I will give it thee, unto the half of my kingdom.

Herod to his daughter
Mark 6:23

READINESS

Prepare ye the way of the Lord, make His paths straight.

Matt. 3:3, Mark 1:3, Luke 3:4
See also Isa. 40:3

This is he, of whom it is written, Behold, I send my messenger before Thy face, which shall prepare Thy way before Thee.

Jesus (he: John the Baptist)
Matt. 11:10, Luke 7:27
See also Mal. 3:1

Elias is come already, and they knew him not.

Jesus
Matt. 17:12

Every valley shall be filled, and every mountain and hill shall be brought low.

Luke 3:5
See also Isa. 40:4

Be ye therefore ready also: for the Son of man cometh at an hour when ye think not.

Jesus
Luke 12:40
See also Matt. 24:44

I am the voice of one crying in the wilderness, Make straight the way of the Lord.
John the Baptist
John 1:23
See also Matt. 3:3, Mark 1:3,
  Luke 3:4

Lift up your eyes, and look on the fields; for they are white already to harvest.
Jesus
John 4:35

Be instant in season, out of season.
2 Tim. 4:2

Gird up the loins of your mind.
1 Pet. 1:13

[*See also* Vigilance]

REBELLION

Whosoever therefore resisteth the power, resisteth the ordinance of God.
Rom. 13:2

They that resist shall receive to themselves damnation.
Rom. 13:2

[*See also* Disobedience, Godlessness, Government, Strife]

REBIRTH

See Born Again, Jesus (Acceptance of).

RECIPROCITY

An eye for an eye, and a tooth for a tooth.
Jesus
Matt. 5:38
See also, e.g., Ex. 21:24

All things whatsoever ye would that men should do to you, do ye even so to them.
Jesus
Matt. 7:12
See also Luke 6:31

He shall have judgment without mercy, that hath showed no mercy.
James 2:13

[*See also* Consequences, Retribution]

REDEMPTION

Behold the Lamb of God, which taketh away the sin of the world.
John the Baptist
John 1:29

The bread that I will give is my flesh, which I will give for the life of the world.
Jesus
John 6:51

Sin shall not have dominion over you: for ye are not under the law, but under grace.
Rom. 6:14

Christ hath redeemed us from the curse of the law.
Gal. 3:13

Thou art no more a servant, but a son.
Gal. 4:7

We have redemption through His blood, even the forgiveness of sins.
Col. 1:14

The blood of Jesus Christ His Son cleanseth us from all sin.
1 John 1:7

[*See also* Kingdom of God, Salvation]

REFUGE

See Safety.

REGRET

There shall be weeping and gnashing of teeth.
Jesus
E.g., Matt. 24:51

He found no place of repentance, though he sought it carefully with tears.
(He: Esau)
Heb. 12:17

REHABILITATION

Put on the new man.
Eph. 4:24

Let him that stole steal no more: but

rather let him labour, working with his hands.
Eph. 4:28

He which converteth the sinner from the error of his way shall save a soul from death.
James 5:20

[*See also* Renewal]

REJECTION

He that despiseth you despiseth me; and he that despiseth me despiseth Him that sent me.
Jesus
Luke 10:16

He that denieth me before men shall be denied before the angels of God.
Jesus
Luke 12:9
See also Matt. 10:33

Depart from me, all ye workers of iniquity.
Jesus
Luke 13:27
See also Matt. 7:23

He came unto His own, and His own received Him not.
John 1:11

Whom He hath sent, Him ye believe not.
Jesus
John 5:38

I am come in my Father's name, and ye receive me not.
Jesus
John 5:43

Hath God cast away His people? God forbid.
Rom. 11:1

[*See also* Abandonment]

RELIANCE

Without me ye can do nothing.
Jesus
John 15:5

Our sufficiency is of God.
2 Cor. 3:5

[*See also* God's Protection, God's Support, Trust]

REMEMBRANCE

This is my body, which is broken for you: this do in remembrance of me.
Jesus
1 Cor. 11:24
See also Luke 22:19

This cup is the new testament in my blood: this do ye, as oft as ye drink it, in remembrance of me.
Jesus
1 Cor. 11:25
See also Luke 22:20

[*See also* Abandonment, History]

RENEWAL

Old things are passed away; behold, all things are become new.
2 Cor. 5:17

Be renewed in the spirit of your mind.
Eph. 4:23

Ye were as sheep going astray; but are now returned unto the Shepherd.
1 Pet. 2:25

I saw a new heaven and a new earth: for the first heaven and the first earth were passed away.
Rev. 21:1

Behold, I make all things new.
Rev. 21:5

[*See also* Born Again, Rehabilitation]

REPENTANCE

Repent, for the kingdom of heaven is at hand.
Jesus
Matt. 4:17
See also Matt. 3:2, Matt. 10:7,
Mark 1:15

I am not come to call the righteous, but sinners to repentance.
Jesus
Matt. 9:13
See also Mark 2:17, Luke 5:32

Bring forth therefore fruits worthy of repentance.
Luke 3:8

Except ye repent, ye shall all likewise perish.
Jesus
Luke 13:3

Rejoice with me; for I have found my sheep which was lost.
Jesus
Luke 15:6

Joy shall be in heaven over one sinner that repenteth, more than over ninety and nine just persons, which need no repentance.
Jesus
Luke 15:7

There is joy in the presence of the angels of God over one sinner that repenteth.
Jesus
Luke 15:10

When thou art converted, strengthen thy brethren.
Jesus
Luke 22:32

Repentance and remission of sins should be preached in His name among all nations.
Jesus
Luke 24:47

Repent, and be baptized every one of you in the name of Jesus Christ.
Acts 2:38

Repent ye therefore, and be converted, that your sins may be blotted out.
Acts 3:19

Pray God, if perhaps the thought of thine heart may be forgiven thee.
Acts 8:22

The baptism of repentance.
Acts 13:24

The goodness of God leadeth thee to repentance.
Rom. 2:4

He found no place of repentance, though he sought it carefully with tears.
(He: Esau)
Heb. 12:17

Cleanse your hands, ye sinners; and purify your hearts, ye double minded.
James 4:8

Remember therefore from whence thou art fallen, and repent.
Jesus
Rev. 2:5

Repent; or else I will come unto thee quickly.
Jesus
Rev. 2:16

[*See also* Forgiveness, Punishment, Rehabilitation, Sin]

REPRESENTATIVES

See Spokesmen, Status.

REPUTATION

A prophet is not without honour, save in his own country, and in his own house.
Jesus
Matt. 13:57
See also Mark 6:4, Luke 4:24

Woe unto you, when all men shall speak well of you!
Jesus
Luke 6:26

A prophet hath no honour in his own country.
John 4:44

Ye know that our record is true.
3 John 12

[*See also* Achievement, Fame, Shame]

RESCUE

See Assistance, Danger, Deliverance.

RESPECT

A prophet is not without honour, save in his own country, and in his own house.
Jesus
Matt. 13:57
See also Mark 6:4, Luke 4:24

A prophet hath no honour in his own country.
John 4:44

If I honour myself, my honour is nothing: it is my Father that honoureth me.
Jesus
John 8:54

God hath showed me that I should not call any man common or unclean.
Acts 10:28

Thou shalt not speak evil of the ruler of thy people.
Acts 23:5
See also Ex. 22:28

Tribute to whom tribute is due; custom to whom custom; fear to whom fear; honour to whom honour.
Rom. 13:7

Walk honestly toward them that are without.
1 Thess. 4:12

Rebuke not an elder, but intreat him as a father.
1 Tim. 5:1

He who hath builded the house hath more honour than the house.
Heb. 3:3

Honour all men.
1 Pet. 2:17

Fear God. Honour the king.
1 Pet. 2:17

Submit yourselves unto the elder.
1 Pet. 5:5

[*See also* Homage]

RESPONSIBILITY

Let the dead bury their dead.
Jesus
Matt. 8:22, Luke 9:60

Every idle word that men shall speak, they shall give account thereof in the day of judgment.
Jesus
Matt. 12:36

He took water, and washed his hands.
(He: Pilate)
Matt. 27:24

His blood be on us, and on our children.
Crowd to Pilate
Matt. 27:25

Unto whomsoever much is given, of him shall be much required.
Jesus
Luke 12:48

He that is faithful in that which is least is faithful also in much.
Jesus
Luke 16:10

Father, forgive them; for they know not what they do.
Jesus
Luke 23:34

The hireling fleeth, because he is an hireling, and careth not for the sheep.
Jesus
John 10:13

Take ye Him, and judge Him according to your law.
John 18:31

Take ye Him, and crucify Him: for I find no fault in Him.
Pilate
John 19:6
See also Luke 23:4

Feed my lambs.
Jesus
John 21:15

Feed my sheep.
Jesus
John 21:16, 17

Lord, lay not this sin to their charge.
Stephen, dying
Acts 7:60

Do thyself no harm: for we are all here.
Acts 16:28

Look ye to it; for I will be no judge of such matters.
Acts 18:15

It is no more I that do it, but sin that dwelleth in me.
Rom. 7:17, 20

Every one of us shall give account of himself to God.
Rom. 14:12

When I became a man, I put away childish things.
1 Cor. 13:11

Bear ye one another's burdens.
Gal. 6:2

Every man shall bear his own burden.
Gal. 6:5

If he hath wronged thee, or oweth thee ought, put that on mine account.
Philem. 18

[*See also* Blame, Burdens, Duty, Guilt]

RESTRAINT

Unto him that smiteth thee on the one cheek offer also the other.
Jesus
Luke 6:29
See also Matt. 5:39

Hast thou faith? have it to thyself before God.
Rom. 14:22

[*See also* Anger, Forgiveness, Patience, Prudence, Revenge, Temptation]

RESURRECTION

The third day He shall rise again.
Jesus
Matt. 20:19, Mark 10:34,
Luke 18:33

God is not the God of the dead, but of the living.
Jesus
Matt. 22:32
See also Mark 12:27, Luke 20:38

He is risen.
Matt. 28:6, Mark 16:6

After that He is killed, He shall rise the third day.
Jesus
Mark 9:31
See also Matt. 17:23

They shall mock Him, and shall scourge Him, and shall spit upon Him, and shall kill Him: and the third day He shall rise again.
Jesus
Mark 10:34
See also Luke 18:33

They are equal unto the angels; and are the children of God.
Jesus
Luke 20:36

Why seek ye the living among the dead?
Luke 24:5

Destroy this temple, and in three days I will raise it up.
Jesus
John 2:19

The hour is coming, in the which all that are in the graves shall hear His voice.
Jesus
John 5:28

They that have done good, unto the resurrection of life; and they that have done evil, unto the resurrection of damnation.
Jesus
John 5:29

Thy brother shall rise again.
Jesus, about Lazarus
John 11:23

I am the resurrection, and the life.
Jesus
John 11:25

Lazarus, come forth.
Jesus
John 11:43

His soul was not left in hell, neither His flesh did see corruption.
Acts 2:31

Him God raised up the third day, and

showed Him openly; Not to all the people, but unto witnesses chosen before of God.
Acts 10:40–41

God raised Him from the dead.
Acts 13:30
See also Acts 17:31

I will give you the sure mercies of David.
Acts 13:34
See also Isa. 55:3

Why should it be thought a thing incredible with you, that God should raise the dead?
Acts 26:8

Who was delivered for our offences, and was raised again for our justification.
Rom. 4:25

If thou shalt confess with thy mouth the Lord Jesus, and shalt believe in thine heart that God hath raised Him from the dead, thou shalt be saved.
Rom. 10:9

If Christ be not raised, your faith is vain; ye are yet in your sins.
1 Cor. 15:17

If in this life only we have hope in Christ, we are of all men most miserable.
1 Cor. 15:19

As in Adam all die, even so in Christ shall all be made alive.
1 Cor. 15:22

The last enemy that shall be destroyed is death.
1 Cor. 15:26

What advantageth it me, if the dead rise not?
1 Cor. 15:32

Death is swallowed up in victory.
1 Cor. 15:54

When Christ, who is our life, shall appear, then shall ye also appear with Him in glory.
Col. 3:4

The dead in Christ shall rise first.
1 Thess. 4:16

Remember that Jesus Christ of the seed of David was raised from the dead.
2 Tim. 2:8

I am He that liveth, and was dead.
Jesus
Rev. 1:18

I am alive for evermore.
Jesus
Rev. 1:18

I saw the souls of them that were beheaded for the witness of Jesus, and for the word of God.
Rev. 20:4

Blessed and holy is he that hath part in the first resurrection: on such the second death hath no power.
Rev. 20:6

I saw the dead, small and great, stand before God.
Rev. 20:12

Death and hell delivered up the dead which were in them: and they were judged every man according to their works.
Rev. 20:13

[*See also* Christ Eternal, Eternal Life]

RETRIBUTION

He that killeth with the sword must be killed with the sword.
Rev. 13:10

Reward her even as she rewarded you, and double unto her double according to her works.
(her: Babylon)
Rev. 18:6

Out of His mouth goeth a sharp sword, that with it He should smite the nations.
Rev. 19:15

[*See also* Forgiveness, God's Anger, Judgment, Punishment, Revenge]

REVELATION

No man knoweth the Son, but the Father; neither knoweth any man the Father, save

the Son, and he to whomsoever the Son will reveal Him.
Jesus
Matt. 11:27
See also Luke 10:22

Flesh and blood hath not revealed it unto thee, but my Father which is in heaven.
Jesus
Matt. 16:17

I that speak unto thee am He.
Jesus
John 4:26

I speak to the world those things which I have heard of Him.
Jesus
John 8:26

I have not spoken of myself; but the Father which sent me.
Jesus
John 12:49
See also John 14:10

He that hath seen me hath seen the Father.
Jesus
John 14:9

All things that I have heard of my Father I have made known unto you.
Jesus
John 15:15

I have appeared unto thee for this purpose, to make thee a minister and a witness.
Jesus to Saul
Acts 26:16

REVENGE

Whosoever shall smite thee on thy right cheek, turn to him the other also.
Jesus
Matt. 5:39

Give me here John Baptist's head.
Matt. 14:8
See also Mark 6:25

Unto him that smiteth thee on the one cheek offer also the other.
Jesus
Luke 6:29

The Son of man is not come to destroy men's lives, but to save them.
Jesus
Luke 9:56

Recompense to no man evil for evil.
Rom. 12:17

Avenge not yourselves.
Rom. 12:19

Vengeance is Mine; I will repay, saith the Lord.
Rom. 12:19

Be not overcome of evil, but overcome evil with good.
Rom. 12:21

See that none render evil for evil unto any man.
1 Thess. 5:15

In flaming fire taking vengeance on them that know not God, and that obey not the gospel.
2 Thess. 1:8

Vengeance belongeth unto Me, I will recompense, saith the Lord.
Heb. 10:30

The great winepress of the wrath of God.
Rev. 14:19

They have shed the blood of saints and prophets, and Thou hast given them blood to drink.
Rev. 16:6

Rejoice over her, thou heaven, and ye holy apostles and prophets; for God hath avenged you on her.
(her: Babylon)
Rev. 18:20

[See also Enemies, Forgiveness, Punishment, Restraint, Retribution]

REVERENCE

Every tongue should confess that Jesus Christ is Lord.
Phil. 2:11

Fear God, and give glory to Him; for the hour of His judgment is come.
Rev. 14:7

Who shall not fear Thee, O Lord, and glorify Thy name?
Rev. 15:4

[*See also* Awe, Fear of God]

REVERSAL

The stone which the builders rejected is become the head of the corner.
Jesus
Mark 12:10
See also Ps. 118:22, Matt. 21:42,
  Luke 20:17

He that is least among you all, the same shall be great.
Jesus
Luke 9:48

The elder shall serve the younger.
Rom. 9:12, Gen. 25:23

Babylon the great is fallen, is fallen, and is become the habitation of devils.
Rev. 18:2

REVOLUTION

See Rebellion, Strife.

REWARD

Blessed are the meek: for they shall inherit the earth.
Jesus
Matt. 5:5
See also Ps. 37:11

Great is your reward in heaven.
Jesus
Matt. 5:12

Thy Father which seeth in secret shall reward thee openly.
Jesus
Matt. 6:6, Matt. 6:18

Every one that asketh receiveth.
Jesus
Matt. 7:8, Luke 11:10

According to your faith be it unto you.
Jesus
Matt. 9:29

Freely ye have received, freely give.
Jesus
Matt. 10:8

He shall reward every man according to his works.
Jesus
Matt. 16:27
See also Ps. 62:12

To sit on my right hand, and on my left, is not mine to give, but it shall be given to them for whom it is prepared of my Father.
Jesus
Matt. 20:23
See also Mark 10:40

He that hath, to him shall be given: and he that hath not, from him shall be taken even that which he hath.
Jesus
Mark 4:25
See also Matt. 13:12, Matt. 25:29,
  Luke 8:18, Luke 19:26

Seek ye the kingdom of God; and all these things shall be added unto you.
Jesus
Luke 12:31
See also Matt. 6:33

When thou makest a feast, call the poor, the maimed, the lame, the blind: And thou shalt be blessed; for they cannot recompense thee.
Jesus
Luke 14:13–14

Thou shalt be recompensed at the resurrection of the just.
Jesus
Luke 14:14

A man can receive nothing, except it be given him from heaven.
John 3:27

He that reapeth receiveth wages, and gathereth fruit unto life eternal.
Jesus
John 4:36

If any man serve me, him will my Father honour.
Jesus
John 12:26

Glory, honour, and peace, to every man that worketh good.
Rom. 2:10

The wages of sin is death; but the gift of

God is eternal life through Jesus Christ our Lord.
Rom. 6:23

All things work together for good to them that love God.
Rom. 8:28

Every man shall receive his own reward according to his own labour.
1 Cor. 3:8

He which soweth bountifully shall reap also bountifully.
2 Cor. 9:6

Whatsoever a man soweth, that shall he also reap.
Gal. 6:7

He that soweth to the Spirit shall of the Spirit reap life everlasting.
Gal. 6:8

In due season we shall reap.
Gal. 6:9

Whatsoever good thing any man doeth, the same shall he receive of the Lord.
Eph. 6:8

Of the Lord ye shall receive the reward of the inheritance.
Col. 3:24

The husbandman that laboureth must be first partaker of the fruits.
2 Tim. 2:6

There is laid up for me a crown of righteousness, which the Lord, the righteous judge, shall give me at that day.
2 Tim. 4:8

Ye have need of patience, that, after ye have done the will of God, ye might receive the promise.
Heb. 10:36

When the chief Shepherd shall appear, ye shall receive a crown of glory that fadeth not away.
1 Pet. 5:4

To him that overcometh will I give to eat of the hidden manna.
Jesus
Rev. 2:17

And I will give him the morning star.
Jesus
Rev. 2:28

They shall walk with me in white: for they are worthy.
Jesus
Rev. 3:4

Him that overcometh will I make a pillar in the temple of my God.
Jesus
Rev. 3:12

[*See also* Blessing, Eternal Life, Profit, Punishment, Success, Victory, Wealth]

RIGHTEOUSNESS

It becometh us to fulfil all righteousness.
Jesus
Matt. 3:15

Blessed are they which do hunger and thirst after righteousness: for they shall be filled.
Jesus
Matt. 5:6
See also Luke 6:21

Blessed are they which are persecuted for righteousness' sake: for their's is the kingdom of heaven.
Jesus
Matt. 5:10

He that receiveth a righteous man in the name of a righteous man shall receive a righteous man's reward.
Jesus
Matt. 10:41

If ye were Abraham's children, ye would do the works of Abraham.
Jesus
John 8:39

Thy heart is not right in the sight of God.
Acts 8:21

The just shall live by faith.
E.g., Rom. 1:17
See also Hab. 2:4

There is none righteous, no, not one.
Rom. 3:10
See also Ps. 14:3, Ps. 53:3

The unrighteous shall not inherit the kingdom of God.
1 Cor. 6:9

If righteousness come by the law, then Christ is dead in vain.
>   *Gal. 2:21*

Ever follow that which is good.
>   *1 Thess. 5:15*

Be not weary in well doing.
>   *2 Thess. 3:13*
>   *See also Gal. 6:9*

Flee also youthful lusts: but follow righteousness, faith, charity, peace.
>   *2 Tim. 2:22*

A sceptre of righteousness is the sceptre of Thy kingdom.
>   *Heb. 1:8*

The fruit of righteousness is sown in peace of them that make peace.
>   *James 3:18*

If ye suffer for righteousness' sake, happy are ye.
>   *1 Pet. 3:14*

Every one that doeth righteousness is born of Him.
>   *1 John 2:29*

Little children, let no man deceive you: he that doeth righteousness is righteous.
>   *1 John 3:7*

All unrighteousness is sin.
>   *1 John 5:17*

They shall walk with me in white: for they are worthy.
>   *Jesus*
>   *Rev. 3:4*

In their mouth was found no guile: for they are without fault before the throne of God.
>   *Rev. 14:5*

Just and true are Thy ways, Thou King of saints.
>   *Rev. 15:3*

Behold a white horse; and he that sat upon him was called Faithful and True.
>   *Rev. 19:11*

[*See also* Evil, Goodness, Integrity, Justice, Self-Righteousness, Sin, Virtue, Wickedness]

RISK

Why stand we in jeopardy every hour?
>   *1 Cor. 15:30*

RITUALS

I will have mercy, and not sacrifice.
>   *Jesus*
>   *Matt. 9:13*
>   *See also Hos. 6:6*

To eat with unwashen hands defileth not a man.
>   *Jesus*
>   *Matt. 15:20*

This people honoureth me with their lips, but their heart is far from me.
>   *Jesus*
>   *Mark 7:6*
>   *See also Matt. 15:8*

He is not a Jew, which is one outwardly.
>   *Rom. 2:28*

He that eateth, eateth to the Lord, for he giveth God thanks.
>   *Rom. 14:6*

The kingdom of God is not meat and drink; but righteousness, and peace, and joy in the Holy Ghost.
>   *Rom. 14:17*

Circumcision is nothing, and uncircumcision is nothing, but the keeping of the commandments of God.
>   *1 Cor. 7:19*

The things which the Gentiles sacrifice, they sacrifice to devils, and not to God.
>   *1 Cor. 10:20*

It is not possible that the blood of bulls and of goats should take away sins.
>   *Heb. 10:4*

[*See also* Circumcision, Sacrifices]

ROBBERY

Thou shalt not steal.
>   *Jesus*
>   *Matt. 19:18*
>   *See also, e.g., Ex. 20:15, Mark 10:19, Luke 18:20*

[See also Crime]

See Love.

SABBATH

The Son of man is Lord even of the sabbath day.
Jesus
Matt. 12:8
See also Mark 2:28, Luke 6:5

It is lawful to do well on the sabbath days.
Jesus
Matt. 12:12
See also Mark 3:4, Luke 6:5

The sabbath was made for man, and not man for the sabbath.
Jesus
Mark 2:27

He that regardeth the day, regardeth it unto the Lord.
Rom. 14:6

SACRIFICE

He that loseth his life for my sake shall find it.
Jesus
Matt. 10:39

Whosoever will save his life shall lose it: and whosoever will lose his life for my sake shall find it.
Jesus
Matt. 16:25
See also Mark 8:35, Luke 9:24

The Son of man came not to be ministered unto, but to minister, and to give His life a ransom for many.
Jesus
Matt. 20:28, Mark 10:45

For God so loved the world, that He gave His only begotten Son, that whosoever believeth in Him should not perish, but have everlasting life.
Jesus
John 3:16
See also John 3:36, John 6:47

The bread that I will give is my flesh, which I will give for the life of the world.
Jesus
John 6:51

The good shepherd giveth his life for the sheep.
Jesus
John 10:11

Greater love hath no man than this, that a man lay down his life for his friends.
Jesus
John 15:13

Glorify Thy Son, that Thy Son also may glorify Thee.
Jesus
John 17:1

Like a lamb dumb before His shearer, so opened He not His mouth.
Acts 8:32
See also Isa. 53:7

Christ died for the ungodly.
Rom. 5:6

Scarcely for a righteous man will one die: yet peradventure for a good man some would even dare to die.
Rom. 5:7

While we were yet sinners, Christ died for us.
Rom. 5:8

This is my body, which is broken for you: this do in remembrance of me.
Jesus
1 Cor. 11:24
See also Luke 22:19

Christ died for our sins.
1 Cor. 15:3

He died for all.
2 Cor. 5:15

Though He was rich, yet for your sakes He became poor, that ye through His poverty might be rich.
2 Cor. 8:9

Ye would have plucked out your own eyes, and have given them to me.
Gal. 4:15

What things were gain to me, those I counted loss for Christ.
Phil. 3:7

With such sacrifices God is well pleased.
Heb. 13:16

He laid down His life for us: and we ought to lay down our lives for the brethren.
1 John 3:16

God sent His only begotten Son into the world, that we might live through Him.
1 John 4:9

They overcame him by the blood of the Lamb.
(him: Satan)
Rev. 12:11

[*See also* Crucifixion, Martyrdom]

SACRIFICES

I will have mercy, and not sacrifice.
Jesus
Matt. 9:13
See also Hos. 6:6

[*See also* Rituals]

SACRILEGE

My house is the house of prayer: but ye have made it a den of thieves.
Jesus
Luke 19:46
See also Matt. 21:13, Mark 11:17

Make not my Father's house an house of merchandise.
Jesus
John 2:16

If any man defile the temple of God, him shall God destroy.
1 Cor. 3:17

SAFETY

He that followeth me shall not walk in darkness.
Jesus
John 8:12

I am with thee, and no man shall set on thee to hurt thee.
Jesus to Paul
Acts 18:10

The Lord shall deliver me from every evil work, and will preserve me unto His heavenly kingdom.
2 Tim. 4:18

The Lord is my helper, and I will not fear what man shall do unto me.
Heb. 13:6
See also Ps. 118:6

[*See also* God's Protection, Peace, Security]

SALUTATIONS

Grace be to you and peace from God our Father.
2 Cor. 1:2

Greet one another with an holy kiss.
2 Cor. 13:12
See also Rom. 16:16

Grace and peace be multiplied unto you through the knowledge of God, and of Jesus our Lord.
2 Pet. 1:2

Grace be with you, mercy, and peace.
2 John 3

Mercy unto you, and peace, and love.
Jude 2

[*See also* Blessings]

SALVATION

Strait is the gate, and narrow is the way, which leadeth unto life, and few there be that find it.
Jesus
Matt. 7:14

The kingdom of heaven is at hand.
Jesus
E.g., Matt. 10:7

The keys of the kingdom of heaven.
Jesus
Matt. 16:19

Whosoever will save his life shall lose it:

and whosoever will lose his life for my sake shall find it.
Jesus
Matt. 16:25
See also Mark 8:35, Luke 9:24

The Son of man is come to save that which was lost.
Jesus
Matt. 18:11

Who then can be saved?
Matt. 19:25, Mark 10:26,
Luke 18:26

He that shall endure unto the end, the same shall be saved.
Jesus
Matt. 24:13, Mark 13:13

The kingdom of God is at hand: repent ye, and believe the gospel.
Jesus
Mark 1:15
See also Matt. 4:17

Suffer the little children to come unto me, and forbid them not: for of such is the kingdom of God.
Jesus
Mark 10:14
See also Matt. 19:14, Luke 18:16

He that believeth and is baptized shall be saved; but he that believeth not shall be damned.
Jesus
Mark 16:16

The Son of man is not come to destroy men's lives, but to save them.
Jesus
Luke 9:56

The Son of man is come to seek and to save that which was lost.
Jesus
Luke 19:10

For God so loved the world, that He gave His only begotten Son, that whosoever believeth in Him should not perish, but have everlasting life.
Jesus
John 3:16
See also John 3:36, John 6:47

God sent not His Son into the world to condemn the world; but that the world through Him might be saved.
Jesus
John 3:17

Salvation is of the Jews.
Jesus
John 4:22

These things I say, that ye might be saved.
Jesus
John 5:34

I am the door: by me if any man enter in, he shall be saved.
Jesus
John 10:9

I am come a light into the world, that whosoever believeth on me should not abide in darkness.
Jesus
John 12:46

I came not to judge the world, but to save the world.
Jesus
John 12:47

No man cometh unto the Father, but by me.
Jesus
John 14:6

None of them is lost, but the son of perdition.
Jesus (son: Judas)
John 17:12

Whosoever shall call on the name of the Lord shall be saved.
E.g., Acts 2:21
See also Joel 2:32

Whosoever among you feareth God, to you is the word of this salvation sent.
Acts 13:26

I have set thee to be a light of the Gentiles, that thou shouldest be for salvation unto the ends of the earth.
Acts 13:47
See also Isa. 49:6

Through the grace of the Lord Jesus Christ we shall be saved.
Acts 15:11

Believe on the Lord Jesus Christ, and thou shalt be saved.
Acts 16:31

The salvation of God is sent unto the Gentiles.
Acts 28:28

The gift of God is eternal life through Jesus Christ our Lord.
Rom. 6:23

If thou shalt confess with thy mouth the Lord Jesus, and shalt believe in thine heart that God hath raised Him from the dead, thou shalt be saved.
Rom. 10:9

Now it is high time to awake out of sleep.
Rom. 13:11

Now is our salvation nearer than when we believed.
Rom. 13:11

I am made all things to all men, that I might by all means save some.
1 Cor. 9:22

Behold, now is the accepted time; behold, now is the day of salvation.
2 Cor. 6:2

By grace are ye saved through faith.
Eph. 2:8

Work out your own salvation with fear and trembling.
Phil. 2:12

God hath not appointed us to wrath, but to obtain salvation.
1 Thess. 5:9

Christ Jesus came into the world to save sinners.
1 Tim. 1:15

God our Saviour.
1 Tim. 2:3

Not by works of righteousness which we have done, but according to His mercy He saved us.
Titus 3:5

Ye have need of patience, that, after ye have done the will of God, ye might receive the promise.
Heb. 10:36

He which converteth the sinner from the error of his way shall save a soul from death.
James 5:20

If the righteous scarcely be saved, where shall the ungodly and the sinner appear?
1 Pet. 4:18

The longsuffering of our Lord is salvation.
2 Pet. 3:15

The Father sent the Son to be the Saviour of the world.
1 John 4:14

Without are dogs, and sorcerers, and whoremongers, and murderers, and idolaters, and whosoever loveth and maketh a lie.
Rev. 22:15

[*See also* Eternal Life, Kingdom of God, Redemption]

SARCASM

See Mockery.

SATAN

If Satan cast out Satan, he is divided against himself; how shall then his kingdom stand?
Jesus
Matt. 12:26
See also Mark 3:26, Luke 11:18

Get thee behind me, Satan: thou art an offence unto me.
Jesus
Matt. 16:23
See also Matt. 4:10, Mark 8:33,
Luke 4:8

How can Satan cast out Satan?
Jesus
Mark 3:23

What have I to do with Thee, Jesus, Thou Son of the most high God?
Mark 5:7
See also Matt. 8:29, Luke 8:28

Even the devils are subject unto us through Thy name.
(Thy: Jesus)
Luke 10:17

I beheld Satan as lightning fall from heaven.
Jesus
Luke 10:18

Ye are of your father the devil, and the lusts of your father ye will do.
Jesus
John 8:44

There is no truth in him.
Jesus
John 8:44

He is a liar, and the father of it.
Jesus
John 8:44

Can a devil open the eyes of the blind?
John 10:21

Now is the judgment of this world: now shall the prince of this world be cast out.
Jesus
John 12:31

Wilt thou not cease to pervert the right ways of the Lord?
Acts 13:10

Ye cannot drink the cup of the Lord, and the cup of devils.
1 Cor. 10:21

We are not ignorant of his devices.
2 Cor. 2:11

A thorn in the flesh, the messenger of Satan to buffet me.
2 Cor. 12:7

Put on the whole armour of God, that ye may be able to stand against the wiles of the devil.
Eph. 6:11

We wrestle not against flesh and blood, but against principalities, against powers, against the rulers of the darkness.
Eph. 6:12

Resist the devil, and he will flee from you.
James 4:7

Be sober, be vigilant; because your adversary the devil, as a roaring lion, walketh about, seeking whom he may devour.
1 Pet. 5:8

He that committeth sin is of the devil; for the devil sinneth from the beginning.
1 John 3:8

He was cast out into the earth, and his angels were cast out with him.
Rev. 12:9

They overcame him by the blood of the Lamb.
Rev. 12:11

Woe to the inhabiters of the earth and of the sea! for the devil is come down unto you.
Rev. 12:12

[*See also* Evil, Exorcism, Temptation]

SATISFACTION

Having food and raiment let us be therewith content.
1 Tim. 6:8

Ye fight and war, yet ye have not, because ye ask not.
James 4:2

Thou sayest, I am rich, and increased with goods, and have need of nothing; and knowest not that thou art wretched, and miserable, and poor, and blind, and naked.
Jesus
Rev. 3:17

[*See also* Complaints, Contentment, Greed, Happiness, Serenity]

SCORN

Is not this the carpenter's son?
Matt. 13:55
See also Mark 6:3

A crown of thorns.
Matt. 27:29, Mark 15:17, John 19:2

The stone which the builders rejected is become the head of the corner.
Jesus
Mark 12:10
See also Ps. 118:22, Matt. 21:42,
* Luke 20:17*

Is not this Jesus, the son of Joseph, whose father and mother we know?
John 6:42

These men are full of new wine.
Acts 2:13

Paul, thou art beside thyself; much learning doth make thee mad.
Festus
Acts 26:24

So is the will of God, that with well doing ye may put to silence the ignorance of foolish men.
1 Pet. 2:15

[*See also* Contempt, Criticism, Mockery]

SCRIPTURE

Man shall not live by bread alone, but by every word that proceedeth out of the mouth of God.
Jesus
Matt. 4:4
See also, e.g., Deut. 8:3, Luke 4:4

I am not come to destroy, but to fulfil.
Jesus
Matt. 5:17

This day is this scripture fulfilled in your ears.
Jesus
Luke 4:21

The law and the prophets were until John: since that time the kingdom of God is preached.
Jesus
Luke 16:16

If ye believe not his writings, how shall ye believe my words?
Jesus, about Moses
John 5:47

These things were done, that the scripture should be fulfilled.
John 19:36

They have fulfilled them in condemning Him.
Acts 13:27

Give attendance to reading, to exhortation, to doctrine.
1 Tim. 4:13

All Scripture is given by inspiration of God.
2 Tim. 3:16

If that first covenant had been faultless, then should no place have been sought for the second.
Heb. 8:7

In that He saith, A new covenant, He hath made the first old.
Heb. 8:13

Blessed is he that readeth, and they that hear the words of this prophecy.
Rev. 1:3

[*See also* Commandments, God's Word, Gospel, Prophecy]

SEARCHING

Seek ye first the kingdom of God, and His righteousness.
Jesus
Matt. 6:33
See also Luke 12:31

Seek, and ye shall find.
Jesus
Matt. 7:7, Luke 11:9

Ye shall seek me, and shall not find me: and where I am, thither ye cannot come.
Jesus
John 7:34

I was found of them that sought me not.
Rom. 10:20
See also Isa. 65:1

The Spirit searcheth all things.
1 Cor. 2:10

I am He which searcheth the reins and hearts.
Jesus
Rev. 2:23

SECOND COMING

The end is not yet.
Jesus
Matt. 24:6
See also Mark 13:7

As the lightning cometh out of the east, and shineth even unto the west; so shall also the coming of the Son of man be.
Jesus
Matt. 24:27
See also Luke 17:24

Of that day and hour knoweth no man,

no, not the angels of heaven, but my
Father only.
Jesus
Matt. 24:36
See also Mark 13:32

Watch therefore: for ye know not what
hour your Lord doth come.
Jesus
Matt. 24:42
See also Matt. 25:13

Be ye also ready.
Jesus
Matt. 24:44

Take ye heed, watch and pray: for ye know
not when the time is.
Jesus
Mark 13:33
See also Matt. 13:23

If the goodman of the house had known
what hour the thief would come, he would
have watched.
Jesus
Luke 12:39
See also Matt. 24:43

Be ye therefore ready also: for the Son of
man cometh at an hour when ye think not.
Jesus
Luke 12:40
See also Matt. 24:44

Then shall they see the Son of man com-
ing in a cloud with power and great glory.
Luke 21:27
See also Matt. 24:30, Mark 13:26

I will come again.
Jesus
John 14:3

If I will that he tarry till I come, what is
that to thee?
Jesus to Peter, about John
John 21:22

When Christ, who is our life, shall appear,
then shall ye also appear with Him in
glory.
Col. 3:4

The Lord Jesus shall be revealed from
heaven with His mighty angels, In flaming

fire taking vengeance on them that know
not God, and that obey not the gospel.
2 Thess. 1:7–8

Let no man deceive you.
2 Thess. 2:3

That day shall not come, except there
come a falling away first, and that man of
sin be revealed, the son of perdition.
2 Thess. 2:3

Unto them that look for Him shall He
appear the second time.
Heb. 9:28

Rejoice, inasmuch as ye are partakers of
Christ's sufferings; that, when His glory
shall be revealed, ye may be glad also with
exceeding joy.
1 Pet. 4:13

When the chief Shepherd shall appear, ye
shall receive a crown of glory that fadeth
not away.
1 Pet. 5:4

The Lord is not slack concerning His
promise.
2 Pet. 3:9

The day of the Lord will come as a thief in
the night.
2 Pet. 3:10
See also, e.g., 1 Thess. 5:2

Behold, the Lord cometh with ten thousands of His saints, To execute judgment
upon all.
Jude 14–15

I will come on thee as a thief.
Jesus
Rev. 3:3
See also Rev. 16:15

Thou shalt not know what hour I will
come upon thee.
Jesus
Rev. 3:3

Blessed is he that watcheth, and keepeth
his garments, lest he walk naked, and they
see his shame.
Rev. 16:15

I saw a new heaven and a new earth: for
the first heaven and the first earth were
passed away.
Rev. 21:1

There shall be no more death, neither

sorrow, nor crying, neither shall there be any more pain: for the former things are passed away.
Rev. 21:4

Behold, I come quickly.
Jesus
Rev. 22:7, 12

[*See also* Apocalypse, End Days, Imminence, Jesus, Judgment Day]

SECRECY

See that no man know it.
Jesus to blind men He healed
Matt. 9:30

Nothing is secret, that shall not be made manifest; neither any thing hid, that shall not be known.
Jesus
Luke 8:17

There is nothing covered, that shall not be revealed; neither hid, that shall not be known.
Jesus
Luke 12:2
See also Matt. 10:26, Mark 4:22

That which ye have spoken in the ear in closets shall be proclaimed upon the housetops.
Jesus
Luke 12:3
See also Matt. 10:27

God knoweth your hearts.
Jesus
Luke 16:15

Every one that doeth evil hateth the light.
Jesus
John 3:20

I have called you friends; for all things that I have heard of my Father I have made known unto you.
Jesus
John 15:15

This thing was not done in a corner.
Acts 26:26

The Spirit searcheth all things.
1 Cor. 2:10

I am He which searcheth the reins and hearts.
Jesus
Rev. 2:23

[*See also* Exposure, God's Knowledge, Mystery]

SECURITY

Foxes have holes, and birds of the air have nests; but the Son of man hath not where to lay His head.
Jesus
Luke 9:58
See also Matt. 8:20

[*See also* God's Protection, Safety]

SEDUCTION

See Temptation.

SELF-AWARENESS

Why beholdest thou the mote that is in thy brother's eye, but considerest not the beam that is in thine own eye?
Jesus
Matt. 7:3
See also Luke 6:41

Examine yourselves, whether ye be in the faith.
2 Cor. 13:5

SELF-CONFIDENCE

See Confidence.

SELF-CONTROL

What I hate, that do I.
Rom. 7:15

The good that I would I do not: but the evil which I would not, that I do.
Rom. 7:19

Be sober, be vigilant; because your adver-

sary the devil, as a roaring lion, walketh about, seeking whom he may devour.
1 Pet. 5:8

[*See also* Anger, Temptation]

SELF-DECEPTION

Professing themselves to be wise, they became fools.
Rom. 1:22

If any man think that he knoweth any thing, he knoweth nothing yet as he ought to know.
1 Cor. 8:2

Thou sayest, I am rich, and increased with goods, and have need of nothing; and knowest not that thou art wretched, and miserable, and poor, and blind, and naked.
Jesus
Rev. 3:17

[*See also* Deception]

SELF-DENIAL

Whosoever will come after me, let him deny himself, and take up his cross, and follow me.
Jesus
Mark 8:34
See also Matt. 16:24, Luke 9:23

Whosoever he be of you that forsaketh not all that he hath, he cannot be my disciple.
Jesus
Luke 14:33

Make not provision for the flesh, to fulfil the lusts thereof.
Rom. 13:14

[*See also* Denial, Self-Control, Temptation, Worldliness]

SELF-HATRED

O wretched man that I am! who shall deliver me from the body of this death?
Rom. 7:24

SELF-INCRIMINATION

Wherein thou judgest another, thou condemnest thyself.
Rom. 2:1

[*See also* Guilt]

SELF-INTEREST

If ye do good to them which do good to you, what thank have ye? for sinners also do even the same.
Jesus
Luke 6:33
See also Matt. 5:46

Sinners also lend to sinners, to receive as much again.
Jesus
Luke 6:34

When thou makest a feast, call the poor, the maimed, the lame, the blind: And thou shalt be blessed; for they cannot recompense thee.
Jesus
Luke 14:13–14

We preach not ourselves, but Christ Jesus the Lord.
2 Cor. 4:5

[*See also* Motivation, Selfishness, Selflessness]

SELF-RIGHTEOUSNESS

Why eateth your Master with publicans and sinners?
Matt. 9:11
See also Luke 5:30

The time cometh, that whosoever killeth you will think that he doeth God service.
Jesus
John 16:2

If He were not a malefactor, we would not have delivered Him up unto thee.
John 18:30

[*See also* Conceit]

SELFISHNESS

I was an hungred, and ye gave me no meat: I was thirsty, and ye gave me no drink.
Jesus
Matt. 25:42

Whosoever shall seek to save his life shall lose it; and whosoever shall lose his life shall preserve it.
Jesus
Luke 17:33
See also Matt. 16:25, Mark 8:35

He that loveth his life shall lose it; and he that hateth his life in this world shall keep it unto life eternal.
Jesus
John 12:25

The merchants of the earth shall weep and mourn over her; for no man buyeth their merchandise any more.
(her: Babylon)
Rev. 18:11

[*See also* Altruism, Greed, Poverty, Underprivileged]

SELFLESSNESS

If I go not away, the Comforter will not come unto you.
Jesus
John 16:7

I have coveted no man's silver, or gold, or apparel.
Acts 20:33

Even Christ pleased not Himself.
Rom. 15:3

[*See also* Altruism, Charity, Generosity, Sacrifice, Self-Interest, Selfishness]

SEPARATION

Whither I go, ye cannot come.
Jesus
John 8:21, John 13:33
See also John 7:34

Who shall separate us from the love of Christ? shall tribulation, or distress, or persecution, or famine, or nakedness, or peril, or sword?
Rom. 8:35

SERENITY

Take my yoke upon you, and learn of me; for I am meek and lowly in heart: and ye shall find rest unto your souls.
Jesus
Matt. 11:29

Peace be with you all that are in Christ Jesus.
1 Pet. 5:14

[*See also* Contentment, Peace, Satisfaction]

SERVANTS

See Employees, Freedom, Slavery, Work.

SERVICE

See Altruism, Charity, Ministry.

SERVICE TO GOD

If any man serve me, him will my Father honour.
Jesus
John 12:26

We should serve in newness of spirit, and not in the oldness of the letter.
Rom. 7:6

He that is called, being free, is Christ's servant.
1 Cor. 7:22

There are differences of administrations, but the same Lord.
1 Cor. 12:5

[*See also* Devotion, Ministry]

SEVERITY

It shall be more tolerable for the land of Sodom in the day of judgment, than for thee.
Jesus
Matt. 11:24
See also Luke 10:14

[*See also* Cruelty]

SEX

See Adultery, Carnality, Celibacy, Fornication, Homosexuality, Immorality, Lust.

SHAME

Whosoever shall be ashamed of me and of my words, of him shall the Son of man be ashamed.
Jesus
Luke 9:26

Thou shalt heap coals of fire on his head.
Rom. 12:20
See also Prov. 25:22

Brother goeth to law with brother, and that before the unbelievers.
1 Cor. 6:6

I am not ashamed: for I know whom I have believed.
2 Tim. 1:12

[*See also* Humiliation]

SHARING

It is not meet to take the children's bread, and to cast it to dogs.
Jesus
Matt. 15:26
See also Mark 7:27

Yet the dogs eat of the crumbs which fall from their masters' table.
Matt. 15:27
See also Mark 7:28

Him they compelled to bear His cross.
(Him: Simon)
Matt. 27:32
See also John 19:17

He that hath two coats, let him impart to him that hath none; and he that hath meat, let him do likewise.
John the Baptist
Luke 3:11

I have called you friends; for all things that I have heard of my Father I have made known unto you.
Jesus
John 15:15

Bear ye one another's burdens.
Gal. 6:2

[*See also* Burdens, Charity, Cooperation, Generosity, Selfishness, Underprivileged]

SHARPNESS

Sharper than any twoedged sword.
Heb. 4:12

SIBLINGS

The elder shall serve the younger.
Rom. 9:12, Gen. 25:23

SICKNESS

See Healing, Miracles.

SIGHT

The light of the body is the eye.
Jesus
Matt. 6:22, Luke 11:34

If thine eye offend thee, pluck it out, and cast it from thee.
Jesus
Matt. 18:9
See also Matt. 5:29, Mark 9:47

It is better for thee to enter into the kingdom of God with one eye, than having two eyes to be cast into hell fire.
Jesus
Mark 9:47
See also Matt. 18:9

There fell from his eyes as it had been scales: and he received sight forthwith, and arose, and was baptized.
(he: Saul)
Acts 9:18

Now we see through a glass, darkly; but then face to face.
1 Cor. 13:12

We walk by faith, not by sight.
2 Cor. 5:7

Anoint thine eyes with eyesalve, that thou mayest see.
Jesus
Rev. 3:18

[*See also* Blindness]

SILENCE

As a thief in the night.
1 Thess. 5:2, 2 Pet. 3:10

When He had opened the seventh seal, there was silence in heaven about the space of half an hour.
Rev. 8:1

[*See also* Speech, Verbosity]

SIN

All manner of sin and blasphemy shall be forgiven unto men: but the blasphemy against the Holy Ghost shall not be forgiven unto men.
Jesus
Matt. 12:31
See also Matt. 12:32, Mark 3:29,
    Luke 12:10

Not that which goeth into the mouth defileth a man; but that which cometh out of the mouth, this defileth a man.
Jesus
Matt. 15:11
See also Mark 7:15

Out of the heart proceed evil thoughts, murders, adulteries, fornications, thefts, false witness, blasphemies.
Jesus
Matt. 15:19
See also Mark 7:21

The spirit indeed is willing, but the flesh is weak.
Jesus
Matt. 26:41
See also Mark 14:38

All these evil things come from within, and defile the man.
Jesus
Mark 7:23

It is better for thee to enter into the kingdom of God with one eye, than having two eyes to be cast into hell fire.
Jesus
Mark 9:47
See also Matt. 18:9

Forgive us our sins.
Jesus
Luke 11:4

There is nothing covered, that shall not be revealed; neither hid, that shall not be known.
Jesus
Luke 12:2
See also Matt. 10:26, Mark 4:22

Sin no more, lest a worse thing come unto thee.
Jesus
John 5:14

He that is without sin among you, let him first cast a stone.
Jesus
John 8:7

Woman, where are those thine accusers?
Jesus
John 8:10

Go, and sin no more.
Jesus
John 8:11

Whosoever committeth sin is the servant of sin.
Jesus
John 8:34

If ye were blind, ye should have no sin.
Jesus
John 9:41

Now they have no cloak for their sin.
Jesus
John 15:22

Pray God, if perhaps the thought of thine heart may be forgiven thee.
Acts 8:22

Thou art in the gall of bitterness, and in the bond of iniquity.
Acts 8:23

Whosoever believeth in Him shall receive remission of sins.
Acts 10:43

Arise, and be baptized, and wash away thy sins.
Acts 22:16

As many as have sinned without law shall also perish without law.
Rom. 2:12

As many as have sinned in the law shall be judged by the law.
Rom. 2:12

They are all under sin.
Rom. 3:9

There is none that doeth good, no, not one.
Rom. 3:12, Ps. 14:3, Ps. 53:3
See also Rom. 3:10

By the law is the knowledge of sin.
Rom. 3:20

All have sinned, and come short of the glory of God.
Rom. 3:23

Where no law is, there is no transgression.
Rom. 4:15

By one man sin entered into the world.
Rom. 5:12

Sin is not imputed when there is no law.
Rom. 5:13

Where sin abounded, grace did much more abound.
Rom. 5:20

He that is dead is freed from sin.
Rom. 6:7

Sin shall not have dominion over you: for ye are not under the law, but under grace.
Rom. 6:14

The wages of sin is death; but the gift of God is eternal life through Jesus Christ our Lord.
Rom. 6:23

I had not known sin, but by the law.
Rom. 7:7

When the commandment came, sin revived.
Rom. 7:9

What I hate, that do I.
Rom. 7:15

It is no more I that do it, but sin that dwelleth in me.
Rom. 7:17, 20

In me (that is, in my flesh,) dwelleth no good thing.
Rom. 7:18

With the mind I myself serve the law of God; but with the flesh the law of sin.
Rom. 7:25

Make not provision for the flesh, to fulfil the lusts thereof.
Rom. 13:14

Whatsoever is not of faith is sin.
Rom. 14:23

Christ died for our sins.
1 Cor. 15:3

Awake to righteousness, and sin not.
1 Cor. 15:34

The sting of death is sin; and the strength of sin is the law.
1 Cor. 15:56

Use not liberty for an occasion to the flesh.
Gal. 5:13

He that soweth to his flesh shall of the flesh reap corruption.
Gal. 6:8

When lust hath conceived, it bringeth forth sin.
James 1:15

Sin, when it is finished, bringeth forth death.
James 1:15

To him that knoweth to do good, and doeth it not, to him it is sin.
James 4:17

A multitude of sins.
James 5:20

He that hath suffered in the flesh hath ceased from sin.
1 Pet. 4:1

Charity shall cover the multitude of sins.
(charity: love)
1 Pet. 4:8

The blood of Jesus Christ His Son cleanseth us from all sin.
1 John 1:7

If we say that we have no sin, we deceive ourselves.
1 John 1:8

If we say that we have not sinned, we make Him a liar.
1 John 1:10

If any man sin, we have an advocate with the Father.
1 John 2:1

Whosoever committeth sin transgresseth also the law: for sin is the transgression of the law.
1 John 3:4

In Him is no sin.
1 John 3:5

Whosoever abideth in Him sinneth not.
1 John 3:6

Whosoever is born of God doth not commit sin.
1 John 3:9

All unrighteousness is sin.
1 John 5:17

Be not partakers of her sins.
(her: Babylon)
Rev. 18:4

Her sins have reached unto heaven, and God hath remembered her iniquities.
(her: Babylon)
Rev. 18:5

[*See also* Adultery, Behavior, Carnality, Confession, Decadence, Depravity, Disobedience, Evil, Forgiveness, Godlessness, Immorality, Punishment, Repentance, Righteousness, Sinners, Wickedness]

SINCERITY

Not every one that saith unto me, Lord, Lord, shall enter into the kingdom of heaven.
Jesus
Matt. 7:21

I will have mercy, and not sacrifice.
Jesus
Matt. 9:13
See also Hos. 6:6

Why call ye me, Lord, Lord, and do not the things which I say?
Jesus
Luke 6:46

They that worship Him must worship Him in spirit and in truth.
Jesus
John 4:24

If God were your Father, ye would love me: for I proceeded forth and came from God.
Jesus
John 8:42

Circumcision is that of the heart, in the spirit, and not in the letter; whose praise is not of men, but of God.
Rom. 2:29

With the heart man believeth unto righteousness.
Rom. 10:10

The kingdom of God is not in word, but in power.
1 Cor. 4:20

Not in tables of stone, but in fleshy tables of the heart.
2 Cor. 3:3

Be ye doers of the word, and not hearers only.
James 1:22

Sanctify the Lord God in your hearts.
1 Pet. 3:15

Let us not love in word, neither in tongue; but in deed and in truth.
1 John 3:18

[*See also* Devotion, Hypocrisy, Rituals]

SINNERS

They that be whole need not a physician, but they that are sick.
Jesus
Matt. 9:12
See also Mark 2:17, Luke 5:31

Sinners also lend to sinners, to receive as much again.
Jesus
Luke 6:34

Christ died for the ungodly.
Rom. 5:6

While we were yet sinners, Christ died for us.
Rom. 5:8

By one man's disobedience many were made sinners.
Rom. 5:19

Christ Jesus came into the world to save sinners.
1 Tim. 1:15

Lovers of pleasures more than lovers of God.
2 Tim. 3:4

The devils also believe, and tremble.
James 2:19

Cleanse your hands, ye sinners; and purify your hearts, ye double minded.
James 4:8

He which converteth the sinner from the error of his way shall save a soul from death.
James 5:20

The error of his way.
James 5:20

They think it strange that ye run not with them to the same excess of riot.
1 Pet. 4:4

God spared not the angels that sinned, but cast them down to hell.
2 Pet. 2:4

Whosoever sinneth hath not seen Him, neither known Him.
1 John 3:6

He that committeth sin is of the devil; for the devil sinneth from the beginning.
1 John 3:8

Whosoever is born of God sinneth not.
1 John 5:18

[*See also* Sin, Wicked People]

SIZE

Which of you by taking thought can add one cubit unto his stature?
Jesus
Matt. 6:27
See also Luke 12:25

A little leaven leaveneth the whole lump.
1 Cor. 5:6, Gal. 5:9

[*See also* Growth, Quantity]

SKEPTICISM

An evil and adulterous generation seeketh after a sign; and there shall no sign be given to it, but the sign of the prophet Jonas.
Jesus
Matt. 12:39
See also Matt. 16:4, Mark 8:12,
*   Luke 11:29*

But whom say ye that I am?
Jesus
Matt. 16:15, Mark 8:29, Luke 9:20

Physician, heal thyself.
Luke 4:23

If they hear not Moses and the prophets, neither will they be persuaded, though one rose from the dead.
Jesus
Luke 16:31

O fools, and slow of heart to believe all that the prophets have spoken.
Jesus
Luke 24:25

If I have told you earthly things, and ye believe not, how shall ye believe, if I tell you of heavenly things?
Jesus
John 3:12

Except ye see signs and wonders, ye will not believe.
Jesus
John 4:48

Had ye believed Moses, ye would have believed me: for he wrote of me.
Jesus
John 5:46

Because I tell you the truth, ye believe me not.
Jesus
John 8:45
See also John 8:46

How can a man that is a sinner do such miracles?
Pharisees, about Jesus
John 9:16

Though ye believe not me, believe the works.
Jesus
John 10:38

Blessed are they that have not seen, and yet have believed.
Jesus
John 20:29

Some believed the things which were spoken, and some believed not.
Acts 28:24

The Jews require a sign, and the Greeks seek after wisdom.
1 Cor. 1:22

Believe not every spirit.
1 John 4:1

[*See also* Belief, Doubt, Faith, Possibility]

SKILL

See Ability.

SLANDER

Do violence to no man, neither accuse any falsely.
Luke 3:14

Their throat is an open sepulchre.
Rom. 3:13

Speak evil of no man.
Titus 3:2
See also James 4:11

[*See also* Lies, Speech]

SLAVERY

We are not children of the bondwoman, but of the free.
Gal. 4:31

Servants, be obedient to them that are your masters.
Eph. 6:5
See also 1 Pet. 2:18

He that leadeth into captivity shall go into captivity.
Rev. 13:10

[*See also* Freedom]

SLEEP

They that sleep sleep in the night; and they that be drunken are drunken in the night.
1 Thess. 5:7

SLOTH

See Laziness.

SNAKES

Be ye therefore wise as serpents, and harmless as doves.
Jesus to disciples
Matt. 10:16

See Conceit.

See Homosexuality.

See Peace, War, Weapons.

Ye shall be sorrowful, but your sorrow shall be turned into joy.
Jesus
John 16:20

Be of good cheer; I have overcome the world.
Jesus
John 16:33

The desolate hath many more children than she which hath an husband.
Gal. 4:27
See also Isa. 54:1

The voice of the bridegroom and of the bride shall be heard no more at all in thee.
Rev. 18:23

There shall be no more death, neither sorrow, nor crying, neither shall there be any more pain: for the former things are passed away.
Rev. 21:4

[*See also* Anguish, Grief, Mourning, Tears]

Fear not them which kill the body, but are not able to kill the soul.
Jesus
Matt. 10:28
See also Luke 12:4

What shall a man give in exchange for his soul?
Jesus
Matt. 16:26, Mark 8:37

What shall it profit a man, if he shall gain the whole world, and lose his own soul?
Jesus
Mark 8:36
See also Matt. 16:26, Luke 9:25

Of His kingdom there shall be no end.
(His: Jesus)
Luke 1:33

Heaven is My throne, and earth is My footstool: what house will ye build Me? saith the Lord.
Acts 7:49
See also Isa. 66:1, Matt. 5:34–35

The earth is the Lord's, and the fulness thereof.
1 Cor. 10:26, 28
See also Ps. 24:1

He must reign, till He hath put all enemies under His feet.
1 Cor. 15:25

Thy throne, O God, is for ever and ever.
Heb. 1:8

A sceptre of righteousness is the sceptre of Thy kingdom.
Heb. 1:8

[*See also* Authority, God's Power, Monarchy]

How can ye, being evil, speak good things?
Jesus
Matt. 12:34

Out of the abundance of the heart the mouth speaketh.
Jesus
Matt. 12:34

A good man out of the good treasure of the heart bringeth forth good things: and an evil man out of the evil treasure bringeth forth evil things.
Jesus
Matt. 12:35

Every idle word that men shall speak, they

shall give account thereof in the day of judgment.
Jesus
Matt. 12:36

By thy words thou shalt be justified, and by thy words thou shalt be condemned.
Jesus
Matt. 12:37

Not that which goeth into the mouth defileth a man; but that which cometh out of the mouth, this defileth a man.
Jesus
Matt. 15:11
See also Mark 7:15

Their throat is an open sepulchre.
Rom. 3:13

Whatsoever ye do in word or deed, do all in the name of the Lord Jesus.
Col. 3:17

Let your speech be alway with grace, seasoned with salt, that ye may know how ye ought to answer every man.
Col. 4:6

Shun profane and vain babblings: for they will increase unto more ungodliness.
2 Tim. 2:16

The word of God is quick, and powerful, and sharper than any twoedged sword.
Heb. 4:12

The tongue is a fire, a world of iniquity.
James 3:6

It defileth the whole body, and setteth on fire the course of nature.
(It: the tongue)
James 3:6

The tongue can no man tame; it is an unruly evil, full of deadly poison.
James 3:8

Out of the same mouth proceedeth blessing and cursing.
James 3:10

He that will love life, and see good days, let him refrain his tongue from evil.
1 Pet. 3:10
See also Ps. 34:13

[*See also* Advice, Candor, Communication, Eloquence, Lies, Persuasion, Preaching, Profanity, Quotations, Slander, Verbosity]

SPEED

That thou doest, do quickly.
Jesus
John 13:27

In the twinkling of an eye.
1 Cor. 15:52

[*See also* Urgency]

SPIES

See Betrayal.

SPIRIT

See Holy Spirit, Inspiration.

SPIRITUALITY

Man shall not live by bread alone, but by every word that proceedeth out of the mouth of God.
Jesus
Matt. 4:4
See also, e.g., Deut. 8:3, Luke 4:4

Lay up for yourselves treasures in heaven, where neither moth nor rust doth corrupt, and where thieves do not break through nor steal.
Jesus
Matt. 6:20

The light of the body is the eye.
Jesus
Matt. 6:22, Luke 11:34

Seek ye first the kingdom of God, and His righteousness.
Jesus
Matt. 6:33
See also Luke 12:31

To give light to them that sit in darkness.
Luke 1:79

Take heed therefore that the light which is in thee be not darkness.
Jesus
Luke 11:35

Except a man be born again, he cannot see the kingdom of God.
Jesus
John 3:3

That which is born of the flesh is flesh; and that which is born of the Spirit is spirit.
Jesus
John 3:6

I have meat to eat that ye know not of.
Jesus
John 4:32

If any man thirst, let him come unto me, and drink.
Jesus
John 7:37

The law is spiritual: but I am carnal.
Rom. 7:14

To be carnally minded is death; but to be spiritually minded is life and peace.
Rom. 8:6

The carnal mind is enmity against God.
Rom. 8:7

Flesh and blood cannot inherit the kingdom of God.
1 Cor. 15:50

Though our outward man perish, yet the inward man is renewed day by day.
2 Cor. 4:16

The things which are seen are temporal; but the things which are not seen are eternal.
2 Cor. 4:18

Having nothing, and yet possessing all things.
2 Cor. 6:10

Put on the new man.
Eph. 4:24

Ye were sometimes darkness, but now are ye light in the Lord.
Eph. 5:8

Seek those things which are above, where Christ sitteth on the right hand of God.
Col. 3:1

Bodily exercise profiteth little: but godliness is profitable unto all things.
1 Tim. 4:8

The darkness is past, and the true light now shineth.
1 John 2:8

[*See also* Born Again, Holy Spirit, Light and Darkness, Materialism, Worldliness]

SPOKESMEN

I am come in my Father's name, and ye receive me not.
Jesus
John 5:43

He that receiveth whomsoever I send receiveth me.
Jesus
John 13:20

He is a chosen vessel unto me, to bear my name.
Jesus, about Saul
Acts 9:15

I am an ambassador in bonds.
Eph. 6:20

SPORTSMANSHIP

See Competition.

STAMINA

See Fortitude.

STATUS

The disciple is not above his master, nor the servant above his lord.
Jesus
Matt. 10:24
See also Luke 6:40

The servant is not greater than his lord; neither he that is sent greater than he that sent him.
Jesus
John 13:16
See also John 15:20

God is no respecter of persons.
Acts 10:34
See also Rom. 2:11

As the Lord hath called every one, so let him walk.
1 Cor. 7:17

If ye have respect to persons, ye commit sin.
James 2:9

[*See also* Appearance, Authority]

STEADFASTNESS

Be not moved away from the hope of the gospel.
Col. 1:23

Hold fast to that which is good.
1 Thess. 5:21

We are not of them who draw back unto perdition; but of them that believe to the saving of the soul.
Heb. 10:39

[*See also* Diligence, Perseverance]

STOICISM

See Acceptance.

STRANGERS

See Hospitality.

STRATEGY

Be ye therefore wise as serpents, and harmless as doves.
Jesus to disciples
Matt. 10:16

[*See also* Planning]

STRENGTH

Upon this rock I will build my church; and the gates of hell shall not prevail against it.
Jesus
Matt. 16:18

The weakness of God is stronger than men.
1 Cor. 1:25

My strength is made perfect in weakness.
Jesus
2 Cor. 12:9

When I am weak, then am I strong.
2 Cor. 12:10

[*See also* Fortitude, Frailty, Weakness]

STRIFE

A man's foes shall be they of his own household.
Jesus
Matt. 10:36

If a house be divided against itself, that house cannot stand.
Jesus
Mark 3:25
See also Matt. 12:35, Luke 11:17

Suppose ye that I am come to give peace on earth? I tell you, Nay; but rather division.
Jesus
Luke 12:51
See also Matt. 10:34

The father shall be divided against the son, and the son against the father; the mother against the daughter, and the daughter against the mother.
Jesus
Luke 12:53
See also Matt. 10:35

After my departing shall grievous wolves enter in among you, not sparing the flock.
Acts 20:29

Of your own selves shall men arise, speaking perverse things.
Acts 20:30

Brother goeth to law with brother, and that before the unbelievers.
1 Cor. 6:6

Be at peace among yourselves.
1 Thess. 5:13

Where envying and strife is, there is confusion and every evil work.
James 3:16

Ye fight and war, yet ye have not, because ye ask not.
James 4:2

[*See also* Arguments, Trouble, Unity, War, War and Peace]

STUBBORNNESS

Having eyes, see ye not? and having ears, hear ye not?
Jesus
Mark 8:18

What I have written I have written.
Pilate
John 19:22

Ye stiffnecked and uncircumcised in heart and ears, ye do always resist the Holy Ghost.
Acts 7:51

The heart of this people is waxed gross, and their ears are dull of hearing, and their eyes have they closed.
Acts 28:27

If ye will hear His voice, harden not your hearts.
Heb. 3:15
See also, e.g., Ps. 95:7–8

[*See also* Impenitence]

SUBMISSION

See Acceptance, Authority, Marriage.

SUCCESS

This is the Lord's doing, and it is marvellous in our eyes.
Jesus
Matt. 21:42
See also, e.g., Ps. 118:23,
Mark 12:11

Many that are first shall be last; and the last first.
Jesus
Mark 10:31
See also Matt. 19:30, Matt. 20:16

The stone which the builders rejected is become the head of the corner.
Jesus
Mark 12:10
See also Ps. 118:22, Matt. 21:42,
Luke 20:17

A man's life consisteth not in the abundance of the things which he possesseth.
Jesus
Luke 12:15

Unto whomsoever much is given, of him shall be much required.
Jesus
Luke 12:48

The hand of the Lord was with them: and a great number believed.
Acts 11:21

The word of God grew and multiplied.
Acts 12:24

It is not of him that willeth, nor of him that runneth, but of God that showeth mercy.
Rom. 9:16

What hast thou that thou didst not receive?
1 Cor. 4:7

[*See also* Achievement, Defeat, Reward, Victory, Wealth]

SUDDENNESS

As the lightning cometh out of the east, and shineth even unto the west; so shall also the coming of the Son of man be.
Jesus
Matt. 24:27
See also Luke 17:24

[*See also* Second Coming]

SUFFERING

Let this cup pass from me.
Jesus
Matt. 26:39

We must through much tribulation enter into the kingdom of God.
Acts 14:22

For the hope of Israel I am bound with this chain.
Acts 28:20

Tribulation worketh patience; And patience, experience; and experience, hope.
Rom. 5:3–4

We are fools for Christ's sake.
1 Cor. 4:10

If in this life only we have hope in Christ, we are of all men most miserable.
1 Cor. 15:19

As ye are partakers of the sufferings, so shall ye be also of the consolation.
2 Cor. 1:7

In labours more abundant, in stripes above measure, in prisons more frequent, in deaths oft.
2 Cor. 11:23

A thorn in the flesh, the messenger of Satan to buffet me.
2 Cor. 12:7

If we suffer, we shall also reign with Him.
2 Tim. 2:12

Though He were a Son, yet learned He obedience by the things which He suffered.
Heb. 5:8

Without shedding of blood is no remission.
Heb. 9:22

Whom the Lord loveth He chasteneth.
Heb. 12:6

We count them happy which endure.
James 5:11

What glory is it, if, when ye be buffeted for your faults, ye shall take it patiently?
1 Pet. 2:20

If, when ye do well, and suffer for it, ye take it patiently, this is acceptable with God.
1 Pet. 2:20

If ye suffer for righteousness' sake, happy are ye.
1 Pet. 3:14

It is better, if the will of God be so, that ye suffer for well doing, than for evil doing.
1 Pet. 3:17

He that hath suffered in the flesh hath ceased from sin.
1 Pet. 4:1

Rejoice, inasmuch as ye are partakers of Christ's sufferings; that, when His glory shall be revealed, ye may be glad also with exceeding joy.
1 Pet. 4:13

[*See also* Anguish, Compassion, Grief, Persecution, Torment]

SUPERSTITION

The gods are come down to us in the likeness of men.
Acts 14:11

[*See also* Idols, Omens]

SUPPORT

See God's Support.

SURVIVAL

I send you forth as sheep in the midst of wolves: be ye therefore wise as serpents, and harmless as doves.
Jesus
Matt. 10:16

If we suffer, we shall also reign with Him.
2 Tim. 2:12

[*See also* Life and Death, Perseverance]

SUSTENANCE

See Bread of Life, Food.

SWEARING

Swear not at all; neither by heaven; for it is God's throne: Nor by the earth; for it is His footstool: neither by Jerusalem; for it is the city of the great King.
Jesus
Matt. 5:34–35

[*See also* Blasphemy, Oaths, Profanity, Promises]

SYMBOLISM

See Omens.

SYMPATHY

He that despiseth you despiseth me; and he that despiseth me despiseth Him that sent me.
> *Jesus*
> *Luke 10:16*

Jesus wept.
> *John 11:35*

Remember them that are in bonds, as bound with them; and them which suffer adversity, as being yourselves also in the body.
> *Heb. 13:3*

[*See also* Comfort, Compassion]

TALENT

See Ability.

TASTE

See Flavor.

TAXATION

If ye love them which love you, what reward have ye? do not even the publicans the same?
> *Jesus*
> *Matt. 5:46*
> *See also Luke 6:32*

Of whom do the kings of the earth take custom or tribute? of their own children, or of strangers?
> *Jesus*
> *Matt. 17:25*

Take, and give unto them for me and thee.
> *Jesus*
> *Matt. 17:27*

Render therefore unto Caesar the things which are Caesar's; and unto God the things that are God's.
> *Jesus*
> *Matt. 22:21*
> *See also Mark 12:17, Luke 20:25*

Exact no more than that which is appointed you.
> *Luke 3:13*

Pay ye tribute also: for they are God's ministers.
> *Rom. 13:6*

Tribute to whom tribute is due.
> *Rom. 13:7*

TEACHING

Whosoever shall do and teach them, the same shall be called great in the kingdom of heaven.
> *Jesus (them: commandments)*
> *Matt. 5:19*

My doctrine is not mine, but His that sent me.
> *Jesus*
> *John 7:16*

Thou therefore which teachest another, teachest thou not thyself?
> *Rom. 2:21*

Be gentle unto all men, apt to teach, patient.
> *2 Tim. 2:24*

Reprove, rebuke, exhort with all long-suffering and doctrine.
> *2 Tim. 4:2*

Speak thou the things which become sound doctrine.
> *Titus 2:1*

We put bits in the horses' mouths, that they may obey us.
> *James 3:3*

[*See also* Education, Guidance, Instruction]

TEARS

Blessed are ye that weep now: for ye shall laugh.
> *Jesus*
> *Luke 6:21*

Woman, why weepest thou?
Jesus to Mary Magdalene
John 20:15

What mean ye to weep and to break mine heart?
Acts 21:13

Rejoice with them that do rejoice, and weep with them that weep.
Rom. 12:15

He found no place of repentance, though he sought it carefully with tears.
(He: Esau)
Heb. 12:17

God shall wipe away all tears from their eyes.
Rev. 7:17

[*See also* Grief, Happiness, Sorrow]

TEMPER

See Anger, Patience, Restraint.

TEMPERANCE

See Behavior, Excess.

TEMPTATION

If Thou be the Son of God, command that these stones be made bread.
Devil to Jesus
Matt. 4:3
See also Luke 4:3

Thou shalt not tempt the Lord thy God.
Jesus
Matt. 4:7, Luke 4:12
See also Deut. 6:16

Lead us not into temptation, but deliver us from evil.
Jesus
Matt. 6:13, Luke 11:4

Wide is the gate, and broad is the way, that leadeth to destruction.
Jesus
Matt. 7:13

Get thee behind me, Satan: thou art an offence unto me.
Jesus
Matt. 16:23
See also Matt. 4:10, Mark 8:33, Luke 4:8

Woe to that man by whom the offence cometh!
Jesus
Matt. 18:7

Why tempt ye me, ye hypocrites?
Jesus
Matt. 22:18
See also Mark 12:15, Luke 20:23

Watch and pray, that ye enter not into temptation.
Jesus
Matt. 26:41
See also Luke 22:40, 46

The spirit indeed is willing, but the flesh is weak.
Jesus
Matt. 26:41
See also Mark 14:38

He that is dead is freed from sin.
Rom. 6:7

Yield yourselves unto God.
Rom. 6:13

What I hate, that do I.
Rom. 7:15

It is no more I that do it, but sin that dwelleth in me.
Rom. 7:17, 20

With the mind I myself serve the law of God; but with the flesh the law of sin.
Rom. 7:25

To avoid fornication, let every man have his own wife, and let every woman have her own husband.
1 Cor. 7:2

We are not ignorant of his devices.
(his: Satan)
2 Cor. 2:11

The flesh lusteth against the Spirit, and the Spirit against the flesh.
Gal. 5:17

Put on the whole armour of God, that ye

may be able to stand against the wiles of the devil.
Eph. 6:11

Blessed is the man that endureth temptation.
James 1:12

God cannot be tempted with evil, neither tempteth He any man.
James 1:13

Resist the devil, and he will flee from you.
James 4:7

The Lord knoweth how to deliver the godly out of temptations.
2 Pet. 2:9

[*See also* Fortitude, Restraint, Self-Control, Self-Denial]

TERROR

The abomination of desolation.
Jesus
Matt. 24:15, Mark 13:14

Every island fled away, and the mountains were not found.
Rev. 16:20

[*See also* Destruction, Fear, Violence]

TESTIMONY

Whosoever therefore shall confess me before men, him will I confess also before my Father which is in heaven. But whosoever shall deny me before men, him will I also deny before my Father which is in heaven.
Jesus
Matt. 10:32–33

The blind see, the lame walk, the lepers are cleansed, the deaf hear, the dead are raised, to the poor the gospel is preached.
Jesus
Luke 7:22
See also Matt. 11:5

Whosoever shall confess me before men, him shall the Son of man also confess before the angels of God.
Jesus
Luke 12:8

I saw, and bare record that this is the Son of God.
John 1:34

If I bear witness of myself, my witness is not true.
Jesus
John 5:31

The works that I do in my Father's name, they bear witness of me.
Jesus
John 10:25

Ye also shall bear witness, because ye have been with me from the beginning.
Jesus
John 15:27

To this end was I born, and for this cause came I into the world, that I should bear witness unto the truth.
Jesus
John 18:37

He that saw it bare record, and his record is true.
John 19:35

If they should be written every one, I suppose that even the world itself could not contain the books that should be written.
John 21:25

Ye shall be witnesses unto me.
Jesus
Acts 1:8

We cannot but speak the things which we have seen and heard.
Acts 4:20

To Him give all the prophets witness.
Acts 10:43

He left not Himself without witness, in that He did good, and gave us rain from heaven.
Acts 14:17

Thou shalt be His witness unto all men.
Acts 22:15

As thou hast testified of me in Jerusalem, so must thou bear witness also at Rome.
Jesus
Acts 23:11

I continue unto this day, witnessing both to small and great.
Paul
Acts 26:22

God is my witness.
Rom. 1:9

Ye are our epistle written in our hearts, known and read of all men.
2 Cor. 3:2

Not in tables of stone, but in fleshy tables of the heart.
2 Cor. 3:3

Walk in wisdom toward them that are without.
Col. 4:5

Be not thou therefore ashamed of the testimony of our Lord.
2 Tim. 1:8

That which we have seen and heard declare we unto you.
1 John 1:3

It is the Spirit that beareth witness, because the Spirit is truth.
1 John 5:6

There are three that bear witness in earth, the Spirit, and the water, and the blood: and these three agree in one.
1 John 5:8

If we receive the witness of men, the witness of God is greater.
1 John 5:9

What thou seest, write in a book, and send it unto the seven churches.
Jesus
Rev. 1:11

Write the things which thou hast seen, and the things which are, and the things which shall be hereafter.
Jesus
Rev. 1:19

[*See also* Evangelism]

TESTING

See Competition.

THANKSGIVING

See Gratitude.

THIRST

Whosoever drinketh of this water shall thirst again: But whosoever drinketh of the water that I shall give him shall never thirst.
Jesus
John 4:13–14

I thirst.
Jesus, on the cross
John 19:28

[*See also* Bread of Life, Deprivation, Hunger]

THOUGHTS

Think soberly.
Rom. 12:3

The Lord knoweth the thoughts of the wise, that they are vain.
1 Cor. 3:20

Gird up the loins of your mind.
1 Pet. 1:13

I am He which searcheth the reins and hearts.
Jesus
Rev. 2:23

[*See also* Attitude, Contemplation, Secrecy]

THREAT

If thou let this man go, thou art not Caesar's friend.
John 19:12

TIME

Mine hour is not yet come.
Jesus
John 2:4
See also John 7:6

Lift up your eyes, and look on the fields; for they are white already to harvest.
Jesus
John 4:35

The night cometh, when no man can work.
Jesus
John 9:4

The fashion of this world passeth away.
1 Cor. 7:31

One day is with the Lord as a thousand years, and a thousand years as one day.
2 Pet. 3:8

Thrust in Thy sickle, and reap.
Rev. 14:15

The time is come for Thee to reap; for the harvest of the earth is ripe.
Rev. 14:15

[*See also* Imminence, Procrastination, Second Coming]

TIMIDITY

When I have a convenient season, I will call for thee.
Felix to Paul
Acts 24:25

God hath not given us the spirit of fear; but of power, and of love, and of a sound mind.
2 Tim. 1:7

[*See also* Confidence, Fear]

TOLERANCE

Why eateth your Master with publicans and sinners?
Matt. 9:11
See also Luke 5:30

O faithless and perverse generation, how long shall I be with you? how long shall I suffer you?
Jesus
Matt. 17:17
See also Mark 9:19, Luke 9:41

Judge not, and ye shall not be judged: condemn not, and ye shall not be condemned.
Jesus
Luke 6:37
See also Matt. 7:1

Forgive, and ye shall be forgiven.
Jesus
Luke 6:37

Let not him which eateth not judge him that eateth.
Rom. 14:3

One man esteemeth one day above another: another esteemeth every day alike. Let every man be fully persuaded in his own mind.
Rom. 14:5

We then that are strong ought to bear the infirmities of the weak.
Rom. 15:1

Receive ye one another, as Christ also received us to the glory of God.
Rom. 15:7

Let no man think me a fool; if otherwise, yet as a fool receive me.
2 Cor. 11:16

For ye suffer fools gladly, seeing ye yourselves are wise.
2 Cor. 11:19

[*See also* Equality, Forgiveness]

TONGUES

The Spirit gave them utterance.
Acts 2:4

We do hear them speak in our tongues the wonderful works of God.
Acts 2:11

These men are full of new wine.
Acts 2:13

He that speaketh in an unknown tongue speaketh not unto men, but unto God: for no man understandeth him.
1 Cor. 14:2

He that speaketh in an unknown tongue edifieth himself; but he that prophesieth edifieth the church.
1 Cor. 14:4

Except ye utter by the tongue words easy to be understood, how shall it be known what is spoken? for ye shall speak into the air.
1 Cor. 14:9

Tongues are for a sign, not to them that believe, but to them that believe not.
1 Cor. 14:22

TORMENT

In those days shall men seek death, and shall not find it; and shall desire to die, and death shall flee from them.
Rev. 9:6

They have no rest day nor night, who worship the beast and his image.
Rev. 14:11

The lake of fire and brimstone.
Rev. 20:10

[*See also* Anguish, Grief, Suffering]

TRADITION

Laying aside the commandment of God, ye hold the tradition of men.
Jesus
Mark 7:8

Ye reject the commandment of God, that ye may keep your own tradition.
Jesus
Mark 7:9
See also Matt. 15:3

As your fathers did, so do ye.
Acts 7:51

[*See also* Heritage, Posterity, Rituals]

TRAITORS

See Betrayal, Loyalty, Treachery.

TRAPS

See Strategy.

TREACHERY

By thy sorceries were all nations deceived.
Rev. 18:23

[*See also* Betrayal, Loyalty]

TRIBULATION

See Suffering.

TRINITY

Go ye therefore, and teach all nations, baptizing them in the name of the Father, and of the Son, and of the Holy Ghost.
Jesus
Matt. 28:19

The grace of the Lord Jesus Christ, and the love of God, and the communion of the Holy Ghost, be with you all.
2 Cor. 13:14

There are three that bear record in heaven, the Father, the Word, and the Holy Ghost: and these three are one.
1 John 5:7

There are three that bear witness in earth, the Spirit, and the water, and the blood: and these three agree in one.
1 John 5:8

[*See also* God, Holy Spirit, Jesus]

TROUBLE

Sufficient unto the day is the evil thereof.
Jesus
Matt. 6:34

This sickness is not unto death, but for the glory of God.
Jesus
John 11:4

Give none offence.
1 Cor. 10:32

[*See also* Assistance, Danger, Escape, God's Protection, Safety]

TRUST

We trust in the living God, who is the Saviour of all men.
1 Tim. 4:10

Cast not away therefore your confidence, which hath great recompence of reward.
Heb. 10:35

[*See also* Betrayal, Faith, God's Protection, Reliance, Safety]

TRUTH

Heaven and earth shall pass away, but my words shall not pass away.
Jesus
Matt. 24:35, Mark 13:31,
Luke 21:33

The law was given by Moses, but grace and truth came by Jesus Christ.
John 1:17

He that doeth truth cometh to the light, that his deeds may be made manifest.
Jesus
John 3:21

God is true.
John 3:33

He that sent me is true, whom ye know not.
Jesus
John 7:28

Ye shall know the truth, and the truth shall make you free.
Jesus
John 8:32

Because I tell you the truth, ye believe me not.
Jesus
John 8:45
See also John 8:46

These are not the words of him that hath a devil.
John 10:21

I am the way, the truth, and the life: no man cometh unto the Father, but by me.
Jesus
John 14:6

Sanctify them through Thy truth.
Jesus
John 17:17

Thy word is truth.
Jesus to God
John 17:17

To this end was I born, and for this cause came I into the world, that I should bear witness unto the truth.
Jesus
John 18:37

Every one that is of the truth heareth my voice.
Jesus
John 18:37

What is truth?
Pilate
John 18:38

We cannot but speak the things which we have seen and heard.
Acts 4:20

Well spake the Holy Ghost by Esaias the prophet unto our fathers.
Acts 28:25

Let God be true, but every man a liar.
Rom. 3:4

We can do nothing against the truth, but for the truth.
2 Cor. 13:8

Behold, before God, I lie not.
Gal. 1:20

Am I therefore become your enemy, because I tell you the truth?
Gal. 4:16

The truth is in Jesus.
Eph. 4:21

Whatsoever things are true, whatsoever things are honest, whatsoever things are just, whatsoever things are pure, whatsoever things are lovely, whatsoever things are of good report; if there be any virtue, and if there be any praise, think on these things.
Phil. 4:8

I have not written unto you because ye know not the truth, but because ye know it.
1 John 2:21

It is the Spirit that beareth witness, because the Spirit is truth.
1 John 5:6

I have no greater joy than to hear that my children walk in truth.
3 John 4

Just and true are Thy ways, Thou King of saints.
Rev. 15:3

Behold a white horse; and he that sat upon him was called Faithful and True.
Rev. 19:11

[*See also* Candor, Credibility, Dishonesty, Honesty, Lies]

U

UNCERTAINTY

See Doubt.

UNDERPRIVILEGED

Ye have the poor with you always.
Jesus
Mark 14:7
See also Matt. 26:11, John 12:8

He hath filled the hungry with good things; and the rich He hath sent empty away.
Luke 1:53

Support the weak.
1 Thess. 5:14

[*See also* Charity, Poverty, Wealth, Widows and Orphans]

UNDERSTANDING

Who hath ears to hear, let him hear.
Jesus
Matt. 13:9, Matt. 13:43
See also, e.g., Matt. 11:15, Mark 4:9, Rev. 13:9

They seeing see not; and hearing they hear not, neither do they understand.
Jesus
Matt. 13:13
See also Isa. 6:9, Isa. 42:20, Acts 28:26

Having eyes, see ye not? and having ears, hear ye not?
Jesus
Mark 8:18

We do hear them speak in our tongues the wonderful works of God.
Acts 2:11

When I was a child, I spake as a child, I understood as a child, I thought as a child: but when I became a man, I put away childish things.
1 Cor. 13:11

Now we see through a glass, darkly; but then face to face.
1 Cor. 13:12

Be not children in understanding.
1 Cor. 14:20

The peace of God, which passeth all understanding.
Phil. 4:7

Anoint thine eyes with eyesalve, that thou mayest see.
Jesus
Rev. 3:18

Let him that hath understanding count the number of the beast.
Rev. 13:18

[*See also* Compassion, Education, Folly, Ignorance, Knowledge, Wisdom]

UNITY

If a kingdom be divided against itself, that kingdom cannot stand.
Jesus
Mark 3:24
See also Matt. 12:25, Luke 11:17

If a house be divided against itself, that house cannot stand.
Jesus
Mark 3:25
See also Matt. 12:35, Luke 11:17

I and my Father are one.
Jesus
John 10:30

All that believed were together, and had all things common.
Acts 2:44

We, being many, are one body in Christ, and every one members one of another.
Rom. 12:5

Is Christ divided?
1 Cor. 1:13

We being many are one bread, and one body: for we are all partakers of that one bread.
1 Cor. 10:17

One Lord, one faith, one baptism.
Eph. 4:5

Both He that sanctifieth and they who are sanctified are all of one.
Heb. 2:11

[*See also* Cooperation]

UNIVERSALITY

There shall be one fold, and one shepherd.
Jesus
John 10:16

Is He the God of the Jews only? is He not also of the Gentiles?
Rom. 3:29

I am made all things to all men, that I might by all means save some.
1 Cor. 9:22

There is neither Jew nor Greek, there is neither bond nor free, there is neither male nor female: for ye are all one in Christ Jesus.
Gal. 3:28

[*See also* Brotherhood]

UNIVERSE

See Heaven and Earth, Nature.

URGENCY

I must work the works of Him that sent me, while it is day.
Jesus
John 9:4

The time is short.
1 Cor. 7:29

[*See also* Speed]

VALUE

Ye are the salt of the earth.
Jesus
Matt. 5:13

If the salt have lost his savour, wherewith shall it be salted? it is thenceforth good for nothing.
Jesus
Matt. 5:13
See also Mark 9:50, Luke 14:34

Give not that which is holy unto the dogs, neither cast ye your pearls before swine.
Jesus
Matt. 7:6

Ye are of more value than many sparrows.
Jesus
Matt. 10:31, Luke 12:7

If a man have an hundred sheep, and one of them be gone astray, doth he not leave the ninety and nine, and goeth into the mountains, and seeketh that which is gone astray?
Jesus
Matt. 18:12
See also Luke 15:4

[*See also* Quality]

VALUES

Lay up for yourselves treasures in heaven, where neither moth nor rust doth corrupt, and where thieves do not break through nor steal.
Jesus
Matt. 6:20

Is not the life more than meat, and the body than raiment?
Jesus
Matt. 6:25
See also Luke 12:23

He that loveth father or mother more than me is not worthy of me: and he that loveth son or daughter more than me is not worthy of me.
Jesus to disciples
Matt. 10:37

Thou savourest not the things that be of God, but those that be of men.
Jesus
Matt. 16:23
See also Mark 8:33

What shall a man give in exchange for his soul?
Jesus
Matt. 16:26, Mark 8:37

What shall it profit a man, if he shall gain the whole world, and lose his own soul?
Jesus
Mark 8:36
See also Matt. 16:26, Luke 9:25

If thy foot offend thee, cut it off: it is better for thee to enter halt into life, than having two feet to be cast into hell.
Jesus
Mark 9:45
See also Matt. 18:8

It is better for thee to enter into the kingdom of God with one eye, than having two eyes to be cast into hell fire.
Jesus
Mark 9:47
See also Matt. 18:9

Take no thought for your life, what ye shall eat; neither for the body, what ye shall put on.
Jesus
Luke 12:22
See also Matt. 6:25

That which is highly esteemed among men is abomination in the sight of God.
Jesus
Luke 16:15

Labour not for the meat which perisheth, but for that meat which endureth unto everlasting life.
Jesus
John 6:27

They loved the praise of men more than the praise of God.
John 12:43

The things which are seen are temporal; but the things which are not seen are eternal.
2 Cor. 4:18

What things were gain to me, those I counted loss for Christ.
Phil. 3:7

Above all these things put on charity, which is the bond of perfectness.
(charity: love)
Col. 3:14

Hold fast to that which is good.
1 Thess. 5:21

He that said, Do not commit adultery, said also, Do not kill.
James 2:11

Know ye not that the friendship of the world is enmity with God?
James 4:4

Buy of me gold tried in the fire, that thou mayest be rich; and white raiment, that thou mayest be clothed.
Jesus
Rev. 3:18

[*See also* Goals, Materialism, Spirituality]

See Arrogance, Conceit.

See Revenge.

They think that they shall be heard for their much speaking.
Jesus (They: heathens praying)
Matt. 6:7

[*See also* Eloquence, Speech]

See Martyrdom, Persecution, Sacrifice.

Be of good cheer; I have overcome the world.
Jesus
John 16:33

Sit Thou on my right hand, Until I make Thy foes Thy footstool.
Acts 2:34–35
See also Ps. 110:1, Matt. 22:44

They which run in a race run all, but one receiveth the prize.
1 Cor. 9:24

Thanks be to God, which giveth us the victory through our Lord Jesus Christ.
1 Cor. 15:57

Whatsoever is born of God overcometh the world.
1 John 5:4

To him that overcometh will I give to eat of the hidden manna.
Jesus
Rev. 2:17

They overcame him by the blood of the Lamb.
(him: Satan)
Rev. 12:11

The Lamb shall overcome them: for He is Lord of lords, and King of kings.
Rev. 17:14

Alleluia: for the Lord God omnipotent reigneth.
Rev. 19:6

He that overcometh shall inherit all things.
Rev. 21:7

[*See also* Confidence, Defeat, Reward, Success]

See Attitude, Perspective.

Take heed that no man deceive you. For many shall come in my name, saying, I am Christ.
Jesus
Matt. 24:4–5
See also Mark 13:6, Luke 21:8

Watch therefore: for ye know not what hour your Lord doth come.
Jesus
Matt. 24:42
See also Matt. 25:13

What, could ye not watch with me one hour?
Jesus
Matt. 26:40
See also Mark 14:37

Watch and pray, that ye enter not into temptation.
Jesus
Matt. 26:41
See also Luke 22:40, 46

Take heed to yourselves.
Jesus
Mark 13:9

Take ye heed, watch and pray: for ye know not when the time is.
Jesus
Mark 13:33
See also Matt. 13:23

Watch ye therefore: for ye know not when the master of the house cometh.
Jesus
Mark 13:35

If the goodman of the house had known what hour the thief would come, he would have watched.
Jesus
Luke 12:39
See also Matt. 24:43

Watch ye therefore, and pray always.
Jesus
Luke 21:36

Take heed therefore unto yourselves, and to all the flock.
Acts 20:28

Now it is high time to awake out of sleep.
Rom. 13:11

Let us not sleep, as do others; but let us watch and be sober.
1 Thess. 5:6

They that sleep sleep in the night; and they that be drunken are drunken in the night.
1 Thess. 5:7

Be sober, be vigilant; because your adversary the devil, as a roaring lion, walketh about, seeking whom he may devour.
1 Pet. 5:8

Look to yourselves, that we lose not those things which we have wrought.
2 John 8

Blessed is he that watcheth, and keepeth his garments, lest he walk naked, and they see his shame.
Rev. 16:15

[*See also* Deception, Readiness]

VINDICATION

Many that are first shall be last; and the last first.
Jesus
Mark 10:31
See also Matt. 19:30, Matt. 20:16

The stone which the builders rejected is become the head of the corner.
Jesus
Mark 12:10

See also Ps. 118:22, Matt. 21:42, Luke 20:17

Sit Thou on my right hand, Until I make Thy foes Thy footstool.
Acts 2:34–35
See also Ps. 110:1, Matt. 22:44

VIOLENCE

All they that take the sword shall perish with the sword.
Jesus
Matt. 26:52
See also Rev. 13:10

Do violence to no man, neither accuse any falsely.
Luke 3:14

Be ye come out, as against a thief, with swords and staves?
Jesus
Luke 22:52

Their feet are swift to shed blood.
Rom. 3:15

Destruction and misery are in their ways: And the way of peace have they not known.
Rom. 3:16–17
See also Isa. 59:7–8

With violence shall that great city Babylon be thrown down.
Rev. 18:21

[*See also* Destruction, Murder, War]

VIRTUE

Whatsoever things are true, whatsoever things are honest, whatsoever things are just, whatsoever things are pure, whatsoever things are lovely, whatsoever things are of good report; if there be any virtue, and if there be any praise, think on these things.
Phil. 4:8

Add to your faith virtue; and to virtue knowledge.
2 Pet. 1:5

[*See also* Goodness, Honesty, Integrity, Kindness, Righteousness]

See Sight.

Your young men shall see visions, and your old men shall dream dreams.
>Acts 2:17
>See also Joel 2:28

Behold, I see the heavens opened, and the Son of man standing on the right hand of God.
>Stephen
>Acts 7:56

They heard not the voice of Him that spake to me.
>Paul
>Acts 22:9

If a spirit or an angel hath spoken to him, let us not fight against God.
>Pharisees, about Paul
>Acts 23:9

Who is worthy to open the book, and to loose the seals thereof?
>Rev. 5:2

[*See also* Future]

Lift up the hands which hang down, and the feeble knees.
>Heb. 12:12

[*See also* Fortitude]

Whatsoever is right, that shall ye receive.
>Jesus
>Matt. 20:7

Be content with your wages.
>John the Baptist to soldiers
>Luke 3:14

The labourer is worthy of his reward.
>1 Tim. 5:18
>See also Luke 10:7

[*See also* Employees]

All they that take the sword shall perish with the sword.
>Jesus
>Matt. 26:52
>See also Rev. 13:10

Such things must needs be.
>Jesus
>Mark 13:7

Armageddon.
>Rev. 16:16

In righteousness He doth judge and make war.
>Rev. 19:11

[*See also* Battle Calls, Defeat, God's Protection, Peace, Strife, Violence, Weapons]

Think not that I am come to send peace on earth: I came not to send peace, but a sword.
>Jesus
>Matt. 10:34
>See also Luke 12:51

[*See also* Peace, War]

Behold, I have foretold you all things.
>Jesus
>Mark 13:23

If the goodman of the house had known what hour the thief would come, he would have watched.
>Jesus
>Luke 12:39
>See also Matt. 24:43

Ye can discern the face of the sky and of

the earth; but how is it that ye do not discern this time?
Jesus
Luke 12:56
See also Matt. 16:3

Sin no more, lest a worse thing come unto thee.
Jesus
John 5:14

If this counsel or this work be of men, it will come to nought: But if it be of God, ye cannot overthrow it.
Acts 5:38–39

Antichrist shall come.
1 John 2:18

Even now are there many antichrists.
1 John 2:18

Receive not of her plagues.
(her: Babylon)
Rev. 18:4

[*See also* Heedfulness, Prudence, Vigilance]

WASTE

Give not that which is holy unto the dogs, neither cast ye your pearls before swine.
Jesus
Matt. 7:6

It is not meet to take the children's bread, and to cast it to dogs.
Jesus
Matt. 15:26
See also Mark 7:27

Gather up the fragments that remain, that nothing be lost.
Jesus
John 6:12

WATER

Doth a fountain send forth at the same place sweet water and bitter?
James 3:11

[*See also* Thirst]

WEAKNESS

God hath chosen the weak things of the world to confound the things which are mighty.
1 Cor. 1:27

Who is weak, and I am not weak? who is offended, and I burn not?
2 Cor. 11:29

Support the weak.
1 Thess. 5:14

[*See also* Fortitude, Strength]

WEALTH

Lay up for yourselves treasures in heaven, where neither moth nor rust doth corrupt, and where thieves do not break through nor steal.
Jesus
Matt. 6:20

Where your treasure is, there will your heart be also.
Jesus
Matt. 6:21, Luke 12:34

The care of this world, and the deceitfulness of riches, choke the word.
Jesus
Matt. 13:22
See also Mark 4:19

If thou wilt be perfect, go and sell that thou hast, and give to the poor, and thou shalt have treasure in heaven: and come and follow me.
Jesus
Matt. 19:21
See also Mark 10:21, Luke 18:22

A rich man shall hardly enter into the kingdom of heaven.
Jesus
Matt. 19:23

It is easier for a camel to go through the eye of a needle, than for a rich man to enter into the kingdom of God.
Jesus
Matt. 19:24, Mark 10:25
See also Luke 18:25

How hard is it for them that trust in riches to enter into the kingdom of God!
Jesus
Mark 10:24
See also Luke 18:24

Woe unto you that are rich! for ye have received your consolation.
Jesus
Luke 6:24

Though He was rich, yet for your sakes He became poor, that ye through His poverty might be rich.
2 Cor. 8:9

We brought nothing into this world, and it is certain we can carry nothing out.
1 Tim. 6:7

They that will be rich fall into temptation and a snare.
1 Tim. 6:9

Be rich in good works.
1 Tim. 6:18

Ye rich men, weep and howl for your miseries that shall come upon you.
James 5:1

The merchants of the earth are waxed rich through the abundance of her delicacies.
(her: Babylon)
Rev. 18:3

[*See also* Greed, Materialism, Money, Poverty, Profit, Sharing, Underprivileged, Values, Worldliness]

WEAPONS

The shield of faith, wherewith ye shall be able to quench all the fiery darts of the wicked.
Eph. 6:16

He that killeth with the sword must be killed with the sword.
Rev. 13:10

[*See also* War, War and Peace]

WICKED PEOPLE

O generation of vipers.
E.g., Matt. 3:7, Luke 3:7

The Lord reward him according to his works.
2 Tim. 4:14

[*See also* Evil, Punishment, Sinners, Wickedness]

WICKEDNESS

Ye serpents, ye generation of vipers, how can ye escape the damnation of hell?
Jesus
Matt. 23:33

What city is like unto this great city!
(city: Babylon)
Rev. 18:18

[*See also* Corruption, Decadence, Depravity, Evil, Good and Evil, Immorality, Punishment, Righteousness, Sin, Sinners]

WIDOWS AND ORPHANS

Honour widows that are widows indeed.
1 Tim. 5:3

Visit the fatherless and widows in their affliction.
James 1:27

[*See also* Compassion]

WILL POWER

See Temptation.

WINE

See Drunkenness, Liquor.

WISDOM

A wise man, which built his house upon a rock.
Jesus
Matt. 7:24

Neither do men put new wine into old bottles: else the bottles break, and the wine runneth out.
Jesus
Matt. 9:17
See also Mark 2:22, Luke 5:37

Wisdom is justified of her children.
Jesus
Matt. 11:19
See also Luke 7:35

Behold, a greater than Solomon is here.
Jesus
Matt. 12:42, Luke 11:31

Ye can discern the face of the sky and of the earth; but how is it that ye do not discern this time?
Jesus
Luke 12:56
See also Matt. 16:3

I will destroy the wisdom of the wise, and will bring to nothing the understanding of the prudent.
1 Cor. 1:19
See also Isa. 29:14

The foolishness of God is wiser than men.
1 Cor. 1:25

Let him become a fool, that he may be wise.
1 Cor. 3:18

The wisdom of this world is foolishness with God.
1 Cor. 3:19
See also 1 Cor. 1:20

If any of you lack wisdom, let him ask of God.
James 1:5

[*See also* Education, Experience, Folly, Fools, Ignorance, Knowledge, Understanding]

WITCHCRAFT

Thou child of the devil, thou enemy of all righteousness.
Acts 13:10

WITNESS

See Perjury, Testimony.

WOMEN

If a woman have long hair, it is a glory to her.
1 Cor. 11:15

Let your women keep silence in the churches: for it is not permitted unto them to speak.
1 Cor. 14:34

If they will learn any thing, let them ask their husbands at home.
1 Cor. 14:35

It is a shame for women to speak in the church.
1 Cor. 14:35

Let the woman learn in silence with all subjection.
1 Tim. 2:11

[*See also* Family, Man and Woman, Mankind, Marriage]

WONDERS

This is the Lord's doing, and it is marvellous in our eyes.
Jesus
Matt. 21:42
See also, e.g., Ps. 118:23,
   Mark 12:11

Ye shall see heaven open, and the angels of God ascending and descending upon the Son of man.
Jesus
John 1:51

Eye hath not seen, nor ear heard, neither have entered into the heart of man, the things which God hath prepared for them that love Him.
1 Cor. 2:9
See also Isa. 64:4

[*See also* Awe, Miracles, Nature]

WORK

Come unto me, all ye that labour and are heavy laden, and I will give you rest.
Jesus
Matt. 11:28

The labourer is worthy of his hire.
Jesus
Luke 10:7
See also Matt. 10:10

One soweth, and another reapeth.
Jesus
John 4:37

We are labourers together with God.
1 Cor. 3:9

Let every man abide in the same calling wherein he was called.
1 Cor. 7:20

Do all to the glory of God.
1 Cor. 10:31

He which soweth sparingly shall reap also sparingly.
2 Cor. 9:6

Whatsoever a man soweth, that shall he also reap.
Gal. 6:7

Of the Lord ye shall receive the reward of the inheritance.
Col. 3:24

Ye serve the Lord Christ.
Col. 3:24

If any would not work, neither should he eat.
2 Thess. 3:10

The labourer is worthy of his reward.
1 Tim. 5:18

The husbandman that laboureth must be first partaker of the fruits.
2 Tim. 2:6

Study to show thyself approved unto God, a workman that needeth not to be ashamed.
2 Tim. 2:15

The cries of them which have reaped are entered into the ears of the Lord.
James 5:4

Servants, be subject to your masters with all fear; not only to the good and gentle.
1 Pet. 2:18
See also Eph. 6:5

[*See also* Cooperation, Diligence, Effort, Employees]

WORLDLINESS

Thou savourest not the things that be of God, but those that be of men.
Jesus
Matt. 16:23
See also Mark 8:33

The children of this world are in their generation wiser than the children of light.
Jesus
Luke 16:8

Ye are from beneath; I am from above: ye are of this world; I am not of this world.
Jesus
John 8:23

Be not conformed to this world.
Rom. 12:2

I would have you wise unto that which is good, and simple concerning evil.
Rom. 16:19

Hath not God made foolish the wisdom of this world?
1 Cor. 1:20

The wisdom of this world is foolishness with God.
1 Cor. 3:19

For though we walk in the flesh, we do not war after the flesh.
2 Cor. 10:3

Set your affection on things above, not on things on the earth.
Col. 3:2

Whosoever therefore will be a friend of the world is the enemy of God.
James 4:4

Love not the world, neither the things that are in the world.
1 John 2:15

If any man love the world, the love of the Father is not in him.
1 John 2:15

They are of the world: therefore speak they of the world.
1 John 4:5

[*See also* Conformity, Materialism, Self-Denial, Spirituality]

Which of you by taking thought can add one cubit unto his stature?
Jesus
Matt. 6:27
See also Luke 12:25

Take therefore no thought for the morrow: for the morrow shall take thought for the things of itself.
Jesus
Matt. 6:34

The care of this world, and the deceitfulness of riches, choke the word.
Jesus
Matt. 13:22
See also Mark 4:19

Take no thought for your life, what ye shall eat; neither for the body, what ye shall put on.
Jesus
Luke 12:22
See also Matt. 6:25

Let not your heart be troubled, neither let it be afraid.
Jesus
John 14:27
See also John 14:1

[*See also* Burdens]

WORSHIP

Thou shalt worship the Lord thy God, and Him only shalt thou serve.
Jesus
Matt. 4:10
See also Deut. 6:13

In vain they do worship me, teaching for doctrines the commandments of men.
Jesus
Matt. 15:9, Mark 7:7
See also Isa. 29:13

Thou shalt love the Lord thy God with all thy heart, and with all thy soul, and with all thy mind. This is the first and great commandment.
Jesus
Matt. 22:37–38
See also Deut. 6:5, Mark 12:29–30,
   Luke 10:27

Ye worship ye know not what.
Jesus
John 4:22

They that worship Him must worship Him in spirit and in truth.
Jesus
John 4:24

Whom therefore ye ignorantly worship, Him declare I unto you.
Acts 17:23

After the way which they call heresy, so worship I the God of my fathers.
Paul
Acts 24:14

When they knew God, they glorified Him not as God.
Rom 1:21

Worship God: for the testimony of Jesus is the spirit of prophecy.
Rev. 19:10

[*See also* Churches, Devotion, God's Temple, Godlessness, Hypocrisy, Idolatry, Idols, Prayer, Rituals]

WORTHINESS

If the house be worthy, let your peace come upon it: but if it be not worthy, let your peace return to you.
Jesus
Matt. 10:13

He that loveth father or mother more than me is not worthy of me: and he that loveth son or daughter more than me is not worthy of me.
Jesus to disciples
Matt. 10:37

He that taketh not his cross, and followeth after me, is not worthy of me.
Jesus
Matt. 10:38
See also Luke 14:27

The labourer is worthy of his hire.
Jesus
Luke 10:7
See also Matt. 10:10, 1 Tim. 5:18

Walk worthy of the Lord.
Col. 1:10
See also 1 Thess. 2:12

Who is worthy to open the book, and to loose the seals thereof?
Rev. 5:2

Worthy is the Lamb that was slain.
Rev. 5:12

[*See also* Value]

WRATH

See Anger.

YOUTH

Your young men shall see visions, and your old men shall dream dreams.
Acts 2:17
See also Joel 2:28

Let no man despise thy youth.
1 Tim. 4:12

Every one that useth milk is unskilful in the word of righteousness: for he is a babe.
Heb. 5:13

[*See also* Age, Children]

ZEAL

Preach ye upon the housetops.
Jesus
Matt. 10:27
See also Luke 12:3

I persecuted them even unto strange cities.
Paul
Acts 26:11

I continue unto this day, witnessing both to small and great.
Paul
Acts 26:22

They have a zeal of God, but not according to knowledge.
Rom. 10:2

I seek not your's, but you.
2 Cor. 12:14

He which persecuted us in times past now preacheth the faith which once he destroyed.
(He: Paul)
Gal. 1:23

It is good to be zealously affected always in a good thing.
Gal. 4:18

Earnestly contend for the faith which was once delivered unto the saints.
Jude 3

[*See also* Devotion, Enthusiasm]

APPENDIX

Contents

The Beatitudes
from The Sermon on the Mount

Blessed are the poor in spirit: for theirs is the kingdom of heaven.

Blessed are they that mourn: for they shall be comforted.

Blessed are the meek: for they shall inherit the earth.

Blessed are they which do hunger and thirst after righteousness: for they shall be filled.

Blessed are the merciful: for they shall obtain mercy.

Blessed are the pure in heart: for they shall see God.

Blessed are the peacemakers: for they shall be called the children of God.

Blessed are they which are persecuted for righteousness' sake: for theirs is the kingdom of heaven.

Blessed are ye, when men shall revile you, and persecute you, and shall say all manner of evil against you falsely, for My sake.

Rejoice, and be exceeding glad: for great is your reward in heaven: for so persecuted they the prophets which were before you.

Matt. 5:3–12
See also Luke 6:20–24

The Lord's Prayer

Our Father which art in heaven, Hallowed be Thy name.

Thy kingdom come. Thy will be done in earth, as it is in heaven.

Give us this day our daily bread.

And forgive us our debts, as we forgive our debtors.

And lead us not into temptation, but deliver us from evil: For Thine is the kingdom, and the power, and the glory, for ever. Amen.

Matt. 6:9–13
See also Luke 11:2–4

On Love
from 1 Corinthians*

Though I speak with the tongues of men and of angels, and have not love, I am become as sounding brass, or a tinkling cymbal.

And though I have the gift of prophecy, and understand all mysteries, and all knowledge; and though I have all faith, so that I could remove mountains, and have not love, I am nothing.

And though I bestow all my goods to feed the poor, and though I give my body to be burned, and have not love, it profiteth me nothing.

Love suffereth long, and is kind; love envieth not; love vaunteth not itself, is not puffed up,

Doth not behave itself unseemly, seeketh not her own, is not easily provoked, thinketh no evil;

Rejoiceth not in iniquity, but rejoiceth in the truth;

Beareth all things, believeth all things, hopeth all things, endureth all things.

Love never faileth: but whether there be prophecies, they shall fail; whether there be tongues, they shall cease; whether there be knowledge, it shall vanish away.

For we know in part, and we prophesy in part.

But when that which is perfect is come, then that which is in part shall be done away.

When I was a child, I spake as a child, I understood as a child, I thought as a child: but when I became a man, I put away childish things.

For now we see through a glass, darkly; but then face to face: now I know in part; but then shall I know even as also I am known.

And now abideth faith, hope, love, these three; but the greatest of these is love.

1 Cor. 13:1–13

---

*In the King James Version of the Bible, "charity" is used as the English translation for the Latin "caritas" and the Greek "agape." Biblical scholars generally agree, however, that "love" is a more accurate translation today. For purposes of this appendix, "love" has been substituted each time the word "charity" ordinarily appears in the KJV, both for purposes of accuracy and to clearly illustrate one of the Bible's most beautiful and renowned passages on love.

KEY-WORD INDEX

Explanation

This Index gives the key words in every quotation in the book (except for "Jesus," "God," and "Lord," which appear too often to make it practical), together with a few adjacent words to provide the context. It serves two purposes.

If you remember certain words from a quotation but cannot remember the entire quotation or its citation, you can look up the word here and locate the page number on which that quotation first appears (it may be placed in other categories as well).

The Index also serves as a supplement to the categories in the book itself. For example, although there is no category titled "heart" in the main section, readers seeking quotations about that word can easily find them with this Key-Word Index.

A

abased
  exalt himself shall be a., 89
  exalteth shall be a., 5
  himself shall be a., 31
abide
  a. in the same calling, 33
ability
  a. which God giveth, 123
able
  a. of these stones, 72
  a. to kill the soul, 18
  a. to save and destroy, 70
  believe ye that I am a., 13
  that is a. to receive, 20
  who shall be a. to stand,
    70
abomination
  a. in the sight of, 119
  a. of desolation, 44
abominations
  the A. of the Earth, 43
abounded
  where sin a., 66
above
  a. where Christ sitteth, 69
  affection on things a., 5
  given thee from a., 10
  I am from a., 77
  perfect gift is from a., 77
  that cometh from a. is a.,
    9
Abraham
  before A. was, 24
  do the works of A., 91
  God of A., 85
  if ye were A.'s children, 91
  seed of A., 104
  seed of A., 104
  up children unto A., 72
absent
  a. from the Lord, 112
  a. in body, 1
  a. in the flesh, 1
abstain
  a. from all appearance, 13
  a. from fleshly lusts, 116
abundance
  a. of the heart, 22
  not in the a. of, 119
  rich through the a., 35
abundant
  labours more a., 136
acceptable
  patiently, this is a., 2
accepteth
  a. no man's person, 7

account
  a. of himself to God, 152
  put that on mine a., 152
  they shall give a., 151
accuse
  a. any falsely, 35
accusers
  where are thine a., 2
Adam
  A. was first formed, 10
  in A. all die, 112
add
  a. to your faith, 61
  a. unto him the plagues,
    138
  can a. one cubit unto, 126
  if any man shall a., 138
administrations
  differences of a. but, 47
admonish
  a. him as a brother, 11
adulterers
  whoremongers and a., 3
adulteries
  out of heart proceed a.,
    126
adulterous
  a. generation, 123
adultery
  a. in his heart, 3
  committeth a., 48
  divorced committeth a., 3
  do not commit a., 27
  dost thou commit a., 3
  his wife to commit a., 3
  man should not commit a.,
    3
  marry another, commit a.,
    48
  not commit a., 3
  not commit a. said also, 4
  she committeth a., 3
advantage
  a. then hath the Jew, 26
advantageth
  what a. it me, 147
adversary
  agree with thine a., 8
  your a. the devil, 162
adversity
  them which suffer a., 30
advocate
  a. with the Father, 97
affection
  a. on things above, 5
afraid
  be a. for he beareth, 63
  be not a., 27

be not a., 51
  be not a. only believe, 59
  neither let it be a., 27
  not a. of them that kill,
    126
again
  brother shall rise a., 152
  except a man be born a.,
    18
  He shall rise a., 152
  I will come a., 164
  ye must be born a., 18
against
  not a. us is for us, 4
  not with me is a. me, 97
  who can be a. us, 31
age
  he is of a., 120
  that are of full a., 120
agree
  a. with thine adversary, 8
air
  birds of the a., 87
  speak into the a., 29
alas
  a. a. that great city, 40
alike
  esteemeth every day a., 21
alive
  Christ shall all be made a.,
    112
  I am a. for evermore, 24
  said that He was a., 6
all
  a. be made alive, 112
  a. have sinned, 117
  a. shall know Me, 3
  a. that ever I did, 98
  a. things are delivered, 97
  a. things are delivered, 2
  a. things are lawful, 12
  a. things are of God, 73
  a. things are possible, 13
  a. things are possible, 1
  a. things are possible, 72
  a. things to a. men, 3
  by Him a. things consist,
    12
  by Him a. things created,
    36
  Christ is a. and in a., 100
  endureth a. things, 114
  He died for a., 37
  He is before a., 12
  He that built a. things, 2
  let a. things be done, 12
  possessing a. things, 60
  sanctified are a. of one, 85

Spirit searcheth a., 86
alleluia
    a. for the Lord, 73
alms
    do not a. before men, 22
    have, and give a., 23
    when thou doest a., 22
    when thou doest thine a.,
        22
alone
    for I am not a., 105
    I am not a., 112
    let Him thus a., 118
    live by bread a., 78
Alpha
    I am A. and Omega, 12
always
    but me ye have not a., 139
    have the poor a., 139
    I am with you a., 24
am
    be as I a., 53
    I a. what I a., 22
ambassador
    a. in bonds, 94
ambassadors
    a. for Christ, 123
Anathema
    let him be A., 38
angel
    if an a. hath spoken, 1
angels
    a. were cast out, 132
    confess before the a., 3
    denied before the a., 75
    entertained a. unawares, 6
    equal unto the a., 6
    heaven open, and the a.,
        70
    lower than the a., 117
    not the a. of heaven, 164
    ordained by a., 28
    presence of the a., 94
    seen of a., 100
    spared not the a., 6
    tongues of men and of a.,
        50
    vision of a., 6
    we shall judge a., 6
    with His mighty a., 75
anger
    not your children to a., 23
    put off all these; a., 12
angry
    a. with his brother, 6
anguish
    remembereth no more the
        a., 16

anoint
    a. thine eyes with, 169
    fastest, a. thine head, 62
anointed
    a. me to preach, 52
another
    do we look for a., 48
    love one a., 12
    love one to a., 25
    one day above a., 21
answer
    know how ye ought to a.,
        35
antichrist
    a. shall come, 6
    is a. that denieth, 7
antichrists
    are there many a., 6
Apollos
    planted, A. watered, 38
    who is A., 110
apostles
    rejoice ye holy a., 154
apparel
    silver, or gold, or a., 96
appeal
    a. unto Caesar, 10
appear
    a. not unto men to fast, 62
    a. righteous unto men, 7
    a. the second time, 164
    a. unto men to fast, 90
    a. with Him in glory, 153
    when Christ shall a., 153
appearance
    according to the a., 7
    from all a. of evil, 13
appeared
    a. for this purpose, 124
appeareth
    a. for a little time, 126
appointed
    a. a day, 105
    a. us to wrath, 105
    that which is a. you, 80
arise
    a. and be baptized, 11
    a. and go into Damascus,
        124
    a. and make thy bed, 83
    men a. speaking perverse,
        15
Armageddon
    A., 44
armies
    compassed with a., 51
armour
    a. of God, 73

a. of light, 77
    whole a. of God, 162
arrayed
    not a. like the lilies, 7
art
    graven by a. and man's, 75
ascending
    angels a. and descending,
        71
ashamed
    a. of me and of my words,
        78
    a. of the testimony, 100
    hope maketh not a., 87
    I am not a., 32
    let him not be a., 25
    not a. of the gospel, 78
    on Him shall not be a., 14
    Son of man be a., 78
    that needeth not be a., 45
ask
    a. and it shall be given,
        140
    a. and ye shall receive, 82
    a. any thing in my name,
        99
    a. in my name, 71
    a. in prayer, believing, 13
    a. of me, I will give, 143
    a. the Father in my name,
        99
    a. their husbands, 195
    because ye a. amiss, 126
    because ye a. not, 141
    he is of age; a., 120
    know not what ye a., 127
    lack wisdom, let him a.,
        195
    need of, before ye a., 71
    of him they will a., 58
    son a. bread, 106
    to them that a. Him, 68
    whatsoever we a. we, 141
    ye a. and receive not, 126
asketh
    every one that a., 140
    give to him that a., 18
asps
    poison of a., 82
astray
    one of them be gone a.,
        137
    seeketh that which is a.,
        137
asunder
    let not man put a., 48
athirst
    let him that is a. come, 55

unto him that is a., 43
audience
  fear God, give a., 84
author
  a. of confusion, 21
  Jesus the a. and, 100
authority
  a. over the man, 10
avenge
  a. not yourselves, 154
avenged
  God hath a. you on her,
    154
avoid
  a. foolish questions, 34
awake
  a. to righteousness, 12
  time to a., 161
away
  if I go not a., 86
  put a. his wife, 3

B

babblings
  profane and vain b., 64
babe
  for he is a b., 92
babes
  as newborn b., 74
  out of the mouth of b., 23
Babylon
  away beyond B., 58
  B. be thrown down, 76
  B. came in remembrance,
    146
  B. the great is fallen, 40
  B. the Great, the Mother,
    43
  that great city B., 40
back
  if any man draw b., 11
  looking b. is fit, 45
baptism
  b. of repentance, 11
  one b., 11
Baptist
  John B.'s head, 154
baptize
  b. you with the Holy, 11
  Christ sent me not to b.,
    56
baptized
  arise, and be b., 11
  arose, and was b., 34
  b. you with water, 11
  believeth and is b., 11
  hinder me to be b., 11

repent, and be b., 11
baptizing
  b. them in the name, 55
Barabbas
  not this man, but B., 24
barbarian
  B. Scythian, bond nor, 53
  speaketh a b., 29
barbarians
  Greeks, and to the B., 85
battle
  prepare himself to the b.,
    11
beam
  cast out the b., 36
  the b. in thine own eye, 16
bear
  they b. witness of me, 2
  to b. my name, 56
bearing
  b. His cross, 1
beast
  the number of the b., 57
  worship the b. and his, 92
beaten
  synagogues ye shall be b.,
    135
beautiful
  appear b. outward, 7
  b. are the feet, 78
bed
  arise, and make thy b., 83
  rise, take up thy b., 83
befall
  things that shall b. me, 49
before
  b. Abraham was, 24
  b. faith came, 28
  b. God, I lie not, 186
  He is b. all things, 12
beginning
  b. of the world, 68
  b. was the Word, 11
  been with me from the b.,
    56
  every man at the b., 88
  heard from the b., 114
  I am the b. and the end, 12
  sinneth from the b., 162
begotten
  b. through the gospel, 78
  gave His only b., 54
  name of the only b., 13
  only b. Son into the, 100
behaviour
  be in b. as becometh, 13
beheaded
  the souls of them b., 119

behind
  get thee b. me, Satan, 64
behold
  b. the man, 2
  b. thy mother, 103
  woman, b. thy son, 63
being
  move, and have our b., 111
believe
  all men will b., 118
  b. in God b. also in me, 14
  b. in thine heart, 101
  b. not every spirit, 14
  b. not his writings, 38
  b. not me, b. the works, 14
  b. not that I am He, 121
  b. not, yet He abideth, 14
  b. on the Lord Jesus, 14
  b. on the name of His, 28
  b. that Jesus Christ is, 14
  b. that Thou art Christ,
    101
  b. that ye receive, 59
  b. to the saving of the, 39
  b. ye that I am able, 13
  be not afraid, only b., 59
  cometh to God must b., 14
  devils also b., 63
  earthly things and ye b., 13
  except I see I will not b.,
    49
  for them that b. not, 144
  how shall they b., 14
  how shall ye b., 13
  how shall ye b. my words,
    38
  little ones that b., 23
  Lord, I b., 14
  not to them that b., 185
  repent ye, and b., 78
  sent, Him ye b. not, 121
  slow of heart to b., 144
  that b. are justified, 14
  wonders, ye will not b., 13
  work of God, that ye b., 49
  ye b. me not, 173
believed
  all that b. were, 188
  as thou hast b. so be, 59
  b. on in the world, 100
  great number b., 34
  had ye b. Moses, 14
  know whom I have b., 32
  ministers by whom ye b.,
    110
  nearer than when we b.,
    161
  not b. in the name, 13

not seen and yet have b.,
  14
some b. the things, 137
spoken, and some b. not,
  137
ye would have b. me, 14
believeth
  and b. on Him that sent,
    13
  b. all things, 114
  b. in Him shall receive, 66
  b. in Him should not, 160
  b. in Him should not per-
    ish, 39
  b. not is condemned, 13
  b. not on me, but on Him,
    14
  b. not shall be damned, 38
  b. on me shall never, 43
  he that b. in me, 14
  he that b. on me, 14
  husband that b. not, 14
  liveth and b. in me, 14
  possible to him that b., 1
  that b. and is baptized, 11
  that b. not God, 14
  that b. not the Son, 13
  to every one that b., 78
  who b. that Jesus is, 121
  whomsoever b. on Him, 14
  with the heart man b., 14
  world, that whosoever b.,
    52
believing
  ask in prayer, b., 13
  faithless, but b., 49
belly
  make thy b. bitter, 16
beloved
  b. which was not b., 72
  Lord, my dearly b., 45
  this is My b. Son, 97
  this is My b. Son, 121
beneath
  ye are from b., 77
benevolence
  unto the wife due b., 117
berries
  fig tree bear olive b., 33
beseech
  love's sake I b., 110
betray
  eateth with me shall b.,
    15
  one of you shall b., 15
betrayed
  b. into the hands, 15
  Son of man is b., 15

betrayest
  b. thou the Son of man, 15
betrayeth
  b. me is at hand, 15
  hand of him that b., 15
better
  b. for thee to enter, 83
  b. if the will of God be, 2
  b. that a millstone, 23
  b. to enter halt into, 38
  b. to marry than to burn,
    21
  blessed of the b., 10
  not in marriage doeth b.,
    21
between
  b. us and you there is a, 84
beware
  b. lest any man spoil, 41
  b. of covetousness, 80
  b. of false prophets, 41
  b. of the scribes, 91
  b. ye of the leaven, 91
bewitched
  who hath b., 41
bind
  b. on earth shall be, 139
  they b. heavy burdens, 90
birds
  b. of the air, 87
bishop
  b. must be blameless, 110
  office of a b., 5
bits
  b. in the horses', 129
bitter
  make thy belly b., 16
  sweet water and b., 33
  wives, and be not b., 118
bitterness
  gall of b., 53
black
  one hair white or b., 128
blade
  first the b., 80
blasphemed
  b. among the Gentiles, 91
blasphemeth
  that b. against the Holy, 16
blasphemies
  out of heart proceed b.,
    126
blasphemy
  all manner of sin and b.,
    16
  b. against the Holy Ghost,
    16
  put off all these; b., 12

bless
  b. and curse not, 38
  b. them that curse, 38
  b. them which persecute,
    38
  being reviled, we b., 2
blessed
  b. and holy is he that, 40
  b. are the dead which, 40
  b. are the meek, 89
  b. are the merciful, 120
  b. are the peacemakers,
    133
  b. are the persecuted, 107
  b. are the poor, 89
  b. are the pure in heart,
    146
  b. are they called, 82
  b. are they that do, 111
  b. are they that have not,
    14
  b. are they that hear, 78
  b. are they that mourn, 27
  b. are they which hunger,
    156
  b. are they whose, 66
  b. are ye that weep, 109
  b. are ye, when men, 33
  b. art thou among women,
    102
  b. he that keepeth, 130
  b. is He that cometh, 121
  b. is he that readeth, 144
  b. is he that watcheth, 164
  b. is the man, 66
  b. is the man that, 182
  less is b., 10
  more b. to give, 5
  thou shalt be b., 20
blessing
  same mouth proceedeth b.,
    17
blind
  b. guides which strain, 91
  b. lead the b., 17
  b. see, 81
  b. ye should have no sin,
    95
  eyes of the b., 2
  I was b. now I see, 58
  poor and b. and naked,
    120
  the lame, the b., 20
blood
  b. be on us, 151
  b. of bulls, 66
  b. of Jesus, 17
  b. of the new testament, 17

b. upon your own heads, 81
but by water and b., 11
by the b. of the Lamb, 159
drink His b., 29
drinketh my b., 54
drinketh my b., 98
flesh and b., 107
flesh and b. hath not, 101
given them b. to drink, 119
innocent of the b., 16
moon into b., 51
new testament in my b., 29
nigh by the b. of Christ, 25
not against flesh and b., 52
purchased with His own b., 49
redemption through His b., 66
shed the b. of saints, 119
Spirit, water, and b., 183
swift to shed b., 57
without shedding of b., 17

blotted
sins may be b. out, 34

bloweth
b. where it listeth, 127

boast
if thou b. thou bearest, 17

bodies
b. are the members of, 18

bodily
b. exercise profiteth, 76
fulness of the Godhead b., 47

body
absent in b., 1
against his own b., 66
b. is of Christ, 9
b. is the temple, 18
b. not for fornication, 18
b. of this death, 6
b. shall be full of, 22
b. what ye shall put on, 65
b. without the spirit, 40
bear in my b. the marks, 136
defileth the whole b., 175
glorify God in your b., 18
head of the b., 10
home in the b., 112
kill the b. and after, 126
kill the b. but are not, 18
light of the b., 18
members of His b., 100
my b. to be burned, 23
nor yet for your b., 119
one b. in Christ, 26

one bread, and one b., 64
take, eat; this is my b., 29
the b. than raiment, 119
this is my b. which is, 29
whole b. should be cast, 38
ye are the b. of Christ, 25
yourselves in the b., 30

bond
b. nor free: but Christ, 53
b. of iniquity, 53
b. of perfectness, 114
neither b. nor free, 53

bondage
same is he brought in b., 67

bonds
ambassador in b., 94
remember my b., 94
remember them in b., 30

bondwoman
children of the b., 85

bones
members of His b., 100

book
b. of this prophecy, 144
out of the b., 144
plagues in this b., 138
prophecy of this b., 130
seest, write in a b., 18
the b. of life, 39
worthy to open the b., 127

books
b. that should be written, 18

born
b. of God overcometh, 76
b. of God sinneth not, 172
b. of the flesh is, 15
b. of the Spirit is, 15
end was I b., 102
except a man be b., 11
except a man be b. again, 18
had not been b., 15
I was free b., 67
righteousness is b. of, 157
that loveth is b. of God, 115
the Christ is b. of God, 121
unto you is b. this day, 25
who is b. of God doth, 18
ye must be b. again, 18

borrow
from him that would b., 18

bottles
b. break, and the wine, 194

must be put into new b., 11
new wine into old b., 194

bottomless
b. pit, 84

bought
b. with a price, 67

bound
b. in heaven, 139
b. in the spirit, 49
b. unto a wife, 48
b. with this chain, 94
ready not to be b. only, 44
word of God is not b., 78

bountifully
soweth b. shall reap, 45

bow
every knee should b., 87

bowed
b. His head, 37

bramble
b. bush gather, 33

branches
holy, so are the b., 85
vine, ye are the b., 9

brass
become as sounding b., 50

bread
b. he shall live forever, 19
b. of God is He, 18
b. that I will give, 148
day our daily b., 65
he that eateth b., 15
I am the b. of life, 18
I am the living b., 19
not live by b. alone, 78
not live by b. alone, 163
one b. and one body, 64
partakers of that one b., 64
son ask b., 106
stones be made b., 21
take the children's b., 168

break
b. mine heart, 181
bottles b. and wine, 194

breastplate
b. of faith, 13

breath
to all life, and b., 70

brethren
least of these my b., 22
love as b., 13
men, b. and fathers, 106
mother and my b. are, 62
our lives for the b., 159
perils among false b., 51
strengthen thy b., 51
ye are b. why do ye, 8

bride
    voice of the b., 42
bridegroom
    voice of the b., 42
bright
    the b. and morning star, 101
brimstone
    lake of fire and b., 146
broad
    b. is the way, 38
broken
    body, which is b., 29
brokenhearted
    heal the b., 42
brother
    admonish him as a b., 11
    and hateth his b., 76
    angry with his b., 6
    b. beloved, 64
    b. goeth to law with b., 109
    b. shall rise again, 152
    b. trespass, 36
    hateth his b., 19
    have thy b.'s wife, 3
    loveth God love his b., 19
    loveth his b., 114
    loveth not his b., 19
    mote out of thy b.'s eye, 36
    mote that is in thy b.'s, 16
    reconciled to thy b., 22
    the same is my b., 62
    who hateth his b. is a, 82
    withdraw from every b., 29
brotherly
    b. love continue, 19
build
    b. my church, 177
    if I b. again, 81
    intending to b. a tower, 138
    what house will ye b., 26
builded
    every house is b. by, 2
    he who hath b., 2
builders
    stone which the b., 132
built
    b. his house on a rock, 138
    b. his house on the sand, 138
    but He that b. all, 2
    without a foundation b., 4
bulls
    blood of b., 66
burden
    bear his own b., 152

burdens
    b. grievous to be borne, 19
    bear ye one another's b., 19
    bind heavy b., 90
    touch not the b. with, 19
burn
    better to marry than b., 21
    offended, and I b., 51
burned
    b. in their lust, 87
    give my body to be b., 23
burning
    b. and a shining light, 96
bury
    dead b. their dead, 151
    field, to b. strangers, 20
bush
    bramble b., 33
bushel
    put it under a b., 145
business
    about my Father's b., 49
    do your own b., 13
buy
    b. of me gold tried, 61
buyeth
    no man b. their, 6

C

Caesar
    appeal unto C., 10
    art not C.'s friend, 184
    C.'s judgment seat, 25
    nor yet against C., 95
    render therefore unto C., 25
    things which are C.'s, 25
    we have no king but C., 116
Cain
    gone in the way of C., 76
calf
    hither the fatted c., 20
call
    c. any man common, 151
    c. His name Emmanuel, 103
    c. His name Jesus, 102
    c. His name Jesus, 102
    c. no man your father, 70
    c. not thou common, 146
    c. on the name of, 8
    c. them My people, 72
    rich unto all that c., 70
    why c. ye me Lord, 41

called
    as the Lord hath c., 33
    c. us unto uncleanness, 85
    c. you friends, 67
    c. you unto His kingdom, 69
    he that is c., 67
    many are c., 113
    that is c. in the Lord, 15
    they with Him are c., 61
    vocation ye are c., 25
    wherein he was c., 33
callest
    why c. thou me good, 77
calleth
    faithful is He that c., 70
calling
    abide in the same c., 33
    c. of God, 17
    prize of the high c., 30
came
    c. from God, 99
    c. not to judge, 105
    c. unto His own, 8
camel
    easier for a c. to go, 106
    swallow a c., 91
candle
    light of a c. shall, 42
    men light a c., 145
candlestick
    bushel, but on a c., 145
captives
    deliverance to the c., 42
captivity
    shall go into c., 106
    that leadeth into c., 106
carcase
    wheresoever the c., 21
care
    c. of the church, 26
    c. of the world, 78
    take c. of him, 77
carefully
    sought it c. with, 148
careth
    c. for things of world, 45
    c. not for the sheep, 44
    he that is unmarried c., 44
carnal
    c. mind is enmity, 20
    spiritual: but I am c., 20
carnally
    c. minded is death, 9
carpenter
    this the c.'s son, 98
carry
    c. you beyond Babylon, 58

certain we can c., 40

cast
be thou c. into the sea, 59
body c. into hell, 38
c. away His people, 104
c. into hell fire, 83
c. it from thee, 16
c. it to dogs, 168
c. not away your, 32
c. off the works, 77
c. out devils, 82
c. out devils, 58
c. out the beam, 36
c. out the mote, 36
c. ye your pearls, 188
cut it off, and c., 16
feet to be c. into hell, 38
let him first c. a stone, 2
pluck it out, and c., 38
poor widow hath c. more,
68
power to c. into hell, 38
Satan c. out Satan, 58

cause
angry without a c., 6
but for this c., 124
c. came I into the world,
102

causeth
c. his wife to commit, 3

cease
c. to pervert, 62

ceasing
pray without c., 141

chain
bound with this c., 94

charge
sin to their c., 66

charity
above all things have c.,
114
angels, and have not c., 50
be sound in faith, in c., 13
burned, and have not c.,
23
c. edifieth, 31
c. envieth not, 114
c. never faileth, 114
c. out of a pure heart, 114
c. shall cover the, 114
c. suffereth long, 114
c. vaunteth not, 114
faith, hope, c., 60
greatest of these is c., 60
lusts: but follow c., 13
not c. I am nothing, 60
put on c., 114
things be done with c., 114

with a kiss of c., 64

chasten
I love, I rebuke and c., 46

chasteneth
father c. not, 24
the Lord loveth he c., 23

chastening
no c. for the present, 37
the c. of the Lord, 2

cheek
on thy right c. turn, 65
smiteth thee on the one c.,
65

cheer
be of good c., 51
be of good c., 27
be of good c., 27

cheerful
loveth a c. giver, 9

chickens
a hen gathereth her c., 110

chief
whosoever will be c., 89

child
c. I spake as a c., 24
c. of the devil, 57
delivered of the c., 16
kingdom as a little c., 24
receive one little c., 23
thought as a c., 24
understood as a c., 24
virgin shall be with c., 102

childish
put away c. things, 152

children
all the c. of God, 53
angels and are the c. of, 6
become as little c., 34
blood be on our c., 151
c. in understanding, 120
c. keep yourselves from, 92
c. let no man deceive, 157
c. obey your parents, 24
c. obey your parents, 129
c. of disobedience, 47
c. of light, 25
c. of the bondwoman, 85
c. of the day, 25
c. of this world are, 196
c. ought not to lay, 132
c. walk in truth, 24
called the c. of God, 133
desolate hath more c., 24
good gifts unto your c., 68
henceforth be no more c.,
48
if ye were Abraham's c., 91
justified of her c., 195

love the c. of God, 115
malice be ye c., 57
of c. or of strangers, 180
of God, as dear c., 12
parents for the c., 132
provoke not your c., 6
provoke not your c., 23
same unto us their c., 78
stones to raise up c., 72
suffer the little c., 23
take the c.'s bread, 168
than the c. of light, 196
to love their c., 118
walk as c. of light, 12
we are c. of God, 24
weep for your c., 80
you, and to your c., 86

choke
c. the word, 78

chosen
but I have c. you, 24
c. the foolish things, 64
c. the weak things, 193
c. vessel unto me, 56
c. you twelve, 15
few are c., 113
they with Him are c., 61
witnesses c. before of, 144
ye have not c. me, 24

Christ
ambassadors for C., 123
as C. also hath loved, 12
as C. loved the church, 114
as ye have received C., 12
being free, is C.'s, 67
believe on C., 14
belong to C., 27
blood of C., 25
blood of C. cleanseth, 17
body is of C., 9
bring us unto C., 28
by faith in C., 53
C. also received, 64
C. being raised, 24
C. came into the world,
100
C. died for our sins, 37
C. died for the ungodly, 37
C. died for us, 37
C. hath made us free, 67
C. hath redeemed, 28
C. is all, 100
C. is dead in vain, 28
C. is God's, 14
C. is the head of the, 118
C. is the Son of God, 14
C. liveth in me, 100
C. maketh thee whole, 83

■ 211 ■

C. pleased not Himself, 5
C. sent me not to, 56
C. sitteth on the right, 69
C. the same yesterday, 21
C. the Saviour of the, 13
C. the Son of the living,
103
C. to come out of her, 58
C. we shall be saved, 160
C. who is our life, 153
C.'s sake hath forgiven, 66
calling of God in C., 30
church subject unto C.,
118
confess that C. is Lord, 3
counted loss for C., 102
crucified with C., 37
dead in C. shall, 25
denieth that Jesus is C.,
111
do all things through C., 1
even as C. forgave, 66
fools for C.'s sake, 122
good soldier of C., 136
gospel of C., 78
grace that is in C., 67
head of C. is God, 10
head of every man is C.,
10
hope in C., 153
if any man be in C., 18
if C. be not raised, 60
in C. I have begotten, 78
in C. neither circumcision,
26
in C. shall all be alive, 112
in the name of Jesus C., 83
instructors in C., 18
is C. divided, 188
judgment seat of C., 53
judgment seat of C., 105
life is hid with C., 102
live godly in C., 76
love of C., 44
members of C., 18
name of C. happy are ye,
136
not be the servant of C., 8
not ourselves, but C., 142
partakers of C.'s, 164
peace be with you in C.,
17
preach C. crucified, 37
preach unto you, is C., 121
rejoice in C., 15
revelation of C., 78
Saviour, which is C., 103
saying, I am C., 62

sweet savour of C., 25
that Jesus is the C., 121
the man C., 74
Thou art the C., 101
to live is C., 112
truth C. is preached, 69
truth came by Jesus C., 28
will of God in C., 79
word of C., 74
ye are all one in C., 15
ye are C.'s, 14
ye are the body of C., 25
Christian
man suffer as a C., 25
persuadest me to be a C.,
50
Christians
disciples were called C.,
25
Christs
false C., 84
church
build my c., 177
c. is subject unto, 118
care of the c., 26
Christ also loved the c.,
114
edifieth the c., 29
feed the c. of God, 49
head of the body, the c.,
10
is the head of the c., 118
speak in the c., 26
churches
silence in the c., 26
Spirit saith unto c., 84
unto the seven c., 18
circumcision
c. availeth any thing, 26
c. is nothing, 26
c. is that of the heart, 26
c. nor uncircumcision, 53
c. which is outward, 7
profit is there of c., 26
we are the c., 15
cities
even unto strange c., 136
city
c. Babylon be thrown, 76
c. had no need of, 71
c. of the great king, 128
c. of the great King, 97
c. set on an hill, 110
c. set on an hill, 62
like unto this great c., 194
perils in the c., 39
that great c. Babylon, 40
what c. is like unto, 194

clay
potter power over the c.,
140
clean
c. through the word, 85
canst make me c., 59
heads; I am c., 81
ye are not all c., 15
cleanse
c. the lepers, 138
c. your hands, 146
cleansed
lepers are c., 81
what God hath c., 146
cleanseth
c. us from all sin, 17
cleave
c. to which is good, 12
cloak
let him have thy c., 68
no c. for their sin, 57
closed
eyes have they c., 92
closet
enter into thy c., 140
closets
spoken in the ear in c., 58
clothed
c. with humility, 90
naked, and ye c. me, 30
clothing
love to go in long c., 91
to you in sheep's c., 41
cloud
coming in a c., 164
clouds
c. they are without, 22
wells without water, c.,
22
coals
heap c. of fire, 168
coat
take away thy c., 68
coats
he that hath two c., 168
cock
before the c. crow, 43
immediately the c. crew,
43
cold
neither c. nor hot, 29
would thou wert c. or, 52
come
antichrist shall c., 6
behold, I c. quickly, 165
c. from God, 47
c. in my Father's name, 9
c. on thee as a thief, 164

consisteth
c. not in the abundance, 119

consolation
also of the c., 179
received your c., 194

consuming
God is a c. fire, 70

contain
world could not c., 18

contend
earnestly c. for the, 61

content
c. with such things as, 33
c. with your wages, 192
let us be c., 80
therewith to be c., 5

contentment
godliness with c., 33

continue
c. in my word, 46
c. unto this day, 182

contradiction
without all c., 10

contrary
c. to the law, 58

convenient
c. season, 184

converted
except ye be c., 34
repent, and be c., 34
when thou art c., 51

converteth
c. the sinner from the, 149

corn
c. in the ear, 80

corner
done in a c., 165
head of the c., 132

corners
c. of the streets, 90

corrupt
c. tree bringeth forth, 22
evil communications c., 22
moth and rust doth c., 119
moth nor rust doth c., 175

corruptible
obtain a c. crown, 30

corruption
of the flesh reap c., 116
sown in c., 18

cost
counteth the c., 138

counsel
if this c. be of men, 41

counsellor
who hath been His c., 108

count
c. him not as an enemy, 11
c. number of the beast, 57

counted
c. loss for Christ, 102

counteth
c. the cost, 138

country
honour in his own c., 150
save in his own c., 144

course
finished my c., 2

courteous
brethren, be c., 13

covenant
c. had been faultless, 36
He saith, a new c., 36
mediator of the new c., 120

covenants
c. of promise, 44

covered
sins are c., 66
there is nothing c., 165

covet
shalt not c., 53
thou shalt not c., 53

coveted
c. no man's silver, 96

covetousness
beware of c., 80

craftiness
cunning c., 48

created
by Him all things c., 36
man c. for the woman, 116

Creator
creature more than the C., 91

creature
c. of God is good, 65
he is a new c., 18
served the c. more, 91

cried
c. out, saying, crucify, 37

cries
c. of them which have, 196

crooked
c. shall be made, 130

cross
bear His c., 19
bearing His c., 1
come down from the c., 121
enemies of c. of Christ, 75
glory, save in the c., 17
take up his c., 4
take up the c., 4

that taketh not his c., 4

crow
before the cock c., 43

crown
a c. of life, 55
c. of righteousness, 156
c. of thorns, 162
obtain a corruptible c., 30
receive a c. of glory, 156

crownedst
c. him with glory, 117

crucified
c. with Christ, 37
preach Christ c., 37
would not have c., 37

crucify
saying, c. Him, c., 37
take ye Him, and c., 124

crumbs
dogs eat of the c., 168

crying
neither sorrow, nor c., 40
voice of one c., 104
voice of one c. in the, 35

cubit
can add one c., 126

cunning
c. craftiness, 48

cup
c. is the new testament, 29
c. of water, 27
c. pass from me, 178
c. which my Father, 1
cannot drink the c. of, 4
Lord, and the c. of devils, 4

curse
bless them that c., 38
bless, and c. not, 38
redeemed us from the c., 28

curseth
c. father or mother, 132

cursing
blessing and c., 17

custom
c. to whom c., 63
take c. or tribute, 180

cut
c. it off, 16
foot offend thee, c., 38

cymbal
become a tinkling c., 50

D

daily
day our d. bread, 65
exhort one another d., 51

Damascus
  arise, and go into D., 124
damnation
  escape the d. of hell, 38
  resist shall receive d., 148
  resurrection of d., 38
damned
  believeth not shall be d.,
    38
damsel
  d. is not dead, 111
danced
  ye have not d., 39
danger
  d. of the judgment, 6
dare
  would even d. to die, 40
darkly
  see through a glass, d., 26
darkness
  abide in d., 52
  d. comprehended it not, 52
  d. is past, 52
  full of d., 22
  in Him is no d., 70
  is in d., 19
  light be not d., 22
  light, lest d. come, 108
  light shineth in d., 52
  men loved d., 56
  rulers of the d., 52
  shall not walk in d., 14
  that sit in d., 52
  turn them from d., 56
  turned into d., 51
  walketh in d., 92
  works of d., 77
  ye were sometimes d., 102
darts
  d. of the wicked, 60
daughter
  loveth d. more than me, 62
  mother against the d., 62
David
  Christ of the seed of D.,
    153
  sure mercies of D., 16
  the offspring of D., 101
day
  appointed a d., 105
  children of the d., 25
  continue unto this d., 182
  d. and hour knoweth, 163
  d. He shall rise again, 37
  d. is this scripture, 122
  d. is with the Lord as, 133
  d. of His wrath is come, 70
  d. of salvation, 161

d. of the Lord will come,
    164
d. shall not come, 164
esteemeth every d. alike,
    21
give us this d., 65
him up at the last d., 54
in the d. of judgment, 151
is born this d., 25
no rest d. nor night, 92
not be shut by d., 83
notable d. of the Lord, 51
one day above another, 21
plagues come in one d.,
    138
raised up the third d., 144
regardeth the d., 87
renewed d. by d., 67
rise the third d., 152
seven times in a d., 66
Sodom in d. of judgment,
    93
sufficient unto the d., 68
third d. He shall rise, 152
thousand years as one d.,
    133
us, who are of the d., 13
while it is d., 49
withstand in the evil d.,
    73
days
  and see good d., 57
  d. of vengeance, 105
  d. shall men seek death, 40
dead
  blessed are the d. which,
    40
  Christ is d. in vain, 28
  d. and your life is hid, 102
  d. are raised, 81
  d. bury their d., 151
  d. in Christ shall, 25
  d. is freed from sin, 40
  d. to the law, 28
  d. while she liveth, 93
  d. yet shall he live, 14
  damsel is not d., 111
  faith without works d., 40
  hell delivered up the d.,
    105
  if the d. rise not, 147
  if we be d. with Him, 100
  living among the d., 152
  not the God of the d., 70
  raise the d., 82
  raise the d., 153
  raised from the d., 24
  raised from the d., 153

raised Him from the d.,
    153
raised Him from the d.,
    101
rose from the d., 137
saw the d. small and, 105
that liveth and was d., 153
without the spirit is d., 40
without works is d., 42
deadly
  full of d. poison, 175
deaf
  d. hear, 81
  d. to hear, 81
death
  abideth in d., 19
  body of this d., 6
  carnally minded is d., 9
  d. and hell delivered up,
    105
  D. and Hell followed, 7
  d. and hell were cast, 40
  d. is swallowed up in, 40
  d. mourning and famine,
    138
  d. of the testator, 40
  d. shall flee from them, 40
  d. where is thy sting, 40
  die the d., 132
  die the d., 145
  enemy destroyed is d., 40
  faithful unto d., 55
  not taste of d. till, 39
  save a soul from d., 149
  second d. hath no power,
    40
  shall be no more d., 40
  shall men seek d., 40
  shall never see d., 39
  sickness is not unto d., 71
  sin bringeth forth d., 40
  sorrowful, even unto d., 6
  sting of d. is sin, 40
  this is the second d., 40
  wages of sin is d., 54
  worthy of d., 95
deaths
  in d. oft, 136
debtor
  d. both to the Greeks, 85
debtors
  forgive our d., 65
debts
  forgive us our d., 65
deceit
  philosophy and vain d., 41
deceitfulness
  d. of riches, 78

deceive
children, let no man d., 157
d. you with vain words, 41
heed that no man d., 62
let no man d., 31
let no man d., 164
lie in wait to d., 48
no sin, we d. ourselves, 95

deceived
be not d., 60
heed that ye be not d., 41
were all nations d., 41

deceiveth
nothing, he d. himself, 31

decently
all things be done d., 12

declare
d. His generation, 85
Him d. I unto you, 92
seen and heard declare we, 85

decrease
but I must d., 125

deed
love in d. and in truth, 42
ye do in word or d., 42

deeds
d. may be made manifest, 41
d. were evil, 56
partaker of his evil d., 35
without d. of the law, 42

deep
well is d., 127

defence
d. of the gospel, 78
fathers, hear ye my d., 106

defile
d. the temple of God, 159
within, and d. the man, 169

defiled
and conscience is d., 9
unto them that are d., 9

defileth
d. not a man, 146
d. the whole body, 175
into the mouth d. a man, 65
out of mouth d., 65

defraud
d. not, 27

delicacies
abundance of her d., 35

deliver
d. me from every evil, 159
d. me from the body, 6
d. the godly out of, 42

d. us from evil, 56

deliverance
preach d., 42

delivered
all things are d., 2
all things are d. unto, 97
d. for our offences, 153
d. Him up unto thee, 2
d. of the child, 16
d. out of the mouth, 42
envy they had d., 53
that d. me unto thee, 81

deliverer
the D., 103

den
d. of thieves, 26

denied
d. before the angels, 75

denieth
d. the Father and the, 7
liar but he that d., 111
that d. me before men, 75
whosoever d. the Son, 43

deny
d. before my Father, 42
d. me thrice, 43
He cannot d. Himself, 14
He will also d. us, 33
if we d. Him, 33
in works they d. Him, 42
let him d. himself, 4
whosoever shall d. me, 42
yet will I not d., 21

depart
d. from me, 31
d. from me, all ye, 29
let him d., 75
unbelieving d., 75

departing
after my d. shall, 177

descending
d. like a dove, 85
d. upon the Son of man, 71
I saw the Spirit d., 86

desire
d. to be first, 5
d. when ye pray, 59
though I d. to glory, 17

desireth
straightway d. new, 95

desirous
d. of vain glory, 5

desolate
d. hath more children, 24

desolation
abomination of d., 44
d. thereof is nigh, 51

despair
perplexed, but not in d., 4

despise
d. not prophesyings, 144
d. not thou the, 2
d. the other, 115
let no man d., 198

despiseth
d. me d. Him that sent, 46
d. not man but God, 47
d. you d. me, 46

despitefully
d. use you, 29

destroy
d. the wisdom of the, 31
d. this temple, 44
him shall God d., 159
not come to d., 68
not come to d., 121
to kill, and to d., 36
to save and to d., 70

destroyed
cast down, but not d., 4
faith which once he d., 21
last enemy d. is, 40
the things which I d., 81

destruction
d. and misery, 88
end is d., 75
leadeth to d., 38

device
by art and man's d., 75

devices
ignorant of his d., 162

devil
child of the d., 57
d. is come, 162
d. open the eyes, 2
d. shall cast some into, 4
d. sinneth from beginning, 162
he hath a d., 116
of your father the d., 56
one of you is a d., 15
resist the d., 162
sin is of the d., 162
wiles of the d., 162
words of a d., 116
your adversary the d., 162

devils
cast out d., 82
cast out d., 58
cup of d., 4
d. also believe, 63
even the d. are subject, 161
sacrifice to d., 75
the habitation of d., 40

die

as in Adam all d., 112
d. at Jerusalem for, 44
d. in your sins, 121
d. the death, 132
d. we are the Lord's, 112
flesh, ye shall d., 20
in me shall never d., 14
let him d. the death, 145
refuse not to d., 95
righteous man will one d., 39
shall desire to d., 40
though I should d., 21
to d. is gain, 112
tomorrow we shall d., 138
which d. in the Lord, 40
would even dare to d., 40

died

Christ d. for our sins, 37
Christ d. for the ungodly, 37
d. unto sin once, 37
He d. for all, 37
in that He d., 37
yet sinners, Christ d., 158

dieth

d. no more, 24
no man d. to himself, 40
worm d. not, 84

difference

no d. between the Jew, 53

differences

d. of administrations, 47

differeth

one star d., 83

discern

d. the face of the sky, 192
d. the signs of the, 45
hypocrites, ye can d., 45
not d. this time, 193

disciple

cannot be my d., 44
d. is not above his, 45
enough for the d., 5

disciples

d. called Christians, 25
know that ye are my d., 25
then are ye my d., 46

discouraged

anger, lest they be d., 23

disfigure

they d. their faces, 90

disobedience

children of d., 47
one man's d., 66

disobedient

for the lawless and d., 109

disorderly

brother that walketh d., 29

disputations

doubtful d., 34

disputings

without murmuring and d., 2

dissimulation

love be without d., 114

distress

tribulation, or d., 44

ditch

both fall into the d., 17

diversities

d. of gifts, 1

divided

d. against himself, 161
d. against itself, 79
d. against itself, 177
father d. against the, 62
is Christ d., 188

divideth

d. his sheep, 24

division

nay; but rather d., 133

divorced

marry her that is d., 3

do

and d. not the things, 41
d. all things through, 1
d. all without murmurings, 2
d. and thou shalt live, 113
d. as I have done, 12
d. that I would not, 16
d. to you, d. ye also to, 12
d. ye even so to them, 12
doest, d. quickly, 15
fear what man shall d., 32
go, and d. thou likewise, 77
know not what they d., 66
men should d. to you, 12
my name, I will d. it, 99
no more I that d. it, 152
no more I that d. it, 16
they say, and d. not, 90
ye d. it heartily, 50

doctrine

become sound d., 48
d. is not mine, 48
every wind of d., 48
longsuffering and d., 133
teaching for d., 84
to exhortation, to d., 48

doers

d. of the law, 41
d. of the word, 42

doest

that thou d. do quickly, 15

doeth

none that d. good, 35
sayings of mine, and d., 41
sayings of mine, and d., 46
that heareth, and d. not, 4

dog

d. is turned to his own, 11

dogs

cast it to d., 168
d. eat of the crumbs, 168
holy unto the d., 188
without are d. and, 41

doing

suffer for well d., 2
this is the Lord's d., 178

dominion

glory and d. forever, 73
glory and d. forever, 100
sin shall not have d., 79

done

believed, so be it d., 59
do as I have d., 12
not d. in a corner, 165
Thy will be d., 70

door

before thee an open d., 131
entereth in by the d., 110
I am the d., 103
standeth before the d., 93
voice, and open the d., 102

double

d. minded man is, 94
d. unto her d. her works, 57

doubt

wherefore didst thou d., 48

doubtful

d. disputations, 34

doubting

without wrath and d., 141

dove

descending like a d., 85
from heaven like a d., 86

doves

harmless as d., 173
harmless as d., 39

down

come d. from the cross, 121
d. but not destroyed, 4
gods are come d., 123

dream

old men shall d. dreams, 49

dreams

old men shall dream d., 49

drink
   and ye gave me d., 30
   and ye gave me no d., 37
   cannot d. the cup of the, 4
   come unto me, and d., 43
   d. His blood, 29
   d. in my name, 27
   d. it, in remembrance, 29
   given them blood to d.,
     119
   if he thirst give him d., 52
   let us eat and d., 138
   not meat and d., 86
   shall I not d. it, 1
   what ye shall d., 119
drinketh
   d. my blood, 54
   d. my blood, 98
   d. of this water, 54
drunk
   d. of the wine of wrath, 35
   d. old wine, 95
   not d. with wine, 49
drunken
   they that be d. are d., 75
dry
   walketh through d., 56
dull
   d. of hearing, 92
dumb
   d. before His shearer, 120
   d. to speak, 81
dwell
   He will d. with them, 74
   word of Christ d., 74
dwelleth
   commandments d. in Him,
     130
   d. in love d. in God, 115
   d. no good thing, 20
   d. not in temples, 26
   drinketh my blood, d., 98
   God d. in him and he in,
     76
   God d. in us, 115
   Him d. all the fulness, 47
   sin that d., 152
   sin that d., 16
   Spirit of God d. in, 86
dwelt
   flesh, and d. among us, 98

E

eagles
   e. be gathered, 21
ear
   blade, then the e., 80

full corn in the e., 80
he that hath an e., 84
man have an e. let him, 144
nor e. heard, 17
spoken in the e., 58
earnestly
   e. contend for the faith, 61
ears
   e. are dull, 92
   e. hear ye not, 178
   fulfilled in your e., 122
   His e. are open unto, 73
   that hath e. to hear, 96
   the e. of the Lord, 196
   uncircumcised in e., 75
   who hath e. to hear, 84
earth
   Abominations of the E., 43
   and that are in e., 36
   bind on e. shall be, 139
   cast out into the e., 132
   come to give peace on e.,
     133
   e. is My footstool, 26
   e. is the Lord's, 49
   e. it is His footstool, 128
   e. shall pass away, 24
   e. were passed away, 83
   ends of the e., 34
   father upon the e., 70
   harvest of the e. is, 120
   heaven and e. to pass, 28
   house upon the e., 4
   inhabiters of the e., 162
   inherit the e., 89
   is taken from the e., 85
   kings of the e., 180
   Lord of heaven and e., 26
   made heaven, and e., 36
   of the kings of the e., 103
   on e. peace, good will, 19
   power on e. to forgive, 65
   salt of the e., 22
   saw a new e., 83
   send peace on e., 192
   sky and of the e., 193
   swear not by the e., 96
   that bear witness in e., 183
   things on the e., 5
   Thy will be done in e., 70
   treasures upon e., 119
   vessels of e., 47
earthly
   if I told you e., 13
earthquakes
   great e. shall be, 7
easier
   e. for a camel to go, 106

e. for heaven and earth, 28
east
   cometh out of the e., 163
   star in the e., 86
easy
   e. to be understood, 29
eat
   dogs e. of the crumbs, 168
   e. of the hidden manna,
     156
   e. the flesh of the Son, 29
   e. with unwashen hands,
     146
   let us e. and drink, 138
   man e. of this bread, 19
   meat to e. that ye know,
     176
   neither should he e., 90
   rise Peter; kill and e., 65
   take, e. this is my body, 29
   what ye shall e., 119
   what ye shall e., neither, 65
eateth
   e. me, even he shall live,
     29
   e. to the Lord, 87
   e. with me shall betray, 15
   he that e., 87
   judge him that e., 184
   let not him which e., 184
   that e. bread with me, 15
   that e. my flesh, 98
   whoso e. my flesh, 54
   why e. your Master, 55
edifieth
   charity e., 31
   e. the church, 29
effect
   faith of God without e., 73
elder
   e. shall serve younger, 64
   rebuke not an e., 4
   submit unto the e., 4
elders
   e. that rule well, 27
elect
   to seduce the e., 84
Eli
   E. E. lama sabachthani, 6
Elias
   E. is come already, 3
Emmanuel
   call His name E., 103
empty
   rich He hath sent e., 30
end
   e. is at hand, 7
   e. is destruction, 75

e. is not yet, 133
e. of the commandment, 114
endure unto the e., 160
even unto the e., 24
His kingdom shall be no e., 24
hope to the e., 137
the beginning and the e., 12
the e. shall be saved, 16
this e. was I born, 102
ends
e. of the earth, 34
endure
count them happy which e., 82
e. hardness, 136
that e. unto the end, 160
endureth
e. all things, 114
he that e. to the end, 16
meat which e., 18
that e. temptation, 182
word of the Lord e., 74
enemies
e. of the cross, 75
e. under His feet, 174
love your e., 52
enemy
count him not as an e., 11
e. because I tell you, 187
e. hunger, feed him, 52
e. of all righteousness, 57
last e. destroyed is, 40
world is the e. of God, 115
enmity
carnal mind is e., 20
of the world is e. with, 32
enter
better to e. halt into, 38
e. into the kingdom, 107
e. into the kingdom, 107
e. into the kingdom, 83
e. into the kingdom, 54
e. into the kingdom, 11
e. into thy closet, 140
e. kingdom of God, 106
e. not into temptation, 181
grievous wolves e., 177
he shall not e., 24
if any man e., 99
not e. into the kingdom, 34
through tribulation e., 107
wilt e. into life, 27
entered
by one man sin e., 94

entereth
e. in by the door, 110
entertain
to e. strangers, 6
entertained
e. angels unawares, 6
envieth
charity e. not, 114
envy
e. they had delivered, 53
envying
where e. and strife is, 32
Ephphatha
E. that is, be opened, 82
epistle
e. written in our hearts, 183
equal
e. unto the angels, 6
which is just and e., 51
error
e. of his way, 172
escape
accounted worthy to e., 7
e. the damnation of hell, 38
esteem
e. them very highly, 26
esteemed
highly e. among men, 119
esteemeth
e. every day alike, 21
eternal
blood, hath e. life, 54
e. life through Jesus, 54
fruit unto life e., 54
given to us e. life, 54
keep it unto life e., 111
lay hold on e. life, 54
no murderer hath e. life, 127
perish, but have e. life, 39
things not seen are e., 119
Eve
first formed, then E., 10
ever
See "Forever"
everlasting
endureth unto e. life, 18
hath e. life, 13
have e. life, 160
reap life e., 54
unworthy of e. life, 24
every
not e. one that saith, 107
evidence
e. of things not seen, 61

evil
abhor that which is e., 12
against them that do e., 57
all appearance of e., 13
bear witness of the e., 2
being e. speak good, 36
bringeth forth e. fruit, 22
bringeth forth e. things, 22
confusion and every e., 32
day is the e. thereof, 68
deeds were e., 56
deliver us from e., 56
do that which is e., 63
doeth e. hath not seen, 76
e. against you falsely, 33
e. and adulterous, 123
e. come from within, 169
e. communications, 22
e. for e., 154
e. in your hearts, 56
e. man out of e., 22
e. which I would not, 97
eschew e. and do good, 24
every one that doeth e., 56
follow not which is e., 24
good works but to the e., 79
heart proceed e., 126
his tongue form e., 57
if I have spoken e., 2
if thine eye be e., 22
if ye, being e. know, 68
is thine eye e., 52
keep you from e., 61
me from every e. work, 159
not lust after e., 43
overcome e. with good, 77
partaker of his e. deeds, 35
render e. for e., 154
rise on the e. and the, 76
root of all e., 57
simple concerning e., 77
speak e. of no man, 173
speak e. of the ruler, 79
suffer for e. doing, 2
tempted with e., 182
they that have done e., 38
this is an e. generation, 56
unruly e. full of, 175
withstand in the e. day, 73
wrath upon him that doeth e., 79
exact
e. no more than, 80
exalt
whosoever shall e. himself, 89
exalted
e. with His right, 99

himself shall be e., 89
himself shall be e., 5
himself shall be e., 31
exalteth
  e. himself shall be, 5
  that e. himself shall be, 31
examine
  e. yourselves, 61
excess
  same e. of riot, 32
  wine, wherein is e., 49
exchange
  in e. for his soul, 96
execute
  revenger to e. wrath, 79
exercise
  e. profiteth little, 76
  herein do I e., 32
exhort
  e. one another daily, 51
  e. with longsuffering, 133
expedient
  all things are not e., 12
experience
  and e. hope, 87
  and patience, e., 87
eye
  beam that is in thine e., 16
  e. for an e., 148
  e. hath not seen, 17
  e. of a needle, 106
  e. offend thee, pluck, 16
  if thine e. be evil, 22
  is thine e. evil, 52
  kingdom with one e., 83
  light of body is the e., 18
  mote in thy brother's e., 16
  mote of thy brother's e., 36
  out of thine own e., 36
  right e. offend thee, 38
  twinkling of an e., 175
eyes
  anoint thine e. with, 169
  devil open the e., 2
  e. have they closed, 92
  e. of the Lord, 73
  e. see ye not, 178
  fell from his e., 34
  lift up your e., 131
  marvellous in our e., 178
  mine e. have seen Thy, 33
  open their e., 52
  plucked out your own e.,
    45
  tears from their e., 181
  two e. to be cast into, 83
eyesalve
  thine eyes with e., 169

F

fables
  old wives' f., 127
face
  but then f. to f., 26
  discern f. of the sky, 192
  discern the f. of sky, 45
  f. of all people, 33
  f. of the Lord, 57
  messenger before Thy f.,
    122
  wash thy f., 62
faces
  disfigure their f., 90
fadeth
  glory that f. not, 156
fail
  tittle of the law to f., 28
faileth
  charity never f., 114
faith
  according to your f., 59
  add to your f. virtue, 61
  all men have not f., 61
  ask in f., 61
  be sound in f., 13
  before f. came, 28
  breastplate of f., 13
  but by the f. of Jesus, 28
  by f. ye stand, 60
  by works was f. made, 42
  children of God by f., 53
  contend for the f., 61
  f. as a grain of mustard, 59
  f. cometh by hearing, 60
  f. hath made thee whole,
    59
  f. hath saved, 59
  f., hope, charity, 60
  f. in God, 59
  f. is the substance of, 61
  f. is vain, 60
  f. of God without effect, 73
  f. of the saints, 2
  f. should not stand, 60
  f. to be healed, 83
  f. which worketh by love,
    26
  f. without works, 42
  finisher of our f., 100
  follow after f., 69
  follow righteousness, f., 13
  fruit of the Spirit is f., 86
  good fight of f., 61
  great is thy f., 59
  hast thou f.?, 60
  I have kept the f., 2

increase our f., 59
justified by f., 42
justified by f., 28
live by f., 60
not by f. only, 42
not found so great f., 59
not of f. is sin, 60
now preacheth the f., 21
O thou of little f., 48
O ye of little f., 59
of f. unfeigned, 114
one f., 11
prayer of f., 83
profession of our f., 61
righteousness of f., 60
saved through f., 60
shield of f., 60
so f. without works is, 40
stand fast in the f., 44
though I have all f., 60
void the law through f., 28
walk by f., 12
weak in the f., 34
whether ye be in the f., 61
without f. it is, 61
ye of little f., 48
faithful
  but the Lord is f., 116
  f. also in much, 33
  f. in that which is least, 33
  f. is He that calleth, 70
  f. unto death, 55
  f. witness, 103
  God is f., 75
  good and f. servant, 8
  He is f. and just, 31
  that sat was called F., 61
  they with Him are f., 61
  yet he abideth f., 14
faithless
  f. and perverse generation,
    75
  f. but believing, 49
fall
  both f. into the ditch, 17
  heed lest he f., 31
  lightning f. from heaven,
    161
  through their f., 104
fallen
  Babylon the great is f., 40
  from whence thou art f.,
    11
falling
  a f. away first, 164
false
  bear f. witness, 134
  beware of f. prophets, 41

feareth

  whosoever among you f., 63

fearful

  f. O ye of little faith, 59

  f. thing to fall, 70

feast

  makest a f. call the, 20

feasts

  uppermost rooms at f., 91

fed

  f. you with milk, 50

feeble

  lift up the f. knees, 32

feebleminded

  comfort the f., 30

feed

  enemy hunger, f., 52

  f. my lambs, 122

  f. the church, 49

  f. the flock of God, 110

  f. the poor, 23

  Lamb shall f. them, 74

feet

  enemies under His f., 174

  f. are swift, 57

  f. of them that preach, 78

  f. to be cast into hell, 38

  paths for your f., 13

  trample under their f., 95

fell

  f. from his eyes, 34

fellowcitizens

  f. with the saints, 25

fellowship

  f. is with the Father, 64

  f. one with another, 13

female

  neither male nor f., 53

Festus

  mad, most noble F., 116

fetch

  come themselves and f., 35

few

  f. are chosen, 113

  f. there be that find it, 12

  labourers are f., 55

field

  lilies of the f., 7

  potter's f., 20

  treasure hid in a f., 107

fields

  look on the f., 131

fiery

  quench all the f. darts, 60

fig

  f. tree bear olive, 33

fight

  f. and war yet ye, 141

  f. the good f., 61

  fought a good f., 2

  not f. against God, 1

figs

  men do not gather f., 33

filled

  f. with the Spirit, 49

  for they shall be f., 156

  valley shall be f., 122

filthy

  f. communication, 12

  f. lucre, 125

  not for f. lucre, 126

find

  f. rest unto your souls, 27

  few there be f. it, 12

  for my sake shall f. it, 53

  life for my sake shall f., 111

  seek death, and not f., 40

  seek me and shall not f., 163

  seek, and ye shall f., 45

  that we shall not f. Him, 127

findeth

  he that seeketh f., 5

  seeking rest and f. none, 56

finding

  ways past f. out, 71

finger

  f. into the print, 48

fingers

  burdens with your f., 19

  with one of their f., 90

finish

  f. His work, 124

  sufficient to f. it, 138

finished

  f. my course, 2

  it is f., 39

  sin, when it is f., 40

finisher

  f. of our faith, 100

fire

  cast into hell f., 83

  cast into the lake of f., 39

  coals of f., 168

  f. is not quenched, 84

  f. never quenched, 84

  f. taking vengeance, 154

  God is a consuming f., 70

  gold tried in the f., 61

  into the lake of f., 40

lake of f. and brimstone, 146

little f. kindleth, 12

setteth on f., 175

tongue is a f., 57

first

  Adam was f. formed, 10

  dead shall rise f., 25

  f. and great command-ment, 27

  f. and the f. last, 53

  f. be reconciled, 22

  f. cast out, 36

  f. heaven and the f., 83

  f. the blade, 80

  He hath made the f. old, 36

  I am the f. and the last, 12

  if that f. covenant had, 36

  last; and the last f., 54

  last shall be f., 87

  last shall be f., 53

  man desire to be f., 5

  many that are f., 54

  must f. come to pass, 7

  seek ye f. the kingdom, 69

  the f. resurrection, 40

fishers

  f. of men, 45

fishes

  five loaves, and two f., 48

fit

  f. for the kingdom of, 45

fixed

  great gulf f., 84

flame

  tormented in this f., 84

fled

  every island f. away, 44

flee

  devil will f., 162

  f. also youthful lusts, 13

  f. fornication, 66

  f. from idolatry, 91

  warned you to f., 53

fleeth

  hireling f., 44

flesh

  absent in the f., 1

  born of the f. is f., 15

  bread is my f., 148

  eat the f. of the Son, 29

  f. and blood, 107

  f. and blood hath not, 101

  f. is as grass, 69

  f. is weak, 67

  f. lusteth against the, 88

  f. profiteth nothing, 86

f. the law of sin, 20
in my f. dwelleth no, 20
live after the f., 20
lust of the f., 12
manifest in the f., 100
members of His f., 100
no f. be justified, 28
occasion to the f., 67
of f. reap corruption, 116
outward in the f., 7
perfect by the f., 11
provision for the f., 166
soweth to his f. shall, 116
Spirit against the f., 88
suffered in the f., 171
that are after the f. do, 20
that eateth my f., 98
they that are in the f., 20
things of the f., 20
thorn in the f., 162
trouble in the f., 118
twain shall be one f., 117
walk in the f., 32
war after the f., 32
whoso eateth my f., 54
Word was made f., 98
wrestle not against f., 52
ye are not in the f., 60
ye judge after the f., 7
fleshy
  f. tables of the heart, 135
flock
  and to all the f., 191
  fear not, little f., 107
  feed the f. of God, 110
  not sparing the f., 177
flower
  f. falleth away, 74
  glory of man as the f., 69
foes
  f. Thy footstool, 57
  man's f. shall be they,
    177
fold
  not of this f., 55
  there shall be one f., 25
follow
  come and f. me, 22
  cross, and f., 4
  f. his steps, 100
  f. me, 46
  f. me, 110
  f. me, and I will make, 45
  f. not that which is, 24
  f. peace with all men, 8
  f. that which is good, 157
  the cross, and f. me, 4
  them, and they f. me, 4

followers
  be ye f. of me, 12
  f. of God, 12
followeth
  f. after me is not, 4
  f. me shall not walk, 14
food
  having f. and raiment, 80
fool
  as a f. receive me, 7
  become a f. that he may,
    89
  I shall not be a f., 17
  no man think me a f., 7
foolish
  avoid f. questions, 34
  f. man, which built, 138
  f. questions avoid, 34
  f. the wisdom of the, 196
  f. things of the world, 64
  ignorance of f. men, 42
foolishness
  f. of God is wiser, 195
  unto the Greeks f., 37
  world is f. with God, 195
fools
  circumspectly, not as f., 12
  f. and slow of heart, 144
  f. for Christ's sake, 122
  suffer f. gladly, 65
  wise, they became f., 31
foot
  if thy f. offend, 38
footstool
  earth is My f., 26
  earth; for is His f., 128
  foes Thy f., 57
for
  if God be f. us, 31
forbid
  away His people? God f.,
    104
  come unto me, and f., 23
  faith? God f., 28
  God f. that I should, 17
  man f. water, 11
foreigners
  no more strangers and f.,
    25
foretold
  f. you all things, 144
forever
  abide with you f., 27
  bread, he shall live f., 19
  Christ the same f., 21
  Father be glory f., 140
  glory and dominion f., 73
  glory both now and f., 100

power, and the glory, f., 55
Thy throne is f., 24
will of God abideth f., 43
forgave
  even as Christ f., 66
forgetful
  be not f. to, 6
forgive
  f. and ye shall be, 65
  f. men their trespasses,
    65
  f. our debtors, 65
  f. us our debts, 65
  f. us our sins, 65
  f. us our sins, 31
  f. you your trespasses, 80
  f. your trespasses, 81
  Father, f. them, 66
  Father will also f., 65
  if he repent, f., 36
  if ye do not f. neither, 80
  power on earth to f., 65
  repent; thou shalt f., 66
  stand praying, f., 80
forgiven
  and ye shall be f., 65
  blasphemy shall be f., 16
  cheer; thy sins be f., 51
  Christ's sake hath f., 66
  Ghost it shall not f., 16
  iniquities are f., 66
  it shall be f. him: but, 16
  it shall not be f., 85
  not be f. unto men, 16
  sins are f., 66
  thine heart may be f., 150
  to whom little is f., 65
forgiveness
  f. of sins, 66
  preached unto you the f.,
    66
forgotten
  not one of them is f., 71
formed
  Adam was first f., 10
former
  f. things passed away, 40
fornication
  body is not for f., 18
  except it be for f., 48
  flee f., 66
  he that committeth f., 66
  saving for cause of f., 3
  to avoid f., 66
  wrath of her f., 35
fornications
  out of heart proceed f.,
    126

forsake
  never leave thee, nor f., 1
forsaken
  persecuted, but not f., 4
  why hast Thou f., 1
forsaketh
  f. not all that he hath, 44
forty
  f. years suffered He, 103
fought
  f. a good fight, 2
found
  f. Him, of whom Moses, 122
  f. my sheep, 82
  f. of them that sought, 34
  mountains were not f., 44
foundation
  f. of God standeth sure, 70
  that without a f. built, 4
fountain
  athirst of the f. of, 43
  doth a f. send forth, 33
fountains
  living f. of waters, 74
foxes
  f. have holes, 87
fragments
  gather up the f., 193
frankincense
  f. and myrrh, 69
free
  bond nor f. but Christ, 53
  bondwoman, but of the f., 85
  called, being f., 67
  Christ hath made us f., 67
  f. from all men, 122
  I was f. born, 67
  neither bond nor f., 53
  Son shall make you f., 67
  truth shall make you f., 67
  ye shall be f. indeed, 67
freed
  f. from sin, 40
freely
  f. ye have received, 68
  received, f. give, 68
freeman
  the Lord's f., 15
friend
  art not Caesar's f., 184
  f. of the world is the, 115
friends
  called you f., 67
  life for his f., 67
friendship
  f. of the world is, 32

fruit
  bring forth f., 56
  bringeth forth evil f., 22
  bringeth forth good f., 22
  f. of righteousness is, 134
  f. of the Spirit is, 86
  f. unto life eternal, 54
  known by his own f., 41
  peaceable f., 46
  tree is known by his f., 22
  trees whose f. withereth, 22
fruits
  bring forth therefore f., 41
  by their f. ye shall, 2
  f. that thy soul lusted, 5
  partaker of the f., 156
fulfil
  becometh us to f., 49
  destroy, but to f., 68
  not f. the lust of, 12
fulfilled
  f. the law, 28
  f. them in condemning, 122
  fathers, God hath f., 78
  law is f. in one word, 28
  prophets might be f., 122
  scripture f. in your, 122
  scripture should be f., 122
  written may be f., 105
fulness
  and the f. thereof, 49
  dwelleth all the f., 47

G

gain
  contentment is great g., 33
  g. the whole world, 96
  to die is g., 112
  what things were g., 102
Galilee
  art thou also of G., 124
gall
  g. of bitterness, 53
garden
  cast into his g., 80
garment
  touch His g., 59
garments
  keepeth his g. lest he, 164
gate
  strait is the g., 12
  wide is the g., 38
gates
  g. of hell, 177
  g. shall not be shut, 83

gather
  g. the clusters, 105
  g. they grapes, 33
  g. up the fragments, 193
  thorns men do not g., 33
gathered
  eagles be g., 21
  g. together in my name, 63
gathereth
  as a hen g. her chickens, 110
gave
  g. Himself for me, 100
  g. His only begotten Son, 54
generation
  declare His g., 85
  evil and adulterous g., 123
  faithless and perverse g., 75
  fear Him from g. to g., 63
  g. of vipers, 56
  g. of vipers, 38
  g. seek after a sign, 143
  g. wiser than the children, 196
  this is an evil g., 56
  untoward g., 35
Gentiles
  blasphemed among the G., 91
  I will go unto the G., 57
  is He not also of the G., 70
  light of the G., 34
  name shall the G. trust, 97
  preached unto the G., 100
  salvation come unto G., 104
  sent unto the G., 56
  we turn to the G., 24
  which the G. sacrifice, 75
gentle
  g. unto all men, 106
  to the good and gentle, 2
gentleness
  fruit of the Spirit is g., 86
ghost
  gave up the g., 37
  See also "Holy Ghost"
gift
  come and offer thy g., 22
  g. of God, 79
  g. of God is, 54
  g. of God may be, 23
  g. that is in thee, 1
  good g. is from above, 77
  man hath his proper g., 94
  perfect g. is from, 77
  unspeakable g., 79

gifts
diversities of g., 1
g. and calling of God, 17
g. unto your children, 68
presented unto Him g., 69
gird
g. up the loins, 148
give
and I will g. you rest, 19
ask of me, I will g., 143
bread that I will g., 148
g. and it shall be given, 5
g. for the life of the, 148
g. good gifts, 68
g. good things to them, 68
g. him a stone, 106
g. him the morning star, 156
g. me here John, 154
g. not which is holy, 188
g. to him that asketh, 18
g. to the poor, 53
g. unto thee the keys, 107
g. unto them for me, 180
g. unto your servants, 51
g. us this day, 65
g. you another Comforter, 27
have, and g. alms, 23
heart, so let him g., 23
in every thing g. thanks, 79
is not mine to g., 9
more blessed to g., 5
my name, He will g., 99
new commandment I g., 28
peace I g. unto you, 27
received, freely g., 68
such as I have g. I, 23
what shall a man g. in, 96
given
ask, and it shall be g., 140
be g. him from heaven, 69
cup my Father hath g., 1
give, and it shall be g., 5
much is g. of him, 130
to him shall be g., 113
giver
loveth a cheerful g., 9
giveth
g. his life, 44
g. life unto the world, 18
he that g. do it with, 23
gladly
suffer fools g., 65
glass
through a g. darkly, 26

glorieth
g. let him glory, 17
glorified
Father may be g., 71
g. Him not as God, 75
God is g. in Him, 71
she hath g. herself, 17
Son of man g., 71
Son of man should be g., 71
glorify
Father, g. Thy name, 71
g. God in your body, 18
g. Thy Son, 71
shall not g. Thy name, 140
Thy Son also may g., 71
glory
all to the g. of God, 2
another star in g., 83
appear with Him in g., 153
come short of the g., 117
crownedst him with g., 117
death, but for the g., 71
desirous of vain g., 5
fear God, and give g., 105
forbid that I should g., 17
g. and dominion forever, 100
g. honour, and peace, 41
g. in the highest, 70
g. is in their shame, 75
g. of God did lighten it, 71
g. of man, 69
g. that fadeth not, 156
g. to God in the highest, 140
His g. shall be revealed, 164
image and g. of God, 116
let him g. in the Lord, 17
nor of men sought we g., 140
power and great g., 164
power, and the g., 55
received up into g., 100
received us to the g., 64
seeketh his own g., 17
Solomon in all his g., 7
though I desire to g., 17
to Him be g., 100
to Him g. and dominion, 73
unto His kingdom and g., 69
unto our Father be g., 140
what g. is it, 37
woman is the g. of, 116
ye are our g., 69

gnashing
weeping and g. of teeth, 6
weeping and g. of teeth, 148
gnat
strain at a g., 91
go
g. and do thou likewise, 77
g. thou and preach, 49
g. with him twain, 34
g. ye into all the world, 46
to g. a mile, 34
whither I g. ye know, 83
whither will He g., 127
goats
blood of bulls and g., 66
sheep from the g., 24
god
g. is their belly, 75
Godhead
fulness of the G., 47
G. is like unto gold, 75
godliness
follow after g., 69
g. is profitable, 143
g. with contentment, 33
mystery of g., 76
godly
all that will live g., 76
deliver the g., 42
gods
g. are come down, 123
they be no g. which, 92
goeth
not that which g. into, 65
gold
g. and frankincense, 69
g. have I none, 23
g. tried in the fire, 61
Godhead is like unto g., 75
man's silver, or g., 96
vessels of g., 47
Gomorrah
tolerable for Sodom and G., 75
good
and see g. days, 57
be of g. cheer, 51
be of g. cheer, 27
be of g. cheer, 27
bringeth forth g., 22
bringeth forth g. fruit, 22
callest thou me g., 77
cleave to which is g., 12
corrupt g. manners, 22
creature of God is g., 65
desireth a g. work, 5
do g., 13

do g. unto all men, 5
dwelleth no g. thing, 20
eschew evil, and do g., 24
evil and on the g., 76
evil, because I am g., 52
evil, speak g., 36
fast to that which is g., 77
filled the hungry with g., 30
follow that which is g., 157
follow that which is g., 24
for a g. man some would, 40
g. and gave us rain, 147
g. conscience before God, 32
g. for a man not to, 21
g. for nothing, 64
g. gift is from above, 77
g. man out of the g., 22
g. shepherd, 103
g. that I would, 97
g. thing any man doeth, 77
g. thing come, 38
g. tidings of great joy, 81
g. to be zealously, 198
g. to them that hate, 12
g. to them which do g., 12
g. treasure of the heart, 22
g. tree bringeth forth, 22
g. will toward men, 19
give g. gifts unto, 68
give g. things to them, 68
law is g. if, 109
man that worketh g., 41
none g. but one, 77
none that doeth g., 35
not only to the g., 2
of a g. conscience, 114
overcome evil with g., 77
see your g. works, 41
set forth g. wine, 88
terror to g. works, 79
that doeth g. is of God, 76
that knoweth to do g., 77
they that have done g., 38
whatsoever are of g. report, 191
wise to that which is g., 77
work together for g., 60
goodman
g. of the house, 21
goodness
fruit of the Spirit is g., 86
g. of God leadeth, 77
goods
all my g. to feed the, 23

gospel
begotten through the g., 78
believe the g., 78
but to preach the g., 56
defence of the g., 78
g. must be published, 55
g. should live of the g., 12
g. which was preached, 78
hope of the g., 78
if our g. be hid, 75
my sake and the g.'s, 78
not ashamed of the g., 78
obey not the g., 154
poor the g. is preached, 81
preach any other g., 84
preach not the g., 26
preach the g., 46
preach the g., 52
preach the g., 78
unto us was the g., 72
grace
but g. and truth came, 28
by g. are ye saved, 60
by the g. of God, 22
g. and peace be multiplied, 108
g. be to you, 159
g. be with them that, 17
g. be with you, 17
g. did much more abound, 66
g. is no more g., 79
g. of Christ be with you, 17
g. of Christ be with you, 185
g. of the Lord, 160
g. unto the humble, 90
g. which was bestowed, 22
giveth g. to the humble, 90
grow in g., 109
if by g. then, 79
speech be alway with g., 35
strong in the g., 67
under g., 79
word of His g., 16
grain
faith as a g. of mustard, 59
g. of mustard seed, 80
grapes
bush gather they g., 33
g. are fully ripe, 105
grass
flesh is as g., 69
g. withereth, 74
man as the flower of g., 69
grave
be sober, g., 13

g. where is thy victory, 40
graven
g. by art, 75
graves
that are in the g. shall, 93
great
Babylon the G., 43
both to small and g., 182
city of the g. King, 97
done to me g. things, 16
first and g. commandment, 27
found so g. faith, 59
g. house there are not, 47
g. is the mystery, 76
g. is thy faith, 59
g. is your reward, 118
g. prophet is risen, 10
g. shepherd of the sheep, 103
how g. a matter a little, 12
like unto this g. city, 194
same shall be called g., 27
same shall be g., 80
the dead, small and g., 105
whosoever will be g., 5
greater
g. he that prophesieth, 29
g. is He that is in you, 100
g. love hath no man, 67
g. than he that sent, 53
g. than Solomon is here, 98
God is g. than our heart, 71
hath the g. sin, 81
My Father is g., 9
no g. joy than to, 24
servant is not g., 53
greatest
g. of these is charity, 60
he that is g. among you, 110
least to the g., 3
Greek
neither G. nor Jew, 53
neither Jew nor G., 53
the Jew and the G., 53
Greeks
debtor both to the G., 85
G. seek after wisdom, 144
unto the G. foolishness, 37
greet
g. with an holy kiss, 159
g. ye one another with, 64
grew
g. and waxed a great, 80
word of God g., 56

grievous
   burdens g. to be borne, 19
   g. to be borne, 90
gross
   heart is waxed g., 92
grow
   field, how they g., 7
   g. in grace, 109
   word, that ye may g., 74
grudging
   hospitality without g., 88
guide
   except some man g. me, 50
guides
   blind g. which strain, 91
guile
   mouth was found no g., 95
guilty
   he is g. of all, 47
gulf
   great g. fixed, 84

H

habitation
   the h. of devils, 40
hair
   man have long h., 7
   one h. white or black, 128
   woman have long h., 7
hairs
   the very h. of your head,
      71
half
   h. of my kingdom, 143
hallowed
   h. be Thy name, 70
halt
   enter h. into life, 38
hand
   betrayeth me is at h., 15
   end is at h., 7
   h. into His side, 49
   h. of a mediator, 28
   h. of him that betrayeth,
      15
   h. of the Lord was with, 34
   h. to the plough, 45
   hour is at h., 15
   kingdom of God is at h.,
      160
   know what thy right h., 22
   let not thy left h., 22
   Lord is at h., 73
   My h. made all these, 36
   of heaven is at h., 107
   of heaven is at h., 159
   on the right h. of God, 118

reach hither thy h., 49
right h. offend, 16
sat on the right h., 8
sit Thou on my right h., 57
time is at h., 93
time is at h., 93
to sit on my right h., 9
hands
   cleanse your h., 146
   eat with unwashen h., 146
   h. I commend my spirit, 1
   h. of sinners, 15
   h. of the living God, 70
   h. on the sick, 82
   laid His h. on, 83
   lift up the h. which, 32
   lifting up holy h., 141
   over the works of Thy h.,
      117
   see in His h., 48
   temples made with h., 26
   water, and washed his h.,
      151
   which are made with h.,
      92
   working with his h., 36
hang
   hands which h. down, 32
hanged
   millstone h. about his, 23
happy
   h. are ye if ye do, 82
   of Christ, h. are ye, 136
   sake, h. are ye, 157
   them h. which endure, 82
hard
   how h. is it, 54
harden
   h. not your hearts, 94
   h. not your hearts, 14
harlots
   Babylon Mother of H., 43
harm
   do thyself no h., 152
harmless
   h. as doves, 173
   h. as doves, 39
harvest
   h. of the earth is ripe, 120
   h. truly is plenteous, 55
   white already to h., 131
hate
   do good to them that h.,
      12
   either he will h., 115
   if the world h., 82
   if the world h. you, 136
   what I h. that do I, 165

hated
   h. me before it h. you, 82
   h. of all men for my, 16
hateth
   and h. his brother, 19
   and h. his brother, 76
   evil h. the light, 56
   h. his brother is a, 82
   h. his life, 111
   h. me h. my Father, 52
head
   bowed His h., 37
   coals on his h., 168
   fastest, anoint thine h.,
      62
   h. of all principality, 10
   h. of Christ is God, 10
   h. of every man is, 10
   h. of the body, 10
   h. of the church, 118
   h. of the corner, 132
   hairs of your h. are all, 71
   John Baptist's h., 154
   swear by thy h., 128
   where to lay His h., 87
heads
   blood upon your own h.,
      81
heal
   h. the brokenhearted, 42
   h. the sick, 138
   physician, h. thyself, 36
healed
   every one of them and h.,
      83
   faith to be h., 83
   h. every one, 83
   h. wist not who it was, 5
   pray that ye may be h., 141
   servant shall be h., 59
hear
   as I h. I judge, 104
   before it h. him, 2
   blessed are they that h., 78
   deaf h., 81
   deaf to h., 81
   ears to h. let him h., 84
   ears to h. let him h., 96
   ears, h. ye not, 178
   fathers, h. ye my defence,
      106
   graves shall h. His, 93
   greater joy than to h., 24
   h. and understand, 84
   h. O Israel, 126
   h. them speak, 185
   h. what the Spirit, 84

h. without a preacher, 50
have an ear, let him h.,
144
hearing they h. not, 92
Him shall ye h. in all, 10
if any man h. my voice,
102
if they h. not Moses, 137
if will h. His voice, 14
man be swift to h., 6
pleased; h. ye Him, 121
sheep h. my voice, 4
that h. the words of, 144
which h. the word, 62
heard
all things I have h., 154
h. for much speaking, 140
h. not the voice, 192
message that ye h., 114
nor ear h., 17
seen and h. declare we, 85
shall be h. no more, 42
they that have not h., 56
things seen and h., 182
which I have h. of Him,
154
whom they have not h., 14
hearers
doers, and not h., 42
not the h. of the law, 41
hearest
h. the sound thereof, 127
heareth
he that h. my word, 13
of God h. God's words, 9
that h. and doeth not, 4
that h. these sayings, 46
truth h. my voice, 186
whosoever h. these, 41
hearing
dull of h., 92
faith cometh by h., 60
h. by the word of, 60
h. they hear not, 92
hearken
h. unto you more, 32
heart
abundance of the h., 22
adultery in his h., 3
believe in thine h., 101
break mine h., 181
but their h. is far, 4
charity out of a pure h.,
114
circumcision is of the h.,
26
entered into the h., 17
fleshy tables of the h., 135

God greater than our h.,
71
h. be troubled, 27
h. is not right, 9
h. man believeth, 14
h. of this people, 92
meek and lowly in h., 27
out of the h. proceed, 126
pure in h., 146
purposeth in his h., 23
slow of h. to believe, 144
there will your h. be, 115
thought of thine h., 150
treasure of the h., 22
uncircumcised in h., 75
with all thy h., 44
hearts
evil in your h., 56
harden not your h., 94
harden not your h., 14
knoweth the h., 34
knoweth your h., 71
laws into their h., 28
purify your h., 146
rule in your h., 134
sanctify Lord in your h.,
45
searcheth the h., 71
searcheth the h., 100
written in our h., 183
heat
on them, nor any h., 34
heathen
repetitions, as the h., 140
heaven
bound in h., 139
came down from h., 98
came down from h., 19
cometh down from h., 18
created, that are in h., 36
earth, as it is in h., 70
easier for h. and earth, 28
Father which art in h., 70
Father which is in h., 134
Father which is in h., 22
Father which is in h., 62
Father which is in h., 101
Father which is in h., 80
Father which is in h., 81
Father which is in h., 68
Father which is in h., 13
Father which is in h., 70
first h. and the first, 83
from h. like a dove, 86
gave us rain from h., 147
given him from h., 69
h. and earth shall pass, 24
h. is My throne, 26

hast made h., 36
joy shall be in h., 94
lightning fall from h., 161
Lord of h., 26
Master in h., 51
names are written in h., 81
not the angels of h., 164
peace in h. and, 70
received up into h., 8
rejoice over her thou h.,
154
revealed from h., 75
saw a new h., 83
signs from h., 7
silence in h. about, 10
sinned against h., 31
sins reached unto h., 76
swear by h., 128
swear neither by h., 128
swear not, neither by h., 96
that bear record in h., 185
treasure in h., 54
treasures in h., 175
ye shall see h., 70
your reward in h., 118
See also "Kingdom of
Heaven"
heavenly
h. Father will also, 65
preserve me unto His h.,
159
tell you of h., 13
heavens
see the h. opened, 118
heaviness
joy to h., 109
heavy
labour and are h. laden,
19
Hebrews
H. so am I, 104
heed
h. that be not deceived, 41
h. what thou doest, 106
take h. therefore, 22
take h. therefore, 191
take h. to yourselves, 190
take ye h., 141
heel
lifted up his h., 15
hell
body cast into h., 38
cast into h. fire, 83
cast them down to h., 6
death and h. were cast, 40
Death, and H. followed, 7
feet to be cast into h., 38
gates of h. shall not, 177

h. delivered up the dead, 105

not left in h., 152

power to cast into h., 38

the damnation of h., 38

helmet

for an h. the hope of, 13

help

h. Thou mine unbelief, 48

helper

Lord is my h., 32

hen

as a h. gathereth her, 110

here

for we are all h., 152

heresy

way which they call h., 84

heretick

man that is an h., 34

hid

h. that not be known, 165

h. that shall not be, 165

hill cannot be h., 110

hill cannot be h., 62

if our gospel be h., 75

life is h. with Christ, 102

treasure h. in a field, 107

hidden

eat of the h. manna, 156

high

maketh men h. priests, 35

Son of the most h., 161

highest

glory in the h., 70

glory to God in the h., 140

hill

city set on an h., 110

city set on an h., 62

h. shall be brought low, 122

hire

worthy of his h., 196

hireling

because he is an h., 44

h. fleeth, 44

hold

h. fast to that, 77

holes

foxes have h., 87

holiness

behaviour as becometh h., 13

h. without which no man, 8

uncleanness, but unto h., 85

holy

greet with an h. kiss, 159

h. h. h. Lord God, 55

h. is he that hath part, 40

h. is His name, 16

H. One and the Just, 103

h. to the Lord, 32

h. unto the dogs, 188

if the root be h., 85

is h. so be ye h., 85

lifting up h. hands, 141

rejoice ye h. apostles, 154

temple of God is h., 14

Thou only art h., 85

with an h. kiss, 67

Holy Ghost

baptize you with the H., 11

baptizing in name of H., 55

blasphemeth against the H., 16

blasphemy against the H., 16

Comforter which is the H., 86

communion of the H., 185

Father, Word, and H., 185

giving them the H., 34

joy in the H., 86

receive ye the H., 16

resist the H., 75

speaketh against the H., 85

temple of the H., 18

well spake the H., 144

home

h. in the body, 112

honest

whatsoever things are h., 191

honestly

walk h. toward, 151

willing to live h., 32

honey

in thy mouth sweet as h., 16

honour

and give h. to Him, 82

glory, h. and peace, 41

h. all men, 151

h. is nothing, 140

h. the king, 79

h. thy father and mother, 27

h. thy father and mother, 132

h. to whom h., 63

h. unto the wife, 118

h. widows that are, 194

him will my Father h., 46

him with glory and h., 117

if I h. myself, 140

more h. than the house, 2

prophet hath no h. in, 150

prophet is not without h., 144

receive not h. from men, 8

worthy of double h., 27

honoureth

Father that h. me, 140

h. me with their lips, 4

h. not the Son h. not, 3

hope

and experience, h., 87

faith, h., charity, 60

h. maketh not ashamed, 87

h. of Israel, 94

h. of salvation, 13

h. of the gospel, 78

h. that is seen is not h., 87

h. to the end, 137

judged for the h., 136

life only we have h., 153

of whom ye h. to receive, 5

promise, having no h., 44

saved by h., 87

hoped

substance of things h., 61

hopeth

h. all things, 114

horse

behold a pale h., 7

behold a white h., 61

horses

bits in the h.' mouths, 129

Hosanna

H., 140

hospitality

h. without grudging, 88

hot

neither cold nor h., 29

thou wert cold or h., 52

hour

behold, the h. cometh, 93

came I unto this h., 124

cometh at an h. when, 147

h. is at hand, 15

h. is come, 71

h. is coming, 93

h. is not yet come, 184

h. knoweth no man, 163

h. of His judgment is, 105

h. the thief would come, 21

h. your Lord doth come, 164

in jeopardy every h., 136
know what h. I will come,
164
one h. is thy judgment, 40
the space of half an h., 10
watch with me one h., 45
house
an h. of merchandise, 159
begin at the h. of God, 105
builded the h. hath more,
2
every h. is builded by, 2
goodman of the h., 21
h. be divided, 177
h. cannot stand, 177
h. is the h. of prayer, 26
h. upon a rock, 138
h. upon the earth, 4
h. upon the sand, 138
how to rule his own h., 26
if the h. be worthy, 16
in a great h. there are, 47
in his own h., 144
in my Father's h. are, 27
lost sheep of the h., 103
make not my Father's h.,
159
master of the h. cometh,
51
more honour than the h., 2
what h. will ye build, 26
household
of his own h., 177
housetops
preach ye upon the h., 142
proclaimed upon the h., 58
how
h. shall this be, 48
howl
rich men, weep and h., 194
humble
giveth grace to the h., 90
grace unto the h., 90
h. yourselves in the, 90
he that shall h. himself, 89
humbleth
h. himself shall be, 5
h. himself shall be, 31
humility
clothed with h., 90
h. of mind, 89
hundred
his number is Six h., 57
if a man have h. sheep,
137
hunger
blessed are they which h.,
156

h. no more, 33
if thine enemy h., 52
to me shall never h., 43
hungred
h. and ye gave me meat, 30
h. and ye gave me no, 37
hungry
filled the h., 30
hurt
set on thee to h., 159
husband
h. is the head of the, 118
h. put away his wife, 48
h. render unto the wife,
117
h. that believeth not, 14
please her h., 45
put away her h., 3
sanctified by the h., 14
than she which hath h.,
24
unbelieving h., 14
woman have her own h.,
66
husbands
ask their h. at home, 195
h. love your wives, 118
subjection to your h., 118
submit unto your h., 118
to love their h., 118
wives be to their own h.,
118
hypocrisy
Pharisees, which is h., 91
within ye are full of h., 7
hypocrites
and Pharisees, h., 91
as the h. do, 22
h. ye can discern, 45
tempt ye me, ye h., 181

I

idle
every i. word that men,
151
idolaters
without are dogs, and i.,
41
idolatry
flee from i., 91
idols
keep yourselves from i., 92
ignorance
i. of foolish men, 42
through i. ye did, 37
ignorant
i. of his devices, 162

ignorantly
i. worship, 92
ill
love worketh no i., 114
image
i. and glory of God, 116
the beast and his i., 92
impossible
i. to please Him, 61
nothing shall be i., 1
nothing shall be i., 72
with men it is i., 117
impute
Lord will not i. sin, 66
imputed
sin is not i., 109
incorruptible
crown; but we an i., 30
incorruption
raised in i., 18
increase
but God gave the i., 38
he must i. but I, 125
i. our faith, 59
incredible
thought a thing i., 153
infirmities
bear the i. of the weak, 22
infirmity
priests which have i., 35
inhabiters
i. of the earth and, 162
inherit
i. the kingdom, 107
overcometh shall i., 61
shall i. the earth, 89
unrighteous shall not i.,
107
inheritance
reward of the i., 156
iniquities
hath remembered her i., 76
i. are forgiven, 66
iniquity
bond of i., 53
full of hypocrisy and i., 7
workers of i., 29
world of i., 57
inn
room for them in the i.,
102
innocent
i. of the blood, 16
inspiration
Scripture is given by i.,
163
instant
i. in season, 148

instruct
  that he may i. Him, 71
instructors
  ten thousand i. in Christ,
    18
interpretation
  of any private i., 144
inward
  i. man is renewed, 67
Isaac
  God of I., 85
island
  i. fled away, 44
Israel
  faith not in I., 59
  hear, O I., 126
  hope of I., 94
  master of I., 92
  sheep of the house of I.,
    103
Israelite
  I also am an I., 104
Israelites
  I. so am I, 104

J

Jacob
  God of J., 85
jeopardy
  stand we in j., 136
Jerusalem
  die at J. for, 44
  J. compassed with armies,
    51
  J. for it is the city, 128
  J. J. thou that killest, 97
  spirit unto J., 49
  testified of me in J., 35
Jew
  advantage hath the J., 26
  between the J. and the, 53
  he is not a J., 7
  neither Greek nor J., 53
  neither J. nor Greek, 53
Jews
  I might gain the J., 3
  is He the God of the J., 70
  J. a stumblingblock, 37
  J. have I done no wrong,
    25
  J. I became as a Jew, 3
  J. require a sign, 144
  King of the J., 98
  King of the J., 103
  salvation is of the J., 160
Job
  patience of J., 133

John
  J. Baptist's head, 154
  prophets were until J., 107
joined
  God hath j. together, 48
Jonas
  sign of the prophet J., 123
Joseph
  Jesus, the son of J., 162
joy
  glad with exceeding j., 164
  good tidings of great j., 81
  j. in the Holy Ghost, 86
  j. in the presence of, 94
  j. may be full, 82
  j. shall be in heaven, 94
  j. to heaviness, 109
  no greater j. than to, 24
  Spirit is love, j., 86
  turned into j., 87
  ye are our glory and j., 69
joyous
  no chastening be j., 37
Judas
  J. Iscariot, 15
judge
  adulterers God will j., 3
  as I hear, I j., 104
  came not to j., 105
  doth j. and make war, 105
  I j. no man, 7
  j. Him according to, 151
  j. him that eateth, 184
  j. me after the law, 58
  j. my judgment is true, 105
  j. not according to, 7
  j. not and ye shall not, 36
  j. not that ye be not, 16
  j. righteous judgment, 7
  j. standeth before the, 93
  j. the world, 105
  j. yourselves unworthy, 24
  law j. any man before, 2
  Lord, the righteous j., 156
  more than unto God, j., 32
  no j. of such matters, 25
  saints shall j., 14
  we shall j. angels, 6
  with what judgment ye j.,
    36
  ye j. after the flesh, 7
judged
  j. by the law, 105
  j. every man according,
    105
  j. for the hope, 136
  judge, ye shall be j., 36
  that ye be not j., 16

where I ought to be j., 25
  ye shall not be j., 36
judgest
  j. another man's servant, 8
  wherein thou j. another, 37
  who art thou that j., 37
judgeth
  Father j. no man, 9
  that j. me is the Lord, 10
  the Lord God who j., 146
judgment
  committed all j. unto, 9
  danger of the j., 6
  day of j. than for thee, 93
  execute j. upon all, 145
  hour of His j. is come, 105
  I stand at Caesar's j., 25
  if I judge my j. is true, 105
  in the day of j., 75
  in the day of j., 151
  j. must begin at, 105
  j. of this world, 105
  j. seat of Christ, 53
  j. seat of Christ, 105
  j. without mercy, 38
  judge righteous j., 7
  my j. is just, 104
  one hour is thy j. come, 40
  with what j. ye judge, 36
judgments
  righteous are His j., 105
  righteous are Thy j., 146
  unsearchable are His j., 71
just
  give that which is j., 51
  Holy One and the J., 103
  j. and true are Thy ways,
    157
  j. before God, 41
  j. shall live by faith, 60
  my judgment is j., 104
  ninety nine j. persons, 94
  resurrection of the j., 5
  sendeth rain on the j., 76
  whatsoever things are j.,
    191
justification
  raised again for our j., 153
justified
  all that believe are j., 14
  doers shall be j., 41
  j. by faith, 42
  j. by faith, 28
  j. by the law, 28
  j. in the name, 106
  j. in the Spirit, 100
  not j. by the works, 28
  shall no flesh be j., 28

wisdom is j., 195
words thou shalt be j., 104
works a man is j., 42
justifieth
it is God that j., 106

K

keep
if ye love me, k. my, 99
k. His saying, 43
k. my commandments, 129
k. my words, 101
k. the commandments, 27
k. you from evil, 61
k. your own tradition, 91
keepeth
k. not His commandments, 47
k. not my sayings, 47
keys
k. of the kingdom, 159
kill
adultery, do not k., 27
afraid of them that k., 126
do not k., 4
fear not them which k., 18
k. Him: and the third, 37
k. the soul, 18
rise, Peter; k. and eat, 65
to steal, and to k., 36
killed
after that He is k., 152
k. hath power to cast, 38
k. with the sword, 153
killest
k. the prophets, 97
killeth
k. you will think, 136
letter k., 28
that k. with the sword, 153
kind
k. one to another, 12
suffereth long and is k., 114
kindleth
little fire k., 12
king
city of the great k., 128
King
city of the great K., 97
king
He is K. of k., 57
honour the k., 79
K. of K. and Lord of, 103
K. of the Jews, 98
K. of the Jews, 103
no k. but Caesar, 116

kingdom
and k. against k., 7
called you unto His k., 69
comest into Thy k., 34
half of my k., 143
His heavenly k., 159
how shall then his k., 161
k. be divided, 79
k. cannot stand, 79
k. is not of this world, 9
k. there shall be no end, 24
pleasure to give the k., 107
sceptre of Thy k., 157
Son coming in His k., 39
thine is the k. and the, 55
Thy k. come, 70
kingdom of God
cannot enter into the k., 11
cannot see the k., 18
enter into the k., 54
enter into the k., 107
fit for the k., 45
inherit the k., 107
k. cometh not with, 107
k. is at hand, 160
k. is come nigh, 107
k. is not in word, 107
k. is not meat, 86
k. is preached, 107
k. is within you, 107
k. with one eye, 83
not inherit the k., 107
preach the k., 49
receive the k., 23
rich man to enter k., 106
seek first the k., 69
seek ye the k., 107
such is the k., 23
kingdom of heaven
enter into the k., 107
enter into the k., 107
for their's is the k., 107
great in the k., 27
k. is at hand, 107
k. is at hand, 159
k. like unto a merchant, 20
k. like unto treasure, 107
keys of the k., 159
not enter into the k., 34
their's is the k., 89
kings
before rulers and k., 135
k. of the earth, 180
prince of the k. of, 103
kiss
greet with an holy k., 159
k. that same is He, 15
Son of man with a k., 15

with a k. of charity, 64
with an holy k., 67
knee
every k. should bow, 87
knees
lift up the feeble k., 32
knew
and they k. him not, 3
because it k. Him not, 25
when they k. God, 75
world k. Him not, 8
knock
k. and it shall be, 140
k. and it shall be, 131
knocketh
k. it shall be opened, 50
know
all shall k. Me, 3
and k. what he doeth, 2
as he ought to k., 108
but because ye k. it, 4
father and mother we k., 162
for you to k. the times, 68
fruits ye shall k. them, 2
if I k. not the meaning, 29
if ye k. these things, 82
Jesus I k., 10
k. God but in works, 42
k. Him for I am from Him, 108
k. Him, and keep His, 43
k. how to give good, 68
k. I the Father, 108
k. not a man, 48
k. not Him that sent, 108
k. not how to rule, 26
k. not this man, 43
k. not what hour, 164
k. not what shall be, 68
k. not what they do, 66
k. not what ye ask, 127
k. not when the master, 51
k. not when the time, 141
k. nothing by myself, 89
k. that this is the, 13
k. them which labour, 26
k. thy works, 52
k. what hour I will come, 164
k. ye are my disciples, 25
let not thy left hand k., 22
meat to eat that ye k., 176
on them that k. not God, 154
one thing I k., 58
Paul I k., 10
say, I k. Him not, 43

see that no man k., 125
sinner or no, I k. not, 58
that saith, I k. Him, 47
the way ye k., 83
we k. in part, 92
whither I go ye k., 83
whom ye k. not, 70
worship ye k. not what, 92
ye k. not the truth, 4
ye shall k. the truth, 67
knowest
k. not that thou art, 119
k. the commandments, 27
knoweth
as the Father k. me, 108
born of God, and k. God, 115
day and hour k., 163
Father k. what things ye, 71
God k. all things, 71
k. any man the Father, 108
k. not these things, 92
k. not whither he goeth, 92
k. nothing yet as he, 108
k. the hearts, 34
k. them that are His, 15
k. what is the mind, 71
k. your hearts, 71
Lord k. how to deliver, 42
Lord k. the thoughts of, 68
loveth not k. not God, 82
man think that he k., 108
no man k. the Son, 108
that k. to do good and, 77
things of God k. no man, 70
world k. us not, 25
knowing
unto Jerusalem, not k., 49
knowledge
and to virtue k., 61
grow in the k. of our, 109
k. puffeth up, 31
law is k. of sin, 28
not according to k., 92
speech, yet not in k., 50
through the k. of God, 108
known
had they k. it, 37
hid that shall not be k., 165
hid that shall not be k., 165
I have made k. unto you, 154
if ye had k. me, ye, 98
k. by his fruit, 22

k. by his own fruit, 41
k. lust, except the law, 53
k. my Father also, 98
k. sin, but by the law, 28
k. the mind of the Lord, 108
k. the mind of the Lord, 71
k. unto God, 68
k. what hour the thief, 21
k. what is spoken, 29
peace have they not k., 88
seen Him, neither k. Him, 100
your requests be made k., 141

L

labour
according to his own l., 51
all ye that l., 19
know them which l., 26
l. not for the meat, 18
let him l. working, 36
labourer
l. is worthy, 196
l. is worthy, 59
labourers
but the l. are few, 55
l. together with God, 122
laboureth
husbandman that l., 156
labours
l. more abundant, 136
laden
labour and are heavy l., 19
laid
l. His hands, 83
lake
cast into the l. of fire, 39
into the l. of fire, 40
l. of fire and brimstone, 146
lama
Eli, Eli, l. sabachthani, 6
lamb
blood of the L., 159
L. are the temple temple, 74
L. is the light, 71
L. of God, 98
L. shall overcome them, 57
L. which is in the midst, 74
like a l. dumb before, 120
marriage of the L. is, 101

marriage supper of the L., 82
worthy is the L. that was slain, 37
lambs
feed my l., 122
send you forth as l., 39
lame
l. be turned out, 13
l. walk, 81
maimed, the l., 20
lament
weep and l., 37
lamented
ye have not l., 39
last
am the first and the l., 12
first shall be l., 54
first, and the first l., 53
him up at the l. day, 54
l. and the l. first, 54
l. enemy destroyed is, 40
l. shall be first, 87
l. shall be first, 53
same shall be l., 5
latchet
l. of whose shoes, 104
laugh
weep now: for ye shall l., 109
woe unto you that l., 109
laughter
l. be turned to mourning, 109
law
according to your l., 151
are not under the l., 79
brother goeth to l. with, 109
by the l. then Christ is, 28
contrary to the l., 58
curse of the l., 28
deeds of the l., 42
doers of the l., 41
flesh the l. of sin, 20
fulfilled the l., 28
hearers of the l., 41
judge me after the l., 58
judged by the l., 105
justified by the l., 28
kept under the l., 28
known lust except the l., 53
known sin, but by the l., 28
l. am dead to the l., 28
l. and the prophets were, 107

loveth his life shall l., 111
not l. his reward, 27
save his life shall l., 111
save his life shall l., 53
shall l. his life shall, 53
loseth
l. his life for my sake, 53
loss
I counted l. for Christ, 102
lost
hid to them that are l., 75
l. sheep, 103
none of them is l., 104
save that which was l., 98
save that which was l., 98
sheep which was l., 82
that nothing be l., 193
Lot
remember L.'s wife, 47
love
abide in my l., 129
and l. one another, 28
and peace, and l., 17
breastplate of l., 13
brotherly l. continue, 19
but to l. one another, 114
faith which worketh by l.,
26
Father, ye would l. me, 99
follow after l., 69
for them that l. Him, 17
God is l., 82
good to them that l., 60
grace with them that l., 17
hate the one, and l., 115
he that will l. life, 57
how can he l. God, 19
husbands, l. your wives,
114
husbands, l. your wives,
118
if a man l. me, 101
if a man say, I l. God, 76
if we l. one another, 115
if ye l. me, keep my, 99
if ye l. them which l., 52
in l. dwelleth in God, 115
in the l. of God, 13
l. as brethren, 13
l. casteth out fear, 63
l. for their work's sake, 26
l. hath no man, 67
l. Him, because He first, 70
l. is of God, 115
l. not the Lord, 38
l. not the world, 32
l. of God, 185
l. of God perfected, 130

l. of money is, 57
l. of the Father is not, 115
l. one another, 12
l. one another, 28
l. one to another, 25
l. salutations, 91
l. serve one another, 5
l. the children of God, 115
l. the Lord with all, 27
l. their husbands, 118
l. thy neighbour, 19
l. thy neighbour as, 28
l. to pray standing, 90
l. worketh no ill, 114
l. your enemies, 52
l.'s sake I beseech, 110
let l. be without, 114
let us l. one another, 115
man l. the world, 115
many as I l. I rebuke, 46
not l. in word, 42
ought to l. one another, 37
power, and of l., 32
separate us from the l., 44
Spirit is l., 86
to l. their children, 118
walk in l., 12
we should l. one another,
114
when we l. God, 115
with a rod, or in l., 10
loved
as Christ also hath l., 12
as Christ l. the church, 114
as I have l. you, 28
because He first l. us, 70
God so l. the world, 54
if God so l. us, 37
l. darkness rather than, 56
l. the praise of men, 31
loveth me shall be l., 63
Son of God, who l. me,
100
lovely
whatsoever things are l.,
191
lovers
l. of pleasures, 138
more than l. of God, 138
loveth
he that l. another, 28
l. a cheerful giver, 9
l. father more than me, 62
l. God l. his brother, 19
l. his brother, 114
l. his wife l. himself, 114
l. me not keepeth not, 47
l. me shall be loved, 63

l. not his brother, 19
l. not knoweth not God, 82
l. son more than me, 62
that l. his life, 111
that l. is born of God, 115
that l. not his brother, 19
the same l. little, 65
whom the Lord l. He, 23
whosoever l. a lie, 41
low
hill shall be brought l., 122
lower
little l. than angels, 117
lowly
meek and l. in heart, 27
lucre
filthy l., 125
not for filthy l., 126
lukewarm
because thou art l., 29
lump
leaveneth the whole l.,
33
lust
burned in their l., 87
fulfil the l. of the, 12
I had not known l., 53
l. and have not, 43
l. hath conceived, 43
looketh on a woman to l.,
3
not l. after evil, 43
passeth away, and the l.,
43
lusted
fruits that thy soul l., 5
lusteth
flesh l. against the, 88
lusts
abstain from fleshly l., 116
flee also youthful l., 13
fulfil the l., 166
l. of your father, 56
walking after own l., 30

M

mad
I am not m., 116
learning make thee m., 50
maimed
call the poor, the m., 20
make
m. His paths straight, 147
male
m. that openeth the womb,
32
neither m. nor female, 53

malefactor
if He were not a m., 2
malice
m. be ye children, 57
put off all these; m., 12
mammon
serve God and m., 30
man
a righteous m.'s reward, 88
accepteth no m.'s person, 7
any m. be in Christ, 18
authority over the m., 10
behold the m., 2
by art and m.'s device, 75
by one m. sin entered, 94
call no m. your father, 70
come out of the m., 58
defileth not a m., 146
despiseth not m. but God, 47
double minded m. is, 94
every m. a liar, 186
every m. shall bear, 152
evil m. out of evil, 22
Father judgeth no m., 9
foolish m. which built, 138
for a good m. some would, 40
for a righteous m., 39
for I am a sinful m., 31
glory of m., 69
glory of the m., 116
good m. out of the good, 22
good thing any m. doeth, 77
gospel is not after m., 78
greater love hath no m., 67
He shall reward every m., 41
head of every m. is, 10
head of the woman is m., 10
heed that no m. deceive, 62
hour knoweth no m., 163
I have coveted no m.'s, 96
I judge no m., 7
I know not this m., 43
I myself also am a m., 89
if a m. keep my saying, 39
if a m. think himself to, 31
if any m. draw back, 11
if any m. serve, 46
if any m. thirst, 43
is builded by some m., 2
know not a m., 48
let no m. deceive, 31

let no m. deceive, 164
let no m. deceive, 157
let no m. deceive you, 41
let no m. trouble me, 136
let this m. go, 184
like unto a merchant m., 20
m. be born again, 18
m. be born of water, 11
m. can do these miracles, 74
m. can receive nothing, 69
m. can serve two masters, 115
m. common or unclean, 151
m. created for the woman, 116
m. desire the office, 5
m. desire to be first, 5
m. eat of this bread, 19
m. forbid water, 11
m. hath his proper gift, 94
m. have an hundred, 137
m. have his own wife, 66
m. have long hair, 7
m. having put his hand, 45
m. is justified by, 42
m. is not justified by, 28
m. is not of the woman, 36
m. is preached, 66
m. know not how to rule, 26
m. love not Christ, 38
m. of sin be revealed, 164
m. shall not live by, 78
m. shall not live by, 163
m. that is a sinner, 22
m. that is an heretick, 34
m. who art thou that, 9
m. will sue, 68
m.'s foes shall be they, 177
m.'s life consisteth, 119
made for a righteous m., 109
make you fishers of m., 45
manner of m. is this, 10
mouth defileth a m., 65
name of a righteous m., 88
neither knoweth any m., 108
no m. can come to me, 14
no m. can come unto me, 79
no m. can shut it, 131
no m. cometh unto the, 81
no m. is justified by, 28

no m. knoweth the Son, 108
no m. shall see the, 8
no m. shall set on thee, 159
not fear what m. shall, 32
not m. for the sabbath, 158
not this m. but, 24
of God knoweth no m., 70
of whom a m. is overcome, 67
outward m. perish, 67
owe no m. any thing, 114
peace, to every m., 41
prayer of a righteous m., 141
profit a m., 96
put on the new m., 148
received it of m., 78
receiveth a righteous m., 88
rich m. shall hardly, 107
rich m. to enter into, 106
sabbath was made for m., 158
see that no m. know, 125
spirit gone out of a m., 56
tempteth He any m., 182
to every ordinance of m., 109
together, let not m. put, 48
violence to no m., 35
were judged every m., 105
what is m. that Thou, 94
what m. is there of you, 106
what shall a m. give in, 96
whatsoever a m. soweth, 50
when I became a m., 152
when no m. can work, 51
wise m. which built, 138
within and defile the m., 169
woe to that m. by whom, 96
woman for the m., 116
wrath of m. worketh, 6
wretched m. that I am, 6
See also "Son of Man"
manifest
deeds may be made m., 41
m. by the light, 58
m. in the flesh, 100
not be made m., 165
manna
eat of the hidden m., 156

manner
  all m. of sin, 16
  m. of man is this, 10
  say all m. of evil, 33
manners
  corrupt good m., 22
  suffered He their m., 103
mansions
  house are many m., 27
many
  Legion: for we are m., 56
  m. are called, 113
  m. as received Him, 13
  m. that are first, 54
  m. were made sinners, 66
Maranatha
  m., 99
mark
  m. them which walk, 125
  press toward the m., 30
marketplaces
  salutations in the m., 91
marks
  body the m. of the Lord,
    136
marriage
  giveth her in m., 21
  m. of the Lamb is come,
    101
  m. supper of the Lamb, 82
  not in m. doeth better, 21
married
  m. careth for the things, 44
  m. to another, 3
marrieth
  away his wife, and m., 48
marry
  better to m. than burn, 21
  fornication, and m., 48
  m. her that is divorced, 3
marvel
  m. not if the world hate,
    136
  m. ye at this, 10
marvellous
  m. in our eyes, 178
marvelous
  and m. are Thy works, 71
master
  is not above his m., 45
  m. of Israel, 92
  m. of the house cometh, 51
  shall be as his m., 1
  that he be as his m., 5
  why eateth your M., 55
  ye also have a M., 51
masters
  fall from their m.', 168

no man can serve two m.,
  115
subject to your m., 2
meaning
  m. of the voice, 29
measure
  m. ye mete, 32
  stripes above m., 136
measured
  mete, it shall be m., 32
meat
  he that hath m., 168
  hungred and ye gave me
    m., 30
  kingdom of God is not m.,
    86
  labour not for the m., 18
  life more than m., 119
  m. is to do the will, 124
  m. to eat that ye know,
    176
  m. which endureth, 18
  milk, and not with m., 50
  strong m. belongeth, 120
  worthy of his m., 51
  ye gave me no m., 37
mediator
  hand of a m., 28
  m. between God and men,
    74
  m. is not a m. of one, 120
  m. of the new covenant,
    120
meek
  blessed are the m., 89
  m. and lowly in heart, 27
meekness
  follow after m., 69
  fruit of Spirit is m., 86
meet
  not m. to take, 168
members
  bodies are the m. of, 18
  m. of His body, 100
  m. one of another, 26
  m. one of another, 64
  of thy m. should perish, 38
men
  all m. have not faith, 61
  all m. will believe, 118
  all things to all m., 3
  appear not unto m., 62
  appear unto m. to fast, 90
  be forgiven unto m., 16
  be not ye servants of m.,
    67
  be patient toward all m.,
    133

between God and m., 74
by the sleight of m., 48
commandments of m., 84
confess me before m., 13
confess me before m., 3
denieth me before m., 75
destroy m.'s lives, 121
every idle word that m.,
  151
free from all m., 122
gentle unto all m., 106
God is stronger than m.,
  177
God is wiser than m., 195
good unto all m., 5
good will toward m., 19
hated of all m. for my, 16
highly esteemed among m.,
  119
hold the tradition of m.,
  46
honour all m., 151
if I yet pleased m., 8
if this work be of m., 41
ignorance of foolish m., 42
in understanding be m., 57
life was the light of m., 98
light so shine before m., 41
likeness of m., 123
Lord, and not unto m., 50
loved the praise of m., 31
m. have committed much,
  58
m. it is impossible, 117
m. leaving the natural, 87
m. light a candle, 145
m. loved darkness, 56
m. most miserable, 153
m. ought always to pray,
  141
m. put new wine, 194
m. shall speak well, 64
m. should do to you, 12
m. should do to you, 12
m. their trespasses, 65
m. with m. working, 87
maketh m. high priests, 35
may be seen of m., 90
nor of m. sought we, 140
not honour from m., 8
not lied unto m., 46
obey God rather than m.,
  10
of God is with m., 74
old m. shall dream, 49
praise is not of m., 26
rich m. weep and howl,
  194

mountains
into the m. and seeketh, 137
m. were not found, 44
that I could remove m., 60

mourn
blessed are they that m., 27
for ye shall m., 109
merchants shall m., 6

mourned
m. unto you, 39

mourning
death, m. and famine, 138
laughter be turned to m., 109

mouth
confess with thy m., 101
heart the m. speaketh, 22
in thy m. sweet as honey, 16
into the m. defileth, 65
m. goeth a sharp sword, 86
m. proceedeth blessing, 17
m. was found no guile, 95
opened He not His m., 120
out of the m. defileth, 65
out of the m. of babes, 23
out of the m. of God, 163
out of the m. of lion, 42
out of your m., 12
spue thee out of my m., 29

mouths
bits in the horses' m., 129

move
in Him we live, and m., 111
not m. them with one, 90

much
faithful also in m., 33
him shall be m. required, 130
m. is given, of him, 130
men have committed m., 58
unjust also in m., 33

multiplied
grace and peace be m., 108
word of God grew and m., 56

multitude
voice of a great m., 52

murder
shalt do no m., 126

murderer
m. hath eternal life, 127
who hateth is a m., 82

murderers
without are dogs, and m., 41

murders
evil thoughts, m., 126

murmur
neither m. ye, 30

murmurers
m. complainers, walking, 30

murmurings
do all without m., 2

must
things m. needs be, 7
told thee what thou m., 49

mustard
grain of m. seed, 59
grain of m. seed, 80

myrrh
frankincense, and m., 69

mystery
m. of godliness, 76

N

nails
print of the n., 48

naked
n. and ye clothed me, 30
poor and blind and n., 120
walk n. and they see, 164

nakedness
famine, or n. or peril, 44

name
all in the n. of the, 42
ask any thing in my n., 99
ask in my n., 71
ask the Father in my n., 99
baptizing them in the n., 55
be preached in His n., 55
believe on the n. of His, 28
call His n. Emmanuel, 103
call His n. Jesus, 102
call on the n. of, 8
come in my Father's n., 9
cometh in the n. of the, 121
command thee in the n., 58
die for the n. of, 44
do in my Father's n., 2
drink in my n., 27
Father, glorify Thy n., 71
forgiven for His n.'s, 66
gathered in my n., 63
hallowed be Thy n., 70
hated for my n.'s sake, 16

holy is His n., 16
in the n. of Jesus, 11
justified in the n., 106
little child in my n., 23
many shall come in my n., 62
my n. shall they cast, 58
n. is Legion, 56
n. of a prophet, 88
n. of a righteous man, 88
n. of God is blasphemed, 91
n. of Jesus every knee, 87
n. shall the Gentiles trust, 97
n. was called Jesus, 102
not believed in the n., 13
not glorify Thy n., 140
power, or by what n., 10
reproached for the n. of, 136
shalt call His n. Jesus, 102
to bear my n., 56
unto us through Thy n., 161

names
n. are written in heaven, 81

narrow
n. is the way, 12

nation
n. shall rise against n., 7

nations
He should smite the n., 86
n. have drunk of the, 35
name among all n., 55
published among all n., 55
teach all n., 55
were all n. deceived, 41

natural
n. use of the woman, 87
women did change the n., 87

nature
course of n., 175
that which is against n., 87

Nazareth
good thing come out of N., 38
Jesus Christ of N., 83
Jesus of N., 103

neck
hanged about his n., 23

need
and have n. of nothing, 119
n. not a physician, 8
no n. of the sun, 71

things ye have n. of, 71
needle
eye of a n., 106
needs
things must n. be, 7
neglect
n. not the g., 1
neighbour
love thy n. as thyself, 28
love thy n. as thyself, 19
truth with his n., 64
worketh no ill to his n., 114
nests
birds have n., 87
new
all things are become n., 21
full of n. wine, 162
he is a n. creature, 18
He saith, a n. covenant, 36
make all things n., 149
mediator of n. covenant, 120
n. commandment I give, 28
n. testament in my blood, 29
n. wine into old bottles, 194
n. wine must be put, 11
of the n. testament, 17
put on the n. man, 148
saw a n. earth, 83
saw a n. heaven, 83
straightway desireth n., 95
wine must be put into n., 11
write no n. commandment, 28
newborn
as n. babes, 74
newness
n. of spirit, 9
nigh
desolation thereof is n., 51
draw n. to God, 61
kingdom of God is come n., 107
n. by the blood, 25
word is n., 78
night
drunken in the n., 75
n. cometh, 51
no rest day nor n., 92
shall be no n., 83
sleep in the n., 75
thief in the n., 164

thief in the n., 169
ninety
leave the n. and nine, 137
n. and nine just persons, 94
none
n. of them is lost, 104
n. that doeth good, 35
there is n. righteous, 117
to him that hath n., 168
nothing
carry n. out, 40
charity, I am n., 60
circumcision is n., 26
good for n., 64
knoweth n. yet as he, 108
let n. be done through, 5
man can receive n., 69
n. against the truth, 186
n. and yet possessing, 60
n. into this world, 40
n. shall be impossible, 1
n. shall be impossible, 72
of mine own self do n., 1
profiteth me n., 23
something, when he is n., 31
Son can do n. of Himself, 1
there is n. covered, 165
will bring to n. the, 31
without me ye can do n., 2
nought
men, it will come to n., 41
now
even n. already is it, 7
glory n. and for ever, 100
n. is the accepted time, 161
n. is the day, 161
number
great n. believed, 34
his n. is Six hundred, 57
the n. of the beast, 57
numbered
head are all n., 71

O

oath
swear not by any other o., 96
obedience
learned He o., 100
o. of one, 66
obedient
servants, be o., 173

obey
not o. the truth, 41
o. God rather than men, 10
o. not the gospel, 154
o. your parents, 24
o. your parents in all, 129
that they may o. us, 129
winds and the sea o., 10
observation
cometh not with o., 107
obtain
run, that ye may o., 30
occasion
liberty for an o., 67
offence
conscience void of o., 32
give none o., 35
man by whom the o. come, 96
Satan: thou art an o., 64
offences
delivered for our o., 153
offend
eye o. thee, pluck, 16
if thy foot o., 38
o. one of these little, 23
right eye o. thee, 38
right hand o., 16
yet o. in one point, 47
offended
o. any thing at all, 95
who is o. and I burn, 51
offender
if I be an o., 95
office
man desire the o., 5
offspring
root and the o. of David, 101
old
drunk o. wine, 95
hath made the first o., 36
o. men shall dream, 49
o. things are passed, 21
o. wives' fables, 127
put new wine into o., 194
oldness
o. of the letter, 9
olive
fig tree bear o. berries, 33
Omega
I am Alpha and O., 12
omnipotent
the Lord o. reigneth, 73
once
died unto sin o., 37

one
  add o. cubit unto his, 126
  and watereth are o., 35
  are all of o., 85
  being many are o., 64
  but o. receiveth prize, 30
  called every o., 33
  every o. that asketh, 140
  God is o., 74
  good, no, not o., 35
  I and my Father are o., 47
  Lord God is o., 126
  mediator of o., 120
  members o. of another, 64
  none good but o., 77
  not o. is forgotten, 71
  o. baptism, 11
  o. body in Christ, 26
  o. bread, and o. body, 64
  o. fold, and o. shepherd,
    25
  o. hour is thy judgment, 40
  o. Lord o. faith, 11
  o. man esteemeth, 21
  o. man's disobedience, 66
  o. mediator between God,
    74
  o. of them be gone astray,
    137
  o. of you shall betray, 15
  o. sinner that repenteth,
    94
  o. such little child, 23
  obedience of o., 66
  offend in o. point, 47
  that o. should perish, 38
  there is but o. God, 74
  there is o. God, 74
  there is o. lawgiver, 70
  these three are o., 185
  twain shall be o., 117
  voice of o. crying, 35
  watch with me o. hour, 45
  ye are all o. in, 15
only
  gave His o. begotten Son,
    54
  o. begotten Son into, 100
open
  before thee an o. door, 131
  devil o. the eyes, 2
  o. their eyes, 52
  throat an o. sepulchre, 173
  voice, and o. the door, 102
  ye shall see heaven o., 70
opened
  Ephphatha, that is, be o.,
    82

knock and it shall be o.,
    140
knock and it shall be o.,
    131
knocketh it shall be o., 50
o. He not His mouth, 120
o. the seventh seal, 10
see the heavens o., 118
openeth
  o. the womb, 32
openly
  reward thee o., 73
opportunity
  as we have therefore o., 5
oracles
  committed the o. of God,
    104
  speak as the o., 142
ordained
  o. by angels, 28
  powers that be are o., 10
order
  done decently and in o., 12
ordinance
  resisteth the o. of, 148
  submit to every o., 109
ought
  o. to say, If the Lord, 21
out
  o. of the man, 58
  they went o. from us, 116
outward
  appear beautiful o., 7
  circumcision which is o., 7
  o. man perish, 67
outwardly
  Jew, which is one o., 7
  o. appear righteous, 7
overcame
  o. him by the blood, 159
overcome
  Lamb shall o. them, 57
  o. the world, 27
  of whom a man is o., 67
overcometh
  him that o. will I make,
    156
  o. shall inherit, 61
  o. the world, 76
  to him that o., 156
overthrow
  be of God, ye cannot o., 41
owe
  o. no man any thing, 114
oweth
  or o. thee ought, 152
own
  came unto His o., 8

P

pain
  be any more p., 40
pale
  behold a p. horse, 7
paradise
  be with me in p., 16
parents
  but p. for the children, 132
  children, obey your p., 24
  children, obey your p., 129
  lay up for the p., 132
part
  know in p., 92
  prophesy in p., 92
partaker
  p. of her sins, 33
  p. of his evil deeds, 35
partner
  count me therefore a p., 67
pass
  let this cup p., 178
  must first come to p., 7
  p. from hence to you, 84
passed
  old things are p., 21
passeth
  fashion of this world p., 21
  world p. away, 43
past
  darkness is p., 52
paths
  make His p. straight, 147
  p. for your feet, 13
patience
  and p. experience, 87
  follow after p., 69
  need of p., 133
  p. and the faith of, 2
  p. of Job, 133
  p. of the saints, 133
  run with p., 29
  sound in charity, in p., 13
  tribulation worketh p., 87
patient
  apt to teach, p., 106
  p. toward all men, 133
patiently
  ye shall take it p., 37
Paul
  P. I know, 10
  P. thou art beside, 50
  who then is P., 110
pay
  p. ye tribute, 10
peace
  and p. be multiplied, 108

be at p. among, 134
came not to send p., 192
come to give p., 133
come to send p. on earth, 192
confusion, but of p., 21
earth p. good will, 19
glory, honour, and p., 41
God of p. be with you, 17
gospel of p., 78
he is our p., 100
hold not thy p., 51
let the p. of God, 134
lusts: but follow p., 13
mercy unto you, and p., 17
p. and joy in the Holy, 86
p. be with you in Christ, 17
p. from God our Father, 159
p. have they not known, 88
p. I give unto, 27
p. I leave with you, 27
p. in heaven and, 70
p. of God, which passeth, 33
p. one with another, 63
p. return to you, 16
p. with all men, 8
p. with God through, 33
sown in p. of them that, 134
Spirit is love, joy, p., 86
spiritually minded is p., 9
with you, mercy, and p., 17
worthy, let your p. come, 16
peaceable
p. fruit, 46
peacemakers
blessed are the p., 133
pearls
p. before swine, 188
seeking goodly p., 20
people
be to Me a p., 72
call them My p., 72
cast away His p., 104
face of all p., 33
feared the p., 145
not to all the p. but, 144
p. honoureth me, 4
save His p. from, 97
they shall be My p., 72
which were not My p., 72
perdition
draw back unto p., 39

revealed the son of p., 164
son of p., 104
perfect
be ye therefore p., 134
every one that is p., 1
found thy works p., 42
if thou wilt be p., 22
in heaven is p., 134
made p. by the flesh, 11
p. gift is from above, 77
p. love casteth out fear, 63
strength is made p. in, 90
works was faith made p., 42
perfected
love of God p., 130
Thou hast p. praise, 23
perfectly
made p. whole, 59
perfectness
bond of p., 114
peril
nakedness, or p. or, 44
perils
p. in the city, 39
p. in the sea, 39
p. in the wilderness, 39
perish
believeth should not p., 39
believeth should not p., 160
money p. with thee, 23
outward man p., 67
p. but Thou remainest, 24
p. without law, 28
shall all likewise p., 39
take the sword shall p., 191
that one should p., 38
perisheth
meat which p., 18
pernicious
follow their p. ways, 62
perplexed
p. but not in despair, 4
persecute
bless them which p., 38
revile you, and p., 33
they will also p. you, 135
use you, and p. you, 29
persecuted
being p. we suffer, 2
blessed are the p., 107
have not your fathers p., 136
if they have p. me, 135
p. but not forsaken, 4

p. them even unto strange, 136
p. us in times past, 21
persecutest
Jesus whom thou p., 136
Saul, why p., 136
persecution
p. or famine, 44
shall suffer p., 76
person
accepteth no man's p., 7
blood of this just p., 16
persons
ninety and nine just p., 94
respect of p. with God, 63
respect to p., 35
respecter of p., 93
persuaded
p. in his own mind, 21
p. though one rose from, 137
persuadest
p. me to be a Christian, 50
perverse
p. generation, 75
speaking perverse things, 15
pervert
cease to p., 62
pestilence
famines, and p., 7
Peter
P. and upon this rock, 25
rise, P. kill, and eat, 65
Pharisee
I am a P., 85
son of a P., 85
Pharisees
leaven of the P., 91
scribes and P., 91
philosophy
man spoil you through p., 41
physician
need not a p., 8
p. heal thyself, 36
pillar
a p. in the temple, 156
piped
we have p. unto you, 39
pit
bottomless p., 84
pitiful
brethren, be p., 13
place
I go to prepare a p., 54
no p. of repentance, 148
places
walketh through dry p., 56

plagues
add unto him the p., 138
p. come in one day, 138
receive not of her p., 57
planted
I have p., 38
planteth
p. and he that watereth, 35
please
flesh cannot p., 20
how he may p. his wife, 45
how he may p. the Lord, 44
impossible to p. Him, 61
may p. her husband, 45
pleased
Christ p. not Himself, 5
if I yet p. men, 8
in whom I am well p., 97
in whom I am well p., 121
sacrifices God is p., 42
pleasure
Father's good p., 107
she that liveth in p., 93
soul shall have no p., 11
pleasures
lovers of p., 138
plenteous
harvest truly is p., 55
plough
hand to the p., 45
pluck
p. it out, 38
p. it out and cast, 16
plucked
p. out your own eyes, 45
point
offend in one p., 47
poison
full of deadly p., 175
p. of asps, 82
pool
p. of Siloam, 83
poor
blessed are p. in spirit, 89
feast, call the p., 20
feed the p., 23
give to the p., 54
gospel to the p., 52
p. always with you, 139
p. and blind and naked, 120
p. widow hath cast more, 68
p. with you always, 187
remember the p., 23
to the p. the gospel is, 81

your sakes He became p., 99
possesseth
things which he p., 119
possessing
p. all things, 60
possible
all things are p., 13
all things are p., 1
all things are p., 72
not p. that the blood of, 66
seduce, if it were p., 84
potter
p. power over the clay, 140
p.'s field, 20
poverty
His p. might be rich, 99
power
all principality and p., 10
but in the p. of God, 60
by what p. or by what, 10
couldest have no p., 10
gave He p. to become, 13
kingdom, and the p., 55
not in word, but in p., 107
on the right hand of p., 57
p. but of God, 10
p. of God unto salvation, 78
p. of His might, 35
p. of Satan, 56
p. over the clay, 140
p. to cast into hell, 38
resisteth the p., 148
second death hath no p., 40
Son of man hath p., 65
spirit of fear; but of p., 32
with p. and great glory, 164
powerful
word of God is p., 21
powers
p. that be are ordained, 10
subject unto higher p., 10
wrestle against p., 52
praise
if there be any p., 33
loved the p. of men, 31
men more than the p. of, 31
p. is not of men, 26
p. the Lord, 140
Thou hast perfected p., 23
pray
heed, watch and p., 141
love to p. standing, 90

men ought always to p., 141
p. every where, 141
p. for them which, 29
p. God, if perhaps the, 150
p. in an unknown tongue, 141
p. one for another, 141
p. without ceasing, 141
watch and p., 181
watch ye and p. always, 141
when ye p. believe that, 59
prayer
house of p. but ye have, 26
open unto their p., 73
p. and supplication, 141
p. of a righteous man, 141
p. of faith, 83
watch unto p., 7
whatsoever ye ask in p., 13
prayest
p. enter into thy closet, 140
prayeth
spirit p. but my, 141
praying
stand p. forgive, 80
preach
anointed me to p., 52
but to p. the gospel, 56
feet of them that p., 78
go thou and p., 49
p. any other gospel, 84
p. Christ crucified, 37
p. deliverance, 42
p. not the gospel, 26
p. the gospel, 46
p. the gospel should, 12
p. the word, 78
p. ye upon the housetops, 142
we p. not ourselves but, 142
whom I p. unto you, 121
preached
be p. in His name among, 55
Christ is p., 69
gospel which was p., 78
kingdom of God is p., 107
p. unto the Gentiles, 100
poor the gospel is p., 81
through this man is p., 66
to us was the gospel p., 72
preacher
hear without a p., 50

■ 244 ■

preacheth
now p. the faith which, 21
prepare
p. a place for you, 54
p. himself to the battle, 11
p. Thy way before Thee,
122
p. ye the way of the Lord,
147
prepared
p. before the face, 33
p. of my Father, 9
things which God hath p.,
17
presence
p. of the angels, 94
present
no chastening for the p.,
37
p. in spirit, 1
preserve
lose his life shall p., 53
press
p. toward the mark, 30
pretence
in p. or in truth, 69
prevail
hell shall not p., 177
price
bought with a p., 67
priests
law maketh men high p.,
35
prince
p. of the kings of, 103
p. of this world, 105
right hand to be a P.,
99
principalities
wrestle against p., 52
principality
head of all p., 10
print
p. of the nails, 48
prison
I was in p. and ye came,
30
put in p. are standing, 53
shall cast some into p., 4
shut up in p., 34
prisons
p. more frequent, 136
private
of any p. interpretation,
144
prize
one receiveth the p., 30
p. of the high calling, 30

proceed
heart p. evil, 126
proclaimed
p. upon the housetops, 58
profane
p. and old wives', 127
p. and vain babblings, 64
profess
p. that they know God, 42
professing
p. themselves to be wise,
31
profession
p. of our faith, 61
profit
p. is of circumcision, 26
what shall it p. a man, 96
words to no p., 8
profitable
godliness is p., 143
p. for thee that one, 38
profiteth
bodily exercise p., 76
flesh p. nothing, 86
p. me nothing, 23
promise
covenants of p., 44
hope of the p., 136
p. is unto you, 86
p. which was made, 78
receive the p., 133
slack concerning His p.,
143
wait for the p., 86
proper
man hath his p. gift, 94
prophecy
book of this p., 144
p. of the Scripture, 144
the sayings of the p., 130
the spirit of p., 197
words of this p., 144
prophesieth
greater is he that p., 29
p. edifieth the church, 29
prophesy
p. in part, 92
prophesying
p. serveth not, 144
prophesyings
despise not p., 144
prophet
by Esaias the p., 144
name of a prophet, 88
p. hath no honour in, 150
p. is not without honour,
144
p. is risen up among, 10

receive a p.'s reward, 88
receiveth a p., 88
sign of the p. Jonas, 123
speaketh the p., 122
that Thou art a p., 3
truth this is the P., 122
prophets
and the p. did write, 122
believe all that the p., 144
beware of false p., 41
blood of saints and p., 119
false p., 84
give all the p. witness, 182
killest the p., 97
not Moses and the p., 137
p. have not your fathers,
136
scriptures of the p., 122
the p. were until John, 107
ye holy apostles and p.,
154
proud
God resisteth the p., 90
God resisteth the p., 90
prove
p. all things, 144
provision
p. for the flesh, 166
provoke
p. not your children, 6
p. not your children, 23
prudent
understanding of the p.,
31
publicans
do not even the p., 52
with p. and sinners, 55
published
gospel must first be p., 55
puffed
charity is not p. up, 114
puffeth
knowledge p. up, 31
purchased
p. with His own blood, 49
p. with money, 23
pure
blessed are the p., 146
charity out of a p., 114
is nothing p., 9
keep thyself p., 35
p. all things are p., 9
whatsoever things are p.,
191
purify
p. your hearts, 146
purpose
appeared for this p., 124

purposeth
as he p. in his heart, 23
put
body what ye shall p. on,
65

Q

quench
q. all the fiery darts, 60
q. not the Spirit, 61
quenched
fire is not q., 84
fire never q., 84
questions
avoid foolish q., 34
foolish and unlearned q.,
34
quick
word of God is q., 21
quickeneth
Spirit that q., 86
quickly
behold, I come q., 165
doest, do q., 15
with thine adversary q.,
8
quiet
study to be q., 13

R

race
which run in a r., 30
with patience the r., 29
raiment
and the body than r., 119
having food and r., 80
take ye thought for r., 7
white r. that thou be, 61
rain
good, and gave us r., 147
r. on the just and the, 76
raise
r. him up at the last day,
54
r. the dead, 82
stones to r. up children, 72
that God should r., 153
three days I will r., 44
raised
Christ be not r., 60
dead are r., 81
r. again for our, 153
r. from the dead, 24
r. Him from the dead, 153
r. Him from the dead, 101
r. up the third day, 144

ransom
give His life a r., 5
read
r. of all men, 183
readest
understand what thou r.,
50
readeth
blessed is he that r., 144
reading
give attendance to r., 48
ready
be ye also r., 164
be ye therefore r., 147
r. not to be bound only, 44
reap
due season we shall r., 133
in Thy sickle, and r., 105
of flesh r. corruption, 116
r. also bountifully, 45
r. also sparingly, 50
r. life everlasting, 54
soweth, that shall he r., 50
time for Thee to r., 120
reaped
them which have r., 196
reapeth
r. receiveth wages, 54
soweth, and another r., 34
rebuke
many as I love, I r., 46
r. not an elder, 4
reprove, r. exhort with,
133
them that sin r., 23
trespass against thee r., 36
receive
able to r., 20
ask, and r. not because,
126
ask, and ye shall r., 82
believe that ye r. them, 59
believing, ye shall r., 13
let him r., 20
man can r. nothing, 69
name, and ye r. me not, 9
of whom ye hope to r., 5
r. a prophet's reward, 88
r. as much again, 166
r. him as myself, 67
r. my spirit, 118
r. not honour from men, 8
r. one such little child, 23
r. the kingdom of God, 23
r. the promise, 133
r. the reward, 156
r. ye one another, 64
right, that shall ye r., 58

same shall he r., 77
that thou didst not r., 178
to give than to r., 5
whatsoever we ask, we r.,
141
whosoever shall r. me, 86
received
as many as r. Him, 13
as ye have r. Christ, 12
freely ye have r., 68
His own r. Him not, 8
r. up into glory, 100
r. up into heaven, 8
r. with thanksgiving, 65
r. your consolation, 194
receiveth
but one r. the prize, 30
every one that asketh r.,
140
he that r. me r. Him, 101
in my name r. me, 23
r. a prophet, 88
r. a righteous man, 88
r. not me but Him, 86
r. who I send r. me, 55
reapeth r. wages, 54
recompence
r. of reward, 32
recompense
for they cannot r. thee, 20
I will r. saith the Lord,
154
r. to no man evil, 154
recompensed
r. at the resurrection, 5
reconciled
r. to thy brother, 22
record
his r. is true, 85
I saw, and bare r., 47
our r. is true, 87
saw it bare r., 85
three that bear r., 185
recover
sick, and they shall r., 82
redeemed
r. us from the curse, 28
redemption
r. through His blood, 66
refuse
r. not to die, 95
r. profane and old wives',
127
refused
nothing to be r., 65
regardeth
r. it unto the Lord, 87
that r. the day, 87

reign
He must r., 174
we shall also r., 179
reigneth
the Lord omnipotent r., 73
reins
searcheth the r. and, 100
reject
r. the commandment, 91
second admonition r., 34
rejected
which the builders r., 132
rejoice
and I therein do r., 69
but world shall r., 37
let us be glad and r., 82
r. as partakers of, 164
r. because your names, 81
r. evermore, 20
r. in Christ, 15
r. in his light, 96
r. in the Lord, 82
r. in the Lord alway, 20
r. not, that the spirits, 81
r. over her thou heaven, 154
r. with me, 82
r. with them that do r., 51
remain
fragments that r., 193
remainest
perish; but Thou r., 24
remember
r. from whence thou art, 11
r. Lot's wife, 47
r. me when Thou comest, 34
r. my bonds, 94
r. the poor, 23
r. the words of, 78
r. them in bonds, 30
remembered
hath r. her iniquities, 76
remembereth
r. no more the anguish, 16
remembrance
drink it, in r. of me, 29
this do in r. of me, 29
remission
for the r. of sins, 17
of blood is no r., 17
r. of sins, 66
repentance and r. of, 55
remove
and it shall r., 59
mountain, r. hence to, 59

removed
mountain, be thou r., 59
rend
turn again and r. you, 95
render
r. therefore unto Caesar, 25
renewed
be r. in the spirit, 9
inward man is r., 67
repay
come again, I will r., 77
is Mine; I will r., 154
repent
except ye r. ye shall, 39
if he r. forgive, 36
r. and be baptized, 11
r. for the kingdom, 107
r. or else I will, 150
r. thou shalt forgive, 66
r. ye therefore, 34
r. ye, and believe, 78
thou art fallen, and r., 11
repentance
baptism of r., 11
but sinners to r., 142
fruits worthy of r., 41
just persons, need no r., 94
leadeth thee to r., 77
no place of r., 148
of God are without r., 17
r. and remission of sins, 55
repenteth
one sinner that r., 94
repetitions
use not vain r., 140
repliest
man who art thou that r., 9
report
things are of good r., 33
reproached
r. for the name of, 136
reprove
r. rebuke, exhort with, 133
requests
r. be made known, 141
required
of him shall be much r., 130
resist
r. the devil, 162
r. the Holy Ghost, 75
that r. shall receive, 148
resisteth
God r. the proud, 90
r. the ordinance, 148
r. the power, 148

respect
no r. of persons, 63
r. to persons, 35
respecter
no r. of persons, 93
rest
I will give you r., 19
no r. day nor night, 92
r. unto your souls, 27
r. yet for a little season, 133
seeking r. and findeth, 56
resurrection
I am the r., 54
r. of the just, 5
the first r., 40
unto the r. of damnation, 38
unto the r. of life, 38
return
let your peace r., 16
returned
r. unto the Shepherd, 75
reveal
Son will r. Him, 108
revealed
blood hath not r. it, 101
His glory shall be r., 164
man of sin be r., 164
r. from heaven, 75
that shall not be r., 165
revelation
taught it, but by the r., 78
revenger
r. to execute wrath, 79
revile
men shall r., 33
reviled
being r. we bless, 2
revived
commandment came, sin r., 28
reward
a righteous man's r., 88
great is your r., 118
love you, what r. have, 52
not lose his r., 27
r. every man according, 41
r. her even as she r., 57
r. him according to, 145
r. of reward, 32
r. of your Father, 22
r. thee openly, 73
receive a prophet's r., 88
receive his own r., 51
receive the r., 156
they have their r., 90
worthy of his r., 59

rewarder
He is a r. of them that, 14
rich
    merchants are waxed r., 35
    poverty might be r., 99
    r. fall into temptation, 5
    r. He hath sent empty, 30
    r. in good works, 42
    r. man shall hardly enter,
       107
    r. man to enter kingdom,
       106
    r. men, weep and howl,
       194
    r. unto all that call, 70
    that thou mayest be r., 61
    thou sayest, I am r., 119
    though He was r., 99
    woe unto you that are r.,
       194
riches
    deceitfulness of r., 78
    trust in r. to enter, 54
right
    Christ sitteth on the r., 69
    exalted with His r., 99
    heart is not r., 9
    if thy r. hand offend, 16
    know what thy r. hand, 22
    on the r. hand of God, 118
    on thy r. cheek, turn, 65
    r. eye offend thee, 38
    r. hand, and on my left, 9
    r. in the sight of, 32
    r. to the tree of life, 111
    sat on the r. hand, 8
    sit on the r. hand, 57
    sit Thou on my r., 57
    the r. ways of the Lord, 62
    whatsoever is r., 58
righteous
    a r. man's reward, 88
    come to call the r., 142
    doeth righteousness is r.,
       157
    fervent prayer of a r., 141
    in the name of a r., 88
    judge r. judgment, 7
    Lord are over the r., 73
    Lord, the r. judge, 156
    many be made r., 66
    not made for a r. man, 109
    outwardly appear r., 7
    r. are His judgments, 105
    r. are Thy judgments, 146
    r. scarcely be saved, 75
    receiveth a r. man, 88
    scarcely for a r., 39

there is none r., 117
righteousness
    awake to r., 12
    believeth unto r., 14
    but follow r., 13
    crown of r., 156
    enemy of all r., 57
    every one that doeth r.,
       157
    follow after r., 69
    fruit of r. is sown, 134
    fulfil all r., 49
    God, and His r., 69
    he that doeth r. is, 157
    if r. come by the law, 28
    in r. He doth judge, 105
    judge the world in r., 105
    man worketh not the r., 6
    not by works of r., 42
    not meat and drink but r.,
       86
    peaceable fruit of r., 46
    persecuted for r.' sake, 107
    r. of faith, 60
    sceptre of r., 157
    suffer for r.' sake, 157
    thirst after r., 156
    word of r., 92
riot
    same excess of r., 32
riotous
    with r. living, 40
ripe
    grapes are fully r., 105
    harvest is r., 120
rise
    brother shall r. again, 152
    dead shall r. first, 25
    false prophets shall r., 84
    if the dead r. not, 147
    r. Peter; kill, and eat, 65
    r. take up thy bed, 83
    r. the third day, 152
    r. up and walk, 83
    sun to r. on the evil, 76
    third day He shall r., 152
    third day He shall r., 37
risen
    great prophet is r., 10
    He is r., 152
rock
    house upon a r., 138
    upon this r. I will, 177
rod
    with a r. or in love, 10
Roman
    man is a R., 106
    man that is a R., 106

Rome
    bear witness also at R., 35
room
    no r. in the inn, 102
rooms
    uppermost r. at feasts, 91
root
    bearest not the r., 17
    but the r. thee, 17
    if the r. be holy, 85
    no r. they withered, 13
    r. and the offspring of, 101
    r. of all evil, 57
rose
    r. from the dead, 137
rough
    r. ways shall be made, 130
rude
    r. in speech, 50
rule
    let the elders that r., 27
    man know not how to r.,
       26
    peace of God r., 134
    walk by the same r., 35
ruler
    speak evil of the r., 79
rulers
    brought before r., 135
    r. are not a terror, 79
    r. of the darkness, 52
run
    r. in a race r. all, 30
    r. that ye may obtain, 30
    r. with patience, 29
    strange that ye r. not, 32
runneth
    break, and wine r. out, 194
    nor of him that r., 121
rust
    r. doth corrupt, 119
    r. doth corrupt, 175

S

sabachthani
    Eli, Eli, lama s., 6
sabbath
    do well on the s., 158
    Lord even of the s., 158
    not man for the s., 158
    s. was made for man, 158
sacrifice
    Gentiles s., 75
    mercy and not s., 157
    s. to devils, 75
sacrifices
    s. God is well pleased, 42

cast into the s., 59
cast into the s., 23
of the earth and the s., 162
perils in the s., 39
walking on the s., 123
wave of the s., 49
winds and the s., 10
seal
opened the seventh s., 10
seals
worthy to loose the s., 127
search
s. the scriptures, 122
searcheth
s. the hearts, 71
s. the reins and hearts, 100
Spirit s. all things, 86
season
convenient s., 184
in due s. we shall reap, 133
instant in s. out of s., 148
rest yet for a little s., 133
willing for a s. to, 96
seasoned
s. with salt, 35
seasons
times or the s., 68
seat
at Caesar's judgment s., 25
judgment s. of Christ, 53
judgment s. of Christ, 105
seats
s. in the synagogues, 91
second
appear the s. time, 164
s. death hath no power,
40
sought for the s., 36
this is the s. death, 40
secret
nothing is s., 165
seeth in s., 73
seduce
wonders to s. the elect, 84
see
blind s., 81
blind, now I s., 58
cannot s. the kingdom, 18
eyes, s. ye not, 178
for they shall s. God, 146
no man shall s. the Lord, 8
s. in His hands, 48
s. that no man know, 125
s. through a glass, 26
s. your good works, 41
seeing s. not, 92
spoken of, they shall s., 56
that thou mayest s., 169

young men shall s., 49
seed
grain of mustard s., 59
grain of mustard s., 80
s. of Abraham, 104
s. of Abraham, 104
seeing
s. see not, 92
seek
let no man s. his own, 5
s. a sign, 56
s. after a sign, 143
s. after wisdom, 144
s. and ye shall find, 45
s. me and shall not find,
163
s. not mine own will, 69
s. not to be loosed, 48
s. not your's, but you, 28
s. those things, 69
s. to save his life, 53
s. ye first the kingdom, 69
s. ye the kingdom of God,
107
s. ye the living among, 152
shall men s. death, 40
Son of man is come to s.,
98
them that diligently s., 14
whom s. ye, 95
seeketh
he that s. findeth, 5
s. after a sign, 123
s. his own glory, 17
s. that which is astray, 137
seeking
s. goodly pearls, 20
s. rest and findeth none, 56
seen
brother whom he hath s.,
19
evidence of things not s.,
61
evil hath not s. God, 76
eye hath not s., 17
for to be s. of men, 90
God whom he hath not s.,
19
hope that is s., 87
may be s. of men, 90
not s. and yet believed, 14
s. and heard declare we, 85
s. His star, 86
s. me hath s. the Father, 47
s. of angels, 100
s. strange things, 123
sinneth hath not s. Him,
100

things which are s. are, 119
things which we have s.,
182
write which thou hast s.,
96
seest
s. write in a book, 18
seeth
s. in secret, 73
which he s. the Father do,
1
world s. me no more, 39
sell
s. that thou hast, 53
s. that ye have, 23
selves
own s. shall men arise, 15
send
Behold I s. my messenger,
122
s. you forth as sheep, 39
so s. I you, 124
sent
as my Father hath s., 124
believeth on Him that s.,
13
but Him that s. me, 86
but the Father which s., 9
Father which hath s. me,
14
from Him, and He hath s.,
108
greater than he that s., 53
He whom God hath s., 9
know not Him that s., 108
not mine but His that s., 48
on Him that s. me, 14
on Him whom He hath s.,
49
receiveth Him that s. me,
101
s. but unto the lost, 55
s. not His Son into, 98
that s. me is true, 70
whom He hath s., 121
will of Him that s., 124
will of Him that s. me, 98
works of Him that s., 49
separate
s. them one from another,
24
s. us from the love, 44
sepulchre
throat is an open s., 173
sepulchres
whited s., 7
serpents
be ye wise as s., 39

be ye wise as s., 173
ye s. ye generation of, 38
servant
above a s., 64
and s. of all, 5
art no more a s., 25
free, is Christ's s., 67
good and faithful s., 8
judgest another man's s., 8
let him be your s., 89
made myself s. unto all, 122
not be the s. of Christ, 8
not now as a s., 64
s. above his lord, 45
s. as his lord, 5
s. is not greater, 53
s. is the Lord's freeman, 15
s. of the Lord must not, 34
s. shall be healed, 59
shall be your s., 110
sin is the s. of sin, 169
servants
be not ye s. of men, 67
give unto your s., 51
s. be obedient, 173
s. be subject to, 2
serve
by love s. one another, 5
elder shall s. younger, 64
Him only shalt thou s.,
126
if any man s. me, 46
mind I myself s., 20
of God, and s. tables, 122
s. God and mammon, 30
s. in newness of spirit, 9
s. the Lord Christ, 196
s. two masters, 115
served
s. the creature more, 91
serveth
among you as He that s.,
89
service
think he doeth God's., 136
serving
s. the Lord, 89
seven
s. times in a day, 66
seventh
opened the s. seal, 10
seventy
until s. times seven, 65
shame
naked and see his s., 164
sharper
s. than twoedged sword,
168

shearer
dumb before His s., 120
shed
blood which is s., 17
s. the blood of saints, 119
shedding
without s. of blood, 17
sheep
as a s. to slaughter, 39
careth not for the s., 44
come to you in s.'s, 41
feed my s., 122
great shepherd of the s.,
103
life for the s., 44
lost s., 103
man have an hundred s.,
137
other s. I have, 55
s. going astray, 75
s. hear my voice, 4
s. in midst of wolves, 39
s. not having a shepherd,
110
s. shall be scattered, 110
s. which was lost, 82
shepherd divideth his s.,
24
shepherd of the s., 110
shepherd
chief S. shall appear, 156
fold, and one s., 25
good s., 103
great s. of the sheep, 103
returned unto the S., 75
s. divideth his sheep, 24
s. of the sheep, 110
sheep not having a s., 110
smite the s., 110
shield
s. of faith, 60
shine
let your light so s., 41
of a candle shall s., 42
of the moon, to s., 71
shineth
light s. in darkness, 52
s. even unto the west, 163
true light now s., 52
shining
burning and a s. light, 96
shoes
latchet of whose s., 104
whose s. I am not worthy,
80
short
sinned, and come s., 117
time is s., 131

shortly
s. I must put off, 40
shoulders
lay them on men's s., 90
showed
God hath s. me that, 151
shun
s. profane and vain, 64
shut
no man can s. it, 131
shall not be s. by day, 83
sick
faith shall save the s., 83
heal the s., 138
lay hands on the s., 82
s. and ye visited me, 30
they that are s., 8
sickle
thrust in Thy s., 105
sickness
s. is not unto death, 71
side
my hand into His s., 49
thrust it into my s., 49
sight
abomination in the s. of,
119
faith, not by s., 12
in the s. of the Lord, 90
right in the s. of, 32
right in the s. of God, 9
s. forthwith, and arose,
34
s. of God, 28
sights
fearful s. and great, 7
sign
Jews require a s., 144
no s. be given, 123
s. of the prophet Jonas,
123
seek a s., 56
seek after a s., 143
seeketh after a s., 123
tongues are for a s., 185
signs
except ye see s., 13
s. of the times, 45
shall show s. and, 84
sights and great s., 7
silence
let your women keep s., 26
to s. the ignorance of, 42
was s. in heaven, 10
woman learn in s., 50
woman to be in s., 10
Siloam
pool of S., 83

silver
  coveted no man's s., 96
  like unto gold, or s., 75
  s. and gold have I none, 23
  thirty pieces of s., 15
  vessels of gold and s., 47
simple
  s. concerning evil, 77
simplicity
  do it with s., 23
sin
  all manner of s. and, 16
  blind ye have no s., 95
  but s. that dwelleth, 16
  by one man s., 94
  came, s. revived, 28
  ceased from s., 171
  cleanseth us from all s., 17
  cloak for their s., 57
  died unto s. once, 37
  flesh the law of s., 20
  freed from s., 40
  go, and s. no more, 169
  God doth not commit s.,
    18
  hath the greater s., 81
  he that is without s., 2
  His steps: Who did no s.,
    100
  I do it, but s., 152
  I had not known s., 28
  if any man s., 97
  in Him is no s., 100
  knowledge of s., 28
  lay not this s. to, 66
  Lord will not impute s., 66
  lust bringeth forth s., 43
  man of s. be revealed, 164
  not of faith is s., 60
  righteousness, and s., 12
  s. bringeth forth death, 40
  s. is not imputed, 109
  s. is of the devil, 162
  s. is the transgression, 171
  s. no more, 169
  s. rebuke before all, 23
  s. shall not have dominion,
    79
  say that we have no s., 95
  servant of s., 169
  sting of death is s., 40
  strength of s. is, 40
  taketh away the s., 98
  they are all under s., 117
  to persons, ye commit s.,
    35
  unrighteousness is s., 157
  wages of s., 54

where s. abounded, 66
whosoever committeth s.,
    169
whosoever committeth s.,
    171
sincerity
  love Christ in s., 17
sinful
  for I am a s. man, 31
sinned
  all have s., 117
  angels that s., 6
  s. against heaven, 31
  s. in the law, 105
  s. without law, 28
  say that we have not s., 91
sinner
  converteth the s., 149
  merciful to me a s., 34
  one s. that repenteth, 94
  s. do such miracles, 22
  ungodly and the s. appear,
    75
  whether He be a s., 58
sinners
  but s. to repentance, 142
  hands of s., 15
  law made for s., 109
  many were made s., 66
  s. also do even the same,
    12
  s. also lend to s., 166
  while we were yet s., 158
  with publicans and s., 55
  world to save s., 100
sinneth
  abideth in Him s. not, 130
  born of God s. not, 172
  fornication s. against, 66
  s. from the beginning, 162
  s. hath not seen Him, 100
sins
  blood take away s., 66
  Christ died for our s., 37
  cover the multitude of s.,
    114
  die in your s., 121
  earth to forgive s., 65
  forgive us our s., 65
  forgive us our s., 31
  forgiveness of s., 66
  forgiveness of s., 66
  if we confess our s., 31
  multitude of s., 170
  partakers of her s., 33
  people from their s., 97
  remission of s., 55
  remission of s., 66

s. are covered, 66
s. are forgiven, 66
s. may be blotted out, 34
s. reached unto heaven, 76
shed for remission of s., 17
thy s. be forgiven, 51
wash away thy s., 11
ye are yet in your s., 60
sister
  same is brother, and s., 62
sit
  s. on the right hand, 57
  s. Thou on my right, 57
  that s. in darkness, 52
  to s. on my right hand, 9
sittest
  s. thou to judge, 58
sitteth
  by Him that s. thereon,
    128
  s. not down first, 138
six
  his number is S. hundred,
    57
sky
  discern face of the s., 192
  face of the s., 45
slack
  Lord is not s., 143
slain
  worthy is the Lamb that
    was s., 37
slaughter
  as a sheep to s., 39
sleep
  awake out of s., 161
  let us not s., 191
  they that s. s. in the, 75
sleepeth
  is not dead, but s., 111
sleight
  s. of men, 48
slow
  s. of heart to believe, 144
  s. to speak, 6
  s. to wrath, 6
small
  the dead, s. and great, 105
  witnessing both to s., 182
smite
  s. the shepherd, 110
  s. thee on thy right, 65
smiteth
  s. thee on the one cheek,
    65
smitten
  commandest me to be s.,
    58

smooth
    ways shall be made s., 130
sober
    be s. be vigilant, 162
    be s. grave, 13
    let us watch and be s., 191
    of the day, be s., 13
    s. and watch unto prayer, 7
    young women to be s., 118
soberly
    think s., 89
soberness
    words of truth and s., 116
Sodom
    land of S. than for thee, 93
    more tolerable for S., 75
soldier
    good s. of Christ, 136
Solomon
    greater than S., 98
    S. in all his glory, 7
something
    s. when he is nothing, 31
son
    believeth not the S., 13
    blood of Christ His S., 17
    bring forth a s., 102
    bring forth a s., 102
    bring forth a s. and, 102
    Christ is the S. of God, 14
    Christ, the S., 103
    Christ, the S. of God, 101
    Father sent the S., 100
    Father, and of the S., 55
    Father, save the S., 108
    fellowship is with His S.,
        64
    glorified in the S., 71
    glorify Thy S., 71
    His only begotten S., 54
    honoureth not the S., 3
    if his s. ask bread, 106
    if thou be the S. of God,
        21
    if Thou be the S. of God,
        121
    Jesus, the s. of Joseph, 162
    judgment unto the S., 9
    life is in His S., 54
    loveth s. more than me, 62
    no man knoweth the S.,
        108
    no more servant but a s.,
        25
    on the name of His S., 28
    only begotten S., 13
    only begotten S. into, 100
    s. against the father, 62

S. also may glorify, 71
S. can do nothing of, 1
s. of a Pharisee, 85
S. of God who loved me,
    100
s. of perdition, 104
S. of the most high, 161
S. shall make you free, 67
S. will reveal Him, 108
sent not His S. into, 98
that acknowledgeth the S.,
    102
that denieth the S., 7
that hath the S. hath, 102
that Jesus is the S., 76
the s. of perdition, 164
this is My beloved S., 97
this is My beloved S., 121
this is the S. of God, 47
this the carpenter's s., 98
though He were a S., 100
truly this was the S., 3
truth Thou art the S., 47
what s. is he whom, 24
whosoever denieth the S.,
    43
woman, behold thy s., 63
son of man
    a word against the S., 16
    betrayest thou the S., 15
    coming of the S., 163
    flesh of the S., 29
    now is the S. glorified, 71
    S. also confess before, 3
    S. came not to be, 5
    S. cometh at an hour, 147
    S. coming in a cloud, 164
    S. hath not where to lay,
        87
    S. hath power, 65
    S. is betrayed, 15
    S. is betrayed, 15
    S. is come, 98
    S. is come to seek, 98
    S. is Lord of sabbath, 158
    S. is not come, 121
    S. should be glorified, 71
    S. sit on the right, 57
    S. standing on the right,
        118
    s. that Thou visitest, 94
    see the S. coming in, 39
    shall the S. be ashamed, 78
    the S., 103
sons
    are the s. of God, 86
    to become the s. of God,
        13

sorcerers
    without are dogs, and s.,
        41
sorceries
    by thy s. were all, 41
sorrow
    s. shall be turned to, 87
    shall be no more s., 40
    torment and s. give her, 17
sorrowful
    soul is exceeding s., 6
    ye shall be s., 87
sought
    nor of men s. we glory,
        140
    s. it carefully with, 148
    that s. Me not, 34
soul
    in exchange for his s., 96
    kill the s., 18
    lose his own s., 96
    My s. have no pleasure, 11
    s. be subject unto, 10
    s. exceeding sorrowful, 6
    s. was not left, 152
    save a s. from death, 149
    saving of the s., 39
    that thy s. lusted after, 5
    war against the s., 116
    with all thy s., 44
souls
    find rest unto your s., 27
    s. of them beheaded, 119
sound
    an uncertain s., 11
    do not s. a trumpet, 22
    hearest the s. thereof, 127
sower
    s. soweth the word, 55
soweth
    s. and another reapeth, 34
    s. bountifully, 45
    s. sparingly shall, 50
    s. to the Spirit shall, 54
    that s. to his flesh, 116
    whatsoever a man s., 50
sown
    s. in corruption, 18
    s. in peace, 134
spake
    well s. the Holy Ghost,
        144
spared
    s. not the angels, 6
sparing
    not s. the flock, 177
sparingly
    soweth s. shall reap, 50

■ 253 ■

sparrows
are not five s. sold for, 71
more value than many s.,
94
speak
be not afraid, but s., 51
dumb to s., 81
evil, s. good things, 36
I s. to the world, 154
if any man s., 142
it is not ye that s. but, 96
s. a word against the, 16
s. as the oracles, 142
s. every man truth, 64
s. evil of no man, 173
s. evil of the ruler, 79
s. forth the words, 116
s. in our tongues, 185
s. in the church, 26
s. into the air, 29
s. the word only, 59
s. they of the world, 62
s. thou the things, 48
slow to s., 6
that s. unto thee am He,
121
though I s. with the, 50
we cannot but s. the, 182
when s. well of you, 64
word that men shall s., 151
speaketh
Father which s. in you, 96
heart the mouth s., 22
of whom s. the prophet,
122
s. against the Holy, 85
s. in an unknown tongue,
29
s. not unto men, 29
s. of himself seeketh, 17
s. shall be a barbarian, 29
s. the words of God, 9
s. with tongues, 29
speaking
heard for their much s.,
140
s. perverse things, 15
speech
rude in s., 50
s. be alway with grace, 35
speed
biddeth him God s. is, 35
spendest
s. more, when I come, 77
spin
neither do they s., 7
spirit
also walk in the S., 12

begun in the S., 11
believe not every s., 14
body without the s., 40
body, and in your s., 18
born of the S. is s., 15
bound in the s., 49
but the same S., 1
commend my s., 1
filled with the S., 49
flesh, but in the S., 60
fruit of the S. is, 86
hear what the S. saith, 84
I saw the S. descending, 86
if a s. hath spoken, 1
if we live in the S., 12
justified in the S., 100
led by the S., 86
lusteth against the S., 88
man, thou unclean s., 58
mind of the S., 71
newness of s., 9
of the S. reap life, 54
poor in s., 89
present in s., 1
quench not the S., 61
receive my s., 118
S. against the flesh, 88
s. and not the letter, 26
S. gave them utterance,
184
s. giveth life, 28
s. indeed is willing, 67
S. is truth, 86
S. of God descending, 85
S. of God dwelleth, 86
S. of our God, 106
S. of the Lord, 67
S. of your Father, 96
s. of your mind, 9
s. prayeth but my, 141
S. searcheth all things, 86
S. that beareth witness, 86
S. that quickeneth, 86
S. the water and blood,
183
soweth to the S. shall, 54
that are after the S., 20
the s. of fear, 32
the s. of prophecy, 197
things of the S., 20
walk in the S., 12
water and of the S., 11
when the unclean s., 56
with you in the s., 1
worship God in the s., 15
worship Him in s., 171
spirits
rejoice not, that the s., 81

spiritual
law is s., 20
spiritually
s. minded is life, 9
spit
s. upon Him, and shall, 37
spoil
s. you through philosophy,
41
spoken
angel hath s., 1
if I have s. evil, 2
known what is s., 29
not s. of myself, 9
s. in the ear, 58
that the prophets have s.,
144
to whom He was not s. of,
56
word which I have s., 85
stand
by faith ye s., 60
faith should not s., 60
house cannot s., 177
kingdom cannot s., 79
s. and am judged, 136
s. before the judgment,
53
s. before you whole, 83
s. fast in the faith, 44
s. fast in the Lord, 45
s. fast in the Lord, 61
s. fast, and hold, 49
s. praying, forgive, 80
s. up; I myself, 89
s. we in jeopardy, 136
shall then his kingdom s.,
161
the dead, s. before God,
105
who shall be able to s., 70
standeth
foundation of God s., 70
thinketh he s. take heed,
31
standing
s. in the synagogues, 90
s. in the temple, 53
Son of man s., 118
there be some s. here, 39
star
bright and morning s., 101
give him the morning s.,
156
one s. differeth from, 83
seen His s., 86
stature
one cubit unto his s., 126

staves
thief with swords and s., 9
steadfast
be ye s., 45
steal
break through and s., 119
but for to s., 36
kill, do not s., 27
shalt not s., 36
that stole s. no more, 36
where thieves do not s., 175
Stephen
stoned S., 124
steps
follow his s., 100
steward
blameless, as the s., 110
stiffnecked
s. and uncircumcised, 75
sting
death, where is thy s., 40
s. of death is sin, 40
stomach
wine for thy s.'s, 112
stone
first cast a s., 2
give him a s., 106
s. graven by art, 75
s. which the builders, 132
tables of s., 135
works do ye s. me, 2
stoned
s. Stephen, 124
should have been s., 145
stones
able of these s., 72
command that these s., 21
stonest
the prophets, and s., 97
straight
crooked shall be made s., 130
make His paths s., 147
s. paths for your feet, 13
s. the way of the Lord, 104
strain
s. at a gnat, 91
strait
s. is the gate, 12
strange
even unto s. cities, 136
seen s. things, 123
stranger
s. and ye took me in, 30
strangers
field, to bury s., 20
of children, or of s., 180

s. from the covenants, 44
to entertain s., 6
ye are no more s., 25
streets
corners of the s., 90
strength
s. is made perfect, 90
s. of sin is, 40
strengthen
s. thy brethren, 51
strengtheneth
Christ which s., 1
strife
be done through s. or, 5
envying and s. is, 32
strifes
that they do gender s., 34
stripes
s. above measure, 136
strive
of the Lord must not s., 34
s. not about words, 8
strong
be s. in the Lord, 35
s. in the grace, 67
s. is the Lord who, 146
s. meat belongeth, 120
we that are s., 22
weak, then am I s., 177
stronger
God is s. than men, 177
study
s. to be quiet, 13
s. to show thyself, 45
stumblingblock
unto the Jews a s., 37
subject
even the devils are s., 161
s. unto higher powers, 10
spirits are s. unto, 81
subjection
silence with all s., 50
submit
s. to every ordinance, 109
s. unto the elder, 4
wives, s. yourselves, 118
substance
faith is the s. of, 61
wasted his s. with, 40
sucklings
mouth of babes and s., 23
sue
s. thee at the law, 68
suffer
being persecuted, we s., 2
how long shall I s. you, 48
if we s., 179
if ye s. for, 157

man s. as a Christian, 25
s. fools gladly, 65
s. for well doing, 2
s. not a woman to teach, 10
s. the little children, 23
when ye do well, and s., 2
which thou shalt s., 35
suffered
s. He their manners, 103
s. in the flesh, 171
things which He s., 100
suffereth
charity s., 114
sufferings
partakers of Christ's s., 164
partakers of the s., 179
sufficiency
s. is of God, 1
sufficient
s. to finish it, 138
s. unto the day, 68
sun
no need of the s., 71
s. down upon your wrath, 6
s. light on them,, 34
s. shall be turned, 51
s. to rise on the evil, 76
supper
marriage s. of the Lamb, 82
supplication
by prayer and s., 141
support
s. the weak, 187
sure
s. mercies of David, 16
swallow
s. a camel, 91
swallowed
death is s. up in, 40
swear
he that s. by heaven, 128
neither s. by thy head, 128
s. not at all, 128
s. not by heaven, 96
sweareth
s. by the throne, 128
sweet
in thy mouth s. as honey, 16
s. savour of Christ, 25
s. water and bitter, 33
swift
s. to hear, 6
s. to shed blood, 57

swine
   pearls before s., 188
sword
   beareth not s. in vain, 63
   killeth with the s., 153
   mouth goeth a sharp s., 86
   or peril, or s., 44
   perish with the s., 191
   send peace, but a s., 192
   sharper than twoedged s., 168
   take the s. shall perish, 191
swords
   thief with s. and staves, 9
synagogues
   chief seats in the s., 91
   s. ye shall be beaten, 135
   standing in the s., 90

T

tabernacle
   put off this my t., 40
   t. of God is with men, 74
table
   from their masters' t., 168
   with me on the t., 15
tables
   not in t. of stone, 135
   of God, and serve t., 122
   t. of the heart, 135
taken
   from him shall be t., 113
   hath not shall be t., 113
taketh
   that t. not his cross, 4
talketh
   it is He that t., 121
tame
   tongue can no man t., 175
tarry
   come and will not t., 133
   t. till I come, 10
   t. ye here, and watch, 27
taste
   not t. of death till, 39
taught
   neither t. it, but by, 78
   which ye have been t., 49
teach
   dost thou t. us, 8
   men, apt to t., 106
   shall do and t. them, 27
   suffer not a woman to t., 10
   t. all nations, 55
   t. the young women, 118

teachers
   false t. among you, 84
teachest
   t. thou not thyself, 4
   which t. another, 4
teaching
   t. for doctrines, 84
tears
   mind, and with many t., 89
   sought carefully with t., 148
   wipe away all t., 181
teeth
   and gnashing of t., 6
   and gnashing of t., 148
tell
   not t. whence it cometh, 127
temperance
   fruit of Spirit is t., 86
temperate
   be sober, grave, t., 13
tempest
   clouds carried with a t., 22
temple
   against the t., 95
   body is the t., 18
   defile the t. of God, 159
   destroy this t., 44
   Lord and Lamb are the t., 74
   pillar in the t., 156
   saw no t. therein, 74
   standing in the t., 53
   t. of God is holy, 14
   t. of the living God, 73
   which t. ye are, 14
   ye are the t. of God, 14
temples
   dwelleth not in t., 26
temporal
   things seen are t., 119
tempt
   t. ye me, ye hypocrites, 181
   thou shalt not t., 21
   why t. ye God, 21
   why t. ye me, 8
temptation
   enter not into t., 181
   lead us not into t., 56
   rich fall into t., 5
   that endureth t., 182
temptations
   godly out of t., 42
tempted
   t. with evil, 182

tempteth
   t. He any man, 182
terrified
   commotions, be not t., 7
terror
   rulers are not a t., 79
testament
   blood of the new t., 17
   cup is the new t., 29
   where a t. is, 40
testator
   death of the t., 40
testified
   t. of me in Jerusalem, 35
testimony
   ashamed of the t., 100
   t. of Jesus is the, 197
thank
   good to you, what t., 12
   receive, what t. have ye, 5
thanks
   giveth God t., 87
   in every thing give t., 79
   t. be to God, 54
   t. be unto God, 79
thanksgiving
   received with t., 65
   supplication with t., 141
thefts
   out of heart proceed t., 126
thief
   as a t. in the night, 164
   come on thee as a t., 164
   t. cometh not but for, 36
   t. in the night, 169
   t. with swords and staves, 9
   what hour the t., 21
thieves
   den of t., 26
   t. do not break through, 175
   where t. break through, 119
things
   the t. that be of God, 189
think
   an hour when ye t. not, 147
   killeth you will t., 136
   t. himself something, 31
   t. me a fool, 7
   t. not that I am come, 192
   t. on these things, 33
   t. soberly, 89
   t. that he knoweth, 108

t. they shall be heard, 140
wherefore t. ye evil, 56
thinketh
that t. he standeth, 31
third
raised up the t. day, 144
rise the t. day, 152
t. day He shall rise, 152
t. day He shall rise, 37
thirst
give him shall never t., 54
I t., 103
if any man t., 43
if he t. give him drink, 52
no more, neither t., 33
shall never t., 43
t. after righteousness, 156
water shall t. again, 54
thirsty
t. and ye gave me drink, 30
t. and ye gave me no, 37
thirty
t. pieces of silver, 15
thorn
t. in the flesh, 162
thorns
crown of t., 162
of t. men do not gather,
33
thought
morrow shall take t., 68
t. a thing incredible, 153
t. as a child, 24
t. for your life, 65
t. of thine heart, 150
take no t. for the morrow,
68
take no t. for your life, 119
take ye t. for raiment, 7
which of you by taking t.,
126
thoughts
heart proceed evil t., 126
t. of the wise, 68
thousand
day is as a t. years, 133
t. instructors in Christ,
18
t. years as one day, 133
thousands
ten t. of His saints, 145
three
t. days I will raise, 44
t. that bear record, 185
t. that bear witness, 183
there t. are one, 185
thrice
deny me t., 43

throat
t. is an open sepulchre,
173
throne
fault before the t., 95
for it is God's t., 128
heaven is My t., 26
in the midst of the t., 74
sweareth by the t., 128
Thy t. is for ever, 24
thrust
t. in Thy sickle, 105
thunderings
voice of mighty t., 52
tidings
t. of great joy, 81
time
appear the second t., 164
for a little t. and then, 126
high t. to awake, 161
John: since that t., 107
know not when the t., 141
not discern this t., 193
now is the accepted t., 161
t. cometh, 136
t. is at hand, 93
t. is at hand, 93
t. is come for Thee to, 120
t. is short, 131
times
discern signs of the t., 45
for you to know the t., 68
persecuted us in t. past, 21
until seventy t. seven, 65
tittle
t. of the law to fail, 28
today
Christ the same t., 21
seen strange things t., 123
t. shalt thou be with me,
16
while it is called T., 51
together
all things work t., 60
toil
t. not, neither do they, 7
told
t. me all that ever I, 98
tolerable
more t. for Sodom, 75
more t. for the land of, 93
tomorrow
for t. we die, 138
tongue
every t. should confess, 3
refrain his t. from evil, 57
speaketh in an unknown t.,
29

t. can no man tame, 175
t. is a fire, 57
t. words easy to be, 29
unknown t., 141
tongues
speak in our t., 185
speaketh with t., 29
t. are for a sign, 185
t. of men and of angels, 50
tooth
t. for a t., 148
torment
t. and sorrow give her, 17
tormented
t. in this flame, 84
touch
not to t. a woman, 21
touched
as many as t., 59
tough
t. His garment, 59
tower
intending to build a t., 138
tradition
hold the t. of men, 46
keep your own t., 91
traditions
hold the t., 49
trample
t. them under their feet, 95
transgression
no law is, there is no t., 109
sin is the t. of, 171
transgressions
added because of t., 109
transgressor
make myself a t., 81
treasure
evil man out of evil t., 22
t. hid in a field, 107
t. in heaven, 54
t. of the heart, 22
where your t. is, 115
treasures
t. in heaven, 175
t. upon earth, 119
tree
and waxed a great t., 80
corrupt t. bringeth, 22
every good t., 22
fig t. bear olive, 33
right to the t. of life, 111
t. is known by his fruit, 22
t. is known by his own, 41
trees
t. whose fruit withereth, 22
trembling
with fear and t., 161

trespass
  brother t., 36
  t. against thee seven, 66
trespasses
  Father forgive your t., 80
  forgive men their t., 65
  forgive your t., 81
tribulation
  t. or distress, 44
  t. worketh patience, 87
  through much t., 107
tribute
  earth take custom or t., 180
  pay ye t., 10
  t. to whom t. is due, 180
tried
  that ye may be t., 4
trouble
  let no man t. me, 136
  t. in the flesh, 118
troubled
  heart be t., 27
true
  called Faithful and T., 61
  God is t., 70
  his record is t., 85
  I am the t. vine, 9
  just and t. are Thy ways, 157
  let God be t., 186
  my judgement is t., 105
  our record is t., 87
  sent me is t., 70
  t. and righteous are, 146
  t. are His judgments, 105
  t. light now shineth, 52
  whatsoever things are t., 191
  witness is not t., 36
trumpet
  do not sound a t., 22
  t. give an uncertain, 11
trust
  shall the Gentiles t., 97
  t. in riches to enter, 54
  t. in the living God, 186
truth
  because I tell the t., 173
  but for the t., 186
  children walk in t., 24
  for I will say the t., 17
  I am the way, the t., 99
  I tell you the t., 187
  in pretence, or in t., 69
  lie is of the t., 111
  love in deed and in t., 42
  not obey the t., 41

nothing against the t., 186
sanctify through Thy t., 85
speak every man t., 64
Spirit is t., 86
t. came by Jesus, 28
t. cometh to the light, 41
t. I say unto you, 68
t. is in Jesus, 187
t. shall make you free, 67
t. this is the Prophet, 122
t. Thou art the Son, 47
that is of the t. heareth, 186
there is no t. in him, 162
what is t., 186
witness unto the t., 102
word is t., 74
words of t., 116
worship in spirit and in t., 171
ye know not the t., 4
ye shall know the t., 67
turn
  cheek, t. to him other, 65
  t. again and rend you, 95
  t. from these vanities, 92
  t. not thou away, 18
twain
  go with him t., 34
  t. shall be one, 117
twelve
  chosen you t., 15
twinkling
  t. of an eye, 175
two
  he that hath t. coats, 168
  no man can serve t., 115
twoedged
  sharper than t. sword, 168

U

unawares
  entertained angels u., 6
unbelief
  help Thou mine u., 48
  u. make the faith, 73
unbelievers
  before the u., 109
unbelieving
  u. depart, let him, 75
  u. husband is sanctified, 14
uncertain
  trumpet give an u. sound, 11
uncircumcised
  stiffnecked and u., 75

uncircumcision
  circumcision nor u., 53
  nor u. but faith, 26
  u. is nothing, 26
unclean
  any man common or u., 151
  man, thou u. spirit, 58
  nothing u. of itself, 9
  to be u. to him it is u., 9
  u. spirit is gone, 56
uncleanness
  called us unto u., 85
under
  put it u. a bushel, 145
understand
  have not heard shall u., 56
  hear, and u., 84
  neither do they u., 92
understandest
  u. what thou readest, 50
understandeth
  for no man u., 29
understanding
  children in u., 120
  him that hath u., 57
  passeth all u., 33
  u. be men, 57
  u. is unfruitful, 141
  u. of the prudent, 31
understood
  u. as a child, 24
  words easy to be u., 29
unfruitful
  understanding is u., 141
ungodliness
  increase unto more u., 64
ungodly
  Christ died for the u., 37
  u. and for sinners, 109
  where shall the u., 75
unjust
  on the just and the u., 76
  u. also in much, 33
  u. in the least, 33
unknown
  speaketh in an u. tongue, 29
unmarried
  u. careth for the things, 44
unrighteous
  u. shall not inherit, 107
unrighteousness
  all u. is sin, 157
unsearchable
  u. are His judgments, 71

unseemly
working that which is u., 87

unspeakable
u. gift, 79

unstable
double minded man is u., 94

until
u. seventy times seven, 65

untoward
u. generation, 35

unwise
wise, and to the u., 85

unworthy
u. of everlasting life, 24

uppermost
u. rooms at feasts, 91

use
change the natural u., 87
despitefully u. you, 29
u. not vain repetitions, 140

usurp
nor to u. authority over, 10

utterance
Spirit gave them u., 184

V

vain
Christ is dead in v., 28
deceive with v. words, 41
desirous of v. glory, 5
faith is v., 60
grace bestowed not in v., 22
not the sword in v., 63
profane and v. babblings, 64
use not v. repetitions, 140
v. they do worship, 84
wise, that they are v., 68

vainglory
through strife or v., 5

valley
v. shall be filled, 122

value
v. than many sparrows, 94

vanisheth
and then v. away, 126

vanities
turn from these v., 92

vapour
v. that appeareth, 126

vengeance
days of v., 105
flaming fire taking v., 154

v. belongeth unto Me, 154
v. is Mine, 154

vessel
as unto the weaker v., 118
he is a chosen v., 56

vials
the v. of the wrath of, 70

victory
giveth us v. through, 54
grave, where is thy v., 40
swallowed up in v., 40

vigilant
be sober, be v., 162

vine
I am the true v., 9
I am the v., 9
the clusters of the v., 105

violence
v. to no man, 35
with v. shall that city, 76

vipers
generation of v., 56
generation of v., 38

virgin
v. shall be with child, 102

virtue
add to your faith v., 61
if there be any v., 33
to v. knowledge, 61

vision
v. of angels, 6

visions
young men shall see v., 49

visit
v. the fatherless, 194

visited
sick, and ye v. me, 30

visitest
son of man, that Thou v., 94

vocation
walk worthy of the v., 25

voice
graves shall hear His v., 93
heard not the v., 192
if will hear His v., 14
meaning of the v., 29
my v. and open the door, 102
sheep hear my v., 4
truth heareth my v., 186
v. of a great multitude, 52
v. of many waters, 52
v. of one crying, 35
v. of one crying, 104
v. of the bridegroom, 42

void
v. the law through faith, 28

vomit
turned to his own v., 11

W

wages
content with your w., 192
reapeth receiveth w., 54
w. of sin is death, 54

wait
lie in w. to deceive, 48
w. for the promise, 86

walk
also w. in the Spirit, 12
children w. in truth, 24
every one, so let him w., 33
lame w., 81
mark them which w., 125
rise up and w., 83
shall not w. in darkness, 14
take up thy bed, and w., 83
w. as children of light, 12
w. by faith, 12
w. by the same rule, 35
w. circumspectly, 12
w. honestly toward, 151
w. in love, 12
w. in the flesh, 32
w. in the light, 13
w. in the Spirit, 12
w. in wisdom, 183
w. while ye have light, 108
w. with me in white, 146
w. worthy of God, 69
w. worthy of the Lord, 12
w. worthy of the vocation, 25
w. ye in Him, 12

walked
leaped and w., 83

walketh
that w. disorderly, 29
w. in darkness, 92
w. through dry places, 56

walking
w. on the sea, 123

war
fight and w. yet ye, 141
hear of w. and, 7
judge and make w., 105
w. after the flesh, 32
w. against the soul, 116

warned
w. you to flee, 53

wash
w. away thy sins, 11

w. in the pool of, 83
w. thy face, 62
washed
water, and w. his hands,
151
wasted
w. his substance with, 40
watch
heed, w. and pray, 141
let us w. and be, 191
tarry ye here, and w., 27
w. and pray, 181
w. therefore: for ye, 164
w. with me one hour, 45
w. ye therefore, 51
w. ye therefore and pray,
141
watched
come, he would have w.,
21
watcheth
blessed is he that w., 164
water
baptized you with w., 11
but by w. and blood, 11
clouds without w., 22
drinketh of this w., 54
here is w., 11
living w., 54
man be born of w., 11
man forbid w., 11
not by w. only, 11
Spirit, w. and blood, 183
sweet w. and bitter, 33
take w. of life freely, 55
w. and washed his hands,
151
w. of life freely, 43
w. that I shall give, 54
w. to drink in my name,
27
wells without w., 22
watered
planted, Apollos w., 38
watereth
planteth and he that w., 35
waters
living fountains of w., 74
sitteth upon many w., 43
voice of many w., 52
wavereth
w. is like a wave, 49
wavering
ask in faith, nothing w.,
61
faith without w., 61
waves
w. of the sea, 49

way
be turned out of the w., 13
broad is the w., 38
error of his w., 172
go thy w., 83
I am the w., 99
in the w. of Cain, 76
make straight the w., 104
narrow is the w., 12
prepare Thy w. before, 122
prepare ye the w. of the,
147
the w. ye know, 83
w. they call heresy, 84
ways
just and true are Thy w.,
157
misery are in their w., 88
pervert the right w. of, 62
rough w. made smooth,
130
their pernicious w., 62
unstable in all his w., 94
w. past finding out, 71
weak
flesh is w., 67
gain the w., 3
infirmities of the w., 22
support the w., 187
w. became I as w., 3
w. in the faith, 34
w. then am I strong, 177
w. things of the world, 193
who is w. and I am not, 51
weaker
as unto the w. vessel, 118
weakness
made perfect in w., 90
w. of God is stronger, 177
wealth
every man another's w., 5
weary
w. in well doing, 133
w. in well doing, 157
weep
blessed are ye that w.,
109
merchants shall w., 6
w. and lament, 37
w. not for me, but w., 80
w. with them that w., 51
what mean ye to w., 181
ye rich men, w., 194
ye shall mourn and w., 109
weepest
woman, why w., 27
weeping
w. and gnashing of teeth, 6

w. and gnashing of teeth,
148
well
lawful to do w., 158
suffer for w. doing, 2
w. done, thou good, 8
w. is deep, 127
weary in w. doing, 157
when ye do w. and suffer,
2
wells
w. without water, 22
went
w. to God, 47
wept
Jesus w., 180
west
shineth even unto the w.,
163
what
w. have I to do with, 161
where
w. to lay His head, 87
white
behold a w. horse, 61
not make one hair w., 128
w. already to harvest, 131
w. raiment, that thou be,
61
walk with me in w., 146
whited
w. sepulchres, 7
whither
w. I go ye know, 83
w. I go, ye cannot, 8
who
w. art Thou, Lord, 92
whole
Christ maketh thee w.,
83
faith hath made thee w.,
59
garment, I shall be w., 59
made perfectly w., 59
stand here before you w.,
83
they that be w., 8
w. body should be cast, 38
whore
great w. that sitteth, 43
whoremongers
w. and adulterers, 3
without are dogs, and w.,
41
wicked
fiery darts of the w., 60
wickedness
whole world lieth in w., 77

wide
  w. is the gate, 38
widow
  poor w. hath cast more, 68
widows
  honour w. that are w., 194
  w. in their affliction, 194
wife
  bound unto a w., 48
  have thy brother's w., 3
  he that loveth his w., 114
  His w. hath made herself,
    101
  honour unto the w., 118
  how he may please his w.,
    45
  husband put away his w.,
    48
  is sanctified by the w., 14
  man have his own w., 66
  put away his w., 3
  put away his w., 48
  putteth away his w., 48
  remember Lot's w., 47
  render unto the w. due,
    117
  the head of the w., 118
  unbelieving w., 14
wilderness
  crying in the w., 35
  crying in the w., 104
  manners in the w., 103
  perils in the w., 39
wiles
  w. of the devil, 162
will
  better, if the w. of God, 2
  done the w. of God, 133
  good w. toward men, 19
  meat is to do the w., 124
  not my w. but Thine, 74
  not to do mine own w., 98
  not what I w., 1
  say, If the Lord w., 21
  seek not mine own w., 69
  shall do the w. of my, 62
  so is the w. of God, 42
  the w. of God in Christ, 79
  Thy w. be done, 70
  w. of God abideth forever,
    43
  w. of Him that sent me, 98
  w. of the Father, 69
  w. of the Lord be done, 1
  whoever w. let him take,
    55
willeth
  not of him that w., 120

willing
  spirit indeed is w., 67
wind
  driven with the w., 49
  every w. of doctrine, 48
  w. bloweth where it, 127
winds
  carried about of w., 22
  w. and the sea obey, 10
wine
  bottles break, and w., 194
  drunk old w., 95
  drunk with w., 49
  full of new w., 162
  new w. into old bottles,
    194
  new w. must be put, 11
  set forth good w., 88
  the w. of the wrath, 35
  use a little w., 112
winepress
  great w. of the wrath, 70
wings
  chickens under her w., 110
wipe
  w. away all tears, 181
wisdom
  any of you lack w., 195
  foolish the w. of this, 196
  Greeks seek after w., 144
  in the w. of men, 60
  w. is justified, 195
  w. of the wise, 31
  w. of this world is, 195
  walk in w., 183
wise
  be ye w. as serpents, 39
  be ye w. as serpents, 173
  both to the w., 85
  confound the w., 64
  fool, that he may be w., 89
  not as fools, but as w., 12
  professing to be w., 31
  seeing ye yourselves w., 65
  thoughts of the w., 68
  w. in your own conceits,
    31
  w. man, which built, 138
  w. to that which is good,
    77
  wisdom of the w., 31
wiser
  God is w. than men, 195
  w. than the children of,
    196
with
  not w. me is against me,
    97

withdraw
  w. yourselves, 29
withered
  no root, they w. away, 13
within
  evil things come from w.,
    169
without
  toward them that are w.,
    183
  toward them that are w.,
    151
  w. Him was not any thing,
    36
withstand
  that I could w. God, 1
witness
  a minister and a w., 124
  also shall bear w., 56
  bare them w., 34
  bear false w., 134
  bear w. also at Rome, 35
  beheaded for the w. of,
    119
  do not bear false w., 27
  faithful w., 103
  give all the prophets w.,
    182
  God is my w., 87
  if I bear w. of myself, 36
  not Himself without w.,
    147
  receive not our w., 13
  receive the w. of men, 36
  Spirit that beareth w., 86
  that bear w. in earth, 183
  thefts, false w., 126
  they bear w. of me, 2
  w. is not true, 36
  w. of God is greater, 36
  w. of the evil, 2
  w. unto all men, 182
  w. unto the truth, 102
  was sent to bear w., 104
witnesses
  unto w. chosen before, 144
  ye shall be w., 182
witnessing
  w. both to small, 182
wives
  Christ, so let the w., 118
  husbands, love your w.,
    114
  husbands, love your w.,
    118
  old w.' fables, 127
  w. be in subjection, 118
  w. submit yourselves, 118

woe

second w. is past, 39

w. is unto me, 26

w. to that man by whom, 96

w. unto that man, 15

w. unto them, 76

w. unto you that are rich, 194

w. unto you that laugh, 109

w. unto you when all men, 64

w. unto you ye lawyers, 91

w. unto you, scribes, 91

wolves

are ravening w., 41

as sheep in midst of w., 39

forth as lambs among w., 39

grievous w. enter, 177

woman

head of the w. is man, 10

if a w. shall put away, 3

let the w. learn in, 50

looketh on a w. to lust, 3

man created for the w., 116

man is not of the w., 36

man not to touch a w., 21

natural use of the w., 87

suffer not a w. to teach, 10

w. behold thy son, 63

w. for the man, 116

w. have her own husband, 66

w. have long hair, 7

w. is the glory of, 116

w. where are thine, 2

w. why weepest, 27

womb

conceive in thy w., 102

openeth the w., 32

women

blessed art thou among w., 102

shame for w. to speak, 26

w. did change natural, 87

w. keep silence, 26

w. to be sober, 118

wonderful

w. works of God, 185

wonders

except ye see signs and w., 13

signs and w. to seduce, 84

wood

silver, but also of w., 47

word

beginning was the W., 11

beheaded for the w. of, 119

but by every w. of God, 78

choke the w., 78

clean through the w., 85

continue in my w., 46

doers of the w., 42

every idle w. that men, 151

he that heareth my w., 13

hearing by the w. of, 60

in w. of deed, do, 42

law fulfilled in one w., 28

leave the w. of God, 122

let the w. of Christ, 74

live but by w. of God, 163

not in w. but in power, 107

not love in w., 42

preach the w., 78

sincere milk of the w., 74

sower soweth the w., 55

speak the w. only, 59

that hear the w. and, 78

the Father, the W. and, 185

unskilful in the w., 92

w. against the Son of, 16

w. is nigh, 78

w. is truth, 74

W. of God, 103

w. of God grew, 56

w. of God is not bound, 78

w. of God is quick, 21

w. of His grace, 16

w. of the Lord edureth, 74

w. of this salvation, 63

W. was God, 11

W. was made flesh, 98

W. was with God, 11

which hear the w., 62

whoso keepeth His w., 130

words

ashamed of me and my w., 78

by thy words thou shalt be, 104

deceive you with vain w., 41

from the w. of the book, 144

heareth God's w., 9

keep my w., 101

not the w. of him that, 116

remember the w. of, 78

shall ye believe my w., 38

speaketh the w. of God, 9

strive not about w., 8

w. easy to be understood, 29

w. of this prophecy, 144

w. of truth, 116

w. shall not pass away, 24

w. shalt be condemned, 104

work

are not ye my w. in the, 15

desireth a good w., 5

finish His w., 124

if any would not w., 90

in the w. of the Lord, 45

love for their w.'s sake, 26

no man can w., 51

this w. be of men, 41

w. of God that ye believe, 49

w. out your salvation, 161

w. the works of Him, 49

w. together for good, 60

workers

w. of iniquity, 29

worketh

man that w. good, 41

wrath of man w. not, 6

working

w. with his hands, 36

workman

w. is worthy of his meat, 51

w. that needeth not be, 45

works

according to his w., 41

according to his w., 145

according to their w., 105

all their w. they do, 90

be rich in good w., 42

believe the w., 14

by w. was faith made, 42

do not ye after their w., 90

do the w. of Abraham, 91

double according her w., 57

faith without w., 42

found thy w. perfect, 42

I know thy w., 52

known are all His w., 68

marvellous are Thy w., 71

men may see your good w., 41

no more of w., 79

not by w. of, 42

set him over the w., 117

so faith without w. is, 40

terror to good w., 79

w. a man is justified, 42

wronged
if he hath w., 152
wrote
for he w. of me, 14

Y

yea
let your y. be y., 96
years
day is as a thousand y., 133

yesterday
Christ the same y., 21
yield
y. yourselves unto God, 181
yoke
take my y. upon you, 101
young
y. men shall see, 49
y. women to be sober, 118
younger
elder shall serve y., 64

youth
man despise thy y., 198
youthful
flee also y. lusts, 13

Z

zeal
z. of God but not, 92
zealously
good to be z., 198